TRUE STORIES

OF

SEGREGATION:

AN AMERICAN LEGACY

TRUE STORIES

OF

SEGREGATION: AN AMERICAN LEGACY

by

Robert Ewell Greene

R.E. Greene, Publisher

Fort Washington, Maryland, 1998

Copyright © 1998 by Robert Ewell Greene
ALL RIGHTS RESERVED
Published in 1998 by R.E. Greene Publisher
Fort Washington, Maryland
Library of Congress Catalog No. 98-093761
ISBN-0945 733-16-X

Selection of Cover

I have selected this cover painting because I deeply believe that in the final analyses, the most oppressed, discriminated and segregated American Minorities have been the Native and Black Americans. The legacy of segregation still affects these two minorities greatly in 1998. Even though this book highlights many segregated experiences of people of color, I still must acknowledge the nexus of the Native American and the Black American over many years.

ILLUSTRATION CREDITS

I thank you again, my loving sister, Ruth Greene Richardson, for another outstanding cover painting. I am honored to use this picture because your artistic expertise was acknowledged by the Pittsburgh Federal Executive Board, Native American Heritage Committee, when you received the Third Place award in their Fourth American Art Contest.

To David and the memory of Robert II, who were blessed to be born in the early years of integration.

TABLE OF CONTENTS

AUTHOR'S PREFACE

ACKNOWLEDGMENTS

CHAPTER	PAGE
1 INTRODUCTION	1
2 SEGREGATION	20
3 BLACK CULTURE - GENETIC DIVERSITY	199
4 MILITARY	299
5 MEMORIES OF SEGREGATION	321
6 MEMORIES OF INTEGRATION	335
7 A PICTORIAL REVISIT	342
SEGREGATED YEARS	343
BIBLIOGRAPHY	487
INDEX	497

PREFACE

I have a strong belief that many Americans and foreigners have a very limited awareness of the realities of legal segregation and discrimination in America prior to the 1960's. Perhaps age plays a great part in people's not knowing about the way of life that existed at one time for the real American minority, the "Colored, Negro, Afro American, Black and African American". Therefore, I have revisited the years that I and others have lived in a segregated America.

I have reviewed the 24 books that I have written, obtained personal interviews, and used my military experiences, including the establishment and serving as the first director of the United States Army Europe Race Relations School in Germany, 1972-1974, to write these true stories of segregation in the United States.

I also believe that the general public has a great understanding of the Civil Rights Movement of the 1960's, but a very minimal knowledge of segregation. This book presents facts, both glorious and inglorious. It also attempts to balance those omissions which by design or otherwise have prevented an actual historical presentation of people of color during segregation.

I have written this book to assist Blacks, Whites, Native Americans, Hispanics, Asians, and others in understanding how millions of Blacks have lived and died under the legal system of segregation in our nation.

Robert Ewell Greene
July 25, 1998

ACKNOWLEDGEMENTS

I wish to express my sincere gratitude to Janice Lucile Wood Hunter for her caring, patience, understanding and superb administrative and immense stenographic contributions to this book.

I sincerely thank Madlyn Calbert for her outstanding scholarly expertise in the grammatical editing and proof reading of this book.

I also wish to express my appreciation to the following people for their contributions in making this book possible.

Harriet Allen	Stevie D. Jones
Antone Bailey	Harold Johnson
Bertha Evans	C.A. Ross
Bill Grant	Edward D. Sloan
Adam Greene	Terry Strother
David Greene	Almyra Wills
Janice Wood Hunter	
Kimberly Cherié Hunter	

My appreciation is also hereby expressed to the wonderful persons who have assisted me and their names may have been inadvertently omitted.

R.E.G.

CHAPTER 1

INTRODUCTION

I decided to write this book because I believe that many Blacks, Hispanics, Asians, Native Americans and Europeans do not really understand the true historical experiences of living as a Black, colored or Negro during the years of enforced segregation and discrimination in America prior to the 1960's. Therefore, I will be discussing my personal life experiences from childhood to maturity and recalling every story possible that relates to segregation and discrimination. I will also relate true stories that others have shared with me from their living in a segregated America. I will include many instances that I have researched over some thirty years that will depict valid stories of segregation.

I will present my credentials to write this book on segregation by discussing my childhood, genetic heritage, and adult life to including living day and night in an integrated military society for twenty years, 1955 to 1975.

I was born on July 18, 1931, just one year after one of the worst economic depressions, to the late Ruth N. Conway Greene and Arthur Alonzo Greene Sr. Doctor Joseph Trigg, first Black member of Syracuse University's rowing crew and a graduate of Howard University's Medical School of Medicine, delivered me at 7:56 a.m. I weighed between 10-12 pounds and was the fifth and last child born to my parents. The late Arthur A. Greene Jr., was my older brother. He attended Springfield College, Massachusetts, and studied physical education. During World War II, he served with General George Patton's Third US Army in Belgium, France and Germany. Arthur's medical unit was alerted one day to report to an accident involving a jeep. Upon arriving at the scene with an ambulance, Arthur observed that another ambulance was carrying away an injured person who was the famed General George Patton. Arthur A. Greene Jr. served proudly in a segregated medical unit during World War II.

Ruth Cecelia Greene Richardson is my oldest sister. She is a graduate of St. Louis University and Washington University, St. Louis, Missouri. She has devoted over thirty years of her life to molding young people. Ruth was a social worker, Executive Director of a neighborhood center and the Three Rivers Youth Center in Pittsburgh, Pennsylvania. She is a talented and superb artist and is the mother of a successful son, William Arthur Boler who is a graduate of Yale and Harvard Universities and a classmate of actress Angela Bassett.

Phyllis Wilma Greene McAfee, the third eldest child is a graduate of Milliken University, Decatur, Illinois and the University of Illinois, majoring in home economics. She is a retired teacher, counselor and vice principal in San Francisco,

California school system. She is married to Major Travis McAfee and they are the parents of two daughters, Michelle and Monica and one son, the late Michael McAfee.

Daisy Annie Greene Sanford is my youngest sister and is a graduate of Harris-Stowe College, St. Louis, Missouri, and the University of Illinois. She taught elementary school for many years. Daisy is married to Dr. Johnson Sanford, MD., and they are the parents of three daughters, Comelia, Karla and Jaymie.

My mother, Ruth N. Conway Greene was born in Washington, D.C. to Ewell Conway Sr. and Annie Pryor Conway. Annie was a mulatto who was born in Williamsburg, Virginia. A second cousin, who has been blessed with some eighty years of life related the following genealogical information to me using the oral tradition about my grandfather's parents. Cousin Harriet Johnson Allen said that her mother, Mary Magdalene Conway Johnson, told her that her grandfather was an English Jewish man and her grandmother was a brown skin Egyptian woman. The two had arrived from England many years ago and settled in Yazoo, Mississippi where Mary M. Conway Johnson and her brother, my maternal grandfather, Ewell Conway and a brother Daniel Conway were born, Aunt Mary's mother died when she were very young and her father brought the children to Washington, D.C. It is believed that he had a business in Alexandria, Virginia or Washington, D.C. The children were placed in the care of a Black woman named Sarah Smith or Aunt Sarah, she raised Mary and Ewell. There was no mention by cousin Harriet of Daniels where abouts as a youngster. She did recall an incident that occurred when she was around fourteen years of age, Harriet and her mother were attending church service at a Bishop Turpins' Pentecostal Church in Baltimore, Maryland, one Sunday. Aunt Mary was told by an usher that there was a white man asking for her at the back door of the church. When Aunt Mary arrived at the back door, she was surprised to see a tall slender handsome man who did look as though he was white. The man was her older brother, Daniel Conway. He talked briefly with her and said "I just wanted to see my baby sister." Aunt Mary never saw her brother Daniel again. It has been said that he was passing as a white man and had obtained sufficient finances to have a business and possibly was living in the Caribbean. On several occasions, I had the pleasure of meeting my Great Aunt Mary. She was a very religious woman who believed very deeply on her Jesus. She attended the Pentecostal Church for many years and was highly respected by the Bishop, Ministers, Elders and her church members for her outstanding Christian character and personality. She was a very attractive woman who was able to exceed three scores and ten years, living to the age of 100.

My grandfather, Ewell Conway, was of short stature, light brown skin and did show some Jewish features. He was a produce salesman or huckster who sold fruits and vegetables. He was one of the first Blacks to have a produce stand in the old "O"

Street Market in Northwest Washington, D.C. He was active in the old Nineteenth Street Baptist Church in Georgetown and was President of the Men's Club. Annie and Ewell Conway were the parents of Ewell, Bessie, Esther, Ruth, Mercer, Burnetta and Maria Conway.

My father, Arthur A. Greene Sr. was born in St. Louis, Missouri, the son of Adam Green and Cecelia Spears Green. Adam Green was the son of a 16 years old slave and a white man, possibly named John Green, who was the father of Adam's brother and sisters, namely, Sylvia, of a very dark complexion with distinctive characteristics of her African mother. Phyllis and Tyler were able to pass as white as was Adam. After the Civil War, they decided to leave Evergreen, Alabama and disappeared in the white population.

Adam was a very tall man with an aggressive manner, who spoke out when he felt it was necessary. One day he went into the town of Evergreen, Alabama, and asked the postmaster for the mail belonging to his white father, John Greene. The white postmaster told him "no nigger can come in here asking for a white man's mail. My paternal grandmother, Cecelia Spears Green had brown skin and reflected the genetic representation of her African, Indian and European heritage. She was the daughter of a mulatto man who was half Negro, with a mixture of white and Seminole Her mother was half Black and half Seminole. Their parents were Manassa Sr. (Sandy) and Hannah Spears. Their son Manassa, Jr. was a member of the Reorganized Church of Jesus Christ of Latter Day Saints in the 1870's, while living in Brewton, Alabama. I confirmed this information in May, 1998, when I called his surviving daughter, Ms. Bertha Evans of St. Louis, Missouri, who is 93 years of age. She said to me again that her mother would attend the Baptist Church but her father was a member of the Mormon Church in Alabama in the early 1870's. Some of the Spears left Alabama in the mid 1870's and moved to an area of St. Louis County called Meacham Park, Kirkwood, which was a subdivision. Today it is a part of Kirkwood, Missouri. Later my grandparents settled in the area of South St. Louis, Missouri known as "Italian Hill", an Italian community. They raised twelve children who had various skin colors from dark to light brown. One son, Joseph, could pass for white. My grandmother's sisters Jane and Sarah, along with their brothers, Manassa Sandy, Uriah, Alonzo, and Walter remained in Meacham Park. Jane Spears Perkins was a mulatto who was the mother of Helen, Henry and Moses Perkins. Moses had distinctive Jewish features and it is strongly believed that his father was Jewish.

Manassa Sandy Spears Jr. was married to Sophia St. James Spears. She was of African, Indian and European decent, her father was French Canadian. Sandy and Sophia were the parents of Stella, Helen, Sadie, Eugene, Arthur, Allena, Allen, Viola, Bertha and Oliver Spears.

Walter Spears married a Josephine (Josey) Spears who was white. They were the parents of Helen, Florence, and Frank. Frank was an automobile mechanic who could pass for white. When I met him at the age of twelve years, I thought he was a white man.

Sadie Spears Bailey was the mother of Clifford, Juanita and Antone who have light complexions. Sarah Spears Farris was the mother of Freddie, Leslie, and Walter Farris. Alonzo Spears Sr. was the father of Mollie and Alonzo Jr. who married Robina Spears of Kirkwood, Missouri.

The Meacham Park community honored the late Sandy Manassa Spears Jr. by naming a street in his honor, "Spears Avenue". My second cousin Bertha told me in 1993, that her grandfather, Manassa Spears Sr., after the death of his wife, Hannah, married again. It is said that at the age of 80 years, he became the father of Della Spears. Cousin Bertha said Della resembled the Spears and some half sisters.

I was very fortunate at the age of twelve years to visit St. Louis, Missouri, and Brazil, Indiana, a small town between Terre Haute and Indianapolis, Indiana. In St. Louis and St. Louis County I met some of my father's relatives that I have written about and also my father's sisters and brothers. I was able to meet my father's brothers Joseph and Robert Martin, my name sake, and his sisters, Daisy, Katie, Wilma, Mae, Rosie and Sadie. Aunt Kate was the mother of Edward Palmer. Aunt Wilma Belle moved to New Brunswick, New Jersey and for a brief period lived in Washington, D.C. working for the family of Rudolph Kaufman, an executive for the former Washington Star newspaper. I was very grateful to him for responding to my request when I called from Fort McClellan, Alabama, on February 23, 1965 and had a friend of my father, Mr. Everett Jeffries to deliver an obituary paper to be published concerning my father's death. I told Mr. Jeffries, to tell Mr. Kaufman that Aunt Bee's brother Arthur had died. When I arrived in Washington and obtained the newspaper, he had printed a nice article about my father. This was during the period when most white newspapers did not print many Black obituaries. My father's sisters worked for many years in the home of Jewish and white wealthy families. My father was the only child of 12 children to graduate from high school and college. He obtained a degree in law in 1923 from Howard University School of Law and in 1925 was the first known Black in Brazil, Indiana, Clay County, to pass the bar to practice law. Nevertheless, he decided to return to Washington, D.C. and become a physical education director because of his love for sports.

In 1958, a Caucasian lady in Kansas City, Missouri, Mrs. Pearl Mayo, formerly of Evergreen, Alabama, Conecuh County told my father that she was his distant cousin from Alabama. She was called Mrs. Pearl affectionately. She stated that she grew up on the same plantation where my grandfather Adam Green had lived as a slave.

She also said that she was a very little girl but remembered Adam and that she was related to the Mayo's of Alabama who lived in the Evergreen-Brewton areas. She had a son who owned a foot health store in Arkansas. Mrs. Pearl Mayo was present at my wedding on July 4, 1959 in Kansas City, Missouri and gave me a present of some valuable glass. Later she gave my Dad a copy of some legal deeds which of course were invalid in 1959 which stated that my white great grandfather John Green, had left his son Adam, several thousand acres of valuable timber land. He probably was never aware of the deeds when he migrated to St. Louis in the 1870's.

I spent my early childhood years in the neighborhood where I was born on "O" Street, N.W. between North Capitol and First Streets near Margaret Washington, Vocational and Dunbar High Schools. I could go through the alley and see 6 Hanover Street where my mother was born and raised. I could go through another alley and see my first elementary school, John Mercer Langston, which was across the street from Cook Elementary School. When my family moved from O Street to 2707 Sherman Avenue between Fairmont Street and Girard Street and about two blocks from Howard University, I realized in later years that we lived in a very diverse class of Black families from low middle class to high upper class. I remember that some of our neighbors on our block and surrounding streets were representative of homeowners who were government employees, domestic workers, cab drivers, lawyers, architects, college professors, educators, dentists, physicians and business men and women. I also can recall the street boundaries that separated Blacks from whites. In the 1940's there were few Black families that lived on Thirteen and Fourteenth Streets and on the increasing number blocks. When I delivered the *Washington Post* newspaper in the morning and collected old discarded newspapers to take to the junk yard, most of my customers were white. An all white hospital, Garfield a block away and across the street on Eleventh Street N.W., from Cardozo High School, then a white Central High School which had one known celebrated alumnus, the late FBI Director, Edgar Hoover. Interesting enough, my second cousin Moses Perkins was born in Garfield hospital during the segregated period. There were times when Garfield hospital would admit critical ill Black patients instead of having them to be carried to the all Black hospital, Howard University's Freedmen's hospital.

I attended James Monroe Elementary school on Georgia Avenue and Columbia Road until the sixth grade. When I graduated, I was enrolled at Banneker Junior high school on Euclid street between Sherman and Georgia Avenues. The students who attended Banneker in those days were not from all over the city or representative of Black youngsters from various geographical areas of the city. My classmates were mainly the children of government workers, postal employees, lawyers, dentists, physicians, foreign diplomats of color, college professors, nurses, teachers and some lower middle class wage earners. When I attended the wake this year, in Rankin Chapel, Howard University for the late President of Howard, Dr. James Nabrit

Sr., I met his son James Nabrit Jr., my former classmate who I had not seen since I was fourteen years of age and his classmate at Banneker. Of course, he did not remember me, but when I started to call some names of our class mates who were also present at Monroe Elementary, there was no doubt to him that I was his classmate in the early 1940's. I called off the names of Joan Bunche, Yvonne White, James and Hugh Robinson and the son of the Ambassador from Haiti to the United States and several others. He then pointed to the back of the Chapel and said there is another classmate who was now a judge in Detroit, Michigan. When I went back to the Chapel entrance, I introduced myself as his formal classmate. We talked briefly and during our conversation, I related to him a personal memory that I have never forgotten which is most illustrative of the color obsession that existed within the Black community during the period of segregation. This true story is quite foreign to many Blacks today, young and senior. My father was a graduate lawyer, but he was known by many professionals who frequented the Twelfth YMCA as the physical director and later program secretary as Art or Arthur Greene. He was known to many professionals including physicians, dentists, college professors, physical education directors, such as Johnny Burr (for whom the Howard University Physical Education building is named) and Educators. This story was probably my first exposure to really understanding the class color obsession in the Black community in the 1940's. At the young age of 14 years, I was assigned to a homeroom and attended classes with students whose parents in most cases were hard working citizens who were not representative of a high professional white collar status. Ironically, some of the students were brown skin like me or darker. Very few, if any, were light skin or "high yellow in color". One day the principal, Mrs. Obezine Walker called me to her office. She said Robert Greene, I did not know that you were Arthur A. Greene of the YMCA's son. You are in the wrong home room and class section. You will be reassigned to Dr. Eaton's class room immediately. When I reported to Dr. Eaton's class room honestly that was my initial introduction to what I called the color obsession in a Black society and it was from that day that I did not do like some of my personal friends and other Blacks over the years, become temporarily "color blind". When I entered the classroom, I observed only four brown skin or light brown skin students in the classroom, the others could almost pass for white. This was the prelude to what I would experience in future years. In the early 1950's, at the age of 19 years, my step mother introduced me to my cousin by marriage and she invited me to a young people's cotillion in Philadelphia, Pennsylvania. I was invited to stay overnight with the family of my cousin's date, in Germantown, Pennsylvania. He was a brown skinned young man. When we arrived at the affair, I observed a room filled with mulatto youngsters, the same color of my cousin, and there were present 6 brown skin youngsters, including me and my host. There was one attractive brown skin young lady who was the daughter of a Black Philadelphia bank president. I have not seen my cousin in 46 years when we were sitting on the beach at the exclusive Martha's Vineyard retreat of many professional and celebrity Blacks who owned beach homes on Oak Bluffs, Massachusetts.

My step mother's family owned a lovely home there for years. I did not see the movie called the "Wedding", based on Dorothy West's novel, of life at Martha's Vineyard however, I read several reviews and talked to people who had seen the movie which explores a possible interracial marriage that my cousin told me when we were gazing into the ocean that she would never marry a Black man and I have heard in recent years that she is married to her second white husband. My step mother told me that her two children's birth certificates had their race as white. One of the children was married to a white Broadway producer. My cousin's youngest sister married a very dark skin Black man who was the son of a Black Virginia University College Professor. My step mother informed me that her sisters and brothers were very concerned about the wedding because of the groom's skin color. However, they were a little pleased when they learned that the groom had received a doctorate in chemistry from Purdue University in Indiana. The cousin later divorced her husband and reputedly now has a white companion. Their brother left Pennsylvania, is now married to a white woman and lives in New England. I will be discussing other true stories about color obsession in this manuscript.

My father was offered a YMCA job in his home town St. Louis, Missouri, and my family moved to St. Louis in the mid 1940's. Because the school system in St. Louis, Missouri, had the eighth grade in the middle or elementary school, I had to enroll at Cole Elementary School on Enright Street and when I completed the eighth grade, I received my second elementary diploma. My father had introduced me to our principal and told me that he was his former German teacher at Charles Summer High School in the mid 1900's. I still have my diploma and in later years, I realized that I have a distinctive signature on my diploma because my principal's name was John Mercer Langston III, the grandson of the distinguished lawyer and first Black known congressman from the state of Virginia. I enrolled in Charles Sumner High School and fortunately graduated in three and a half years in January 1950.

Recently, I purchased some copies of my year books from Sumner Alumni Association. After reviewing the yearbooks, I am able to recall a typical model school of excellence similar to Dunbar High School in Washington, D.C. and other superb Black high schools throughout the country during the era of segregation. What was Sumner High School like in the 1940's and 1950's?

Charles Sumner High School was one of three Black high schools for Blacks in St. Louis, Missouri, during segregation. The others were Vashon and Washington Technical High Schools. The principal of Sumner who had been there for many years had an organized school with an outstanding faculty and staff who were very competent and dedicated. Two of my teachers were friends of my father and had gone to school with him and another was his physical education teacher who was still teaching at 70 years of age or more. The school curriculum included the major subjects that were being taught at the all white St. Louis Public schools. Even though we learned in a segregated environment, the graduates were able to compete in most colleges. The students desired professions were in education, engineering, drafting, secretarial, music, aviation, medicine, dentistry, pharmacy, nursing, science, physical education, cosmetology, law, armed forces, mortuary science, physics, chemistry, mathematics, sociology, psychology, criminology, carpentry, religion, and photography.

There were more than sufficient extra curriculum activities to provide the student with a wholesome high school experience which also served as a powerful deterrent to mischievous and criminal acts that entrap some young people today. The different clubs, programs and sports activities each had an interested teacher and sponsor that shared with them values, morality, sportsmanship and spiritual guidance. Sumner high school during the period 1946 to 1951, offered the following extra curricular programs: football, basketball, volleyball, baseball, tennis, golf, track, a cappella choir, girls and boys glee clubs, senior band, gym club, drama club, majorettes, rhythm dance club, student council, boosters club, French club, Negro History club, service club, audio visual club, allied youth club (the members would plan and organize barn dances, and other enjoyable activities without the presence of alcohol), scoop club, (the members were reporters who would gather newsworthy items for the colored newspapers, the *St. Louis Argus, St. Louis American* and the *Chicago Defender*), Junior Surplus Business League, Junior Classical League (students would discuss the classical civilization of Greece and Rome), the Pan American League (the League had its headquarters in Miami, Florida with 223 student chapters, 43 were in universities and 181 in high schools), girls athletic association, Hi-Y clubs (YMCA), flag twirlers, and the radio club. During this period, the parents and children of color were not obsessed with a sports mentality believing that a basketball would provide a wealthy career and also that drug sales could support families. We were exposed to an environment that had strong religious, parental and community leadership that, I am sure, kept many of us from going into crime.

I spent some very enjoyable and memorable days at Sumner. I was a member of the student council, audio visual club, H-Y club (YMCA) and a winning track team. I still admire my second place ribbon for the 440 yard dash in a city-wide high school meet and a ribbon for being a member on a first place 440 yard relay team. I was very happy to know that my father was present when I had a track meet because he was my sports, role model. My father loved sports and he was a star in elementary school, high school and college. Today I possess his medals from 1910 to 1922. I did not learn until we moved to St. Louis, Missouri that he ran the 100 yard dash in 1913 in 10.00 flat.

While going to high school, I worked in a Jewish grocery store across the street from my house on Newberry Terrace, until my father bought a store on Eastern and Taylor Avenues and was called the Eastern-Taylor newsstand, and was located in a building that was owned by a Black physician, Dr. William Hill. The building housed our store, the doctor's office, a 905 chain liquor store, a tavern and a cleaners and tailor shop, both owned and operated by Blacks. Our store consisted of an ice cream soda fountain, shoe shine parlor, and a newsstand section. There were also the sales of cigars, cigarettes, candy, Garrets' snuff, shoe laces, handkerchiefs, and other novelties. The newsstand, consisted of newspapers, magazines, and books. Even though, I had heard the noted historian, Carter G. Woodson, speak at Banneker Jr. High School in Washington and had some teachers who would give you some historical information on Negroes past and present, I believe the beginning of my quest to learn more about my cultural heritage began when I started to work after school and on the weekends in my father's store. The store had a wide collection of books for sale that were written by Black authors, male and females. We also carried Black newspapers from all over the country and we had our paper stands located in front of the store so people could see them as they transferred to a street car or bus at the intersections. Along with our white periodicals, we sold the non rated popular girls model magazines which depicted them in swimsuits, our major customers were white men who would tactfully and in a soft voice ask me to get the magazine of their choice. We definitely had integrated sales for that commodity along with many white shoe shine customers.

Since my father had his job as a YMCA secretary in Webster Groves, Missouri, it was necessary for my brother and sisters when possible to work in the store. At the age of 15 years along with my mother, brother Arthur, and sister Phyllis, we actually were responsible for the management of the store. I was even given the responsibility to close up at times and even walked five or more blocks home carrying the daily receipts concealed, of course. That would be impossible today.

I recall a story that illustrates how the community in that neighborhood would show respect for each other, even though some individuals would have criminal tendencies. One day my mother was sitting at the cashier register and a known "wine-O" rushed into the store and said Mrs. Greene, "please lend me a dollar." Quickly, she responded, "I am not going to lend you a dollar." He continued to plead, "please hurry, I must catch the street car that is coming." She finally decided to lend him a dollar. He thanked her and said, "I will repay you." He then boarded the street car that had just arrived. Within 5-10 minutes several police cars had surrounded the liquor store next door, and it was learned that this man had just robbed the 905 liquor store and was carrying some large bills which he probably did not want to give to the street car conductor. Some of those Blacks who had deviant behavior would not in those days rob their own people, especially if they were located in their own neighborhood. I agree, he did perform a criminal act which was wrong, but in those days some Black criminals were discriminant about their victims.

My father told me the most interesting story of how we were able to purchase the store's stock from Mr. and Mrs. Lamar, who were also Black, for 5,000 dollars cash in the 1940's. There was no bank that would have lent him that amount because his equity was probably nothing. He was raising three children still at home and a wife who did not work and, of course, a YMCA's salary was not very much. When he arrived back to St. Louis after many years, he met a very close friend who was the Black political boss for St. Louis. He was Jordan Chambers who owned the Peoples Funeral Home and one of the most lavish and beautiful night club for Blacks in the mid west called the Club Riviera. Mr. Chambers was very fond of my father and always remembered him as Sumner's star athlete in those days. At one time, he was interested in having my father possibly to become the first Black legislator in the Missouri legislative house in Jefferson City, Missouri. He wanted to groom him for the job. He even introduced him to President Harry S. Truman when he had visited Missouri for a political meeting. Jordan Chambers actually paved the way politically for those persons of color who are in the state legislature as well as Congress. My father felt comfortable enough to ask Mr. Chambers for the 5,000 dollars loan. Now I know in this day and time few people, if any to including your immediate family, will give you 5,000 dollars and a note to repay within a reasonable time without any interest. Yes, my father was a personal friend of Mr. Chambers and within sixteen months my father paid Mr. Chambers in full. There were times when Mr. Chambers would be out of town and he would ask my father to go over to the club and assist his manager in closing some nights and realizing that my father was a graduate lawyer he often would ask him some legal advice.

Since I am writing about true stories during segregation, I know the credibility of this source is 100 percent. My mother told me that one day a white police officer at the Tenth Police Station several blocks down the street from the store came in and asked my mother was my father there? She replied, no. He then said I know Mr. Greene is a close friend of Mr. Jordan Chambers, and I would like for him to intervene for me because I know he has a sergeant's promotion available. Now during segregation the political bosses could not suggest or recommend a Black policeman to be promoted to sergeant because that was not possible. The reason A few years later, a neighbor who was a detective and one of the first Black policemen permitted to arrest a white man, made sergeant. Everyone in our block congratulated him because he was our race hero and not some basketball player. Our sports hero was Joe Louis.

Sometimes my sister Phyllis and I would accompany my Dad to Club Rivera and would see some of the most popular entertainers and bands. When I was growing up in Washington, D.C., I was able to go to the Howard Theatre on Fridays to see a stage show and movie. Therefore, I had seen some of the stars at Howard Theatre who also appeared at the St. Louis Club. One day my sister and I were with our Dad when the club had just closed for the night. The star performer asked the manager to call him a cab because he wanted to go over to a ballroom on Olive street where his friend Dizzy Gillespie was playing and he was having an informal party afterwards. The cab appeared to be taking a long time, so my dad offered the star a ride. I had only been driving for about six months and my father suggested that I drive the car. So there I was driving the car with my Dad, sister and the most distinguished singer and pianist, the great Nat King Cole. When we arrived at the Olive Street ballroom, I was quite surprised when Mr. Nat King Cole invited us into the party. There we were able to see other musicians and their friends and also appeared in the party picture which I am still waiting for my sister to find. Yes, it was during the era of segregation that entertainers and celebrities were closer to the people and did not have to be seen with bodyguards and riding in dark tinted windows of a car. I realize that times are different today. I often write about and even discuss it in class, that during segregation, Black people who were considered middle and upper class had a strong bond or nexus possibly due to education, travel and family connection because they would travel from city to city and meet people who were connected through school, fraternity and sorority groups and families. The cohesiveness present on a small scale today but not as great as was when we lived in a closed community with a togetherness and unity that helped us to survive.

An interesting experience occurred when Jesse Owens visited St. Louis to perform at half time during a sports event at the stadium. He would run the 50 yard dash in competition with a horse and beat the horse at the finish line. The next day he was invited to the Pine Street Colored YMCA to participate in a volleyball game in which my father also played. After the game my father introduced me to Jesse Owens. The YMCA Athletic Department would always have new uniforms, socks and shoes for visitors. Jesse Owens said, Robert, I will give you my socks and you can wash them and that will be your souvenir from me. I thanked him greatly and I wore those socks completely out, because I was quite pleased to wear the socks that one of the fastest humans in the world had worn. Now I was around the age of 15 years when I met Jesse Owens. In 1972, I was stationed in Oberramagau, Germany, where I was opening the first U.S. Army Europe Race Relations school. I had learned that the German government was honoring Jesse Owens in Munich at the U.S. Information Service, "America House" and that he would also be honored during the 1972 Olympic games. I decided to contact Mr. Owens in Munich and was successful in having him to be our honored guest for the opening of the school. I told him the story of my first meeting him and wearing the socks he gave me. He introduced me to his wife and other family members and invited me to be his guest at the America House function. I was most honored to be sitting on the front row with Jesse Owens and his family as he observed a movie that was reliving his outstanding performances in Berlin, Germany in 1936. After the event, we went to a reception at the America House and then proceeded with German police escort to his hotel. Unfortunately, the day of the school's opening ceremony, Mr. Owens became ill and I had to tell a large number of television and news media that Jesse Owens would not be coming.

I enjoyed a very interesting and exciting childhood in St. Louis, Missouri. Although most of my high school days were spent working in my father's store, I still was able to have my friends to including one who helped out in the store either selling St. Louis Argus or shining shoes. He is my good friend, Dick Gregory, a great pioneer comedian, activist, and health enthusiast.

After graduation from high school, my primary goal was to attend college. I was given a good briefing by a former alumnus of the University of Illinois to study pre-medicine. I was selected to stay in the Beta Chapter, Kappa Alpha Psi Fraternity house on Third Street in Champaign Urbana, Illinois. There might have been a few Blacks living in the dormitories, but to the best of my knowledge the majority of Black students lived in either a sorority or fraternity house. There were some who lived with Black families who would house students. We did not demand a separate dormitory as some African American students have requested today. There was a lounge in the student union which was called Ebony Lounge by the Black students and this would be our meeting place on campus. I worked with my big brothers in the fraternity evening in a white sorority house. I believe it was called Gamma Gamma Rho and we waited tables for the young ladies who lived there. This was my first introduction to how some young white people really lived in a comfortable environment while attending college.

Unfortunately, when I returned home at the end of semester, my mother had become ill and in about eight to ten months she died. My mother and I were very close, and after her death I decided not to go back to any school. My father sold the store because my sisters were all in college and my brother had married. I decided to look for a job. There was a man at the Presbyterian Church that I attended who had a high government position in the U.S. Army Records Center Personnel Office on Good fellow Boulevard, St. Louis. He was able to obtain a GS-1 rating for me and I was hired as a file clerk. I had worked previously as a driver for the Rhodes Medical Supply and Pharmacy on Eastern Avenue. Jerry Rhodes was the brother-in-law of Howard University School of Pharmacy's Dean, Chauncey Cooper. I also drove briefly for a white drug store, delivering prescriptions and other items. I believed in the work ethic. While working in the government, I also had two part time jobs, one was working as a usher on the weekends at the colored Circle Theatre on Eastern Avenue across from our store.

I contacted a friend of my father's who was a member of the Catholic Interracial Council of St. Louis. He gave me a lead for an orderly's job at the all white St. Luke's

Catholic Hospital. The only Catholic hospital in St. Louis for colored was Old Saint Mary's Infirmary on Papin Street. That is the hospital where my mother died in 1950. It was a very clean hospital and the Catholic Nun Nurses operated a Nursing school for Black young ladies. The care and services were superb.

When I called St. Luke's to inquire about the job, the Catholic sister administrator was very pleased with my interview. However, when I reported to her office in the hospital, she was very honest and frank because she did not realize that she was talking to a person of color. She said they do not have any Black orderlies and that she was very sorry. At a very young age my father discussed the subject of race with me and he was very forward in challenging white people to give him equal access. Many of his friends, just like some of mine, would criticize him as seeing everything as Black and white and never considering a color blind society. I believe I learned what people may call being sensitive from my father who was convicted to his principles and beliefs that would never be compromised. That is probably why he told Mr. Jordan Chambers that he was not interested in politics. Therefore, when the Catholic Nun told me that I could not be hired, I informed her that I would call the gentleman that I knew on the Catholic Interracial Council and tell him what she told me. She quickly said, "well, you are very qualified for the job and I believe that I will give you the job." This hospital was not a training facility for interns or medical students so some procedures had to be performed by the orderlies. I only worked briefly at the hospital, but I did learn to perform the procedures of catherization and prep patients for surgery.

One day my father decided to drive me to the Black university for the state of Missouri. Lincoln University, Jefferson City, Missouri and I obtained an application and was later admitted. He met the Professor of Military Science, Major Herbert L. Tucker, a Washingtonian who as a youngster knew my father at the 12th Street YMCA. Major Tucker played an integral part in guiding me when I was enrolled in the Reserve Officers Training Corps. (ROTC). I am most thankful to my father for literally forcing me to consider the future options of my life and to make a decision that I was interested in making to go back to college. Yes, I owe whatever accomplishments I have made today to the igniting of the fire to succeed by the determined efforts of my father. My Dad cherished education because he probably never forgot his childhood of poverty, hardships and segregation. He was the only child to complete high school and then college. Today, I tell my college students, whether they like to hear or not, that during segregation some of them would never be sitting in a college classroom and they should be thankful that today if they are qualified they can practically do anything they want to do.

During my four years at Lincoln University, I received some assistance from my father, but it was necessary for me to work when I could. We were receiving no Pell grants or some of the many financial aids to students such as loans from banks that some students never repay. I worked one summer on the Santa Fe Railroad in the lowest wage scales and position as a chair car attendant in assisting the porters and cleaning the bathrooms. That summer job had a great impact on my desire to stay in college and graduate because I knew I did not want to spend a life time cleaning toilets and being subservient to many white passengers who did not have the education that I possessed. I also worked as a desk clerk in the college dormitory assisting the housemother.

I joined the Alpha Mu Chapter, Kappa Alpha Psi fraternity and was able to develop good leadership skills. I was honored to be elected by my fraternity brothers twice to serve as the Polemarch or President. I spent many hours in the library studying and was able to graduate in 1955 with a B.S. degree in zoology and a minor in psychology. My father had accepted a job in Kansas City, Missouri as the Executive Director of the Carver Neighborhood Center at 1628 Campbell Street in the heart of the Black inner city. When I graduated from Lincoln I went to Kansas City and obtained a summer job working as a camp counselor for the Black Optimist Summer Camp for Boys. I had already learned that I would not be accepted for medical school in the fall either at Howard University in Washington, D.C. or Meharry Medical College, Nashville, Tennessee. I knew I could not be admitted to the University of Missouri Medical School because of segregation. I did send an application to a medical school in Nova Scotia and I knew that was wishful thinking.

The optimist camp training program was integrated. The Black staff met daily during the training session with white male and female staffers. The last day of training, there was a buffet meal and we had a program which included a classical literature contest for orations. While at Lincoln University, I had completed a course in speech and also was a member of the debating team. Since I was interested in Shakespeare's, Julius Caesar, I decided to compete in the contest. Reaching the finals, I was challenged by a young man who was an English literature major. I was able to recite verbatim the speech of the tribune Marullus whose several lines were:

"Wherefore rejoice? What conquest brings he home?
What tributaries follow him to Rome
To grace in captive bonds his chariot wheels?
You blocks, you stones, you worse than senseless things!"

I can still recall some of those lines. I was claimed the winner and, every Black in the room was very proud of me. When we returned to our segregated camp site I was the talk of the camp. During segregation, many Blacks were happy to see other Blacks succeed and excel especially when they were not expected to. I was competing in an intellectual arena with whites and I was defying the stereotypes.

I was able to work at the Optimist Camp only about a month, because when I was completing papers for my commission as a Second Lieutenant, Corps of Engineers, I did not really read the fine print. I had checked a box indicating that I would desire to report on active duty within 30 days. I graduated on May 30, 1955, and received my orders around 15 June reporting to Fort Belvoir, Virginia, on July 3, 1955.

When I reported to Fort Belvoir I was assigned to the First Engineers Officer Basic Course class (EOBC). We spent two weeks in a leadership and orientation course called Basic Officers Military Orientation Program (BOMOP). The commanding general of Fort Belvoir and the Engineer school had the authority to revoke an officers commission if he did not complete the first two weeks of training satisfactorily. In later years the authority was rescinded.

Our cadre officer was Lt. Parkin, a white first lieutenant who told me and six other Black officers from Lincoln University "You know you are from Lincoln and most of you will probably fail". As I think about his statement some 43 years later, I do not dwell on the racist stereotype, because it served as the greatest motivator for the seven of us to complete the BOMOP course satisfactory. Lincoln University of Missouri did not have an Engineering school, but like the University of Missouri in Columbia, Missouri did. We were representative of diverse majors in college. I was a pre-medicine student and should have been assigned to the Medical Service Corps. I will always remember Mr. and Mrs. Carson who lived in Northeast Washington in 1955. He was the chief messenger for the Chief of the Medical Service Branch, U.S. Army. Mr. Carson hand carried my request to the chief, but unfortunately, he declined my request to be transferred to the Medical Service Corps.

After the BOMOP course, we started the academic portion of our training. I found myself in a class of 90 percent or more graduate engineers from big ten colleges and universities including several Blacks.

The day I received my diploma from the Engineering school, I had the greatest confidence that I could accomplish almost every task assigned. Since I had no idea of concrete and drafting problems, Mrs. Bolding, my Aunt Maria's neighbor, asked her daughter to assist me. Several men from Lincoln did not complete the course. I asked students today what would they do if they had made 80 on a test and when they received their papers back that they failed the test because of the curve grading system. I survived and realized that all Black classrooms were no more and I would be competing in the future in a predominately white military environment. I can recall two racial situations that occurred while at Ft. Belvoir.

When we went to the Rifle Range to qualify on the M-1 rifle, I had never fired any weapon in my life not even a B-B gun, only a toy water pistol. The instructor did give us thorough but brief pre-firing instructions. Each person had a partner beside him on the firing range and was responsible for marking each other's scores. My white partner was from Alabama and was a sharpshooter who had no problem hitting the target. When the scores were turned in, I knew that I had received a zero, because I could hardly hit anything. When I returned to my barracks several whites were telling me and their friends who could not qualify that many classmates who did not hit anything were qualified on paper. Now this was my first month living in an all white environment and I had learned that some people who had been considering me inferior as now by their partners, cheated when it was necessary for their survival. That experience was painful at the time, but as I have matured mentally over the years and become wiser I can not say the white boy from Alabama did not pencil my cards to qualify because he was a southerner. I believe today that he was an honest person who believed that if he could achieve sharpshooter fairly, then I should be able to at least achieve marksmanship. In an indirect way, his honesty might have been a bonus for me because when I returned to the range after receiving some excellent rifle instruction and qualifying as a marksman. Years later, when I took my company to the range and when I was required to qualify on the carbine rifle; I even surprised myself because I received an expert badge. Also, in 1967 after I was promoted to Major, I was riding in a sedan with my Brigade Commander he said, "Greene, I know you are very happy to receive your field grade rank. We sent in a very good efficiency report and I am sure that it helped." Well in my non tactful manner, I told him, "Sir, These scrambled eggs on my hat certainly did not come over easily, but very hard." During the remainder of our ride, the Colonel did not say another word to me.

The other event at the Officers Club, Fort Belvoir occurred at the graduation. Since I had not lived in Washington, D.C. since childhood I knew very few people there except my immediate family. I knew everyone would be bringing a date so I asked a cousin if they knew anyone who would be kind enough to be my platonic date for one night. She introduced me to her friend who worked with her at the Navy Department and she agreed to be my date. The day of the banquet she had to work and told me that we might have to arrive a few minutes late. When we arrived at the banquet everyone was seated and eating their salads. You could hear silverware falling on the floor as some people began to look at us and staring directly at my date who night or day would never be considered anything other than a Negro, Black or mulatto. Some six months later on a field trip in Korea, one of my friends, a white classmate said, "Greene, can I ask you a personal question? " I said, "Yes." He then asked, "Was your date at the banquet a white lady"? I, of course, said, "no" she is Black just like me." Early in my military career I was exposed to people's color obsession and individual thoughts about race. It is a concern that people who never lived in a segregated society do not really understand what it was really like because as I always say a movie and revised sitcoms can not tell the many true stories of segregation that will be shared in this book.

TRUE STORIES OF SEGREGATION

I have enjoyed the assignments that I have had during my twenty years of active duty in the U.S. Army. I will be able to recall true stories from each of my assignments at the following installations in the United States and overseas: Fort Belvoir, Virginia, 1955 and 1957, Korea. 1955, Fort Leavenworth, Kansas, 1958, Fort Detrick, Maryland, 1960, Fort McClellan, Alabama, 1963, Hannau, Germany, 1965, Military District of Washington, 1968, Korea, 1970, and Germany 1972.

There are two assignments where I met my greatest challenges. They were the United States Army Disciplinary Barracks, (USDB), Fort Leaven worth, Kansas and as the Director of the United States Army Europe Race Relations School, Germany. They were challenging assignments because in each instance I was placed in a position quite higher than my grade or rank with the corresponding responsibilities.

I had planned to leave the Army in 1957 because I wanted to try to enter medical school. But I learned that my father had suffered a slight stroke in Kansas City, Missouri and I remained on active duty so that he could receive the best medical care. I was able to list him as my dependent and with the best of care from Walter Reed Army Hospital he was able with God's blessing to live until 1965. One of his doctors was President Eisenhower's personal cardiologist, a Colonel Jones. I was able to receive assistance from the late James C. Evans, former civilian aide to the Secretary of Army, to obtain for me a compassionate assignment to the nearest Army Military Facility near Kansas City, Missouri. Those were the days when very efficient and capable Blacks had real power plus Black power, even during segregation. While in Mr. Evans' Pentagon office, I heard him ask the Engineer Branch's assignment officer why he disapproved my compassionate transfer. After a few minutes of conversation, Mr. Evans told the officer, "Sir, I am interested in Lt. Greene's case and I would like to see his transfer approved". I was given a transfer to Fort Leavenworth, Kansas, and assigned to the Post Engineers office as an assistant post engineer. I was stationed about 40 miles from Kansas City, Missouri. My immediate supervisor, Colonel Clifford, had been promoted to the rank of Lt. Colonel and was reassigned as the Executive Officer to the Post Engineer, Colonel Walter Faiks. At that time, I was performing duties as an engineer inspector for the Post Housing team when they inspected new troops and civilian family housing being released by the contractor to the military. I also inspected the completed construction of the post Nike Missile installations. I was pleased to see a letter of commendation from the post engineer that read: "Lieutenant Greene was selected as an inspector for Nike installations at the post because the assignment required a very capable and well qualified engineer officer".

This meant a great deal to me because I was trained to be a scientist and not an engineer, but I met the challenges. I had additional duties as an assistant fire Marshall and I was on the duty roster. I was required to follow the fire trucks to their destinations. I also had to report with the trucks when an Air Force Hospital plane landed at our airfield. I served as the Post Chemical, biological and Radiological officer, volunteering my assistance, when I was off duty, to train the Post's personnel and the Civil Defense CBR teams of the Leavenworth, Kansas community. I believed I was given the assignment of Post CBR officer because of my science background.

Colonel Clifford needed someone to replace him as the assistant engineer officer at the U.S. Army Disciplinary Barrack, a 800 man facility that included officer and enlisted men of the Army as well as the Air Force.

While serving as the engineering officer at the United States Disciplinary Barrack, I was in charge of 12 civilians, 30 military and 60 inmates who performed duties in the carpentry, masonry electric, machine and painting shops and the power plant. I was one of the few assigned officers who were permitted to visit the cell base "deathrow" and service one building that housed the execution facility. I also was one of the few personnel required to be present during the executions. I had the option of having someone else to represent me because I never had the desire to observe at least three hangings that occurred during my tour of duty there.

I was proud of some major projects that the men completed, namely, the painting of all buildings to include the "death row", all blue. I can recall visiting the inmates on "death row" and asked them to select the colors that they would like for their areas and cells. They agreed to a powder blue color. There were at least seven inmates on "death row" and the majority in 1958 were Black and several of the executions involved Blacks. Therefore, when I listen to some experts on criminal statistics who cause some Black people to become emotional over prison population statistics, I want them to examine the numbers yesterday and today to learn that in some prisons including the USDB at Leavenworth there were large numbers of Black inmates. I served on special courts martial and even as a trial and defense officer. At times, the Army used selective officers for those duties, with the assistance of a military lawyer who would serve as a law officer in the court room.

I had an interesting experience when the military police officer who was assigned as the supervisor of supply and maintenance accompanied me and several civilian engineers on a trip to Reno and McAlster, Oklahoma, where the state prison is located. The post engineer had tasked me to head a team of civilian engineers to plan for installation of the first electric chair in the state of Kansas because the state prison at Lansing was still using their hanging facility in 1958. When our plane was landing by prearrangement in a farmer's field, the white major military police officer turned to me and said, "Greene, the last time that I was in McAlester, Oklahoma three niggers robbed me". There were a few seconds of silence and I said "Well, Major, you belong to me the rest of the day." He apologized. The conversation ended and we never mentioned that incident again. Now this was not in the 1990's when people use home made names such as politically correct. I later learned from a white soldier who really did not like the major, that sometimes when he wanted his assistant, a first sergeant, to call me to his office, he would say "Please, give that Nigger lieutenant a call and ask him to come up to my office".

When I received my orders for transfer to the Chemical Corps and departed for Ft. Detrick, Maryland, I was awarded the Army's Commendation Medal.

I will discuss some of my experiences as the Director of the U.S. Army Europe Race Relations school in another chapter. I have presented in this Introductory chapter some major highlights of my life's experiences and have shown that my early years molded me to be sensitive about the fact that I was a minority American who lived in the days of real segregation and discrimination and had to perform to the best of my abilities. With God's help and my faith in him, I have survived thus far in a changing America.

CHAPTER 2

SEGREGATION

Segregation is a practice that separates an individual or group from another and has been enforced by law in the United States since the infamous Supreme Court ruling, Plessy v. Ferguson, in 1896. There were numerous acts of segregation prior to 1896. I will discuss in this chapter some true stories of segregation in the respective areas of housing, education, religion, medicine, hospitals, public facilities, transportation, employment, business, politics, government, law enforcement, organizations, entertainment, and sports.

I will also discuss in succeeding chapters true stories of segregation that are relevant to today's problems of race relations. These significant subject areas are stereotypes, Black class-culture, shades of color- genetic-diversity, U.S. Army Europe Race Relations School, and memories of segregation and integration.

HOUSING

Real Estate Law 1946

An area in the State of Maryland on route 5 several miles from the present day Southern Maryland Hospital, forbade real estate agents from selling land to persons of color 52 years ago, if the property was located on the main highway.

California's Housing Discrimination

It was necessary to pass the Hawkins Act in 1960 to end racial discrimination in public housing and successive acts had to be passed.

Restrictive Covenants

Around 1938 throughout the nation property owners had entered into legal contracts that barred persons other than Caucasians from living in certain residential areas. These agreements were major methods used in northern and border states to create and sustain existing ghettos for colored, Jews and some other minority groups.

During the years 1946 through 1948 some restrictive covenant cases were appealed to the U.S. Supreme Court. The cases involved Mr. and Mrs. J.D. Shelley, Missouri; Mr. and Mrs. Orsell McGhee, Michigan; Mr. and Mrs. James Hurd, Robert H. Rowe, Herbert E. Savage, Pauline Stewart, all from Washington, D.C. A white real estate broker, Raphael G. Urciola, represented the Blacks. There were numerous

TRUE STORIES OF SEGREGATION

organizations who filed briefs supporting these cases before the Supreme Court. The organizations were the National lawyers Guild, General Council of Congregational Churches, American Jewish Committee, B'nai B'rith, American Indian Citizens League of California, American Veterans Committee, Jewish War Veterans, and the Congress of Industrial Organizations. The National Association of Real Estates Boards filed a brief upholding the validity of the covenants. A Supreme Court decision was announced on May 3, 1948, and the Justices ruled that the federal and state courts could not enforce restrictive covenants which deny persons from owning or occupying property because of race or color.

Today some Americans are surprised when they learn of the mortgage problems that some minorities face when buying a home and also trying to obtain a bank loan. Many of them are not aware of the historical legacy of opposition by real estate companies and their legal efforts to sustain segregation in housing. After the Supreme Court issued the historical ruling in the Shelley and other cases involving restrictive covenants in May, 1948, new methods of discrimination were initiated by those who opposed Blacks occupying houses in certain residential areas. Some of the methods used were: Club membership, a device where no one could buy property in a neighborhood until they were approved by a board of the community club. Some people in Cleveland used a device which prevented sale of property without the consent of the original owner of the land. There was the leasehold system that involved the occupant's leasing the land for 99 years. They could not sell the land without the permission of community leaders. A person would have to live in the area for one year before they could qualify as a purchaser. A broker's agreement was used to keep out Blacks and other minorities. This agreement stated that real estate brokers were not to rent or sell property to certain classes of people. There was a mortgage device in which mortgage lenders agreed not to make loans in an area where minorities could come in large numbers to inconvenience white home owners.

As a young child, I can remember seeing in the neighborhood a white man we called the insurance man who collected fifty cents to a dollar for the monthly term insurance fee. The salesman was from the Metropolitan Insurance Company that was alleged not to sell ordinary insurance policies to people of color. I had heard that it was a racist company. But I was not aware until I did some research on segregated housing in America that there were some actions by the insurance company to support the allegations.

In 1943, there was a device used by the Metropolitan Insurance Company to bar Blacks from housing projects. They constructed the Stuyvesant town in New York City and stated that Negroes were barred from living there. Later this device was used by other companies. I am sure that this information is not known to many persons who really believe that Blacks have reached their equal place on the playing field.

I can never forget that in 1969 when I purchased my home in the Greenbriar area of Fairfax County, Virginia, no mortgage company in that area would give me a loan and it was necessary for my real estate agent to obtain one from out of state. But I can understand why some immigrant groups arriving in America today wave their little stars and stripes flags and say this is a wonderful country, not understanding the need for affirmative action.

The race relations school in Europe had a course in the curriculum called "white thought". It provided the students with a realization of how some white American thought, and they would discuss statements in class and express their honest agreements or non agreements on some beliefs and convictions about race problems. Therefore, when I read the statement of the former board chairman of Metropolitan Insurance Company, I had to understand his reasoning in that day and time and realize that there are many non Blacks today who would make statements similar to that of Mr. Frederick H. Eckert behind closed doors and in the presence of their friends and family. Mr. Eckert justified the company's decision to exclude Blacks in the Stuyvesant community by saying, "Negroes (not today's other minorities) were barred from the housing project because Negroes and whites do not mix; perhaps they will in 100 years and if we brought them into this development it would be to the detriment of the city too, because it would depress all the surrounding property.

Florida Housing Segregation

The year was 1945 and two Negro families were arrested for occupying homes just outside of the "Brownsville community in Miami, Florida. The court said that the families had moved into an area that was restricted to white residents. A state circuit court judge, Stanley Miledge, ruled that there was nothing in the city's zoning ordinance which gave the commissioners the right to confine Negroes to any particular section of the city. He dismissed the case.

There were cities in various states that would tolerate Black families that moved to all white neighborhoods. I remember when I was twelve years old I visited my father's sister the late Mrs. Sadie Durant, in Kansas City. She purchased a nice home in an all white neighborhood in the 3900 block of Wayne Avenue. Some cities had a policy of changing the names of streets when the dividing line separated the Black community from the whites. Because I would board a bus and ride up Vine Street and when the bus reached the intersections of Vine and 21st Street, Vine Street would become Wayne Avenue, and that would commence the all white neighborhood. I always wondered how Aunt Sadie was able to purchase that house during segregation. Now I believe that the wealthy Jewish millionaires for whom she worked for many years, and helping to raise their children, cleaning and cooking for the family might have helped her to purchase the house. As Professor Woodard suggested years ago, Jim Crow does indeed have a strange career.

Alabama Legal Zoning Case

In 1947, Mr. and Mrs. Samuel Matthews had a house built in West Birmingham, Alabama, and were preparing to move to their new house, when the move was prohibited by city authorities. They were told that there was a zoning ordinance that restricted Negroes to certain sections of the city. A concerned local court judge, Clarence Mullins, ruled that the U.S. Supreme Court had declared unconstitutional such ordinances and that the Black family had a legal right to occupy their home.

When Dr. Martin Luther King Jr. went to Chicago, Illinois he realized that there were some whites who committed violent acts in protest against the Civil Rights goals. I consider segregation an American legacy because many Americans are really color blind when they are unaware of what occurred before in America when Dr. King visited Chicago in the mid 1960s. But in 1946, some returning Black veterans who survived the horrors of warfare met some opposition from white Americans when they attempted to enter as residents in the federally owned housing project located in a predominantly white neighborhood. The incident that occurred was known as the Airport Homes Riot.

Airport Homes Riot

Theodore Turner, a Black veteran, tried to move into the project with the assistance of some 500 policemen because some 200 hundred whites attempted to storm the airport homes. Then on December 6, 1946, two other Black veterans were scheduled to move into the project. But whites began to storm the project. There were some 1,800 persons who surrounded the place and fought the police and many women were among the angry crowd. Some white ministers helped the veterans to move their belongings from the trucks into the houses. There was another project riot in Chicago, Illinois, in August 1947, it was called the Fernwood Project Riot.

Fernwood Project Riot

Some Blacks were given permission to live in the project and some 1,000 policemen were assigned to protect them prevent any disturbance; however, an angry mob of some 2,000 whites stormed the project and four policemen were injured. When the mob could not gain entrance to the project they ran out into the streets and began to stone passing automobiles in which Blacks were riding. Some fifty Blacks, men and women had to be treated for injuries at various hospitals. 92 white persons who took part in the riot were prosecuted but not fined or given jail terms. They were put on probation and required to attend five sessions of a series of lectures and discussions on race relations and the rights of minorities. At the conclusion of the lectures they were all discharged.

All White Levitt Town

A white housing developer, William J. Levitt, constructed some homes for working people at a cost of 7,000 dollars with payments of sixty dollars a month. He built the homes in an open community twenty miles from Manhattan, New York. In the late 1950's, it is believed that some Blacks were able to purchase homes in the all white housing development.

The Creation of Kansas City's Ghetto

In the early 1900's, some all Black districts were created and they had names such as "Hicks Hollow and Belvedere" near Independence Avenue. The streets were unpaved with few sidewalks, and Blacks were restricted as to where they could live. Some 8,000 of the city's 24,000 Blacks lived in the bowery between Troust Avenue and Woodland Avenue from 17th street to 25th streets. Many of the Blacks lived in old two and three story houses that had been vacated by white residents or condemned by the city. The land lords were permitted to rent the houses without any interference from city officials.

Falls Church Proposed Ordinance

When the Virginia legislature in 1912 authorized cities and towns to adopt ordinances that would provide for the segregation of the races, the city of Falls Church, Virginia, proposed an ordinance to confine Blacks to a small section of the city. Some courageous Black leaders called a meeting and formed an organization called the "Colored Citizens Protective League (CCPG). A protest letter was written by Edwin B. Henderson, a distinguished physical education teacher in Washington, D.C. and a community activist. He sent letters to the Mayor of Falls Church and each member of the Falls Church Town Commission. The committee secured the legal services of attorneys James A. Cobb and George C. Hayes (a friend of my father). The attorneys were members of the Washington, D.C. National Association for the Advancement of Colored People (NAACP) branch. They filed a law suit to prevent the enforcement of the ordinance. Finally, the Falls Church Town Council abandoned the proposal. The actions by the Colored Protest Committee was the genesis of the Falls Church Rural NAACP branch.

The Segregated FHA

The Federal Housing Administration (FHA) was established in 1934. It had the authority to insure private lending institutions against loss on long term first mortgage home loans and on long secured loans for home repairs. The underwriters' 1936 manual stated it is necessary that properties shall be continued to be occupied by the same social and racial classes. (This was a discriminating clause promoting continued segregation.)

The FHA also supported the use of hills, ravines and highways to bar Blacks from desirable housing and also used a racial covenant form which left blank spaces for the designation of the groups to be excluded. Between the 1934-1950 some 15 million houses were constructed and occupied under the discriminatory policies.

A Racist Blockbusting Policy

During the eras of segregation, some white real estate owners used a device called "blockbusting". They would tell white owners that Blacks would be moving into the neighborhood. This method was used to frighten some whites to sell and move out of the neighborhood. There were some real estate agents that would use a more positive method. In 1969, when I purchased my home in Fairfax County, my real estate lady told me that she had spoken to neighbors in the all white neighborhood and said a "very nice educated Black family will be moving in. There are two little boys and he is a military man". During the time that I lived there, I had the most cordial neighbors that one could ask for. I purchased the house for $40,000 dollars and sold it for $50,000 dollars within two years. It was on the market for only two days. Well, I guess my family did not depreciate the real estate. I can recall a very interesting story. One day I came home from my job at the U.S. Army Biological Warfare Laboratories at Fort Detrick, Maryland, and had a short white lab coat on the backseat of my car. I realized that the grass had not been cut in several weeks, so I got out the lawn mower and cut the grass. Several days later my white neighbors told my wife that she and her husband could not stop laughing because her parents were visiting from North Carolina and while at the dinner table, her father said, "I did not know that you have some wealthy people living in your block because I saw their colored man cutting the grass with his servant's coat on". My white neighbor said that she told her father with a smile on her face, "No, that is a nice colored neighbor, Captain Greene, who had his lab coat on; he is a very smart scientist that is in the

Army. Just another true story of living as a Black in America the beautiful. My late son, Robert II was about six years old and he played with the white girl his same age that lived next door. One day, I was taking a nap and he had awaken me when I heard him reciting a jingle that the little girl next door had taught him. The jingle was: "Eeny, meany, miney mo, catch a nigger by the toe, if he hollers, let him go, eeny meany miney mo" I immediately told Robert to use the word tiger instead of nigger. Sometimes a child's environment will have an effect on what they hear and later in different cultural groups, especially in an integrated society.

A White Hero

I call the late Morris Milgram a hero because in 1969 or earlier, he built some interracial housing developments in Northeast Philadelphia, Pennsylvania, a suburb called New town. He also built housing for some 20,000 people located in the geographical areas of Philadelphia, Boston, Cambridge, Chicago, Princeton, Washington, California, Maryland, New York, Texas and Virginia. He was born in Russia and had been raised on socialist principles. But he believed if people did not live together, soon the world was going to fall apart. Milgram was a partner in a contracting business with his father-in-law in Philadelphia.

Politicians today are being elected to office especially if they are strong conservatives who believe that the federal government is not needed to enforce laws that could be accomplished by the respective states and that states should have the rights to carry on many functions that the government has been doing in the past. However, in the area of housing, many successful programs to eradicate segregation and discrimination in housing were not being created by many states.

Military's Affirmative Housing Programs

The Department of Defense in cooperation with the U.S. Department of Housing and Urban Development produced a booklet for military personnel in 1969. The booklet was called, A Guide to Housing in Washington for Military Personnel". The first paragraph of the booklet said plainly and clearly that Federal Regulations under the President's Executive Order 11063 requires that housing provided with Federal assistance after November 24, 1962 available housing would be without discrimination because of race, color and national origin. The pamphlet also had a list of some ten housing referral offices which provided assistance in finding houses for military personnel. There was housing not on the federal referral listing. However, many of the owners did cooperate with the government in their efforts to implement equal opportunities policies. I visited an off-base housing referral office in 1970 and obtained a list of available housing in Maryland. I asked a fellow officer who was white to call the manager of an apartment complex in Hyattsville and inquire about any available vacancies. The manager said that there was a vacant apartment. He told her that a Captain Greene will come to see her about the apartment. When I visited the manager's office, I was greeted by a cordial white lady who gave me an application and immediately approved my application. Later, I learned from a Black female resident that we were the only two Blacks living in that complex at the time. The residents were friendly and many of them were retired Jewish people including my 91 year old neighbor across the hall. When my sister visited me the manager remarked, "Your brother is a very nice resident and we all like him." I felt very comfortable when I arrived at the apartment to obtain an application because I knew I had the military's support, if I had happened to confront any problems.

White Thoughts on Housing

An upper class white man said in the 1940's that Blacks should have certain sections in the town for themselves because some white people are unfriendly and living in a separate area will make Blacks happy. Another white person said, "I would not object to Blacks living near me if they have the same standards that I have". These statements were made in 1940, and I know that there is a county near Washington, D.C. where some middle and upper class Blacks live in 200-300,000 dollar homes and the majority of residents in some subdivisions are Blacks with a few Asians or Hispanics families. The county is at least 70 percent Black and you wonder if you are over 50 years of age are you seeing a return to a housing segregation pattern that will now be called defacto segregation.

Equal Housing at Colgate, 1931

There have been some white colleges and universities which have admitted Blacks for many years prior to integration in the 1960's. However, there has been an unwritten policy by some colleges and universities that Black students will be housed separately in the dormitory with no roommates or live off campus in a private home owned by people of color. Some African American students lived in the Fraternity and Sorority houses. As late as 1949, the first Black admitted to the U.S. Naval Academy, Annapolis was in a room alone. I would not be surprised that a visit to some predominantly white colleges today would show a pattern of yesteryears' politics on the assignment of rooms. The following true story portrays two Americans of different ethnic groups who were sharing rooms probably ahead of their time.

In 1931, there was an African American student and a Caucasian student who were college roommates at Colgate University. I was pleased to meet the son of the

Caucasian student and was told the following: His father, Thomas D. Mackey III from Michigan was studying at Colgate in 1931. Mackey was a Phi Beta Kappa scholar and later received a Master's Degree in Greek and English. In later years, he became the president of a very successful printing company. Thomas Mackey Jr. said that during the depression years there was one student on campus who appeared to always have some money. He was a very interesting roommate. The roommate of color that shared a room with Thomas D. Mackey Jr., was the Honorable Reverend Adam Clayton Powell Jr., Congressman from New York City.

Military Housing Problems
(Discrimination off Post Housing Germany)

While serving as the Director, United States Army Europe (USAREUR)'s Race Relations School, I was able to obtain a copy of the USAREUR Housing Referral Service Report, April-June 1972. The report provided information relating to discrimination in off post housing. The report included the names of the landlord or agent of the residences, the complaint, date of imposition and reason why they had been placed under restrictive sanctions during the period. There was also a list of the names of landlords who were replaced on the referral list and the date the restriction was lifted. There were lists that indicated the status of racial complaints carried over from preceding periods and a column for the current status and the other list was for racial complaints received and resolved during the current period and also a column showing complaints that were not resolved. Some of the complaints were received from major cities where military troops were stationed. Some of those cities were: Stuttgart, Darmstadt, Giessen, Fulda, Wuerzburg, Nurenberg, Frankfurt, Baumholder, and Mannheim. Some of the German landlords were very frank in expressing why they did not want to rent to Black servicemen and women and their families. Their honest remarks were, "I would like white tenants because of my neighbors' attitudes. Blacks would not be accepted because in this area, when a Black was referred to my apartment, I did not rent it because I was hoping that a Black would never come". An officer that worked for me at the Race Relations School's, was refused an apartment in Wuertemberg. The German who refused him an apartment said that he believed Blacks would not fit in. These words were spoken by the landlord's cousin. An investigation revealed that the lieutenant had not talked to the landlord who said that he might have rented the apartment. Now credit must be given to some German landlords because in some instances there were communication problems, misunderstandings and a few unfavorable incidents involving Black soldiers.

The United States Army Europe (USAREUR) in 1972 was confronted with some racial problems in Germany. One of the problems was off post housing for Black soldiers and their families. The USAREUR command had an efficient housing referral service for off post housing for the soldiers. Where discrimination was observed, the landlords were placed under restrictive sanctions. Some of the sanctions occurred near military installations in the cities of Darmstadt, Frankfurt, Giessen, Goeppingnen, Fuerth, Stuttgart, Nuernberg, Baumholder and Mannheim.

The military initiated positive actions without the tactics of legal loopholes, delay, avoidance, appeasement and justifications that nothing could be done. The commanding general and his staff were able to implement policies and actions that produced immediate results and reduced some of the major housing problems that were affecting the morale of Black soldiers in the command. The following discussion will reveal some of the measures taken.

Some German landlords would sign a government form agreeing to respond to the U.S. government rule of equal opportunity. However, some would still refuse leases to Blacks. They were honest in their reasons when they stated: "I wanted white tenants because of the neighbor's attitudes, Blacks would not be accepted in the area, felt Blacks would not fit in and refused to rent because he is just Black." Some credit must be given to those German landlords who complaints were made, because through the military's investigation and communication between the parties concerned, some cases were resolved and there were revelations of misunderstandings and negative actions of the Black applicant. Considerable progress was made without the intervention of politicians and activities who sometimes exacerbate the problem instead of obtaining a solution.

Segregated Ordinances

San Francisco, California passed a race segregation ordinance in 1890. In the early 1900's, the cities of Baltimore, Maryland, Atlanta, Georgia and Greenville, South Carolina enacted segregation ordinances. The city of Baltimore, Maryland designated all white and all Black in areas where both races lived. There was a Virginia law that designated separate districts for whites and Blacks. It was unlawful for either race to live in the other's district. An ordinance in Richmond, and Ashland, Virginia, and Winston Salem, North Carolina designated a block white if a majority of the residents were white or if there was a colored majority of the residents, the block would be colored. This law was challenged in the courts in 1915.

This discussion on racial problems in housing during segregation highlighted the Black presence because the new minority today were not affected 60-70 years ago.

EDUCATION

Throughout the years, many Black leaders have emphasized the importance of education as a great weapon against discrimination and segregation. The late W.E.B. Dubois once wrote: "If we ever compel the world's respect it will be by the virtue of our head and not our feet."

The problems that exist in the nation's public schools today and the controversies over school choices, vouchers, charter schools, discipline, and scholarship affect Black students and other minorities. When one considers the legal cases of reverse segregation and the passage of legislation to end all affirmative action measures, then we must ask the questions, if we are advancing above the veil of success, what is its impact? And is the impact actually a fear by some non Blacks that we as a people have sighted that economic and political promised land?

The following discussion will highlight some true stories that are relevant to education. These stories will illustrate how long people of color have been challenging the court system and opponents in a quest to obtain equal rights in this country's educational system.

The early 1820's was when the first known Black was given an opportunity to enroll in an all white college, Middleburg College, Vermont. He was Alexander Lucius Twilight. Twilight was the son of Ichabod and Mary Twilight of Bradford, Vermont. As a young boy, he was indentured at one time to a farmer. During the period 1815-21, he was enrolled at Randolph Academy and completed secondary school and two years of college level courses. He was actually the first Black to earn a college degree from an American school. After graduation from Middleburg, his first job was teaching in an Aidcondad Frontier Community, Peru, New York. Twilight married in 1826, Mary Merrill Ladd. He studied theology and received a license to preach in 1829. Later, he taught in Vermont, then a Preceptorship, Orleans County Grammar at Brownington, Vermont. Twilight served briefly in the state legislature 1836-37. It would be another 112 years before another Black man would be elected to the legislature. William Anderson of Shoreham Orchardist was elected in 1948. He also served as principal of an academy prior to his death at the age of 62 years in 1857.

I believe that when we discuss the present day racial problems of our public school system, it is necessary to reflect historically on some cases prior to the 1954 school decision Brown v. Board of Education. Some of the major cases that were argued before federal, appeal and the Supreme Courts during the separate but equal period were:

Cumming v. Board of Education in 1899. The Georgia high schools were closed and the whites retained their schools. Blacks wanted to restrain expenditure of public funds for white schools. The court avoided the issue of segregation.

Berea College v. Kentucky. The court in 1908 upheld as valid law requiring separate public and private schools.

In 1927, the court upheld Mississippi's rights to exclude Asians from white schools in the case Gong Lum v. Rice.

Donald Murray, a Black, was enrolled at the University of Maryland Law School under a court order. In Pearson v. Murray, the Maryland Court of Appeals held that the state must afford equal opportunities in its own institutions, in 1936.

The University of West Virginia Graduate School decided to voluntarily admit Negroes in 1938.

In 1938, the U.S. Supreme Court stated that Missouri was bound to furnish equal facilities within its borders. The University of Missouri was ordered to admit Lloyd Gaines to their Law School, but for some reason he did not appear to enroll.

Ada Lois Sipuel sought admission to the University of Oklahoma Law School, January 1946, but her application was denied because she was a Negro. She asked the University to admit her on the grounds that it was the only state supported school in Oklahoma offering courses toward a law degree. The case reached the Supreme Court; and on January 13, 1947, the court ruled that the state of Oklahoma must afford to Ms. Sipuel and others equal educational facilities, and the state must provide the facilities at the same time they are provided for whites. Judge Ben T. Williams of Oklahoma then ruled that the University must admit Ms. Sipuel at the opening of the second semester or establish a law school for Blacks. Ms. Sipuel appealed again for admission on January 19, 1947. But the next day, she was refused admission. The Board of Regents announced that a law school would be opened on January 26 in Oklahoma as a branch of the state school for Blacks, Langston University. A school was opened in one room with a facility of three white professors. However, Ms. Sipuel did not apply for admission and it is believed no other Black applied for the one room Negro Law School. Later, a former Black faculty member at Langston University, G.W. McLaurin, filed suit in the federal district court in Oklahoma in August 1948 requesting an injunction against the University of Oklahoma to prevent the state and university authorities from denying him admission to the graduate school of education. A three-judge federal court ruled that to deny a Negro admission to the graduate school of education of the university was unconstitutional, since such courses were not available for Negroes elsewhere in the state. The university admitted McLaurin to its graduate classes.

But he was required to sit in a separate room from the main classroom in which the white students sat. He was able to see and hear the professor. When McLaurin filed for a legal relief, the same court ruled that the school was within its rights in separating the races.

In 1948, the University of Delaware announced it would admit Blacks to any graduate courses not offered at Delaware State College for Negroes.

During 1948. the University of Arkansas voluntarily admitted Black to its professional schools.

The legal case Johnson v. Board of Trustees involved the University of Kentucky under court order to open its school to Blacks in 1949.

On May 16, 1946, the NAACP filed a suit on behalf of Herman Marion Sweatt of Texas. The suit was against the board of regents of the University of Texas, compelling the board to admit Sweatt to its law school. The District Court, Travis County, Austin, Texas, decided on June 26, 1946, that Sweatt should receive relief because he had been denied equal protection of the law guaranteed by the Fourteenth Amendment. The court gave the university six months in order to establish a separate and equal law school for Sweatt. It was necessary for the NAACP to go back to court and present evidence to show that the three-room school which had been established was unequal. The court then decided against Sweatt on the grounds that the new school in Austin was equal to the law school at the University of Texas, and Herman Sweatt could not go to the University of Texas because the laws of the state required segregation.

After an appeal to the appellate and Texas Supreme Courts, the NAACP learned that plans were being developed to provide at the new state university for Negroes at Houston in 1948, a law course. Finally in 1950, the U.S. Supreme Court in the case Sweatt v. Painter ordered Herman Sweatt admitted to the University of Texas Law School after ruling the law school at Texas State University for Negroes (Texas Southern) was inferior in the difference of community standing, reputation of faculty, tradition and prestige.

A federal court order in 1951, in the case of McKissick v. Carmichael, opened the University of North Carolina Law School to Blacks.

The University of Tennessee admitted Negroes to its graduate professional, and special schools after a ruling in the case of Gray v. University of Tennessee.

I do not believe that these preceding cases have been included in the school curricula for the average Black who may not understand the relevance of affirmative action.

New England Liberalism

In the early 1900's, there were some liberal New England Colleges who would accept qualified Negroes. However, they would segregate them or not permit them to live in the dormitories and eat in the dining room.

White Leadership

Many Black colleges were under the leadership of white presidents for some years. Howard University, Washington, D.C., was founded in 1867 and did not receive its first Black president until 1926, the late, Dr. Mordecai Wyatt Johnson.

A popular Black university in Richmond, Virginia, had a white president, a Baptist Missionary, who was accused of paying higher salaries to white faculty members than to Black professors with similar academic qualifications.

Racism, California Style

A town called Allensworth, California was founded by a former slave and retired Army Chaplain, Lieutenant Colonel Allen Allensworth in 1908. He was assisted by some other ambitious Blacks. Around 1915, there were some 300 Blacks living in the town. The Calbert and Hackett families were among the early settlers. The late Mrs. Sadie Hackett Calbert was born in 1885 and was brought to California by her mother, a former slave from Roaring River, North Carolina by train to California. They settled in the area of Allensworth. Sadie Hackett Calbert lived to the age of 102 years. She was married to a lay pastor, Rev. William Calbert. Her sister, Mrs Grace Hackett was declined a position as a principal in the California Public schools because she was Black. During those segregated days, her accomplishments as a graduate of a California high school as class valedictorian and San Francisco State College were irrelevant in her situation.

White Benefactor

The segregated years were characterized by assistance for Black education provided by white benefactors. In the 1920's, Julius Rosenwald, president of Sears Roebuck and a multi-millionaire philanthropist of Chicago, Illinois provided schools throughout the south for Blacks and established the Rosenwald Fund. He provided funds for the construction of schools in many counties in Virginia. One two- three room school houses were built. It was necessary at times for Negro parents to pay one half of the teacher's salary for an additional month of service.

Federal Assistance

In 1934, some federal aid was provided to Blacks for school construction. The Public Works Administration (PWA) and Works Program Administration (WPA) funds became available for school construction. Prior to receiving the federal assistance, many of the schools for Blacks in the south were referred to as "shacks".

Maryland's Unequal School Sessions

The State of Maryland in the 1930's had different school session requirements for Blacks and whites. The session requirement for whites was 180 days and for Blacks 160 days. In 1937, the legislature passed some laws changing the Black session requirements to 180 days, this became effective in September, 1939.

Stereotype Literature

The writing style of the noted author Stephen Foster's include a pattern of stereotypic writings about people of color. A great negative effect that it had during segregation was that these writings, read by young white students in elementary classrooms, had a negative affect. The students developed their first impression and awareness of Blacks from this literature. A review of Foster's book *Stephen Foster and Little Dog* published in 1941, included some of these passages and depictions:

> "a song called Git On Board Little Children
> had a picture with the characters using
> the dialect words of De, Dere, Mo, Dis".

There was a picture of a man named Tom who would sing the song, "Swing Low Sweet Chariot." Another picture of Tom showed a Black man in a church. He was painted jet Black. There were also pictures of a Black minstrel, Blacks, dancing and singing on a boat for whites, and a Black on stage with a banjo singing:

TRUE STORIES OF SEGREGATION

"First on de heel tap, den on de toe and ebb'ny
time I turned around I jump Jim Crow".

Foreign Students at Howard, 1944 and 1929

There were foreign students studying at Black universities during the separate but equal period. Some of the foreign students at Howard University in 1944 were from the countries of British New Guiana, British West Indies, Trinidad, Cuba, Grenada, Hawaii, Liberia, Puerto Rico, Panama, Jamaica, and the Virgin Islands. The medical school graduated a Chinese student in the class of 1929. He was Rupert Cyril Sancho, who was living at 59 West 71st, New York City, New York. Sancho became the first known citizen of his race to become an American citizen under the new procedure that was made possible to achieve naturalization citizenship with the appeal of the Chinese Exclusion Act. Rupert Sancho had studied law in Trinidad prior to coming to the United States in 1921. He was able to work his way through Howard University's Medical School.

Truths about Busing

A review of the U.S. Commission On Civil Rights May, 1972, publication has revealed some facts about the controversial topic of busings. I believe that many people today are unaware of these facts.

Students in rural areas were bused for school consolidation, but when school desegregation began, busing became an emotional and controversial problem. In 1958, Warren County, Virginia was one of the seventeen Virginia counties which had no Black high school. The Black students had to attend schools in two neighboring counties. Some Black students had to travel a long distance daily. However there were children who were boarded in the town, rather than travel more than 100 miles daily.

Indian pupils had experienced months at boarding schools. There were some Alaskan children who went to a boarding school in Oklahoma.

Prior to desegregation, thousands of Black and white students in rural areas traveled by bus to their separate schools. When desegregation occurred busing became a national issue with negative overtones, because busing was being used as a desegregation tool. Some northern cities began their experimentation with busing. The cities of Boston, Chicago, Evanston (Ill.) Berkeley, Hartford, and Rochester used busing as a means of increasing school integration. It is interesting that when many non Blacks in New Mexico had two bus routes, 74 miles one way and three 70 miles in each direction, and in Needles, California, a route 65 miles one way and students traveled three hours a day on a bus, remember their daily community had absolutely nothing to do with desegregation a school system or maintaining a racial balance. I wonder how many honorable politicians in a nearby Washington suburb consider these facts when they successful ended their court ordered desegregation plans.

How many people today are aware that during segregation Black children in some cities were denied bus transportation to go to school? Some students walked five miles each way to one room rural schools with one teacher for seven grades, while the white children had buses and modern school buildings. In south Texas the white children were bused out of predominantly Mexican American neighborhoods to an all white school.

Was Meredith the First at Ole Mississippi?

When James Meredith enrolled at the University of Mississippi in 1962 under Federal Court orders and with the assistance of National Guard and active Army Troops, it was said that Meredith was not the first Black to attend the University. A very light skinned Black, Henry Murphy from Atlanta, Georgia, attended the university as a student in the Armed Forces Specialized Program.

Northern Virginia Community College
Eliminates Race Based Scholarships

The year was 1978 and I was present at a faculty and staff meeting at the Annandale Campus of Northern Virginia Community College when the president of the five campuses was discussing statistics on minority enrollments. He did not give the breakdown by race or ethnic groups. I asked a question concerning the overall number because I knew that there were few Blacks enrolled at the Annandale campus but there was a representative number at the Alexandria campus. The president responded to my question by saying that the figures include the Vietnamese, Mexican Americans, Japanese, Chinese, Native Americans and Black students enrolled. That was my introduction and understanding that minorities no longer had a great emphasis on Blacks and Mexican Americans but also many immigrant students who were enrolled at the college, and they were considered minorities in the sense of government equal opportunity benefits. I had no idea that 20 years later a white student would feel that he had been discriminated against.

The five scholarships in question are privately funded. The white student's complaint was based on a 1994 ruling by the 4th Circuit Court of Appeals decision that struck down the Benjamin Banneker Scholarship program at the University of

Maryland, College Park, because it was limited to Black students. There have been other colleges in the Washington area to open their "race based" scholarship programs to students of all races. These legal challenges in 1998 have been initiated by possible innocent white students and possibly knowledgeable attorneys who are using similar legal tactics to dismantle the progress made by many Black people over the years who used the court system to remedy years of discriminatory practices in our education system affecting Blacks, Mexican American and native Americans. "Just some food for thought" or a term I will be using throughout my discussions "nutritional reasoning".

A Questionable Program, 1962
D.C. Public Schools Basic Track

D.C. Public School officials believed it was necessary to address some problems of student performances 36 years ago, some problems which seem endemic to the Washington, D.C. school system in 1998. The following discussion of the 1962 Basic Track program will possibly reveal some of the problems that school administrators are trying to solve today. They will probably be using similar components of the 1962 program, but not using the term track.

The Basic Track Program in the Junior High Schools in 1962 Washington was organized in this manner: The philosophy, organization and general curriculum guidelines were developed by a committee appointed by the Assistant Superintendent for Junior and Senior High Schools. The committee members included principals, teachers, counselors, social workers, clinical psychologists and reading supervisors.

The major philosophy addressed the problems of the student in the basic curriculum: fundamental skills in arithmetic and reading, and mastery of spoken English. The committee addressed other issues that could have contributed to a child's remedial status such as non school oriented conditions and a deprived social background.

There was consideration for the students placed in the basic curriculum because they shared the same curriculum offerings with students in the regular curriculum to the degree that they could profit from them. They also had facilities, teachers and services with other children in the school. The students were able to still be a member of the student body receiving neither more nor less than any other child.
A method of placement was used which included retention, promotion and or graduation in the basic education program.

On May 14, 1959, a Committee on Health and Special Education Service of the Board of Education issued a statement of purpose and objectives which was referred to by the Basic Track committee in 1962. The purpose and objectives were:

> "The aim of the basic program should be upgrading of children. Those who are academically retarded will be placed in a basic program and moved out when their development has reached acceptable standards. Flexibility between the basic and regular program should be stressed. Factors other than IQ such as the achievement level, motivation and interest need to be considered in the placement of pupils."

The Department of Pupil Appraisal made recommendations to the principals for child placement after clinical evaluations. The students would have had a profile of more than three years below grade level in reading and arithmetic and an IQ in the slow to low normal range. Promotion, transfer and graduation was on the basis of achievement commensurate with improvement in the student's adjustment to social situations, demonstrated progress in handling personal problems and the child's development of a wholesome attitude.

The students were expected to earn their promotion; their advancement was not automatic. Basic program student could be graduated from junior high school on successful completion of the ninth grade basic curriculum. The children were expected to received the same diploma as all other graduates and participate in the graduation exercise without any mark of differentiation. The students would be transferred out of the basic classes when the Department of Pupil Appraisal determined that students needed more specialized school placement such as sight or hearing conservation, city-wide social adjustment or the Boys Junior-Senior High School. The principals were required to review the progress of the basic track students once each semester to determine if a change of the curriculum assignment should be made. Students were retained in the basic track only if there was evidence that they could not perform in an adjacent track.

The curriculum of the Basic Track Program assigned pupils to basic track classes in the junior high schools according to mental ages ranging from eight to twelve. Curriculum materials were selected to satisfy the needs students with low mental ages.

The basic classes were organized as follows: the classes were small 18-1 pupil teacher ratio, students were grouped in their academic classes according to ability, and students participated in all activities of the junior high school with other students. Basic classes were organized on the seventh, eighth and ninth grade levels in the same manner as regular classes. There were to be no labels attached to the home room designation. The skills in home economics and industrial arts were taught by regular teachers.

Textbooks were selected on the basis of student psychological appeal and readings levels. An orientation program was necessary for the student's adjustment upon entering the basic class. Levels were established with standards of excellence to be achieved by the students. The levels included a non reader group, ages 7-9, mental ages 4-6; and beginning readers. A primary group included other students ages 9-11, mental ages 5-7; and the book used were primers and included other simple books. The intermediate group ages were 11-13 with mental ages 7-8 read first to third graded materials. The secondary group's ages were 13-16, mental ages 8-12 who read first to fifth grade materials.

In 1962, I was certified to teach in the evening program of D.C. Public Schools. I was recertified in 1969 to teach science courses at night on the high school levels. Later, I was placed on the substitute list. During the period 1962-1980, I taught in the D.C. School System, part-time, either at night or as a part-time substitute. I have substituted at every D.C. high school except two. I was employed as a full-time teacher to teach science on the secondary level and taught until 1993. When I left to return to college teaching in my other major discipline, history. I felt that I had ground level experience concerning student performance in the high schools of now in a controversial school system. I have always used a method of teaching that I personally call "Teach Me to Learn From the Simple to the Complex". I used the method for grades nine through twelve to assist students in improving their reading skills, vocabulary building and comprehension. My teacher evaluations were based partly on my success in the classroom. I was able to sustain an outstanding rating for ten years at one high school. In 1986, I wrote a learning manual on the subject of biology. The manual could be used with most high school biology texts or even a college introductory course.

The special features of the learning manual were instructions to the student on how to prepare a textbook chapter summary, vocabulary building laboratory activities and instructions on how to prepare a science project. I was able to improve student comprehension, assist special education students who at times were "main streamed" and medial achieving to satisfy a minimum of learning objectives. The manual was most valuable in helping students who were absentees and those who entered the class during mid advisories and semesters.

I have been teaching on the college level for the last five years and classroom observations are most revealing. I see today many freshmen entering college with low skills in reading, comprehension and analysis. There are some who still rely on rote memory skills. There are entering freshmen who are enrolled in classes with sophisticated names but actually are classes designed to assist remedial and low levels students who desire to pursue a college education. I sincerely believe that many high schools throughout the nation, especially in cities with a large Hispanic-Black high school student body, need to revisit in this so-called era of integration some of the necessary program that were started during the period of legal segregation and were successful according to the people who took part in the program. Many lay persons and politicians had personal views, statistics, and analyses that recalled in the dismantle of programs such as the Basic Track Program in the District of Columbia. Just more food for thought or "nutritional reasoning".

Comments on Racial Dialogue in Education, 1978

I reviewed several articles in the Northern Virginia Community College Newspaper, *The Parthian Shot*, October 28, 1977. I was interviewed for the articles and expressed my views and optimism 20 years ago about some problems that are prevalent today. One article was on a Black history course. It read: "Black history course now offered and the instructor Robert Greene will discuss the origins of the Afro Americans to the present. Greene said the unfortunate part about Black history or Afro American history is that it has been neglected in the general history curriculum and the socialization of the majority of Americans. During the separate but equal period, even many Black schools did not have the opportunity to include a course of this type. One of the aims of the course is to educate all Americans regardless of their skin color, about the history of the Afro American. Greene is quick to stress that this course is designed for students of all backgrounds and interests. He hopes this course will help to dispel some of the myths and stereotypes concerning Black citizens and provide an intellectual look at Black achievements in medicine and engineering. Greene also voiced his hope that sometime in the near future, Black History will be an accepted alternative to American history as well as a requirement for degrees in nursing, and fire and police sciences. He summed up the interview by saying, "I feel that the overall problems of Blacks and whites in America could be best understood if both sides could look at the situation unbiasedly."

On June 7, 1978, I participated in a campus debate with a colleague on the Bakke case. The newspaper article read: "Bakke Debates Stirs Racial Awareness. Dr. David Michaels, Professor of Business Management and Mr. Robert Greene, History Instructor, debated the issues in the case. Michaels took Bakke's side and argued against given special opportunities to minorities to catch up. He said some minority students had up to thirty points lower than Bakke on admissions tests. Yet, they were admitted to the medical school. The Grade Point Average (GPA) of 2.5 was waived in some cases. There were 16 seats out of 100 students reserved for minority students. He believed everyone should have the same chance. It is especially wrong when a less qualified individual takes a position away from someone more qualified. Greene argued in favor of the university and its special opportunity format. He claimed that it is America's responsibility to help the minorities who have been deprived and held back for years and fell behind the norm. He used the Black man's history in the U.S. as his main example. Greene stated that for 300 years the Blacks were told that they could not read or write and were denied the opportunity to learn. Now the opportunity is here. Yet, it will take one hundred years more before complete equality can be fulfilled. He used symbolism to further his point by telling of a race between a Mercedes and a Volkswagen. If someone gets in that Mercedes and takes off and you are told to wait 15 minutes and then try to catch him in your Volkswagen, you have an example of what is happening in America, today".

Arlington, Virginia Public Schools
Lest We Forget

Black citiizens of Arlington, Virginia in 1958 had to use the legal system in order to attend public schools. This was four years after Brown v. Board of Education Ruling: May 17, 1954. This was also the year when a youngster was one year of age and as fate would have it he would become a lawyer. In 1997, this lawyer was quoted in a newspaper that "he regrets that his daughter was skipped over to fill non white slots in the Arlington, Virginia Traditional School's Kindergarten class. We did not file this suit to prevent affirmative action".

It appears that the Arlington Public School Board had some awareness of previously segregated schools in the city and that they primarily excluded Blacks. Since sometimes the present day minorities, namely Mexican Americans (now included as Hispanics) and Native Americans could assimilate and associate with whites. Now I can understand how a one year old boy would not know this and in his maturation toward adulthood, he would be ignorant of these facts if they were not discussed in his home, school community and possibly in his law school. Therefore, he states in 1997, that there must be a way to devise a legal way to tackle the larger problem of racial and cultural and ethnic diversity in all of the county schools not just the alternative schools. These remarks were stated after an honorable Judge heard a case involving race preferences with some similar thoughts of the Bakke case 20 years ago the precipitator of what was to be and now is.

In 1997, the Arlington School Board was trying to address the problem of integrating minorities into predominantly white class rooms including a kindergarten in a magnet type school that provided a back to basics program and a strict dress code. The school board devised a lottery system whereby they would be able to expand the Traditional Kindergarten to make space for eleven minority students. Some white parents protested and said that the lottery system was illegal citing other legal cases. This lawyer representing the parents filed a legal suit and Judge Albert V. Bryan Jr., a U.S. District Judge handed down a ruling. Judge Bryan ruled that the lottery was unconstitutional because it was weighed in favor of children who were Hispanic or Black who came from low income households. He ordered the eleven minority students to be replaced by eleven white students.

The Arlington School Board voted 4-1 against appealing the federal court ruling. Those members who voted against the appeal said they believed that it was best not to appeal because an even more restrictive opinion could result if they went to the U.S. Court of Appeals in Richmond, Virginia.

When the attorney received his victorious decision he remarked that diversity is hardly a state interest when it violates the Constitution's equal protection clause. it would have been very nice if this ambitious lawyer was around when I went to segregated schools, he could have used his legal mind to say segregation is hardly a state action when it violates the constitution's equal protection clause. I also believe that this same reasoning could apply to ruling of the late Judge Albert V. Bryan Sr. of Alexandria, Virginia. I believed that he was aware of segregated schools in Fairfax County to include Alexandria, Arlington and Falls Church, Virginia. I am sure that he knew that whites were not threatened by eleven Blacks desiring to enter a kindergarten in an all white school. He knew that also schools were legally segregated and that no equal protection clause interpretation included Negroes. But in 1997, Bryan's son would interpret the clause in accordance with the higher rulings by the Supreme Court.

Judge Albert V. Bryan Sr. did demonstrate some concern for affirmative action when he hired a Black bailiff (a minority officer in the U.S. Courts who served as a messenger and usher in the court room). The late James Hugo Wood, a native of Richmond, Virginia, he worked as a bailiff for Judges Lewis and Pollard. Later, he worked for Judge Bryan Sr. in Alexandria, Virginia, serving as a bailff and at times preparing the Judges's lunch. James H. Wood was married to the late Marguerite Anderson Wood of Richmond, Virginia. They are the perents of Margaret Wood Taylor Riley, Shirley Wood Jones, Judith Wood Cole Thomas, Janice Wood Hunter, Joan Wood Gould and Juliet Wood Coates. The Wood children attended segregated schools in Alexandria, Virginia, when Judge Bryan Sr. was sitting on the bench.

Early Equal Opportunity

In 1901, Wiley College in Texas was under the progressive leadership and administration of the late Dr. Matthew Winfred Dogan. The college had received a grant of eighteen thousand dollars for the construction of a Carnegie Library building on the campus. President Dr. Dogan displayed unusual concern, race pride and integrity when he stated "Negroes should have some part in the construction of the library. The white contractors walked away because they would not work with Negro laborers. There was a delay, but eventually the library was constructed with Blacks assisting.

Value of Education

During the period of segregation, many white Americans believed that it was wrong to educate Negroes beyond suitable only for the most menial service and smallest wages. The late Rev. Walter H. Brooks, D.D., former pastor of the Nineteenth Street Baptist Church, Georgetown, once said, "Let the Black man learn to plow with intelligence, let the Black man improve his morals and let the Black man get education, amen":

A Boston Legacy

Senator Charles Sumner of Massachusetts challenged the Boston School System when he said: Separate schools tend to deepen and perpetuate the odious destruction of caste. The Massachusetts Supreme Court ruled that Boston had provided reasonably equal schools for both Blacks and whites. The judge also said that any caste distinction if it exists is not created by law and probably can not be changed by law.

The Bakke Case

When the Regents of the University of California v. Allan Bakke was being argued before the U.S. Supreme Court in 1976, the University's record on graduating Black medical and dental students revealed that the University at Los Angeles graduated its first Black medical student in 1970, 51 years after its founding. Its first Black dental student graduated in 1974, 55 years after its founding.

Characteristics of a Falls Church, Virginia Segregated School 1930's

There was a two room Black school and the teacher taught grades four through seven in one room. She also had to walk to school each day and make a fire in a potbelly stove. The Black teachers received far lower salaries than white teachers with the same qualifications. Teachers of Black children were responsible for janitorial work whereas such service was provided in school for white children.

There was no source for drinking water on the grounds. There were no junior or senior high school for Blacks in the area. Students traveled to Washington or Manassas, Virginia.

They Did Not Wait until 1954

The Mexican American community in Kansas City, Missouri, did not have to wait until 1954 and experience numerous legal battles and mental pain to attend white schools on an equal basis. In 1928, they were able to attend white schools. Previously, some Mexican Americans did attend public schools with Blacks.

Separate Teaching Licenses

The State of Mississippi in 1924 had separate licensing examinations for Negro and white applicants. Virginia at one time employed some white teachers in Negro schools. The States of Florida, Kentucky, Oklahoma, and Tennessee had laws making it a punishable offense to allow white and Black students to be educated together in any school, college or other institutions, public, or private.

Separate But Not Equal

In 1949, the Clarendon County School District, South Carolina, had a Black school where some 22 Black parents had volunteered to haul water from outside pumps and the students used outside toilets. The white schools had modern plumbing and good sanitation. The white students had their own desks while one Black school had no desks. Students in some Black schools had to share desks and tables. The white schools had visual aids, maps, slides and globes. The only visual aids that Blacks had were blackboards.

"One Among Many"

A small Indiana town located between Indianapolis and Terre Haute has a regional school of 1500 students. In 1996, there was only one known Black student. There was one Black teacher who was the first Black high school teacher ever in this city. Today there are few Blacks living in the city. I first visited this city when I was 12 years old and Black students were going to school with whites, but there were no Black teachers. Many Blacks have moved away from this town today; there are a few Black families remaining. The rural county school has about 1500 students with two Blacks' this year one graduated in June with honors and has been accepted at

Purdue University. Her mother is the first and only Black teacher to teach in the town's high school. This small Indiana town is a true replica of the real America when you talk about school integration in places other than large cities where most Blacks reside along with some Hispanics.

A Merit Scholar

I first became aware of the late William Pickens during one of my father's scheduled YMCA Sunday Forums. At that time, I was not aware of some of the experiences of his life as a scholar, graduate of Talledega, Fisk and Yale Colleges. He also had served as a field secretary for the NAACP in the 1920's. Pickens taught at this Alma Mater Talledaga, Wiley College in Texas and Morgan State College (now a University). He also served in the government as a member of the Defense Savings Staff of the United States Treasury Department.

While researching my manuscript for Thomas Sewell Inborden,*Early Educator of Color*, I learned that William Pickens was a friend of Inborden. In a letter that Pickens wrote to Inborden in January, 1940, he expressed his views on opposition to Black economic development. Thomas S. Inborden had written Pickens about some trouble in North Carolina over the matter of a colored manager selected for the cooperative store. Pickens wrote Inborden that he hoped that they would be able to keep the Black manager on the job and if he needed NAACP assistance to contact him. Pickens said the Negro is ruthlessly opposed more economically than in any other area. In 1995, we read about instances where Blacks confront economic opposition, in real estate, mortgage loans and other opportunities for financial assistance.

William Pickens had learned from Inborden that in North Carolina some Black teachers were asked to go to a neighboring town to register Blacks who were enlisting in the military during World War II. He believed it was un American that the whites denied those teachers the use of restrooms in the schools where they were working. Pickens believed that some protests should be made against this type of treatment. He also wrote that this is a great country and a great effort at democracy but we have to fight continually to keep that effort going. He believed that the NAACP was a strong force for democracy. He also said that it is interesting to hear that there are no draft dodgers, so far as we know yet, among the colored people.

The reasons that I have called William Pickens a "Merit Scholar"is that in his younger days while a student, he personally demonstrated his values and goals to succeed in the academic world. This true story can be a lesson to many young Blacks who are constantly becoming obsessed with professional goals in sports and entertainment primarily for financial purposes. William Pickens said that when he arrived at Talladega College as a freshman he had not seen a school test all summer and in preparing for his entrance examination he learned that it was best to learn each daily lesson and then take a period of rest not to cram just before the test and that for the remainder of his school life he prepared for the examination by retiring at eight o'clock the night before. He related a story about a Latin professor who started to test him in Cicero. He read so easily, that the professor closed the book and opened Virgil's Aeneid asking Pickens to read some passages. Pickens said that he read several passages from some books forwards and backwards. He was then passed on to a math class. William Pickens wrote that in the days of segregation some white people had an honest opinion that Blacks characteristically were unmathematical. He said his mathematics teacher asked him to draw the figure and demonstrate the proposition that the "sum of three angles of a triangle is equal to two right angles". When he had solved the problem correctly the professor, who was the college dean, gave him no further examination and enrolled him in the sophomore class; so he never was a freshman. I recently read in the *Washington Post* newspaper an article written by a Japanese reporter about the outstanding scholarship of several Black sisters who had skipped grades and enrolled in predominantly white colleges after graduating from white secondary schools and are children of upper class Black parents. I question whether the writer of the article is aware of the many Black scholars like Pickens who have lived and died and accomplished similar academic pursuits under some different conditions in all Black institutions of learning. We also must remember that they were challenged by all white faculty members in most cases. The conditions and opportunities are present today for Black youngsters to make similar accomplishments to those of Pickens if they establish their goals obsessions, and fantasies. "Just more nutritional reasoning".

When we read about affirmative action and predominantly white law schools and Blacks' academic performance, many journalists and columnists may be aware and maybe not of the outstanding successful graduates of Howard University's Law school over the years. The following true story that occurred during segregation will show how a Howard University graduate of the class of 1923 would take the bar exam in a predominantly white Indiana County in 1925 and successful passed the examination.

Admission to Clay Court Bar
Brazil, Indiana, 1925

In recent years some law school graduates have had difficulty in qualifying to practice law. Howard University School of Law, Washington, D.C. has graduated many African American lawyers, who have distinguished themselves through excellence in the Judicial field.

The small town of Brazil, Indiana, in 1925 did not have any Black practicing attorneys. There was a very successful physician of color in the town. He was the late Dr. Oliver whose descendants today are affiliated with the *Baltimore Afro American* Newspapers. Dr. Oliver knew an African American farmer who had migrated to Brazil, Indiana from St. Louis, Missouri. His name was Joseph Greene, whose descendants are still living in Brazil, Indiana. A son, Adam Richard Greene lives in the family homestead with some members of his family.

Dr. Oliver asked Joseph Greene in 1925 if he thought his brother, Arthur Alonzo Greene, a 1923 graduate of Howard University Law School, would be interested in coming to Brazil, Indiana, to practice law. Joseph Greene wrote his brother, who was living in Washington, D.C., and asked him if he was interested. His brother replied that he was, and came to Brazil, Indiana, in 1925 to apply for admission to the Clay County Bar. During the September term, Clay County Circuit Court, 1925, John W. Baumunk, an attorney at law and member of the Clay County Bar, filed his written petition and application for Arthur A. Greene as an attorney to practice law in the county's courts. In later years Baumunk became a judge and his son was practicing law in Brazil, Indiana in 1990.

A committee of practicing attorneys of the Clay County Bar was appointed by the Clay County Circuit Court to examine Arthur A. Greene as to his qualifications to practice law in the State of Indiana. The committee consisted of attorneys, Kenneth C. Miller, J. Frank Adams and Otto T. Englehart. The committee members filed their report on October 1, 1925. The committee's report stated that they had "examined the said Arthur A. Greene for such purposes, and we do hereby recommend and move his admission to the bar of the Clay Circuit Court."

The judge of the 13th Judicial Circuit Court of Clay County inspected the report and found that Arthur A. Greene was a person of good moral character, a legal voter and of sufficient learning and qualified to practice the law. Judge Hutchinson ordered that Arthur A. Greene be admitted to the Court to practice law upon his taking the proper oath.

Arthur A. Greene appeared in open court and the following oath was duly administered to him.

> *I, Arthur A. Greene, do solemnly swear that I will support the constitution of the United States and of this state, and that I will faithfully and honestly discharge the duties of an attorney-at-law.*
>
> *The final report was read and signed in open court on* October 2, 1925.

The Clay County Circuit Court in 1925 demonstrated a very honest, and equitable approach in admitting an African American to their bar based on his qualifications. Their actions also indicated that Howard University Law School in awarding Greene a degree in 1923, had successfully prepared him for admission to the Indiana Bar in 1995.

Arthur A. Greene did not move to Brazil, Indiana, to practice law. He decided to remain in Washington, D.C. and become a Physical Education Director and Program Secretary for the Washington 12th Street YMCA. In 1990, his son was able to visit the Clay County Court House, Brazil, Indiana, and obtained a true copy of his father's application for admission to the bar. Arthur Alonzo Greene Sr. was probably the first Black American to be admitted to the Clay County Bar, Indiana.

A Principal's Qualifications for A Teacher During Segregation, 1900'S

After returning from a productive trip to the New England states, Principal, Thomas Inborden had the responsibility of selecting some new faculty members and preparing for the approaching fall semester at Brick. He sent letters to Dr. H.B. Frissell, President of Hampton Institute, Virginia, and Dr. Wilson Bruce Evans, Washington, D.C., his wife's cousin. He asked them to assist him in obtaining a Domestic Science teacher for the fall term 1904. His request stated that the lady must be a Christian, positive in Christian life and who has the ability to work with other people. He said that her salary would be twenty dollars a month to start and traveling expenses to school and back home, plus free washing, ironing, room with heat and light and board. T.S. asked Frissell and Evans if they could find such a person and ascertaining if they would come to Brick, and write a letter including age, complexion, school graduated from, teaching experience, and letters of recommendations.

Fisk Students Applaud A Fine Speaker

Prior to the 1930's, many private schools of higher learning in the South had white presidents and sometimes their views on segregation and the overall race problem were conservative. Schools like Fisk University would have an annual speaker's series to expose students to Black leaders, artists and former alumni. In 1917, the students had a speaker who was born in Albany, Georgia, attended the Normal School and was a graduate of Fisk University. He was studying law prior to his enlistment in the Army. He returned to the campus after serving as a lieutenant in

France. A student wrote that he was one of the best speakers, who spoke about what the students could do to overcome prejudices. The students applauded him greatly. The student also wrote that after his speech the college president got up and made a few remarks which indirectly hit his speech. Everybody got his point but they could not avoid facing facts as they were and as the speaker stated them. The speaker was Lt. William L. Dawson, who in later years would become a congressman from the State of Illinois and serve in Congress as one of the most influential political power representing the Black community. Just another true story of Black survival during segregation.

North Carolina's Unequal Schools, 1920's

The newspapers today print editorials and commentaries on vouchers, charter schools and inner city test scores and on a predominant Black county that has ended desegregation plans. I ask how many politicians and school board officials are aware of the realities of separate facilities that were never equal. This true story is a revelation of white and Black education in North Carolina in 1920. A report revealed that the State of North Carolina had 200 accredited white high schools and 17 for the Black children; However a state official honestly remarked that when it came to real public high schools, North Carolina did not have a single one for the Black children.

In 1924, there were 24 accredited high schools for Blacks and only eight were public high schools. The private schools were the pioneers for Black education in North Carolina. The American Missionary Association (AMA) had three high schools in North Carolina; and in 1923, the only accredited school was Brick School, Enfield, North Carolina. The school had maintained a four year course of study with an eight month school year exclusive of holidays. The recitation periods were 45 or more minutes in length and 15 units were required for graduation.

There are some people of color who do not express their race consciousness or concerns in public but this does not necessarily mean that they are content with the status quo. This observation is true even today. The segregated days were a way of life for many educated as well as uneducated Blacks. But there were many who were vocal in their beliefs and convictions. A young student at Fisk University wrote her parents a letter on March 25, 1917. The letter revealed that there was a race-concerned professor at Fisk in 1917. The young lady wrote that "Dr. Morrow told our psychology class that he did not believe in colored people going to things where they were segregated into one corner. He did not encourage any of his students to go to the Nashville Auditorium to hear ex-President Taft. The professor had tried to get Taft to come to the university to speak, but he was not able to come.

"No Greek and Latin for the Students"

The American Missionary Association informed the principal of one of their schools in North Carolina in the 1900's that the Black children in rural North Carolina needed agriculture and not Greek and Latin. The principal and his wife were interested in accreditation of the school and preparing their graduates for college entrance exams. They had introduced courses in Greek and Latin. They were disappointed with the decision of the all white philanthropic organization. However, the principal's wife would tutor some students in private Greek lessons to prepare them for the entrance exams at Fisk University.

A Need for Both Industrial and Academic Education

During the early years of segregation many educators white and Black believed that Black children needed Industrial Education without a major emphasis on the academics. An educator of color, Thomas Sewell Inborden (T.S.) expressed his views in the 1900's. He said, "Industrial education was considered by many educators in the South in 1908 as primary curriculum for Black students." There were some schools that would place a high premium on industrial subjects rather than on the academic curriculum. Inborden's personal philosophy was that there were values and limitations in Industrial Education. He believed Industrial Training could be of value without a certain amount of academic instructions to accompany it. T.S. believed that young students must have a preparation of arithmetic, grammar, reading and drawing. He gave some references and examples of his views on the subject from his own teaching experiences. T.S. said some years prior to 1908, while he was a teacher in a southern school, he noticed that some of the teachers had problems correcting students who were using ungrammatical English phrases. Some years later, he wrote that a distinguished white educator was speaking at a school and said that you can take a boy right out of the woods and in two or three years, they can make steam engines and later become a contractor or leader of his people. Inborden asked the educator, why it was that in order to take a course in any of the best trade schools of the country it was necessary to have a college preparation or at least a first class high school education? The white gentleman replied, Oh, your people do not need that sort of preparation, evidently they were not born with some qualities to learn. This was the feeling of many white educators in the 1900's".

When Blacks showed their desires to open their schools in the South, some citizens in the white community were concerned. This letter to a Black principal supports this fact. The white community had their fears and apprehensions when the Brick School was organized in 1895. The principal received a letter on April 20,

TRUE STORIES OF SEGREGATION

1905 from a white physician, Dr. A.S. Harrison, County Superintendent of Schools and also a druggist. Harrison wrote:

With some misgivings, I have watched the growth and development of your school from its infancy. I recognized that it was an experiment and that the result depended largely upon the management by those actively in charge. I am convinced that the experiment stage has passed and that you are doing a good work for your race and I think I voice the sentiment of the community generally. I have observed that you teach the heart as well as the head. Morality as well as religion. You teach the work of the hand as well as the brain. Thereby putting brains in the hands and you know the combination of brains and muscle in proper proportions is almost sure to succeed, mentally, physically and financially. I note that your pupils are taught that politeness to each other and to the white race is elevating rather than degrading. Honest work makes one more highly thought of especially by the white men. I observed also that you teach cleanliness, a thing most generally lacking in your race. You teach the students to keep their rooms clean and neat. As a physician, I have noticed a very marked improvement in the healthfulness of the place since your occupancy, which I attribute very largely to your clean surroundings and also to your observance of the ordinary rules of hygiene. As Superintendent of Public Instruction for the county, I am glad to say that some of the best teachers have received their training at your school. May you live long to continue this good work and what your assistants are doing for your people. You may rest assured that so long as you continue your present policy, you will have the good wish and moral support of the community in which you live".

Separate Employee Training

A continuous practice and enforcement of segregated activities in North Carolina was quite evident in July 1930 when the school superintendent sent this letter: A janitors school for white janitors who have not attended more than one school will be conducted in Raleigh July 19-23 and one for Negro janitors at Greensboro July 26-30. The county will furnish transportation and expenses paid by the state.

Segregation in Northern Schools

There has been considerable focus on segregation in the South. But the North has a record also of enforcing segregation within their school system during the separate era. These facts will illustrate how this legacy has no geographical favorites.

In 1946, 130 students of Washington University in St. Louis were polled and asked how many favored the admission of Negroes? Eighty five students opposed and eleven were undecided. The poll was taken when some Negro taxpayers filed a law suit against the university charging that since Negroes were denied admission to the school, its tax exemption privileges should be revoked. The university officials announced in July, 1947, that Negroes would be permitted to attend the medical school only. In May, 1948, the university opened the Graduate School of Social Work to Blacks and in May, 1948, Blacks were admitted to the graduate schools of its arts and science departments. My older sister received her masters of social work from the School of Social Work. There were many aggressive and liberal whites who made direct decisions to help break down barriers of segregation in the 1940's.

The late Archbishop Joseph E. Ritter of St. Louis, Missouri, decreed that Negroes would be permitted to attend the five Catholic parochial high schools of the diocese. There were some 700 white parents who did not agree with the Archibishop's decree, and sent a letter to him protesting the action. They also threatened to go to court, just like some Arlington, Virginia citizens have done in 1998. Yes, the legacy still prevails. The brave and God-fearing priest told the protesters that if they entered into a suit, they faced excommunication from the Church. These people did not give up their cause, because they appealed to Archbishop Amleto Ciognani, Apostolic Delegate in Washington, D.C. asking his intercession. He replied that their only method of appeal from the decision was directly to the Vatican. The group decided to end its protests.

The State of New Jersey had segregated junior high schools in Trenton, New Jersey. Two courageous Black women sued in court for the admission of their children to the junior high schools in 1943. They were successful in their suit, and in August, 1945, segregation was abolished in the elementary and high schools.

New Jersey's new state constitution of 1948 outlawed segregation and discrimination in all public schools and institutions.

There were cities in the North and West that had non segregated schools but did not employ Black teachers. The cities of Montclair, New Jersey; Akron, Ohio; San Francisco, California began to hire some Blacks in the late 1940's.

When Black students were accepted at all white universities they faced segregation in the campus social life to include fraternities and sororities. The University of Vermont's Alpha Xi Delta Sorority's chapter admitted a Black student as a pledgee in 1946. She was Crystal Malone of Washington, D.C. the only Black young lady, attending the university. The sorority's parent body asked the chapter to dismiss Ms. Malone as a pledge. In February 1947, the Alpha Xi Delta chapter at

Vermont University withdrew from the national organization because of its policy of barring Negro members.

Since the reconstruction era many whites have given dedicated service to the cause of educating Black youngsters. They have served on the faculty at Black colleges in the South and North. This true story occurred in the early 1970's and one could call it "Reverse Discrimination".

Reverse Discrimination on a Black College Campus

A very personable, distinguished scholar individual was a Caucasian professor with a tenure over 15 years at a predominantly Black university in the early 1970's. This professor was a sincere concerned educator who guided, taught and assisted many African Americans to pursue and complete successfully their earned degrees on the masters and doctorate level. He gave so much of his time that his scholarly presence was an asset to the university's academic family of scholars. Unfortunately, during the student uprisings and protests on college campuses, this wonderful professor became the target of a few so-called Black nationalist students whose goals and ideologies were too controversial. They desired results inconsistent with the overall protest movements goal. These students decided to personally harass and intimidate this professor. The continual harassment eventually prompted the professor to retire because he was moving toward an emotional collapse. These experiences caused him to state and I sincerely believe uncharacteristically:

> In spite of my life long association with Negroes,
> I am becoming prejudiced. I hope that this is not
> the case, but there are times when I feel as though
> my general attitude of resentment and bitterness is
> indicative of a creeping erosion of my general
> attitude of tolerance".

As stated before, I believe that those words have passed away with the times and that his general attitude today is positive. What he has given over many years to African American students cannot and should not be lost in a few moments words of anger. Yes, he was a person who would always hold out his hand and open his heart without regard to color. That was the way it was on that college campus some 28 years ago, however, a few of us were acting out in a negative way.

Religion

Early Afro-American education was supported by the Black communities and church denominations. Some of the churches were: The African Methodist Episcopal (AME), and Zion, Negro Baptist, Colored Methodist Episcopal (later Christian Methodist Episcopal) CME, Christian Church (Disciples of Christ), Church of Christ (Scientist), Presbyterian, U.S. Protestant Episcopal, Roman Catholic, Seventh Day Adventist and United Church of Christ.

Clark University, Atlanta, Georgia was founded in 1870 by the Freedman's Aid Society of the Methodist Episcopal Church. Mrs. Augusta Clark Cole, the daughter of Bishop Clark contributed a large amount for the funding of the University. Therefore, it was decided to name the university, Clark University.

The late Reverend J.W.E. Bowen was the first Afro-American of the Methodist Episcopal Church to receive by study and examination the degree, Doctor of Philosophy from Boston University. He was Professor of Hebrew at Howard University and Professor of Systematic and Historical Theology at Morgan University as well as a Professor at Gammon Theological Seminary, Atlanta, Georgia, for 33 years.

The American Missionary Association had established seventeen academic and normal schools for Blacks throughout the south by 1875. The Association also had established the following colleges/universities. Berea College, Berea, Kentucky; Hampton Institute, Hampton, Virginia; Fisk University, Nashville, Tennessee; Atlanta University, Atlanta, Georgia; Talladega College, Talladega, Alabama; Tougaloo University. Tougaloo, Mississippi; and Straight University, New Orleans, Louisiana. Two of the original members who organized the American Missionary Association in 1846 were Afro-Americans Samuel Cornish and James W.C. Pennington.

Sister Eliza Healy was a nun and the sister of Fathers Patrick Healy, twenty-ninth president of Georgetown University, Alexander Sherwood Healy, and Bishop James Augustine Healy, first known Afro-American bishop in the United States. He had a sister "Mother Mary Magdalene" of the congregation of Notre Dame Order in Montreal, Canada. The Healy's were children of a former mulatto slave woman and an Irish man.

An educator and scientist named Thomas Wyatt Turner challenged the "racist practices in the Catholic Church in the 1920's." He, along with other concerned Black Catholics, was instrumental in organizing the Committee Against the Extension of Race prejudice in the church. In 1924, "the group adopted a constitution and established an organization known as the "Federated Colored Catholics." Turner was the organization's first president. Turner was baptized in the

Catholic faith as an infant. He attended Howard University and received a Preparatory Department Certificate in 1897. Turner received his A.B. Degree from Howard University in 1901. He accepted a scholarship for graduate work in science at Catholic University, Washington, D.C. However, he did not have sufficient money for his education. He then taught at Tuskegee Institute for a year. Turner returned to Maryland and became one of the first Black teachers to teach Black students in Maryland. He attended classes at John Hopkins and Howard Universities. Turner received his Master of Arts from Howard University in 1905. Turner was the first secretary of the Baltimore NAACP Branch in 1910. In 1915, Turner received a Ph.D. in botany from Cornell University while teaching biology at Howard University. He served as Acting Dean of the School of Education, Howard University from 1914 to 1920.

Turner accepted a position at Hampton Institute, Hampton, Virginia. In 1924, he became chairman of the biology department. He was the author of many articles in science and became the first Afro-American to present a paper "before the Virginia Academy of Science." This courageous pioneer in civil rights community activist, and outstanding educator and scientist was honored by Hampton University in 1978. The new Natural Sciences Building was named in his honor in 1976. The Catholic University of America awarded Turner an honorary doctor of science degree when he was 99 years old and blind. Thomas Wyatt Turner died at the age of 101 in 1978.

Church Statistics 1997

An examination of church statistics will indicate that some years after segregation, the churches in America are still showing a form of defacto segregation in the membership.

In 1997, largest Christian denominations were Roman Catholics 61 million, Southern Baptist, 16 million, United Methodist 9 million, National Baptist Church USA 9 million, Church of God in Christ Pentecostal (mostly Black) 6 million, National Baptist Convention of America, Inc. (mostly Black) 5 million, African Methodist Episcopal, 4 million and the Presberyterian Church USA 3 million. (Note: the numbers have been rounded off).

An Outspoken Bishop on Racism

A Black bishop of the Catholic Church, Joseph A. Carroll was the first Black Catholic prelate to speak out openly against racism. He was born in Lafayette, Louisiana. Carroll was the founder of an interracial center in New Haven, Connecticut, in the 1950's. He was the fourth Black to be appointed as a Bishop.

He has served as the Auxillary Archbishop of Newark, New Jersey. In 1979, Carroll wrote a pastoral letter on racism.

12TH Street YMCA Ecumenical Spirit, 1948

The Washington YMCA conducted lenten services for their members and staff by extending invitations to local ministers. Some guest speakers were the Rev. Arthur Elmes, Peoples Congregational Church (My family's church that I attended as a child), Rev. Dillard Brown, St. Lukes Episcopal Church, Rev, W.B. Nash, St. Paul AME Church, and the Rev. Thomas Brooks, Union Methodist Church, Upper Marlboro, Maryland.

Protest at a Christian Building

The name Young Men's Christian Association means that it has some religious principles related to the organization. However, that Christian focus was redirected in December, 1947, when it was necessary for members of the Washington, D.C.'s interracial workshop to form a picket line. The protesters were voicing concern to the central white YMCA concerning discriminatory policies at their building located at 1736 G Street, N.W. Ten protesters under the leadership of Mr. Raymond Ellis and Ms. Lynn Seifer passed out leaflets in front of the YMCA building.

A Historical Note

A former white president of Howard University, Rev. E. Jeremiah Rankin was the author of the famous hymn. "God Be With You, Til We Meet Again".

Segregated Southern Churches

Many Black churches in the South have small cemeteries next to the churches. The white city cemeteries in many cities did not provide space for Black burials. The pain did not stop at death for the relatives of the deceased.

There was an unusual white priest from New England, in Anniston, Alabama. The Catholic priest was the rector or pastor of the Black church, St. Martin's DePorres. He loved his congregation and they loved him. He was a pastor there for many years. The white Catholic Church would not admit Blacks in the 1960's. It is said that when the priest of St. Martin DePorres died the funeral arrangements were handled by a local Black mortuary. He relieved the pain of many parishioners through prayer and his concern for the poor and needy. But still today, some of that pain from the Civil Rights days and the times of segregation lingers on including the water fountains in the department stores. One fountain for Blacks and one fountain for whites; U.S.A., 1964.

The Mormon Church and Blacks

I received some correspondence in December, 1974, while serving as the Race Relations Coordinator for the Munich Military Community in Germany. The Equal Opportunity Program for United States Army Europe required military communities to have a Race Relations Equal Opportunity Council. When I read the minutes of the Council for their meeting of December 5, 1974, the following comments were included. "The comment was made that a fraternal organization which allegedly practices discrimination in the selection of its membership was recently barred usage of the Community Club. The discussion led to comments concerning the fact that Mormon activities are being conducted in the community facilities, in addition to the solicitation of personnel in the housing area to join the Mormon religion. It was pointed out that the Mormon religion discriminates against the holding of certain offices by members of the Black race. Since this discriminatory qualification, which is evidently inherent in the religion, is not consistent with DoD equal opportunity policies, some council members indicated that they do not feel that community facilities should be utilized for the Mormon activities, nor should the Mormons be allowed to solicit membership in the Perlacher Forst Housing Area." The above comments generated more correspondence when a decision had to be obtained as to how one replies to the comments in reference to the Mormon Church. The military has a chain of command that is used to obtain information, concurrences and final decisions concerning a problem or query. There were some eight endorsements to an original letter requesting a decision on this matter. When the acting community commander, a Colonel reviewed the Council's minutes on January 3, 1975, he sent a first endorsement to the minutes to the Chairman, Race Relations/Equal Opportunity Council, European Exchange System, Munich, Germany and made his comments: "The Church of Jesus Christ of Latter Day Saints (Mormon) is an officially recognized church by the Department of Defense and is entitled to the same considerations and use of government facilities as any other church. The issue of Blacks and church priesthood is a theological doctrine and does not violate DoD directives concerning racial discrimination. Membership in the Mormon Church is open to every race or nationally and full fellowship is extended to all. Church missionaries do not proselyte (or try to convert) in the government areas, except on personal invitation and appointment. To prohibit an individual member from telling his neighbor about religious beliefs would be a gross infringement on the right of free speech and freedom of religion".

The Council met again on January 9, 1975 and several Council members expressed their dissatisfaction with the remarks of the acting commander. After some discussion, the Council members agreed that the response did not positively address the issue, "The Mormon Religion discriminates against the holding of certain offices by members of the Black race", and a motion was passed that the matter should be pursued in writing to the Munich Community Chaplain through official military channels. At the council's meeting on February 3, 1975, it was learned that the community chaplain had addressed the Mormon Church matter through channels.

The community chaplain sent a letter to his superior, Community Chaplain, Augsburg, Germany Military Community and the subject for successive correspondence would be "The Mormon Church versus Department of Defense (DoD) policy on racial discrimination". The Munich community chaplain did not avoid the real question that was originally stated in the council meeting, he wrote in his letter: "Does the Mormon Church's prohibition on Blacks from holding the priesthood violate DoD policies and if not how can DoD reconcile the apparent inconsistency?" The chaplain requested that this matter be given urgent consideration so that the controversy could be laid to rest once and for all. His superior at Augsburg, a colonel, forwarded his letter without any comments to Headquarters, U.S. Army VII Corps, Stuttgart, Germany, Office of the Corp Chaplain.

The Corp Chaplain, a Colonel, wrote these comments: "It is suggested that the alleged position of the Church of Jesus Christ of Latter Day Saints with regard to limitations on eligibility for ordination to the priesthood is not unlike the prohibition of women by the Roman Catholic Church. Such matters are deemed theological in nature and not subject to censure by civil authority and by traditional interpretations of the First Amendment of the Constitution of the U.S. of America.

The Corp Chaplain forwarded his endorsement and comments to the Chief, Equal Opportunity Division, HQ U.S. Army Europe Heidelblerg, Germany. The Equal Opportunity Division Chief forwarded the correspondence to the U.S. Army Europe's Chaplain for comments. The executive officer, a lieutenant colonel in the chaplain's office, prepared an endorsement for the Army's command chaplain. The endorsement read: "concur with the second endorsement", which, of course, was the endorsement of the HQ VII Corp Chaplain. The executive officer included these comments for the Army chaplain: "The policy statement of the presidency of the Church of Jesus Christ of the Latter Day Saints provides for full worship privileges for any or all who wish to join the church. Public facilities which have been set aside for worship services may be used by the Church of Jesus Christ of the Latter Day Saints, since there is no indication that the body discriminates as to who may attend its worship services". This endorsement with comments was forwarded back through channels to the Munich Race Relations Council with the final opinons and decision.

I have a copy of a letter that I strongly believe could have influenced the opinons of the VII Corps chaplain and the final decision of the Army Chaplain. In all of this correspondence for consideration, it was only the Munich Community Chaplain, a Major, who addressed and stated so simply that those who raised this controversy and the others who used the classical tactics of verbiage, interpretation theology and policies coupled with our Constitution provisions. This letter was written on December 15, 1969, and is called "Letter of First Presidency Clarifies Church's Position On The Negro". Interestingly enough, the letter actually answers the first original question. The letter read:

December 15, 1969

"To General Authorities, Regional Representatives of the Twelve, State Presidents, Mission Presidents and Bishops.

Dear Brethren:

In view of confusion that has arisen, it was decided at a meeting of the First Presidency and the Quorum of the Twelve to restate the position of the Church with regard to the Negro both in society and in the Church.

First, may we say that we know something of the sufferings of those who are discriminated against in a denial of their civil rights and Constitutional privileges. Our early history as a church is a tragic story of persecution and oppression. Our people repeatedly were denied the protection of the law. They were driven and plundered, robbed and murdered by mobs, who in many instances were aided and abetted by those sworn to uphold the law. We as a people have experienced the bitter fruits of civil discrimination and mob violence.

We believe that the Constitution of the United States was divinely inspired, that it was produced by "wise men" whom God raised up for this "very purpose," and that the principles embodied in the Constitution are so fundamental and important that, if possible, they should be extended "for the rights and protection of all mankind.

In revelation received by the first prophet of the Church in this dispensation, Joseph Smith (1805-1844), the Lord made it clear that it is "not right that any man should be in bondage one to another." These words were spoken prior to the Civil War. From these and other revelations have sprung the Church's deep and historic concern with man's free agency and our commitment to the sacred principles of the Constitution.

It follows, therefore, that we believe the Negro as well as those of other races should have his full constitutional privileges as a member of society and we hope that members of the Church everywhere will do their part as citizens to see that these rights are held inviolate. Each citizen must have equal opportunities and protection under the law with reference to civil rights.

However, matters of faith, conscience, and theology are not within the purview of the civil law. The First Amendment to the Constitution specifically provides that "Congress shall make no law respecting an establishment of religion or prohibiting the free exercise thereof."

The position of The Church of Jesus Christ of latter Day Saints affecting those of the Negro race who choose to join the Church falls wholly within the category of religion. It has no bearing upon matters of civil rights. In no case or degree does it deny to the Negro his full privileges as a citizen of the nation.

This position has no relevancy whatever to those who do not wish to join the Church. Those individuals, we suppose, do not believe in the divine origin and nature of the Church, nor that we have the priesthood of God. Therefore, if they feel we have no priesthood, they should have no concern with any aspect of our theology on priesthood so long as that theology does not deny any man his constitutional privileges.

A word of explanation concerning the position of the Church.

The Church of Jesus Christ of Latter-day Saints owes its origin, its existence, and its hope for the future to the principle of continuous revelation. "We believe all that God has revealed, all that he does now reveal, and we believe that He will yet reveal many great and important things pertaining to the Kingdom of God".

From the beginning of this dispensation, Joseph Smith and all succeeding Presidents of the Church have taught that Negroes, while spirit children of a common Father, and the progeny of our earthly parents Adam and Eve, were not yet to receive the priesthood, for reasons which we believe are known to God, but which he has not made fully known to man.

Our living prophet, President David O. McKay, has said, "The seeming discrimination by the Church toward the Negro is not something which originated with man; but goes back into the beginning with God...

Revelation assures us that this plan antedates man's mortal existence, extending back to man's preexistent state."

President McKay has also said, "Sometime in God's eternal plan the Negro will be given the right to hold the priesthood."

Until God reveals his will in this matter, to him whom we sustain as a prophet, we are bound by that same will. Priesthood, when it is conferred on any man comes as a blessing from God, not of men.

We feel nothing but love, compassion, and the deepest appreciation for the rich talents, endowments, and the earnest strivings of our Negro brothers and sisters. We are eager to share with men of all races the blessings of the gospel. We have no racially segregated congregation.

Were we the leaders of an enterprise created by ourselves and operated only according to our own earthly wisdom, it would be a simple thing to act according to popular will. But we believe that this work is directed by God and that the conferring of the priesthood must await his revelation. To do otherwise would be to deny the very premise on which the Church is established.

We recognize that those who do not accept the principle of modern revelation may oppose our point of view. We repeat that such would not wish for membership in the Church, and therefore the question of priesthood should hold no interest for them. Without prejudice they should grant us the privilege afforded under the Constitution to exercise our chosen form of religion, just as we must grant all others a similar privilege. They must recognize that the question of bestowing or withholding priesthood in the Church is a matter of religion and not a matter of constitutional right.

We extend the hand of friendship to men everywhere and the hand of fellowship to all who wish to join the Church and partake of the many rewarding opportunities to be found therein.

We join with those throughout the world who pray that all of the blessings of the gospel of Jesus Christ may in the due time of the Lord become available to men of faith everywhere. Until that time comes we must trust in God, in his wisdom, and in his tender mercy.

Meanwhile, we must strive harder to emulate his Son, the Lord Jesus Christ, whose new commandment it was that we should love one another. In developing that love and concern for one another, while awaiting revelations yet to come, let us hope that with respect to these religious differences, we may gain reinforcement for understanding and appreciation for such differences. They challenge our common similarities as children of one Father, to enlarge the outreachings of our divine souls.

                        Faithfully your brethren,
                        THE FIRST PRESIDENCY

                        /SS/   Hugh B. Brown
                        /SS/   N. Eldon Tanner"

Athough this matter occurred in the 1970's, we cannot forget that the Mormon's Church policy in place during segregation was still a policy in 1974. I often tell my college students that if they intend to accomplish constructive research they must apply the scholarly tools of accuracy, update and positive verification, and I remind them that as a biologist and historian, I must do those things.

Therefore, I decided to call the Mormon Church's headquarters in Salt Lake City, Utah, on June 12, 1998. I was able to obtain some creditable updated information from a cordial person in their Public Information Office. I was able to learn that this month, June is a 20 year anniversary of a change in policy by which the Mormon

Church began to admit qualified Black church members to the priesthood in June 1978.

This equal opportunity complaint was resolved in 1975 with the command decision made, but the Church finally resolved the Complainant's concern peacefully in 1978. Religion sometimes has its exceptions just as other instiutions did during the segregated years. I decided to call my second cousin on my paternal side, Cousin Bertha Spears Evans of Kirkwood, Missouri, on June 6, 1998. I asked my cousin a question that I have asked several times, but this time I said Cousin Bertha, I am going to mention what you have told me and I just want to be sure; not that I doubt you in anyway. She was able in her keen active sensible mind to recall, again in her 93 years of a blessed life, the following true story:

She said that her father Sandy Manassa Spears Jr. was a member of the Mormon Reorganized Church of Latter Day Saints in Brewton, Alabama at the age of 19 years, prior to his going to Missouri. Her father was a pioneer in the early development of the Meacham Park Community, Kirkwood, Missouri in the late 1870's. He was a successful businessman and real estate agent. In later years, the community honored him by naming a street in his honor, "Spears Avenue". I conclude this discussion with these words. Curious as it may have been, my great Uncle Sandy Spears Jr. might not have been a priest in the Mormon Church in the 1870's in Alabama, however the oral tradition and accepted truth of his daughter at the age of 93 years is a cherished story".

Catholic Sisterhoods

The following Catholic sisterhoods or orders for nuns were established for Afro-American women interested in entering the sisterhoods. The Oblate Sisters of Providence, Baltimore, Maryland, (1829); the Sisters of the Holy Family, New Orleans, La., (1842); The Hand Maids of Mary, New York City, (1916); and The Magdalene Sisters of Good Shepherd Convent, Baltimore, Md., (1922).

Racist Policies Knights of Columbus, 1960

A predominantly white Catholic church in Kansas City, Missouri, had an order of the Knights of Columbus. When an African American man who was married by the church priest asked him for an application to join the Knights of Columbus, he was denied the application. The priest told him that even though it was 1960, he could not be accepted in the all white order. However, he could join the Black counterpart, the Saint Peter Clavier Society. As the Black man departed the rectory building, he glanced in the hallway at a sign that read "God Loves Us All". He probably felt the pain and said to himself, "Yes, he loves us all even when we are sometimes separate from others. But over the years, he was convinced that God loves us all everywhere; however, man in his own flesh separates God's children in a selfish way.

TRANSPORTATION

A Baggage Car Seat

Frederick Douglas was traveling on a train and had to move to the baggage car. Some people went into the baggage car to express their regrets that Douglas had to ride in the baggage car. Douglas told the group: "They cannot degrade Frederick Douglas. The soul that is within me, no man can degrade, I am not the one that is being degraded on account of this treatment but those who are inflicting upon me:

Jim Crow Travel

Some southern trains had a small passenger car immediately behind the coal burning engine for Blacks. Fare was first class when Blacks were traveling by boat between Washington, D.C. and Norfolk, Virginia however they were permitted only below deck and they were close enough to the engine room to hear the sounds of the engine while trying to sleep. When Blacks entered the dining cars on trains, they could purchase a ticket but had to be served meals behind curtains.

Northern Virginia Segregated Transportation

A Black man was entering the rear door of a train in 1919 that was reserved for Blacks at the East Falls Church railroad station on the Arlington and Fairfax Railroad. The man was pulled off the train and not allowed to enter because a white man was boarding the train at the same time. Later a warrant was sworn out against the conductor on a charge of assault upon the Black man. A white man had observed the incident and served as a counsel to the Black. The court room had Blacks sitting on one side and whites on the other side. The conductor had refused to testify. The judge suspended the Black man's case.

When Blacks traveled from Washington, D.C. to Falls Church, they had to ride on a segregated electric trolley car. There were two waiting rooms. The Black room was cold in the winter and sometimes used for baggage and livestock.

I am sure that when many immigrants today arrive in America they board public transportation and take a seat anywhere in the carrier that has a vacant seat. I wonder how many are aware that during segregation of Blacks in America they could not enjoy the privilege that they automatically enjoy today. My discussion will highlight some selected cases in the states of Virginia, South Carolina, and North Carolina. The southern states in the 1930's and 1940's had rigid enforcement of their segregated public transportation carriers generating some court cases by the defendants who were fined for breaking the law. Some of these cases eventually led to a 1944 interstate bus case.

Henderson Case 1942

A Black man, Elmer W. Henderson went into the dining car on a railroad passenger train. The tables reserved for Negroes were occupied by white persons and the other Blacks sitting in the diner, had their tables separated by a drawn curtain and Henderson was told that there were no tables available for him. He filed a complaint against the Southern Railroad with the Interstate Commerce Commission (ICC) charging that his rights had been violated by the railroad's refusal to serve him on two occasions during an interstate trip. The ICC ruled that the railroad might have subjected him to "undue and unreasonable prejudice and disadvantage", but that there was no basis for the awarding of damages and the diner's regulations setting aside certain tables for Blacks did not result in "any substantial inequality of treatment. Mr. Henderson appealed the ICC ruling and filed suit in the Federal District Court Baltimore, Maryland. During the period 1945-1948, his case was being remanded for further trials. Finally in September 1948, the U.S. District Court, Baltimore, Maryland ruled in favor of the Southern railroad and declared that "racial segregation on interstate passengers is not forbidden by the U.S. Constitution". Sometimes the courts would award damages and there would even be compromises between the railroad officials and the Black plaintiffs.

Irene Morgan Interstate Bus Case

A Black lady, Mrs. Irene Morgan was traveling on a Greyhound bus in 1944 from Virginia to Baltimore, Maryland. The white bus driver asked her to move to the rear of the bus. She refused to move and was convicted on a charge of disorderly conduct in the Middlesex County, Virginia's Circuit Court. She was assisted by the NAACP and appealed the court's decision. The Virginia Supreme Court of Appeals upheld the lower courts' decision on the grounds that "the assignment of Negroes to certain seats in a bus does not constitute inequality of treatment. Mrs. Morgan's case went before the U.S. Supreme Court and the court ruled on June 3, 1946. This was a monumental decision during segregation because the court ruled that the "separation of passengers by race in interstate bus travel cannot be accomplished by state statute". There were six Justices of the Court who concurred in the majority opinion. But there was one dissenting vote and Justice Harold H. Burton earned himself a place in history during the separate era, he was not ready for integration. The major highlights of the Supreme Court's rulings were "separation of passengers by race is an undue burden, on interstate commerce and an interstate passenger must shift seats" at times while traveling in Virginia".

I can remember as a teenager in St. Louis attending an interracial social function at a large Episcopal Church. There were Black and young white youth present and there was a cordial discussion on race relations in the mid 1940's. This was my introduction to an aggressive civil rights organization called the Congress of Racial Equality (CORE). Remember this was during segregation and prior to the 1960's civil rights crusade. CORE in 1947 along with the Racial-Industrial Committee of the Fellowship of Reconciliation sponsored a trip through the upper south to see how bus and train companies were complying with the Supreme Court ruling of the Morgan case on June 3, 1946. The organizations called the trip "Journey of Reconciliation". The trip commenced on April 9, 1947 and the mixed group who traveled through the states of Virginia, North Carolina, Tennessee, and Kentucky visited some fifteen cities in the respective states. The trip lasted for two weeks. I believe that those courageous Black and white concerned individuals during the era of segregation should be recognized in 1998, because there were the early monitors of civil rights legislation for public transportation. I have therefore included their names. The white participants were "George Houser, Fellowship Reconciliation, New York; Ernest Bromley, Minister from North Carolina; James Reck, Editor of the Workers Defense League News Bulletin; Igal Roodenko, Horticulturist, New York; Worth Randle, Botanist, Cincinnati, Ohio; Joseph Felmet, Southern Workers Defense League and Homer Jack, the Chicago Council Against Racial and Religious Discrimination, and Louis Adams, Minister from North Carolina". The Blacks were Bayard Rustin, staff of the Fellowship of Reconciliation, New York; Wallace Nelson, Lecturer, New York; Conrad Lynn, Attorney, New York; Andrew Johnson, Student, Cincinnati, Ohio; Dennis Banks, Musician, Chicago, Illinois; William Worthy, New York Council of the Committee for a Permanent Fair Employment Practice Committee; Eugene Stanley, Professor, A and T College, Greensboro, North Carolina; and Nathan Wright, Social Worker, Cincinnati, Ohio. The combined groups conducted twenty-six tests of bus companies, policies, and twelve members were arrested. There were no major incidents; however, in North Carolina and Tennessee, some bus driver asked the Blacks to move their seats. There were several court cases initiated when the state of Virginia's bus attempted to circumvent the court's ruling by adopting their own procedures. The companies had regulations of seating which they said were not a part of state law. This law was challenged by Mrs. Lottie E. Taylor.

Lottie E. Taylor Case

Mrs. Lottie E. Taylor had boarded a Virginia State Line bus and refused to move to the rear of the bus. She was arrested in Fairfax County, Virginia, in September 1946. Taylor was convicted of a disorderly conduct charge and fined five dollars and court costs. The NAACP represented her on an appeal. The circuit court upheld the lower court's ruling that the bus company had a right to ask her to move and that she was convicted of the state's new statute. The Virginia Supreme Court of Appeals reversed the lower courts. On March 1, 1948, the court ruled that "the state's disorderly conduct law could not be used to maintain the separation of races in interstate bus travel in violation of the United States Supreme Court's decision". We must keep in mind that it would take until the mid 1950's for Mrs. Rosa Parks to challenge the interstate segregation of buses in Alabama and the Federal Courts positive judicial ruling would eventually end segregation in the south's public transportation system. I believe that this discussion is most essential for Americans today to be aware of the fact that Blacks living and dead did not receive some of their equal rights on a "silver platter". They humbly, patiently and nonviolently went through the long and arduous steps of the country's legal system even though some in 1998 are crying "reverse discrimination" and are actually trying to reverse the rights that Blacks have labored for so long to attain.

Birmingham, Alabama's Segregated Street Cars

At one time the street cars of Birmingham, Alabama had large screens clamped on the back of a seat to indicate seats for white and Black passengers.

Black Congressman Ejected from Pullman Car

The late Honorable Arthur Mitchell sued the Pullman Company and won a Supreme Court decision. He was ejected from a Pullman car in Arkansas in 1937. The Court's decision declared that the Pullman Company must provide a special Pullman car and dining facilities for Blacks. This incident clearly showed that you could be a Congressman in the United States Congress, but if you were Black you were still subject to the segregated laws of the respective states.

Majority White Express Bus

The District of Columbia's Transit Company in the 1940's originated an Express bus from Silver Springs to the Federal Triangle area in Washington, D.C. In the evening the bus returned to Silver Spring as an express bus. The buses passed through all Black neighborhoods and never stopped at the local stops. The passengers in most cases were comfortable and did not have to fear sitting near urban Blacks. The members of the African American community had to travel several blocks to board a D.C. Transit bus or local street car to travel downtown. The children never saw a Black bus or street car driver in those days.

Train Porters Adopt a New Name

The term "Red Caps" for railroad porters was conceived when James Williams a porter in New York's Central Train Station, "tied a piece of red flannel around his Black cap on Labor Day, 1890, to be more easily identified. He was able to increase his tips when people easily could identify him. Other porters began to sew this type of identification, and eventually the term "Red Caps was adopted for the train porters."

GOVERNMENT

Civilian Conservation Corps (CCC)

President Franklin Delano Roosevelt in the early 1930's shortly after the Great Depression, delivered a message to Congress. He discussed his plan to establish a Civilian Conservation Corps (CCC) that would be used to help the employment problem. The plan was confined to forestry, prevention of soil erosion, flood control and various work projects. The program was outlined by the Secretary of Labor, Francis Perkins, who stated that the CCC would work with major government agencies. The Labor Department was responsible for recruiting and selecting young men for the work force. The War department had the Army responsible for the training and supervision of the new recruits. They were outfitted in war surplus uniforms and housed in military type barracks. The Interior and Agriculture departments were responsible for the selection of projects and were required to provide technical supervision.

> Congress gave the authorization for the camps on April 4, 1933.
> President Roosevelt issued an Executive Order on April 5, 1933.

The order involved the appointment of R. Fechner, an Tennessean who lived in Georgia as the CCC's Executive Director and the establishment of an advisory council of representatives from cooperative agencies. There was a recruitment goal to enroll some 250,000 young men 18-25 years by July 1933. Eventually some 300,000 men were enrolled in 1,400 camps across the nation. There were nine Corps areas. Selection of the youth was on the basic of each state's proportionate population, and most of the enrollees were assigned to projects in their home areas.

The young men received two weeks of physical training and were assigned to 200 man companies and to camps identified by company, number and project code. The project codes were in the areas of forestry, soil conservation, natural parks, military parks and armed forces installations. The camps were closed in 1942.

Blacks were present in the CCC program on a segregated basis. They were in great need of this program because during the Depression, Blacks suffered twice the national average and some two million Black families were on relief. In the North, many Blacks had been employed where work was available. However, after being the last hired they were the first fired. The South had menial jobs for Blacks.

Congress made some attempts to prohibit the CCC from discrimination based on race, color or creed; However, that prevailing legacy of segregation in the 1930's dictated that Blacks would systematically be under represented in the selection process. The Black men who were chosen were placed in segregated camps and supervised by white officers. There were few exceptions to the rule.

The State of Georgia was one of the southern states that practiced segregation in the CCC program. They had ways to avoid enrolling qualified Blacks. There were some enrolling officers who believed that Blacks were fully employed working in the farm land fields. Clark County, Georgia, had a Black population of sixty percent, but no Blacks were selected for the camps. The state officials had refused to enroll Blacks. Later some Blacks were enrolled in the Georgia CCC program. Some Georgia towns refused to have Black CCC camps in their communities. There were some towns in the North, mid and far West who did not want Blacks in their areas. The few Black camps that were established were located on Army posts and federal land areas. The Executive Director CCC issued directives stating all Black enrollees would work in camps within their home states, and they would be enrolled only to fill vacancies in segregated camps. These requirements limited Black enrollment opportunities.

The State of Georgia had 127 CCC camps and only 19 were Black. Thirteen Black companies were located at the Chickamauga National Military Park. The enrollees worked in soil conservation services and private forestry projects. Many were assigned to the Army posts at Forts Benning, Gillen and Stewart, Georgia.

The Black CCC's companies built roads and trails through battlefields at National Military Parks. One CCC camp was named Booker T. Washington. The segregated camps had activities such as intramural sports, basketball, movies, church services, choral groups, drama groups and some offered high school academic classes and vocational training. Some even published a camp newspaper.

The CCC program paid some 20 million allotments to dependents and the total financial cost of the program was 70 million dollars. Lest we forget, there were many Black young men who also made contributions to CCC program accomplishments including installation of telephone lines and building of dams. Gulley trees were planted and numerous eroded acres restored. Blacks fought forest fires and built roads.

The CCC Camp was a major government program that was a success even though it included segregated policies that states had the rights to enforce.

Segregation in a Congressional Restaurant, 1934

I was able to find a newspaper article in the Thomas S. Inborden papers when I was researching his biography. The article was published in the *Grand Rapids Herald* (Michigan), Sunday, March 18, 1934. The title was "30 Negro Students Blocked by Police in Drive to Enter House Restaurant". The article read, "Thirty Howard University students, Negroes, tried for an hour today to obtain admittance to the House restaurant. One student wound up in jail. Incited by the discharge of Harold Covington, Howard student and part-time waiter in the public dining room, for serving a reporter of the (Washington) Afro American Newspaper. The students swept down upon the eating place unmindful of the detail of a dozen armed Capitol police with night sticks, but under orders from the Sergeant at-arms, Kenneth Rommey, that there be no fighting.

The students without a word approached one of the restaurant doors in flying wedge formation where they were met by the restaurant manager P.H. Johnson, "Hold on there", he shouted, his face flushed as he raised his arms across the doorway. and said, "I told you yesterday you could not come in here". What else he said was lost in the ensuing commotion. Some House members, Capitol employees and newspaper men by this time filled every available inch of the passageway not already occupied by police and the students. The students braced themselves against the steady push of the police who brandished their sticks without bringing them down on the protesting heads. The Negroes finally were shunted to a side entrance where they made a last stand by attempting to jam the big revolving glass door.

The demonstration ended when Covington responded to pleas by Harry Parker, a veteran Negro messenger of the Ways and Means Committee to disband peaceably. The police quickly arrested Covington and hustled him off to the nearest downtown precinct station where he was held until a bondsman arranged his release".

This true story of segregation definitely illustrates the climate of segregation in the country 64 years ago, which was actually sanctioned by the members of Congress who had meals in a Capitol segregated restaurant. The story also documents the fact that there were many Blacks who were not content yet did nothing about their being second class citizens when immigrants could come from countries all over the world and receive the same opportunities that the white majority enjoyed. College and secondary classrooms have taught me without any sophisticated poll or study that many Black, white and other students have no idea what segregation was really like in our government facilities. The textbooks today do not include these facts. A few do, but they skirt over the facts. This is why I support a strong thesis that our newly arrived classified minorities should learn more about the Black experience in America prior to the Civil Rights Movement.

The Segregated USO

Prior to the United States official involvement in World War II, there was an organization making plans to play an integral role in the country's defense and morale efforts. The group was the United Services Organization (USO). The government would consider the Black community when planning conferences that could also affect the Black segregated community. In April, 1941, some one thousand leaders were invited to Washington, D.C. to attend a Defense Morale Conference at the Willard Hotel sponsored by the USO. This was the first of its kind during peace time. The conference was presided over by Paul V. McNutt, Federal Security Administration and Coordinator of Health and Welfare activities affecting the National Defense. Among the attendees were some Black leaders; namely, Dr. Mordecai Johnson, Howard University; Frederick Paterson, Tuskegee Institute; Rufus Clement, Atlanta University; Emment Scott, and Robert De Frantz of the National YMCA Council.

During World II, the Black soldiers experienced additional segregation when they left their respective camps, especially in the Nation's Capitol area. The USO and other government related agencies supported segregated policies. My father was a USO director for the colored YMCA located on 12th Street, Northwest, Washington, D.C. His office would receive a special weekly events flyer that was issued for Black soldiers by the Recreation Services Inc., located in the District Building, Room 500. The flyer was prepared in cooperation with the Governmental Defense Agencies and Works Project Administration (WPA) Adult Education Project. A flyer dated December 24, 1941 - January 2, 1942 contained some information that indicates how the Civilian Community came together and were unified in providing services to Black soldiers after they left their segregated camp facilities and then arrived in Washington's segregated Capitol city. The flyer's heading read "The Colored Service Man". The Phyllis Wheatley YWCA on Rhode Island and Ninth Street, N.W.

provided on Tuesdays the activities of, ping pong and badminton. On Wednesday, soldiers who remained at Fort Belvoir would enjoy activities at their recreation hall. Volunteer hostesses from the YWCA, and the Community Center and Playgrounds Department of the District of Columbia, would visit the Army post.

There was a very well planned program for the soldiers on Thursday, December 25, 1941, Christmas Day, sponsored by the 12th Street YMCA and the YWCA. The soldiers enjoyed hobby night, wood-turning, handicraft, shuffle board and music. Dinners were prepared at the YWCA to serve the soldiers. The responsible people who provided their free services were from: Mt. Carmel Baptist Church, 3rd and Eye Street, N.W., pastored by the Rev. W.H. Jernagin; and Mr. Frank Nettingham and Mr. William Butler, 120 Thomas Street, N.W..

On January 1, 1942, 35 servicemen were entertained and served meals at the Wesley Union Church 1107 23rd Street, under the auspices of the American legion Post and their commander J. Franklin Wilson, whom I recall as one of my father's friends. He was affectionately called by his friends "old soldier".

The 12th Street YMCA offered their swimming pool, pocket billiard room, checkers, games in the club room, basketball in the gym, pool and scheduled dances. On Sundays, various area churches provided escort services to their churches. Mr. Shep Allen, manager of the Howard Theatre, would provide tickets for the soldiers to attend the professional stage shows entertainers would also perform at the YMCA.

STEREOTYPES

When people formulate certain images with different meanings, normally negative, and apply them to a particular group, a stereotype has been created. Every ethnic group in America has experienced stereotypes directed toward their group.

African Americans have experienced damaging images and perceptions from stereotypes during segregation and after. These stereotypes are still being used today and not just by whites. Black people themselves, possibly out of ignorance or for financial gains sometimes reenforce particular stereotypes, especially in comic performances.

The following historical true stories of some Black stereotypes suggest that they might be laughing matters for the performers today and their wide audience, but in the years of segregation most people I believe, educated and uneducated Blacks would have concern about negative effects.

Black Face Minstrels

White entertainers in the late 1800's and 1900's have used Black face characters in their minstrel art. The late Israel Iskowitz, was born in Israel, was a master of the Black face. His stage name was Eddie Cantor. He once appeared as a Black face in "Banjo Eyes".

Huckleberry Finn Novel

Mark Twain's , *The Adventures of Huckleberry Finn* uses racial epithets 39 times.

Traits of Negro Characters

A white educator wrote in 1912 his views on the traits of Negro character. He said the Negro "lacks self control, needs restraints, superstitious, sexual indulgent, lacks initiative, and musical, and religious sensitivity".

Black and Korean Proverbs

The word "black" throughout the world has always connoted a meaning of something dark, bad or evil. Several Korean proverbs reflect these meanings.

"Come near to an Indian ink and you will be stained Black"

This proverb is a lesson forbidding a man to associate with bad people for fear of becoming inflicted by their evil influence.

"To distinguish Black from white"

Discriminate between good and bad and distinguish right from wrong to tell which side is right in a dispute.

"The charcoal calls others Black"

A guilty person accuses another of being guilty, the pot calls the kettle Black.

TRUE STORIES OF SEGREGATION

Black Communication

In 1968, a University of Illinois professor wrote a book on Black Communication. There were some articles that discussed the young street corner Negro and the preconceived impressions of some Blacks that people sometimes apply to all Blacks. Some of stereotypes were:

"Blacks love to party, irrational street people, cool, fight at times, hang on corners, hustlers, drop outs, always late. (colored people time, "CPT"). and love to dance. The author included some words that are used in their communication styles. Some of them were: "run a game, work on the mind, put the bump on the cat, running it down, and welfare county money. Today many young people have devised their current street talk or slang.

Sometimes when educators examine Black behavior within the closed or segregated Black culture, the results of course do not represent all Blacks. However, non Blacks will and have relied on their first impressions and also tend to relate them to what they observed on television, especially the comic and sometimes stereotypes acted out by Blacks themselves.

A scholarly study by a white researcher including some Black writers, poets and educators presented some of these characteristics of African Americans. Unfortunately, many of these can add erroneous information, affecting people's beliefs and conclusions about Black values, culture, morals and character. They then form stereotypes. Some believe that Black behavior originates from their African heritage, such as verbal expressions of "Uh huh, uh uh". There are Blacks who communicate with their eyes, facial expressions and sometimes in a dance pattern. Blacks sometimes have a speech slang that originates from the home, street, or school, and many carry it to the college classrooms.

Amos/Andy

There are some people today who believe that the Amos/Andy comedy videos are just funny and have no racial implications. I am sure that they are not aware that the original characters were played in a stereotypical format by two white men, Freeman Gosden and Charles Correll. They were on radio and you could not see them. Years ago, the NAACP complained about the negative images even though the television characters were played by Blacks. The NAACP declared at the 1995 annual convention that "The show showed the Negro and other minority groups in a stereotyped manner and tended to strengthen the conclusion among uniformed or prejudiced people that Negroes and other minorities are inferior, dumb, lazy, and dishonest."

The Amos/Andy show made fun of Black people, the women as fat, loud mouthed and ugly. But many Blacks still turn on the show. Some Blacks would use their justification that the show portrayed Black doctors, lawyers, and people were informed that Black professionals had gone to college. It appeared that Blacks were laughing at the negative images of themselves. The Amos/Andy shows do not seem negative to some people, who dislike the current Black oriented comedies and movies. There appears to be a continuous trend to use Black comedies to portray typical Black sub culture.

The legacy of Black humor and jokes relative to Blacks continues and the instigators always respond "It was not meant to portray any racial undertones. Black stereotypes are also present in foreign countries. The Netherlands or Holland has had its version of "Black Pete or Zwarte Piet". Lately, the stereotype character has been banned from holiday decoration for some 6,000 Amsterdam children because a local school board in 1997 considered it a racial stereotype. The background of Holland's "Black Pete" is that the Christmas tale of St. Nicholas or Sinter Klass lived in sunny Spain not the North Pole, and he was always accompanied by his Moorish helper. (There has been a controversy over the years about the identity of the Moorish people from Northwest Africa who occupied Spain hundreds of years ago; were they considered of Black descent?). There were street processions that attracted thousands of children who would paint their faces Black and put on bright orange and red lipstick to resemble "Black Pete". The "Black Pete" character would speak in broken Creole and perform some minstrel acts. Throughout the world it is natural for people to justify their individual meanings of Black and its relationship to Black people. One person in Holland said that when Pete comes down the chimney he turns Black. Is he a servant or a slave? Is his skin Black from the soot or is he just a Moor? Some Black children from the former Dutch colonial possession, Surinam would insist on painting their faces Black according to one report.

There are many innocent and uniformed people who have no idea whatsoever about the historical tradition of the Netherland's "Black Pete". Last Christmas an educated Black lady with a college degree informed her Black co-worker in a nursery school where they worked that I see no problem in reading the story about "Black Pete" to our youngsters because I believe it has nothing to do with race. The following story is just a sideline, but I am speculating that "Black Pete" had nothing to do with a young Hollander who was working as a hotel manager in Amsterdam in 1997. His awareness and perceptions of Blacks could have come from television, personal experiences or other false impressions of people of color.

My dear and loving son had traveled to Europe with several of his white friends. When they arrived in Amsterdam, my son decided to go into the lobby of a hotel and ask for a room. The manager politely told him in mid day that there were no rooms available. Since I write on the Black experiences very seriously, I do share my writings with my son and also inform him that he must not day-dream and say "well I guess they had no vacant rooms". He definitely knew how to respond to the manager's statement; he returned to the car and asked one of his white friends to inquire about a vacancy. The white youngster went to the desk and a nice young white Dutch lady said, "Yes, we have some rooms. My son and his friend went back to the desk and my son asked for the manager. He asked him, "Why did you tell me that there were no vacancies?" My son was experiencing what I had told him in the past. At that point, my son and his friends found another hotel in Amsterdam and enjoyed their visit. This story is significant because his two white friends were well educated as well as my son and they knew that black skin is international when toleration is the issue. Just another true story of the Black experience abroad and its similarities to America the Beautiful".

A Sports Stereotype

Even today, some people do not feel that Blacks can perform in an excellent manner in the Marathons even though they have participated as early as 1936.

YMCA Marathon Team

"March 1936 - It is possible that the 12th Street YMCA is the only colored marathon team in the country. The YMCA branch had a Marathon team for the past three years under the direction of Physical Education Director, Arthur A. Greene Sr. The runners have increased their aptitudes for distance with leaps and bounds. The Marathon team is the only one of color to participate in the city's mixed track meet. The nurses' care for the exhausted men as they cross the finish line without regard to color. The 12th YMCA had broken the ice. In June, 1938, Edgar Lee, former Washington, D.C. fireman, captured the Seventh Annual YMCA Marathon for the fifth time."

Portraits of Stereotypes

On a visit to African American expositions and festivals, one can find drawings, sketches, paintings and figurines, all memorabilia representing the Black American military in the West during the Indian Campaigns. The military units were the famed Black Cavalryman's 9th and 10th Cavalry regiments, affectionately known as the "Buffalo" soldiers. The dealers and vendors are selling reproduction sketches and recent paintings of these soldiers. These memorabilia are based on the earlier sketches and drawings of a distinguished artist named Frederic Remington, who made some outstanding sketches and drawings of the Black cavalryman. However, his reporting of the known inferiorities in education and social customs of the Black soldiers did not contribute to the acknowledgment of their outstanding traits and achievements. Remington would often write from his interviews with Black troops and use the illiterate dialect or expressions of many Black soldiers who were not fortunate to receive a basic elementary education. Frederic wrote the following in the *Cosmopolitan Magazine,* February 1897. "I know why so many of dem battles is victorious said one trudging darkey to another. "Why?" he asked. Dey march de men so hard to get thar, dat dey is too tired to run away".

Because of my interest in military history and especially the exploits of two support regiments of color, I cannot forget those racist remarks and attitudes of a white artist who could never see a positive scene or conduct an interview with some Black soldier who had received an education and could articulate normal English. However, Remington's attitude and seeming prejudice are still reflected in the views of some Caucasians who continually reenforce negative stereotypes.

Frederic Remington's sketches and drawings have been revived today by new artists and reproduction specialists. The customers today are African Americans and fortunately, Remington captions and demeaning writings are not presently visible in the sales of his creative portraits of a hundred years ago.

Just recently a government organization was attempting to get a message to young Black men everywhere. The public relations office actually believed that the most plausible way to reach those who were school dropouts and out on the streets was to use a slogan that is possibly used by many Blacks. They even justified their actions by saying they had seen it used on Black television shows and by many Blacks. The reality is that the slogan does not represent all Blacks in our cultural and social diversity.

James Weldon Johnson wrote in 1938, "The greater part of white Americans thinks of us in stereotypes, most of them coming to them second-hand by way of the representation of Negro life and character on stage and in certain books. In the main they are exaggerated, false and entirely unlike our real selves." Today, many stereotypes are developed by some whites and even Blacks from viewing television and advertisements. Johnson also said that white people must be educated and taught the truth about our history and culture. It is interesting to learn that James W. Johnson, the composer and former NAACP official would state in 1938 that if would be helpful if our colleges could devise a way of establishing extension courses for white people.

Blacks have been depicted over the years by non Blacks as "lazy, shiftless, unreliable, irresponsible and a good humored buffoon, incapable of moral and mental development. It is unfortunate that some of these untruths have been perpetuated over the years in writings, comments and conversations by some

TRUE STORIES OF SEGREGATION

whites and acted out by some Blacks in comedy and humor on television and in the theatres.

There are some Blacks and non Blacks today who have no knowledge of the impact that the minstrel shows had on stereotypes of Blacks leaving lasting impressions for some people. The Black faced minstrel was a popular form of entertainment for many years, and millions of white Americans developed their own conceptions of Negroes. The Black was represented on the minstrel stage as a "shuffling, happy go lucky, banjo picking, singing, dancing darkey. The minstrel shows would also highlight the Blacks so-called privileged menu of watermelon, possum and chicken.

Early Congressional Stereotypes

The American politicians play an integral part in leadership and local government affairs in their respective states. Many of their constituents depend on their advice and guidance and some really believe the words spoken in their political campaigns and even speeches on the House and Senate floors. During the years 1830 and 1924, two honorable southern senators discussed their personal perceptions of the intellectual abilities and inferiorities of Black Americans and they definitely were stereotypes. Senator John Calhoun said in 1830, "If a Negro could be found who could parse (speak a word) Greek or explain Euclid (the mathematician), I should be constrained to think that he has human possibilities". Those were the words of a South Carolina senator in 1830.

Senator James K. Vardaman from Mississippi delivered a speech in the Senate and said: "The Black man has never written a language. His achievement in architecture is limited to the thatched roof hut or a hole in the ground. He has never had any civilization except that which has been indicated by a superior race, and it is lamentable, (regrettable) that his civilization lasts only so long as he is in the hands of the white man who inculcates it. When left to himself, he has universally gone back to the barbarism of the jungle." We must realize that in 1924, these words were shared by many scholars throughout the world including some educated Africans and Afro Americans in the United States.

Black Occupational Stereotypes

During segregation some whites would express their beliefs about the work skills and character of Negroes. There were beliefs that Blacks were best suited for manual labor, not technical or clerical work. A manager of an oil company in Louisiana said in 1940 that a Negro is like a mule; he moves along at his own speed, and worries about nothing. If you give him a full stomach, he is then happy and becomes too sluggish mentally to do any work. However, said the manager there are some Negroes who are good carpenters, brick masons, mechanics, porters, bell hops and ideal servants. But some of their minds do not act quickly and they are afraid of getting injured.

Southern Common Stereotypes

During slavery and after, especially in the early days of segregation, white southerners had their special vocabulary to describe their faithful Blacks. They would refer to them as "faithful old Negroes, Uncle, Auntie, old Black Joe, field nigger, good nigger, darkie, mammy, house nigger, white nigger (mulatto), coon, cross breed, white man's nigger and Sam". The whites loved their mammy and often referred to her in their songs and poems.

There were some whites who resented the mulatto because he/she reminded them of their wrongs, and at times the mulatto did not fit into their traditional Negro stereotype. One white man said that the difference between mulattoes and Blacks was, "The real nigger is not uppity, the lighter ones have enough white blood to resent what they are or are ambitious to be something else. They talk back to you, argue and carry a chip on their shoulders". Some whites believed that the "modern nigger has a feeling of responsibility and wants the white people' privileges".

Blacks Can Not Learn

There were some whites southerners who actually believed that Blacks could not learn. They would argue that a little Black boy was as bright as a little white boy up to a certain age. They said between 12-15 years, the Black boy could not progress further. But he could merely copy what he saw about him and therefore it was useless to educate him. Then there were some who believed that if he could learn it would be dangerous, would think too much and try to step out of his place. He was born for the white man's use and abuse.

I read an article in the *Journal of Peace Research* in 1973 which addressed racism and stereotypes in children's literature. I have included a summary of the highlights of the article I used in my race relations lectures twenty-five years ago.

Racism in Children's and Young People's Literature

Several years ago when many African Americans and their leaders became alarmed by a certain "slip of the tongue" or in reality actual expression of some Japanese leaders in reference to Blacks, I was not so alarmed, but it reminded me of its etiology or contributing causes. Over the years some children's literature of the Western World has addressed the African and Black in a racist manner. In many children's books, historical treatment of Blacks was characterized by their being associated with "Animal behavior, and instinct." In 1973, twenty years ago, I read a very well researched article on "Racism in Children's and Young People's Literature in the Western World". The author is Noerg Becker of the Hessiche Stiftung Friedens and Konfliktsforschung, Frankfort, Germany. The article is published in the *Journal of Peace Research.*

Becker said that from its very beginning, European culture has associated "good and evil with the color symbolism of white and Black. Hence, middle-high German literature uses the words devil, heathen and Negro as synonyms. Accordingly, the bogey or the Black man". Boulimia, as he is called in Switzerland, can be found in German nursery rhymes. The article stated that a great number of children's books still portray the African and Negro or Black as the colored servant, happy, unable to compete with modern civilization and culture. In 1971, a book on the life of Albert Schweitzer, late medical missionary in Africa depicted him as a dignified father helping his Black children in distress because they are unable to help themselves.

Over the years, the Afro or African American has been characterized and depicted in European literature in a racist manner, wrote Becker. He cited *Uncle Tom's Cabin* which has been a best seller in the Western World. Ironically in 1967, this writer viewed an Uncle Tom motion picture in Germany with German script and produced by a German motion picture studio. Some European children and young people's literature showed Afro Americans as "a minor child, and dependent upon the white man".

There has been a tendency during segregation, and even after for non Blacks to think that African American are not bilingual. The following true story portrays how a distinguished American general's wife was surprised that the butler and cook could master the French language.

"Do You Understand French, Pat"?, asked Mrs. George S. Patton

This true story was related to me by the late Mr. William West of Vienna, Virginia. Mr. West had a cousin named Pat, who was born in Canada and had learned to speak French fluently. He worked as a butler and cook for the late General George

S. Patton and his wife who resided in the Washington area when the General was a young officer. One day while serving the General and his wife, at their home, Mrs. Patton decided to practice her lessons in French, because they were preparing to leave for France. General Patton and his wife were unaware that their butler, Pat, could speak and understood the French language. Therefore, Mrs. Patton stated in French that Pat was a very dark person and quite Black. Later that evening as Pat was opening the car door for Mrs. Patton, he asked her if he could have the afternoon off in the best spoken French. Mrs. Patton was quite surprised and asked Pat, "Do you understand the French language?" When he replied, "Yes", she went into her house to use the phone. She immediately called General Patton and told him what had occurred. The next day, General George S. Patton took Pat over to Washington, D.C. and visited one of the best stores for stoves. The general purchased Pat a stove costing $100 dollars that he was in need of and personally apologized to him about the remarks his wife had made while they were having lunch. Mr. William West stated in 1970 that Pat's relatives still live a few doors from his house and still own the stove. It was one of the best old coal stoves of the early 1900's. I did have the opportunity to relate some of this story to Mrs. Patton's son at a social gathering.

A Watermelon Story

Historically, there had been a popular stereotype that Blacks love their watermelons and artists would draw pictures of Blacks with a watermelon. There were also photographs of Blacks eating watermelons.

My late cousin, Edward Palmer of St. Louis, Missouri, told me when I was a youngster that he once performed in a minstrel show that came to town when he was five years old. His mother received five dollars for his brief career as an actor and singer. Cousin Edward said that two white minstrels with Black face would be singing a watermelon song. There was a large mock up of a water melon on the stage. Cousin Edward was lying inside the mock up and it was closed. When the mock up watermelon opened, he would look up at the audience, wipe his eyes and sing a little song. At sixty years of age, he was still able to sing that little jingle. The verse was: "Please, please go away, do not disturb my slumber deep". Cousin Edward lived until he was 85 years and probably never forgot his early minstrel experience.

I was standing on a large hill in Rome, Italy, in 1967 viewing the beautiful city. I happened to glance at an Italian man nearby who was eating watermelon, I thought about my cousin Eddie at that time and the stereotype and wished that I had my camera in hand, because that Italian was so into eating that watermelon that he had cleaned that rind clear of all the melon. Well, I guess stereotypes can apply to all people. I read in a newspaper in August 1977 that there was the 21st watermelon eating festival contest and many visitors were present and guess what, at none other than Hope Fair Park, Hope, Arkansas. The photo in the paper depicted all white smiling faces.

Some Asian Perceptions

I read in a Filipino magazine some interesting remarks about how some Filipinos see Blacks. The major discussion was about Asians and color. The author said historically some Asians realize that the lighter the skin you are the better chances you have to advance in society. Some people of color began to hate themselves. Some Asians believe the right way is the white way.

There are some older Filipinos who have developed stereotypes about Blacks, possibly because of ignorance or their unfavorable experiences with Blacks.

A true story about a Filipino interracial couple illustrates some of the Asians perceptions about Blacks and how they are changed after people began to communicate and understand each other.

A young Filipino lady came to America in 1985. At one time she believed that she was afraid of Blacks; However, when she met a dark, handsome Black man, she did not see him as Black, but a person she was attracted to. During the dating period, prior to her eventual marriage to the man, she would not tell her parents about him., feeling they would not approve of him. When she finally told her parents, they asked "Why a Black man of all people?" They implied that she had married beneath her social level. Later, the parents accepted her husband and their children. When the family visited the Philippines she prepared her husband about what he could expect. She told him that some people might call him "egot" or GI Joe and most would think that she is a prostitute but that he should just ignore them. The mother told her daughter that she had thought the way she did because she had believed that if you are a Black person you are bad. I wonder how many other Asians believe that stereotype today.

There is a story about a 50 year old Filipino woman who encountered some problems with her children, from a previous marriage in accepting her young Black friend. She would not go out on a date for seven months because she was fearful of what people would say. She also was afraid of Blacks and foreigners prior to meeting the Black man. She said that he was kind to her and would cook, do the house work and take her to the doctors.

These two true stories portray some of the problems and prevailing stereotypes that are still present today. How many other diverse ethnic group really fear Black people or just avoid them retaining early perceptions and borrowed prejudices.

I believe that the years of segregation in America and the negative propaganda that has been transplanted to other countries officially and unofficially have contributed over the years to lasting perceptions of Blacks. This following letter is an example of how stereotypes are developed about Blacks.

"A French Directive"

[To the] French Military Mission stationed with the American Army, August 7, 1918. Secret information concerning the Black American troops.

It is important for French officers who have been called upon to exercise command over Black American troops, or to live in close contact with them to have an exact idea of the position occupied by Negroes in the United States. The information set forth in the following communication ought to be given to these officers and it is to their interest to have these matters known and widely disseminated. It will devolve likewise on the French Military Authorities, through the medium of the Civil Authorities, to give information on this subject to the French population residing in the cantonments occupied by American colored troops.

The American attitude upon the Negro question may seem a matter for discussion to many French minds. But we French are not in our province if we undertake to discuss what some call "prejudice." [recognize that] American opinion is unanimous on the "color question," and does not admit of any discussion.

The increasing number of Negroes in the United States (about 15,0000,000) would create for the white race in the Republic a menace of degeneracy were it not that an impassable gulf has been made between them.

As this danger does not exist for the French race, the French public has become accustomed to treating the Negro with familiarity and indulgence.

This indulgence and this familiarity [These] are matters of grievous concern to the Americans. They consider them an affront to their national policy. They are afraid that contact with the French will inspire to Black Americans aspirations which to them (the whites) appear intolerable. It is of the utmost importance that every effort be made to avoid profoundly estranging American opinion.

Although a citizen of the United States, the Black man is regarded by the white American as an inferior being with whom relations of business or service only are possible. The Black is constantly being censured for his want of intelligence and discretion, his lack of civic and professional conscience, and for his tendency toward undue familiarity.

The vices of the Negro are a constant menace to the American who has to repress them sternly. For instance, the Black American troops in France have, by themselves, given rise to as many complaints for attempted rape as all the rest of the army. And yet the (Black American) soldiers sent us have been the choicest with respect to physique and morals, for the number disqualified at the time of mobilization was enormous.

Conclusion

1. We must prevent the rise of any pronounced degree of intimacy between French officers and Black officer. We may be courteous and amiable with these last, but we cannot deal with them on the same plane as with the white American officer without [the Blacks] them, must not shake hands or seek to talk or meet with them outside of the requirements of military service.

2. We must not commend too highly the Black American troops, particularly in the presence of (white) Americans. It is all right to recognize their good qualities and their services, but only in moderate terms strictly in keeping with the truth.

3. Make a point of keeping the native cantonment population from "spoiling" the Negroes. (White) Americans become greatly incensed at any public expression of intimacy between white women with Black men. They have recently uttered violent protests against a picture in the "Vie Parisienne" entitled *"The Child of the Desert"* which shows a (white) woman in a "cabinet particular" with a Negro. Familiarity on the part of white women with Black men is furthermore a source of profound regret to our experienced colonials who see in it an overweening menace to the prestige of the white race.

Military authority cannot intervene directly in this question, but it can through this civil authorities exercise some influence on the population.

[Signed] Linard

The United States Military was confronted with a problem in 1922 when some Black troops were being transferred back to the states to Fort Riley, Kansas. The following article was written in 1994 and it is another example of how segregation stereotypes and discrimination have been a legacy.

"What About The Mother and Children?"

The United States Military has stationed troops in many areas of the world. Sometimes these troops remain for a number of years. A problem that is often addressed by military and civilians of the host countries is the fraternization of servicemen with ladies of the respective countries. Often a relationship develops into marriage and/or the birth of children out of wedlock. This has occurred since the 1900's and the military has dealt with these situations in World Wars I and II, the Korean War and the Vietnam War. There are many happy and long relations in, marriage between military men of all services with foreign women from Asia and Europe. Their children in the majority of case have adjusted into the American way of life as another American child of military or former military parents.

There is a problem that the U.S. Military has had to address in World War I and II, Korea and Vietnam Wars, especially World War II. With the coming home of African American soldiers from Europe with their French English and Italian brides.

After the wars of conflicts, the countries were left with some brides and/or girl friends who had children fathered by white and Black servicemen. In some countries there were no problems in locating orphanages and adoption centers to accept the children of white Americans. However, that problem of skin color did exist when the mixed babies/children of African American fathers were present. A question that has often been asked is where are the mixed children of African American fathers and their Asian mothers? Also how many children of African fathers actually Asian boarded that mass airlift of young children from Vietnam at the end of the conflict. Today, America has a serious problem finding suitable adoptions for children of black men and mothers from other cultures..

The problems of the disposition of children born to foreign mothers and African American did not originate in 1945. There was some concern as early as 1922. A concerned and thoughtful post commander developed a plan for the disposition of 207 Filipino women and 72 children of the 9th Cavalry and other "colored soldiers". The post commander of headquarters of Camp Stotsenburg, Pampanga, Philippine Islands (P.I.) submitted his plan and recommendations to the commanding general, Philippine Department, Manila (P.I.). The plan classified the wives and non wives and children into four categories:

"<u>First</u>. 37 Filipino women legally married to soldiers, having 56 children by them.

<u>Second</u>. 9 Filipino women not legally married to soldiers but living openly with them and having 16 children by them.

TRUE STORIES OF SEGREGATION

<u>Third</u>. 95 Filipino women legally married to solders but having no children by them.

<u>Fourth</u>. 66 Filipino women and one Japanese not legally married to soldiers but living openly with them and having no children."

The post commander viewed the first category as presenting great difficulty. He believed the U.S. military should not compel, encourage or allow these soldiers to abandon their lawful wives and children. He wrote, "This should not occur merely for the purpose of conforming to a change of policy based on some minor economy or convenience to the government. On the other hand, it seems to be impracticable to take these 37 families to the United States. Transportation having been provided as far as San Francisco, very few soldiers would have the money to pay railroad fare to Fort Riley or Fort Huachuca, and even if they were taken on troop trains no quarters would be provided for them after arrival. Climatic conditions would not suit them, and if their husbands, at some future time, failed to reenlist or were otherwise discharged, these native women and children would be a charge upon the United States". The commander also addressed government policies. He said, "It seems inconsistent with the policy of a generous government to discharge these men for its own convenience without making any provision, or allowing them any opportunity for securing proper employment. I cannot believe that if the facts were understood, the War Department or higher authority on account of color would compel the immediate discharge of high type, faithful and efficient soldiers of long service in such numbers as to embarrass the local labor market and impose an enormous hardship upon them without even giving them an opportunity to complete their current enlistment. Beside this, the insular government would probably object to such a procedure, as a number of such discharged soldiers are already open to the charge of vagrancy".

The post commander saw the third category presented a similar difficulty but to a lesser degree. His reason was that 95 women without children that were easier to handle than the 37 women with children. The 9 women and 16 children of the class two presented a different problem, because these women could not be taken to the United States, unless the men married them and then they could be placed in class one. They would have to provide for them in the P.I.

The commander also believed that the only problem presented by the women in the category four was to get rid of them from the neighborhood unless the men would marry them and place them in class three.

The commander had to address his views of the "so-called paternal slave master when he said, "*We cannot assume that the heart of a colored man is any less sensitive to the destruction of his Black family ties than that of a white man. No decent slave owner in the old south, would consent to the breaking up of families (the slave owner broke up families when he separated them by selling slaves from families), and the whole world was sickened by the sight of Germany's disregard of family ties in Belgium. It is inconceivable that these families should be broken up and abandoned merely to carry out some little unimportant detail of the policy, that can be changed by the stroke of a pen along with hundreds of other changes being made every time a new man gets into a new position".*

The commander decided upon his solution. He said they were based upon the following principles:

First   *We must be governed by the ordering principle of humanity.*

Second   *We must be fair in our treatment of soldiers who have rendered honorable and faithful service.*

Third   *Our plan must be acceptable to the government general in so far as it affects the civil community.*

Fourth   *The efficiency of the army must not be sacrificed*

Fifth   *The plan must be such as to minimize subsequent controversy.*

The post commander solutions were:

"A   *Many of the women and children be sent to the United States as can be properly cared for and that the soldier responsibility for the rest of them be retained in the service in the P.I. until they can be other wise disposed of.*

B   *That a cable be sent to the War Department requesting information as to whether in the case of soldiers without necessary funds, the women and children in category one and the women of category three shall be sent to the United States (U.S.) with the troops and if so that proper arrangements be made for their transportation to the new stations and their accommodations after arrival.*

C   *That a careful canvass should be conducted to determine those men who desire to be discharged and who are prepared to take care of their families in the P.I. These men to be so discharged. A canvass should also determine the native women who are willing to give up their husband and who consent to their husbands return to the U.S. without them. Affidavit to be secured from these women to this effect and the men so returned.*

D   That all men of categories one, two and three not disposed of A, B and C above, be retained in the military service in the Philippines and gradually discharged for the convenience of the government as rapidly as they can obtain suitable employment, or otherwise make their own arrangements for the proper disposition of their family ties. The following assignments are suggested for these men while being retained in the service. A certain number preferably the older non commissioned officers (NCO) could be retained as instructors in the new 26th Cavalry regiment. Of the balance, some could be transferred to the medical department, some to the quartermaster corps and others formed into labor detachments. They could be used as teamsters, orderlies, messengers, mounted military police and on other necessary duty.

E.   That the disposition of the 67 women in category four be held in abeyance until some policy is outlined for the dispositions of others. But that a careful investigation be made of each case with a view to obtaining a release of the man and to adjust all differences as to debts, ownership of property, etc. Then the soldier, could be returned to the United States."

The commanding general, Philippine Department, Fort William McKinley, Rizal, approved the plan. He stated that he had discussed the plan with the governor general who seemed satisfied with the plan.

There is evidence that some parts of the plan were executed because a memorandum to the commanding officer, Fort Riley Kansas from the office of the post commander, headquarters Camp Stotsenburg, P.I., dated October 8, 1922 was received. The subject of the memorandum was *"Relation of certain soldiers of the Ninth Cavalry to native women."*

There were listed on the memorandum the names of one first sergeant who was released from all obligations to a Filipino woman with no children. A staff sergeant was also released from obligations and the Filipino woman with no children would remain in the islands. Two privates were released from all obligations when the Filipino woman signed the affidavits. One of the privates was married and had no children and his wife decided to remain in the P.I. There were two privates who were married and their Filipino wives accompanied them to the United States.

A corporal's Filipino woman friend, not married and no children signed as affidavit refusing to release the soldier from obligations. A sergeant who was not married to a Filipino woman would remain in the P.I. with their one minor three month old child. The sergeant was unable to make an allotment for the Filipino woman because he had an allotment of fifty (50) dollars a month to a wife in the United States. The soldier agreed in writing to send ten (10) dollars a month until April 1924 for support of the child.

There are many inferences that can be made concerning the Ninth Cavalry soldiers and their Filipino wives and friends in 1922. The military viewed the situation as a problem. They were concerned about the welfare of the child and mother and also obligations that the soldiers could confront.

There were no discernible instances of racial factors involved in correspondence reviewed. However, one must be realistic in the view of the climate of racial segregation in America and the white majority in power enforced all facets of segregation where possible from a legal justification. Therefore, I infer that the problem was not a racial one, because from a biological perspective, the military authorities were concerned with two peoples of similar skin color in many cases, simply "people of color". Of course, that can be debatable in America because unfortunately people are classified by sight and descriptions such as "hair, lips and skin color". I ask the question, why weren't some of the procedures used by the military in 1922 considered in relations to those brown babies in France, Germany, England, Korea and Vietnam. Whatever the answer may be, I deeply believe that many citizens of the Filipinos in 1922 probably would have said, a person can be accepted by their character, sincerity, morality and honesty and not be so concerned about one's skin color. I salute the concerned white post commander and his superiors who concurred with his recommendations because they were ahead of their time when concerned about the family and not just welfare and who pays for it.

White Thought

A lesson plan prepared for the Race Relations School in 1973 was called "Contemporary White Thought". The lesson objective was to discuss the varied views of some white majority members concerning racial matters. The students would discuss the material openly and appreciate why some people think the way they do. I have included some highlights from the student handout and some recent researched "white thoughts".

These thoughts were expressed twenty-five years ago and some of these expressions and honest convictions are still heard in 1998. The major difference is that people will state their views loud and clear, and many politicians will express their thoughts, especially if it is what their constituents believe and want to hear. Many of these views and ideas are carryovers from some idealogies and reasoning from the days of segregation.

Contemporary White Thought
Summary of Teaching Points

This supplement has been prepared to serve as a reference for group discussions on the various categories of white thoughts in American life. Students are instructed to read the quoted material and select the one number (quoted paragraph) that they would like to discuss in class. The student should be prepared to comment as to what category the person who made the quoted statement could be assigned.

The following categories could be used to differentiate the varying thoughts of some white Americans:

1. <u>Conservative</u>: One who attempts to maintain and conserve certain traditions and principles of society and his immediate environment. He also prescribes certain guidelines and limits to actions that would initiate change.

2. <u>Moderate</u>: An individual who tends to support recommended changes in society. However, he places limitations on the progress and scope of suggested change.

3. <u>Liberal</u>: A person who feels that society should not stagnate, but should be a continuing rapid change to improve individual and group desires.

4. <u>Militant</u>: An individual who has expressed openly and nonviolently that changes must occur and now. He is characterized by many persons as a radical and possibly an individual to be feared. American who wants to improve his conditions and surroundings and those of his fellow Americans who might represent the American minority. However, a militant can be a dedicated, true-loving American who wants to improve his conditions and surroundings and those of his fellow Americans who might represent the American minority.

White Perceptions

View, 1997

A book published in 1997 by American Heritage Division of Forbes Inc. included an article on 199 things every American should know. There was a reference to Blacks: *"Five Black Trouble Makers"* Denmark Vesey, Sojourner Truth, Frederick Douglas, Marcus Garvey and Malcolm X.

White Flight

"The choice is sometimes simple", said a white man. The whites do not like colored and they do not like whites. One day one Black moved into my neighborhood on a Friday, and I moved out on the following Monday.

White Supremacy Threatened

When rioting occurred in Wichita, Kansas, in 1968, some blue collar white laborers believed that their values were threatened because they were no longer the masters in their own city.

Name Calling

During segregation, the upper class whites would regard poor class whites as low caste and would call them "hillbillies, crackers, clay eaters, pecker woods, wool hats, trash, and low downers. Sometimes, the lower class whites played a great part in denying Blacks voting rights and were members of lynch mobs and responsible for some violence against Blacks.

An Endearing Comment

A white CBS sports analyst in 1977 called a Georgetown University basketball player a "tough monkey" and told the press he meant no offense and I would not apologize. He said the comment had nothing to do with race, it is "an endearing comment".

Young Whites Perceptions

Several years ago a reporter in a major city asked some white students between the ages of 10-12 years who had been participants in an exchange program visits between the inner city and the suburban students to express their beliefs and perceptions of some Blacks and their home environment. Some of the white children wrote:

"If we could go to the same schools, it would bring us together"

"Suburban students have the advantage that most teenangers in the inner city dream of, clean neighborhoods, first rate high schools and own their cars"

"I do not know what I would have accomplished if I had lived in the inner city"

"I wonder do Blacks and whites confront each other because of pride and jealousy"

"Some white students call Black inner city youngsters "GunToting Welfare Needing Punks"

"We have nothing in common with them and no base to form a relationship, because if it occurred it would be detrimental"

"I could not trust the children of the inner city"

"I just could not imagine going through a metal detector to go to school daily"

"I like living in the suburbs; it is clean and I love the smell of flowers"

Negro Patience, 1930

The late South African leader Jan Christian Smuts was visiting New York City, when he said: "The Negro is the most patient of all animals next to the ass".

"My Great Great Grandfather Had a Slave"

In 1997, there was a great discussion in America about an apology for slavery. I received a letter from a white man on January 13, 1982. I met Mr. Duke Doughty at the Eastville Courthouse in Virginia where I was doing some research. He told me that he would send me a copy of a document that had freed a slave of his great great grandfather, Major Dowty. The slave was Leah Reid who was 46 years old. Mr. Doughty was one white man who did not have loss of memory about slavery in his family.

Recognition of a Family Slave

A concerned white lady wrote in July, 1988, to the office of the Corresponding Secretary General, National Society Daughters of the American Revolution. She was Julia Deckard of Bloomington, Indiana, a member of the DAR. She wrote: "I have a letter which my great great grandfather, Jacob Deckard, sent to the Commander of the British Forces in Montreal in 1784. He said that he had purchased a Black slave, Pompey, in 1774 and that the Indians stole him and sold him to a British officer: Mr. Deckard wanted his property returned. Mrs. Julia Deckard stated that Pompey is buried in Monroe County, Indiana with his former master, Jacob Deckard. He was freed for his heroism in the battle of Stoney Point, New York. Mrs. Deckard wrote that "In the book *Black Courage*, I have reason to think Mr. Greene called him Lamb Pomp when he identifies him as being in Colonel Hays' Regiment, New York. Since I have no proof of Pompey's service, perhaps Mr. Greene can tell me more about the sources. I wish to install a DAR Revolutionary Plaque on his grave."

A Staunch Conservative

The late distinguished politician, senator, major general, U.S. Air Force, anti large government, communism, and pro choice will be remembered in history for his outstanding achievements. However, lest we forget he will also be remembered by some Americans for voting against Civil Rights legislation in the 1960's.

PUBLIC FACILITIES

Justifications For Segregation

Some white citizens in New Orleans believe Blacks should be not allowed with whites because they tend to segregate themselves anyway. They are unclean, have an odor, lack morals and are ignorant. They might contaminate white children and their mental differences require separate treatment. Some people actually thought that the Black child's brain was always two years behind that of a white child.

A white theater manager in Philadelphia, Pennsylvania, said " a good class of white people cannot degrade themselves in associating with Blacks in public facilities".

The merchants and businessmen in the 1940's stated that they were not prejudiced, but they were compelled to segregate Blacks because they had to consider the prejudices of their white customers.

TRUE STORIES OF SEGREGATION

A New Jersey Druggist's Remarks

The druggist said that the only contact with them is in the store. Blacks pay for their goods, they are pleasant but they have a body odor that our white customers do not like. I use paper cups and containers for the Blacks.

Early Affirmative Action, 1964

The military had a meeting in New Orleans in April 1964 and the participants were scheduled to stay at a selected hotel. They were instructed to change hotels because a Black National Guard colonel was denied a room. Governor Rockefeller requested that his delegation return to New York City.

In July 1962, the Veterans Administration was instructed to stop doing business with funeral homes who had a policy of segregation.

An Affirmative Directive, 1944

The Adjustant General's Office of the War Department issued a directive on July 8, 1944 to Commanding Generals, Army Air Forces, All Service Commands and the Military District of Washington. The directive referenced a letter dated 5 March 1943 which directed that all personnel regardless of race would be afforded equal opportunity to enjoy recreational facilities on each post, camp and station. The letter of 8 July 1944 was necessary because some installations were not enforcing the provisions of the 1943 directive. The post exchanges were not to be designated for any race. Transportation owned by the government was to be available to all military regardless of race.

The Army Motion Picture Theaters were to serve all personnel regardless of race. The Commander's Inspector Generals were required to conduct periodic inspections to insure that there were no evidence of racial discrimination or direct or indirect violation of War Department policies. All commanders were directed to comply with the directive.

Segregated Glen Echo Park, 1940's

I am sure that young children today as well as years ago loved to go to the amusement park within minutes of their neighborhoods. Some youngsters in the Washington area enjoyed the Glen Echo Park a few miles from their homes either in Virginia, Maryland or Georgetown, Washington, D.C. That was not for me to enjoy or any other American classified Black like me. As a child growing up in Washington, I was not able to visit the park and be admitted to the wooden coaster rides, dips, and the theaters. Now with the National Park Service operating old park facilities for special events, I am sure that the people who visit the area and use what facilities that are still available have no idea that it is a monument to segregation.

Responsible Protesters

The late Mary Church Terrell, a graduate of Oberlin College, Ohio, was a civil rights crusader in the District of Columbia along with noted Attorney Charles Houston and distinguished educator, anatomist, medical doctor and professor, Dr. Montague Cobb were responsible through their protest for the eventual opening of lunch counters in the District's downtown stores and also the National Theater. Ironically, while reviewing the Inborden papers, I discovered an envelope stamped October 20, 1891, Memphis, Tennessee addressed to Mr. and Mrs. Wilson Evans, Oberlin, Ohio. The Evans were the parents of Thomas Inborden's wife Sarah. The invitation read:

> "Mr. Robert R. Church
> requests your presence
> at the marriage of his
> daughter Mary Eliza
> to
> Mr. Robert Heberton Terrell
> Wednesday evening, October twenty eighth
> at six o'clock
> 362 Lauderdale Street
> Memphis, Tennessee"

Robert H. Terrell was from Orange, Virginia, and his father was a White House messenger under President Grant. Terrell was a graduate of Harvard and Howard Universities. In 1902, he was appointed Judge of the Municipal Court, Washington, D.C. The Terrell's represented Black High Society in the early 1900's. Just another true historical note.

Breaking The Barriers - Uline Arena

Today, the sports world claims the outstanding successes of Black athletes in Chicago and Washington, and the players enjoy the millions of dollars they receive and all the benefits of integration in 1998. How many of them are aware or really care that in the Nation's Capitol a major sports facility practiced segregation, the Uline Arena. Are they aware that it was necessary for white and Black leaders to demonstrate their concerns to integrate the facility? Edwin B. Henderson, a physical education teacher and civil rights activist; Eugene Meyer, of the *Washington Post* Newspaper Company, and Eleanor Patterson of the former *Washington Times Herald Newspaper Company* were all instrumental in convincing Michael Uline to open the Uline Arena to Blacks without discrimination. The Arena was used for wrestling, ice hockey, and boxing events.

No Comfort For Black Children

The Kansas City Board of Public Welfare in the early 1900's provided on hot sunny days multiple portable showers with four nozzle heads attached to the fire hydrants for white children on the northside of the city for their comfort.

"There Will Be No Poles On My Land"

An elderly 80 year old Black woman had asked her white neighbor for easement rights to have a telephone installed by a private contract phone company in Brewton, Alabama. The white neighbor told her he would not allow any poles on his land. He also told the phone company the old colored lady did not need to have a phone. Ironically, the Black lady lived 100 years and thanks to God she did not have to dial 911 or emergency.

Northern Dining Policies

There were some instances of interracial dining in large northern cities during segregation. For some special events where Blacks were present, the hotel and restaurants would provide private dining rooms. Some predominantly white organizations would schedule their meetings at facilities that would accept Blacks.

Some northern restaurants would seat Blacks in the rear and often waiters would ignore the Black customers, be rude at times, smash glasses after Blacks had used them and even overcharge Black customers.

Characteristics of Segregated Stores

Normally Blacks were not served in barber and beauty shops, cafeterias, amusement places, and White Castle Hamburger stands. When Blacks would shop at some department stores, they were not allowed to put on clothes or use the dressing rooms, unless there were ones reserved for colored. If a store was very busy, the owners would use their porters and maids to wait on Blacks. The toliet facilities for Blacks were located in the basement. Many of these stores were owned by Jewish merchants. A famous street in Baltimore, Howard Street, at one time did not encourage Black customers to shop and tried to exclude them. When Blacks would enter the store, they would immediately approach them and say this store does not serve Black people. Then there would be some stores that permitted Blacks to enter and purchase articles across the counter, but they were not allowed to try on shoes, hats, gloves and dresses.

The thousands of immigrants that arrive in America today enjoy many privileges of America. What would some of them do if they were confronted with the following legally imposed segregation: discrimination in theaters, skating rinks, bowling alleys, dance halls, baseball parks, and swimming pools and sometimes would be subject to segregated seats and separate ticket windows.

There were some stores where the merchants would change the prices when Blacks would enter the store.

The banks would accept Black people's deposits but refuse to give them loans even though they had security, such as real estate. There were places in the south where there were special teller windows for Black customers.

Segregation In Parks and Playgrounds

Children and their parents just take it for granted that there is a playground or park and if I want to visit the facility, all I have to do is just go there. That was not the way it was just 30-40 years ago for an American minority called Black, because in most southern cities and some northern ones, Black children were not allowed. Again, I remind newly arrived immigrants to the United States how can any sensible person who experienced that kind of discrimination can just forget it? I cannot forget and believe the " Black voices from the graves" would also say like our Jewish friends "Never Again".

The school playgrounds, ball parks and fairgrounds were reserved in the South for white people. In many cities there were no playgrounds provided for Black children at public expense. I can recall visiting my relatives in Brazil, Indiana and the Black children would play on some privately owned land called "Campbell Woods" and when we would walk to town, we passed several nice school playgrounds where white children would be playing. There was no swimming pool in the town for Blacks. I can recall my friend Joe Grissom and the other boys trying to convince me to come into the water after we had traveled through a small abandoned cemetery in the back of the Black community called "Stringtown". The make shift swimming pool was just nature's open pool of a deep but not safe water hole. When I worked on the Sante Fe Railroad, the Black porters and chair car attendants would stay overnight at a nice Black senior citizen's home where she would provide billeting and meals. The town was Wellington, Kansas.

One day as we were leaving to catch our train to work the run to Kansas City, Missouri, we passed the city's swimming pool and there were all Mexican Americans in the pool. A porter told me that the pool was reserved several days a week for the Mexican. Now remember these Mexicans spoke Spanish and were the real Spanish minority from Mexico and not the new designated Hispanics who came from most every country that speaks the Spanish languagre. As these honorable judges will interpret today in civil rights suits and ask "Is there any past evidence of discrimination? Yes, your honors, the Mexicans, Indians, a few Asians and Blacks over the ages of 50 could reply, "Yes, Sir."

Black children in Houston, Texas, at one time had to visit the zoo on special reserved days. There were even parks in some cities where Blacks were not permitted to walk. Some parks would reserve separate areas for Blacks to play tennis and swim. When I was a youngster, on Sunday evenings, we would go to the Sunday Operas in beautiful Forest Park St. Louis, Missouri. We would join our friends who were seated in the back or "Crows Nest" reserved only for Black patrons. The concerts were free and we could see the whites and numerous new minorities enjoying those confortable seats and favorable viewing areas with whites.

Segregated Fox Theatre, St. Louis, Missouri

I read an article in the *St. Louis Post Dispatch* Newspaper, dated Tuesday, October 21, 1997. The article was discussing the 15th anniversary of the rebirth and renovation of St. Louis Memorable Fox Theatre. The theatre was constructed by a theatre magnate, William Fox, at a cost of six million dollars in January, 1929. The theatre seated some 5,000 persons. It was the second largest theater in the country.

One day in the late 1940's my younger sister Daisy and I went up to the ticket box and tried to purchase tickets but it did not happen. That was a personal experience. I will never forget because I knew then that we would have to wait for some months for that picture to come to our all Black neighborhood theatre that I believe was owned by a friendly Jewish man who was mostly in the background. He would permit his Black manager to assume the position of "Mr. Big Shot" and he did manage a good clean and orderly theatre for a middle and upper class Black clientele without the presence of police cars parked outside.

The paper stated that at a special performance on Sunday, the guest artist was Bill Cosby. I am quite sure that his comic act did not have any reference to my experiences and others during the segregated days of the Fox Theatre. I could be wrong. But probably not. Just another true story of the segregated years.

Separate But Equal

In 1964, a private gasoline station in Anniston, Alabama, a few miles away from Fort McClellan, Alabama where the Stars and Stripes was flying so beautifully, had a sign reading "For Whites Only"; yes, a place where one desires to purchase some gasoline.

Theatre Segregation - Washington, D.C.

The Lisner Auditorium owned by George Washington University in 1946 denied admission to Afro Americans. It was the actions of an interracial group of thirty World War II veterans and their guests attempting to attend the play "Blithe Spirit," which focused the issue. The play was being presented by a student dramatic group of the University. In 1947, George Washington University decided to admit Afro Americans to public performances; however, they permitted private groups renting the auditorium to establish their own racial policy.

"You Cannot Use This Restroom"

A young army captain stopped at a Shell gasoline station just a few miles from the city line of Montngomery, Alabama. He told the station attendant to fill it up. He then was moving toward the men's restroom when the white attendant said, "You cannot use that restroom." The captain said, where is the colored restrooms? The attendant told him, we don't have one. The officer said I must use the restroom because I must urinate. The attendant said again, "You cannot use this restroom. The captain paid the attendant for the gas and entered his car and drove away speeding at times and trying to retain his urine. The captain was quite aware that if he urinated anywhere, he was subject to a ticket and arrest by an Alabama state trooper. He continued speeding down the road until he entered a small town and observed a Gulf gasoline station. The captain told the white station attendant that he must urinate immediately. The white station attendant said, "There is the restroom over there." The captain thanked this understanding and kind white station attendant. The captain threw his shell credit card away after writing the Shell Corporation about the incident. They responded by saying "We are sorry, but we only sell the station gas". Later he obtained a Gulf credit card.

Segregation In the "Land of the Morning Calm:, Korea, 1971

A Black army officer in Korea in 1971 was asked by his Colonel to speak to the Black troops since they were upset about a racial incident in the unit. Several night clubs and bars would not permit Black soldiers in the Seoul area. The officer had joined a team consisting of some Psychological Warfare personnel, Military Police and Equal Opportunity officers. The team went out into the village and visited the clubs and saw first hand that Blacks were denied entrance to many clubs while white soldiers could enter freely. Previously, some Black soldiers had protested by marching in front of the Eighth U.S. Army Headquarters in Seoul, Korea. These incidents did not reach the newspapers of America. When the white soldiers asked some bar owners to keep Black soldiers out of the clubs, the Korean business men complied. I ask the question, how many Koreans in America are aware of some very tense moments between some Koreans and Black troops twenty years ago when small riots occurred in a few small villages? The majority of the Korean people greeted Black soldiers and were friendly, somehow a few listened to the racial remarks of some whites and the pain was felt again by Black soldiers when they were told "No", You cannot come in."

I do not think that the Korean representative on the President's racial commission has heard this true story about segregation in her ancestor's land. Just a nutritional reasoning. (food for thought).

An All White Officers Club, Korea, 1971

There was a predominantly, if not all white, military Intelligence Company in Korea that operated their own officers' club. They would give the impression to outsiders that it was for members only. Very few Blacks, if any, were permitted in the club. The club officer was a Black sergeant who managed and ran the club. He had considerable responsibility and authority. Once he invited a Black officer to the club as his guest. The Black officer was able to observe the white officers and their Korean guests in their reserved setting and reminiscent of "Home sweet home."

"Wait Until You Get Home"

A young child is shopping in downtown Washington, D.C. in the 1940's with his mother. She is purchasing some sewing material in a five and dime store when the young boy says, "Mother, I want a hot dog and a drink." She abruptly tells him, "You know better, you will not eat a hot dog from that Jim Crow lunch counter over there in the corner. You just wait until we get home to have our regular Saturday night's hot dog and beans." The little boy was experiencing some pain that foreigners from Europe, Latin America, Korea, Japan, China and even some African nations will never understand, because only the affilicted can feel the pain that lingers on.

Not Even A Take Out Order

An Afro American lieutenant reports to his assignment at Fort McClellan, Alabama in 1964. He was informed by the owner of a restaurant located immediately outside of the post gate that no Blacks were allowed in the restaurant, not even for a take out order.

"A Sales Lady's Courtesy?"

When a Black captain stationed at an Army Fort in the South went to the town's local Sears Roebuck store to return an item, he was told he could not. He then told the white lady who was waiting on him that she must accept the returned item. She again told him no and to return and see the manager if he had any problems. The Black man returned later and while he was waiting to see the manager, a card was pulled from the folder and was lying on the counter. The Black man picked up the card and read "colored man entered the store and complained about an exchange and got smart with a white lady." The white clerk returned and saw the Black man reading the card, and she demanded that he return the card. He refused and she called for the manager. The young manager, a graduate of Auburn University, invited the customer into his office and they discussed the matter. The manager apologized and removed the information from the card. This young manager demonstrated concern, understanding, and respect for his African American customer. He relieved some of that pain of racism.

White Gangs' Enforcement of Segregation

In southern and northern cities, Blacks were not permitted to use municipal public parks. It is unfortunate that when Black and white journalists discuss and write about so-called Black gangs in 1998, they are not aware or just ignore the facts.

"Prior to the 1940's Blacks were excluded from parks in Cincinnati, Ohio; Indianapolis, Indiana; and Chicago, Illinois.

There were the "bungalow gangs" in Indianapolis who would hit Blacks and chase them out of their lily white parks. Some white people in Chicago, Illinois, used ropes and guns to run Blacks from their parks.

Northern Practices of Segregation

During segregation cities in the North would discriminate and segregate Black citizens in public facilities. Blacks were excluded from all public parks in Cincinnati, Ohio and also the Municipal Bath House. Blacks were not admitted to golf courses in Chicago, Illinois. The tactics of exclusion were spelled out. There was a requirement that people who would use the golf courses must be a member of a golf club that was affiliated with the Western Golf Association, a segregated group.

Beach Segregation

Blacks were required to establish their separate beaches and summer resorts. Some were private and other public. There was a beach in Atlantic City for Blacks, (1900-1950's) called "Chicken Bone Beach". In the Maryland area, there were Carrs and Sparrows Beaches where entertainment starring Black popular entertainers would be available on the weekend. Across from these two beaches would be a private beach for the middle and upper class Black society where most of them were home owners and even had an elected mayor of their small residential area. Such a beach was Highland Beach. These beaches are a few miles from the city of Annapolis, Maryland. My late Uncle and Aunt, Ewell and Jesse Conway, owned a private resort called the "Shirley K" that was available for professional Blacks: physicians dentists, lawyers, teachers, ministers and government workers and other professional Blacks who would reserve rooms at the hotel.

The swimming pool was named in honor of Dr. Charles Drew, the noted Black surgeon and blood plasma specialist. They served delicious homemade meals and also had a boat dock. The State of New Jersey had several public and private beaches for Blacks. Some all white beaches would specify a bathing and swimming area for Blacks and there would be privately owned hotels and rooming houses owned by Black proprietors. Many Black churches would sponsor bus trips to these areas in the summer months.

Legal Cases To Integrate Segregated Facilities

Hairston Theatre Case

In 1946, Mrs. Juanita Hairston was removed from her seat in the orchestra section of a theater, Colorado Springs, Colorado. She was requested to move to the balcony. When she sued, the court awarded her 600 dollars damages because of the violations of her civil rights.

Lawrence Swimming Pool Case

Paul Lawrence of Montgomery, West Virginia, filed a suit against the city on behalf of himself and other Blacks in the city because they were denied admission to the city's swimming pool. The swimming pool was leased to a private group that had discriminatory policies. Lawrence's suit contended that the pool was financed by a general revenue bond. The pool had not been used from its completion in 1942 to the beginning of 1946, because of the question of permitting Blacks to use it. Finally in 1948, Judge Ben Moore, Charleston, West Virginia, Federal Court ruled that all citizens must be permitted to use the pool regardless of race or color.

Merryweather Skating Rink Case

Andrew Merryweather of Cincinnati, Ohio, sued the manager of the Sefferino Rollerdrome in Cincinnati in May 1946 because he was refused permission to use the skating rink, in violation of the state civil rights law. I often state that the word "interpretation" has been used by judges during segregation sometimes beyond the actual meanings of the law to appease the majority's desires, especially when the suit involved Blacks' quest for equal justice. In September 1946, Judge Daniel C. Hanley Jr. ruled in the skating rink case that Sefferino had not violated the state laws, Mr. Sefferino stated during the trial that the day Merryweather wanted to use the rink facilities, it was reserved by a private club.

James Culver Swimming Pool Case

There were judges during segregation whose interpretations of the law seemed consistent with the civil rights complaints raised by Black's. One was Federal Judge Joy Seth Hurd of the Appelate Court in Ohio. In July 1947, a Black man, James Culver, filed suit against the municipal officers of Warren, Ohio, because the municipal swimming pool had discriminatory policies. Negroes were permitted to use the pool only once a week. The city had leased the pool to a private club. The Trumbull County Common Pleas Court ruled against Culver. But in July 1948,

Judge Hurd ruled that the private club must permit Blacks to use the pool at any time that it was open.

CORE, Congress of Racial Equality Pickets Chicago Skating Rink

The CORE Civil Rights group was successful in Chicago, Illinois when they challenged a skating rink to admit Black customers. The skating rink was sued by CORE for refusing to admit Blacks. Members of CORE picketed the skating rink. When attendance at the rink was reduced, the rink management decided to admit Blacks.

Palisades Park Case, New Jersey

The Civil Rights Movement of the 1960's has been highly publicized, but few Americans are aware of the many legal cases filed to try to open some public facilities for Blacks in the north during segregation.

Some civil rights groups in 1947 tested the admittance policies of the New Jersey Palisades Park Swimming Pool. The management took the position that the pool was operated by a private club and only club members were admitted. There were nine Blacks and one white who filed suits against the pool authorities asking for damages, charging unlawful arrest and violation of the state civil rights act. However, a Judge William F. Smith of the Federal court in Newark, New Jersey dismissed the suits on the grounds that swimming pools were not included in the state's civil rights act.

Baltimore, Maryland, Golf Course Case

The Baltimore, Maryland Park Board was sued in December 1947 by Charles Law. The Park Board had refused to permit Law to play on the Mt. Pleasant Golf course, which was owned by the city, because he was Black. Law's case contended that the Municipal Park was supported by taxes paid by city residents and the board deprived him of his civil rights in refusing to permit him to use the park's facilities.

Federal Judge W. Calvin Chestnut ruled on June 18, 1948, that the Carroll Park Golf Course for Blacks was not equal to the white golf course, but he would not direct how the officials should solve the problem. The Judge decided that since the number of Black golfers was small, that Negroes would be admitted to golf courses on certain days.

Benjamin Franklin Hotel Cases

Frank Dixon, Maurice and Stanton Callender, Alex Jordan, Homer Gillis and Milford Parker were members of the New York University Track Team in May 1946. They were refused rooms after their reservations had been accepted through the mail at the Benjamin Franklin Hotel, Philadelphia, Pennsylvania. A suit was brought against the hotel. The hotel manager apologized and said that the desk clerk who refused to register the Black athletes did so without authorization. The case was finally dropped.

"Refusal To Ride An Elevator"

Sometimes whites would use the excuse that people become confused about the role Blacks may be playing. A professional Black dancer, Claude Merchant, was not allowed to ride in a passenger elevator at the Tudor Tower, a hotel apartment house located at 25 Tudor City Place, New York City, New York. Merchant filed suit against the hotel for damages under the state's civil rights law. The case was heard before a Black Judge, Francis E. Rivers, on May 25, 1948. The jury found the apartment manager guilty on two counts of violating the civil rights law. Marchant was awarded 500 dollars on each count. The manager's excuse was that he had issued orders to his employees not to discriminate against anyone; however, the two elevator operators thought that Marchant was a delivery man because he was carrying a package; therefore he was directed toward the service elevator, said the manager.

Dougherty's Bar Case

Two Blacks were charged five dollars for a thirty cent drink; and it was alleged that the bartender of Dougherty's bar, Minneapolis, Minnesota, Joseph Jacob had "spit in the glasses" according to the plaintiffs, John Williams and James T. Wardlow. The bartender was sentenced to thirty days in jail or a fine of one hundred dollars. The bartender paid the fine.

The U.S. Military experienced some race related problem in the United States and overseas when Blacks began to integrate the military. There are some incidents that occurred during the period 1950-1975 that have been documented. Some of the stories that I will discuss will include information that I received and some from situations that I experienced while serving as an Equal Opportunity Officer and Director of the United States Army's Race Relations School, Germany. These are true stories that in most cases the American News media in my personal opinion did not deem newsworthy for the readers in "America The Beautiful".

The Stuttgarter Nachricthen daily paper wrote: "Colored people cannot visit dance places or bars in Stuttgart without fear of racial discrimination. In one club some Blacks had to wait outside while five Germans who had arrived after the Blacks were shown to their tables".

"Membership Card Trick"

There were some German clubs that would tell Black soldiers that they needed a card to enter the club. One day, two equal opportunity officers from the U.S. Army VIII Corps visited a club. They were told that they needed a club card. When they asked for one, they were told that there were no more. It was learned that some of the non Black guests said that none of them used a card to enter the club and they never heard about it. This incident was mentioned in the Stuttgart paper.

Tageblat, Heidelberg

The German newspaper reported in their 1 March 1972 edition that there were some definite reasons why five night clubs in the older section of Heidelberg did not admit Blacks. The bar and night clubs owners said: "Sometimes the bar owners are threatened, girls are molested and there have been repeated beatings and stabbings involving Blacks. One bar owner said sometimes whites were troublemakers. Some clubs stated their guests were chosen by their faces. Whoever's nose does not fit is not admitted, and Black noses are the first ones to meet with disapproval. This leads to bitterness and disputes. It's not race; it's business", said one owner.

That statement sounds like some foreigners or new immigrants to America who drive taxicabs and do not pick up potential Black customers. Yes, it is an American legacy also.

It was interesting to read how some newspapers in Germany would understand the military and Blacks' position to desire equal opportunity. A reporter wrote: "Despite understanding the problems of the bar owners banning Blacks from restaurants in the city of Heidelberg, which is open to the world, this cannot be tolerated just because there have been fights involving Blacks. Heidelberg's night club owners wouldn't have any guests if they decided to bar whites from their places any time there was a fight involving whites. The anger of the Blacks affected by this is justified, and the argument that racism could be involved cannot be eliminated.

"No one will blame a proprietor who removes a brawling guest from his place, although this might be difficult sometimes."

"No one will blame him if he uses his domestic authority to protect his place and guests. But it cannot be broadened to the extent the Blacks are turned away as soon as they come in sight; that cannot and should not be tolerated."

Affirmative Dialogue

I was impressed by the thoughtful editorial published by the *Die Rheinnpfalz, Kaiserlautern* 8 May 1972. The thoughts of a 26 year old German might be a lesson to some silent voices in America.

Stuttgart - Are Blacks Inferior Guests?

Stuttgart - Stuttgart's citizens are agitated by a question which many thought had been solved long ago: are Blacks as guests considered lower than whites? And does this justify restaurant owners rejecting visitors merely because they have a different color? This has happened repeatedly -- not just in Stuttgart -- and probably will continue to happen. It is, however, very understandable that incidents like this draw special attention in a city which only recently labeled itself "Partner of the World."

Despite this, there has been an increase recently in reports of Blacks, including American soldiers, being turned away from Stuttgart night clubs. The lord mayor, the press and also the headquarters of the U.S. VII Corps are involved. Office for "Equal Opportunity" emphatically pointed out that "it is offensive and cannot be accepted" when guests are rejected just because they are Americans or Black. Stuttgart's Lord Mayor Klett informed the owners of the affected night clubs that restaurants "which don't like to accept guests with another skin color" are not desired in Stuttgart. The Hotel and Restaurant Association of North Wuerttemberg-North Baden was quick to say that there is the "basic" opinion that skin color is no standard for deciding whether a certain guest is admitted to a restaurant.

"Generally we have nothing against Blacks, provided that they behave right and in the way it is expected from the guests," the owners declared. If this is not adhered to the restaurant owner or his assistant has the right to turn the troublemaker away, no matter if he is white or Black.

Nobody surely will have anything against this. And nobody can surely maintain that whites are generally better behaved than Blacks. However, it is right to say that Blacks who have been rejected once for any reason react much stronger than whites. Seen objectively, the reason is understandable since Blacks have more difficulties because of their color. On the other hand, many Blacks have built up self-confidence, which has resulted in a stronger reaction in cases where they feel they are being treated unjustly.

This should result in the restaurant owners treating the Blacks with more tact and psychological skill, but many owners and businessmen are sure to fail.

What remains is the little word "tolerance" and the effort to be more gracious than has been the case recently. Such graciousness would apply well to citizens of a city trying to be a credible "Partner of the World".

I have been convinced that many German citizens were concerned about the tremendous race and drug problem that was represent in Germany in 1972 in present U.S. military establishments. The command accomplished outstanding results and there was a German-American friendship bond. I have a personal collection of some 25 paper back books on Black Americans ranging from novels, non fiction, civil rights movement and Black celebrities, all written in German. I did not purchase any of these books in stores that had a special section for Black books that one can observe in many book stores in the United States. And who gravitates toward those books, Black people in the majority of cases, not non Blacks. But in Germany the citizens could observe the Black books situated with other books not designated by race. The Germans were attempting to learn something about America's most distinct and controversial minority, Blacks or people of color. Even the German press were concerned about race designation in 1972, while some white Americans in 1998 are trying to justify why race designations as a necessity for the fulfillment of their respective goals. The German felt thusly 26 years ago: A respected journalistic organization urged the German press to stop needlessly identifying American soldiers by race. Of course, the German government just like America was powerless to do anything about the actions of newspapers and magazines. Censorship could not be tolerated. However, some concerned German citizens agreed to forward requests to all news media asking them to avoid citing race except in cases where it had overriding relevance. These efforts were initiated by the Deutscher Presserat, a group of journalists and publishers who were "watchdogs" of the press.

I repeatedly say in this manuscript that segregation is an "American legacy" because the evidence of past incidents and recurring daily vestiges of it are here today. This true story depicts how it was in 1953, just 45 years ago.

During the era of segregation, there were two Black officers who were assigned temporarily at Fort Benning, Georgia for training. Some white officers circulated a petition demanding the Blacks leave. General George C. Marshall denied their request and the two officers remained. One of them wrote the General later and said, "Your quest and courageous firmness in this case has served to hold my belief in the eventual solution of problems which have beset my people in their offtimes pathetic attempts to be Americans". The officer was Colonel Marcus H. Ray. The letter was dated November 4, 1953. Marshall had written on the letter, "a very fine officer".

Even Unto Death, Segregation

Legal segregation involved communities throughout the country maintaining sacred burial grounds or cemeteries on a segregated basis. Some cities would reserve a special area of the cemetery for Blacks, and Black churches mainly in the South would have their cemeteries on the church's property. During the past 30 years, a major part of my research at times has included the visit to many cemeteries in various states locating burial plots of African Americans. Beyond any doubt, I know that there are numerous segregated cemeteries. I have visited Black cemeteries in Mercersburg, Pennsylvania; St. Louis, Missouri; Chambersburg, Pennsylvania, Richmond, Virginia, and many church cemeteries in the South. Over the years, Black funeral directors have owned Black cemeteries. Today in the Nation's Capitol area, Black citizens are continuing to bury in two major Black cemeteries because their families are buried there and they have purchased grave sites. These cemeteries are Lincoln Memorial and Harmony.

Beverly Perea

lst Lieutenant Beverly Perea was born in Mecklenburg, Virginia. He and his wife, Missouri, had one daughter. Perea enlisted in the Army on 25 July 1871, and was assigned at various times to Companies A, I, E, B and M of the 24th Infantry Regiment. Perea served continuously for 31 years; he spent 2 years, 4 months and 16 days in foreign service in the Philippines and 2 months and 7 days in Cuba. He was cited as a 1st Classman in marksmanship in 1897. Perea was appointned 2nd Lieutenant, 7th U.S. Volunteer on 16 September 1898, and 1st Lieutenant on 7 January 1899.

Lieutenant Perea died on 3 April 1915 and is the first known Black officer to be buried with honors in Arlington National Cemetery. Perea's dying wish was to be buried at Arlington. Several newspapers carried the account of his death. A Boston paper published in April 1915 the following: "In response to an appeal of the widow of 1st Lieutenant Beverly Perea, U.S.A., retired, a colored citizen who died at the Cambridge Hospital Saturday, Mayor Curley has requested Secretary of War

Lindley M. Garrison to give permission for the interment of the Lieutenant's remains in the Arlington National Cemetery at Washington."

Mayor Curley's personal appeal to Secretary Garrison was successful, and Lieutenant Perea was buried at Arlington Cemetery on 10 April 1915. While conducting research at Arlington National Cemetery, a guard told me where I could find the gravesite of LTC Alexander Augusta. The gravesite is located near the gate of Ft. Myer, near the Old Chapel. The guard said that in the 1890's that area was undeveloped and that is where they buried some Blacks and even white army nurses. Augusta's grave has an impressive grave stone near several other Black veterans.

Lieutenant Colonel Alexander Augusta

Alexander Augusta was born free on 8 March 1825 in Norfolk, Virginia. He studied medicine under a private tutor in Baltimore, Maryland. Later he studied in Philadelphia, California, and Canada. In 1856, he graduated from Trinity Medical College, Toronto, Canada, with the degree Bachelor of Medicine. He then practiced medicine in Toronto, Canada, and in the West Indies.

In 1862, Augusta moved to Washington, D.C. On 2 October 1863, he was appointed surgeon of the 7th U.S. Colored Troops which were part of the expedition sent to Beaufort, South Carolina. Later he was in charge of a hospital at Savannah, Georgia. On 13 March 1863, he was brevetted (promoted to higher rank without higher pay or greater authority) Lieutenant Colonel, U.S. Volunteers, for meritorious and faithful service, and thus became one of the few Black field grade officers in the Civil War. He was mustered out of the service on 13 October 1866, and resumed the practice of medicine. He married Mary O. Burgoin of Baltimore, Maryland.

Freedman's Village (Arlington National Cemetery)

In 1863, there was located in present day Arlington National Cemetery, a "Freedman's Village, near Arlington Heights, Virginia." The village was a camp for freed and escaped slaves who fled toward the area of Northern Virginia near Arlington. They were commonly referred to as "contraband." The Village gave the slaves food, medical care and some assistance in learning how to read and write. The number of occupants was approximately 3,000 at one time. The Freedman's Village was supervised by the U.S. Freedmen's Bureau. A large number of the Village contraband died from the diseases of "consumption, measles, scarlet fever, and the whooping cough." Approximately 4,000 of the contrabands are buried in Arlington National Cemetery near the stone masonry wall along side Fort Myer,

Virginia. The section is designated as "Section 27". Many of the headstones have a simple inscription "Civilian or citizen; some bear the first names." Also buried in Section 27 and Section 23 are former Army soldiers of color who were members of the United States Colored Troops (U.S.C.T.).

Burial Segregation Virginia Contracts, 1962

In 1962, the Veteran Administration instructed its hospitals throughout the nation to stop signing contracts with funeral directors on a segregated basis. The policy did not affect all hospitals. In Thomasville, Georgia, there was a contract with a funeral home which handled burials for veterans of both races. Four funeral establishments in Augusta, Georgia, stated that they would not bid for contracts on a non discriminatory basis. But a Black funeral home which held the contracts for Blacks, said it would bid for the business. There was great concern whether the white cemeteries would permit a colored undertaker to bury a white person. That is the way it was in some area of Georgia in 1962, only 36 years ago.

"South Carolina Funeral Home Says, No"

The legacy of segregation was present in 1996 when a 73 year old Virginia educator died. When she died in Lancaster, South Carolina, her daughter called a white funeral home and they agreed to accept the body. The daughter wanted to ship her mother back to Virginia for burial. The white funeral director discussed the prices and arrangements over the phone.

A coroner and nurse arrived at the home of the deceased. The nurse told the physician, "We have a problem, because the white mortician could not render his services, because I have just talked to him." Now the deceased was a white woman, but her daughter's genetic makeup was "native American, Black and white. The deceased lady had married a Black man. The daughter was quite perturbed and said, "This is not 100 years ago and I do not understand how people in this day and age can do that". She also said that she just wanted the best for her mother and now she was refused service because of the pigment of her skin". The daughter was able to obtain the services of another funeral home. A positive action was initiated by the South Carolina Board of Funeral Directors, and the mortician's license was suspended for six months, with a 500 dollar fine, and a requirement to receive sensitivity training.

TRUE STORIES OF SEGREGATION

Vietnam Veteran's Denial of Burial in Florida Cemetery, 1970

Pondexteur Williams was a 20 year old veteran who died in Vietnam. When his remains were returned to his home, Fort Pierce, Florida, his family had plans to bury him in a plot donated by a white woman. A white cemetery in the town refused to issue a permit to bury the Black veteran because the contracts for sales of plots contained a white only stipulation. It was necessary for a Federal Court to issue an order for Williams to finally be buried in the all white Florida cemetery. Again, I remind the reader that this was not a Hispanic, Asian or Native American problem. At that time it was simply the continuation of a Black exclusion policy that did not start when the controversy of Affirmative Action became a household subject. "Just more nutritional reasoning".

There has been considerable progress in the acceptance of Blacks by white funeral homes. Some have been doing it in past years. A funeral director in the area of Waldorf, Maryland would serve Black customers, but he had a small building in the back of the funeral home that he used for the Black families.

EMPLOYMENT

Sometimes the military will assign personnel in civilian positions for a brief period. In 1903, just seven years after the 1896 decision legalizing segregation, a Black officer was appointed as an acting park superintendent

Acting Park Superintendent

Captain Charles Young was assigned as the Acting Superintendent of Sequoia and General Grant National Parks, California on May 20, 1903. On June 3, 1903, Young wrote the Secretary of Interior a letter requesting instructions for his new assignment. He also informed the Secretary that he was making preparations for a road improvement project and that it was his intention to follow his predecessors' plans and also initiate measures to prevent trespassing. Young more specifically explained the importance of the road project to the Secretary of Interior in a telegram, dated June 4, 1903. He stated: Request permission to begin work on the giant forest road immediately in Sequoia National Park to be paid from the appropriation fiscal year 1904. Laborers are on the ground now. Many hundreds of dollars will be paid by the government by not waiting until the dry season, July.

Captain Young was responsible for the supervision of the payroll accounts and also directed the activities of the Forest Rangers. He was concerned about the method of payment for the laborers and was interested in expediting payments in order to enable projects to continue. In a letter to the Secretary of Interior dated

June 10, 1903, Young requested permission for the officers in charge of the work projects to vouch for payment of laborer's debts while they were working in the mountains. He felt the accounting system and assurance of contractors paying the laborers could be improved.

Young had been instructed by the Secretary of Interior to submit a brief monthly report of his activities. On June 30, 1903, he wrote the Secretary of Interior the following:

> I think it may be sufficient for this period. I am also working with respect to the private land claims and hope later to report satisfactorily upon the solution of this the greatest concern relative to the parks. The avenues of entrance to the parks are well guarded, my detachments and Forest Rangers efficiently cooperating toward the protection of game and prevention of grazing on public land. The work on the road in General Grant Park begins the first week in July and the Fresno County authorities have kindly consented to aid in connecting with them.

Captain Young's payroll for civilian employees for the month of June consisted of sixty workers; Blacksmith, gang foreman, stump blaster, powderman, cook, driller, timber faller, flow holder and forty laborers. The total expenses incurred were $3,707.62.

Young and his detachment were stationed at the national parks during a period when the government was attempting to purchase additional land for the park $25, an acre). Correspondence of a George W. Stewart, dated January 17, 1904 refers to a project that was completed by several of the Ninth Cavalry soldiers and a park Ranger. The letter said:

> Last summer Park Ranger Ernest Britten assisted by Corporals Mosby and Smith of Troop 1, Ninth Cavalry, made a count of Redwood Trees on N f of NW + of Sec. 6, Tl 16 S. R 30E, M D. being and eighty acre tract within the giant forest and the result showed 185 trees.

Captain Charles Young's duties also included negotiating with the local county authorities, visits to Mount Whitney Reservation and the development of improvement plans. On August 29, 1903, Young submitted the following plan to the Secretary of Interior:

> "I have the honor to state that during the past month work has been pushed with all diligence in the Giant Forest with most

successful results. I am bending every effort toward completing this road into the forest this year and by economizing in the appropriation as much as possible.

1. Completion of the road of last year to S.W. corner of park - the cost of powder, tools and labor estimated at $1500 (This is the most important work in connection with this part for reasons stated hereafter).

2. Cleaning up rubbish and dead and down timber near the big trees and constructing firebrakes on the West and North sides of Park to prevent spread of fire to the park from the engine and log camps of the Sawyer Lumber Company - estimated cost $100.

3. Constructing fence about General Grant Tree and getting out lumber for a small stable for protection of the animals of the Forest Rangers during the winter cost about $100.

4. Continuing as far as the remainder of the appropriations will permit of the main road toward King's Canyon which has been for years an important point of tourist travel because of its scenic value.

I beg that this plan be approved and the expenditure for 1st and 2nd parts thereof be allowed, as they have been about completed by this time as Part 1 includes the only safe wagon travel into the Park.

Captain Young demonstrated his modesty on many occasions during his military career. In writing to the Secretary of Interior about the parks progress he wrote:

The road has been completed into Giant Forest and around to Moro Rock, water has been placed upon the road for convenience of the traveling public and trails are being repaired. I submit that more work has been done, and better work through rougher country than has been done in any two year previous to this. I claim no special credits for this (my emphasis) as it is largely due to the department's permission to allow work to begin early in the season when the ground was moist and where good men were available.

Young was always concerned about his subordinates' welfare, and openly expressions of his feelings on this subject were made. He mentioned to the Secretary of Interior in his correspondence of August 29, 1903, the need for authority to adjust the vouchers and to prevent delay in the payment for work accomplished during the month of August. He indicated his interest in the employees' welfare when he stated:

> An additional reason for this last request will be found in the fact that these men are poor and any delay in their accounts will work great hardships.

In September 1903, a Captain assigned the Ninth Cavalry who was senior to Captain Young as far as date of rank was concerned, was instructed to report to his Troop M, which was assigned at the Sequoia and General Grant National Park. Major General Arthur MacArthur, Commanding General, headquarters, Department of California, selected Captain Lester W. Cornish, Ninth Cavalry to replace Captain Charles Young as Acting Superintendent, Sequoia and General Grant National park, California.

The Secretary of Interior had requested on September 18, 1903 information relating to a list of patented lands in the Parks. Young was instructed to investigate this matter and submit a report. Captain Young forwarded a reply to the Secretary of Interior on September 28, 1903. Young wrote the following:

> I have carefully examined most of the lands, duly considered the offers here with (he forwarded agreements that claimants had concurred with) in connection with the Forest Rangers, the Register of the Land Office and some of the best businessmen of this section, all whom are highly interested in the welfare of the Park and in the purchase by the U.S. at a reasonable figure of these lands; and we all think and submit that the prices asked in the agreement are reasonable and in many cases low. Out of 18 owners in Sequoia National Park the agreements of 13 are herewith submitted, the other 5 with the other agreements it is thought that their claims will not exceed $16,000, while the other claims aggregate $70,734, these with an offer of 160 acres in General Grant Park for $1600, (the only private claim in the Park) will bring the entire claims within $73,000, which amount is but a trifling sum in comparison with the benefits accruing to the government in securing for the nation at least 40,000 Giant Sequoias with innumerable young trees of this species and other timbered and meadow lands all amounting to 3877 acres. The price asked averages about $18 per acre. As the agreements for

> the most important of these lands, that is those in comprising the "Giant Forest," only remain in force for a year, I earnestly urge that immediate steps be taken to effect their purchase.

The Acting Secretary of War informed the Secretary of Interior on September 30, 1903 that the Commanding General, Department of California had selected Captain Lester W. Cornish, Ninth Cavalry, to replace Captain Charles Young as the Parks acting superintendent.

When Captain Cornish assumed the duties of Acting Superintendent of the Sequoia and General Grant National Parks he wrote the Secretary of Interior the following:

> In reference to the report of Captain Charles Young concerning the purchase of private lands in the Sequoia National park, I have the honor to heartily endorse each and every recommendation made by him in his report. Captain Young is to be congratulated upon the remarkable success he has obtained, and I earnestly recommend that his suggestions be carried out in every respect.

Captain Young was always willing to support his subordinates and to honestly admit and defend his actions if they were challenged by his superiors. The Secretary of Interior had inquired about ten days of absence with pay that was granted a Forest Ranger by Captain Young. Young responded to the inquiry by explaining his actions and also offered to repay the government the money paid the Ranger for ten days absence. Captain Young wrote:

> As was stated in my annual report, this Ranger (Ranger L.L. Davis) volunteered to superintend the work of blasting this season on the Giant Forest Road, thereby saving many hundreds of dollars to the government by his good sense, good judgment, and hard work.
>
> At the end of the season because of the ill effects the close contact and long use of the dynamite had worked upon his system and general health, I ordered him away from duty for ten days to rest. He went unwillingly, but I felt that he was too valuable a man in his place here to sacrifice when the rest could put him in his usual form again. So far as he was concerned he was on duty obeying my order as Acting Superintendent of the Parks. I therefore request that my action be approved by the department and if the exigencies of Ranger service will not permit him to have those ten days so richly deserved by him, I <u>shall be</u>

> glad to refund the money paid him by the department for those days. (my emphasis).

Captain Charles Young had performed an outstanding service to the Interior Department within a brief period of almost six months. His adeptness of administration and ability to supervise civilians as well as military personnel contributed to his success. The Adjutant General's office transferred Young on November 2, 1903. He was assigned as a Troop Commander at the Presidio of San Francisco, California.

The Visalia Board of Trade, California showed their appreciation of Captain Young's performance of duty as the Parks' acting superintendent. He was given a citation which was signed by the President and Secretary of the Visalia Board of Trade.

A bill was introduced in the House of Representatives, February 12, 1904 to provide for acquiring the title to certain patented lands in the Sequoia and General Grant National parks in the State of California. The bill was intended to authorize the Secretary of Interior to enter into negotiations with owners of patented lands and claims within the parks. There was a mention of Captain Charles Young in the bill. The referral to Young read:

> As recommended by Captain Charles Young, Acting Superintendent of said parks, in his report to the Secretary of Interior, dated September twenty-eight nineteen hundred and three.

Government Segregation

In 1913, segregation was present in the Bureau of Engraving, Printing Office, Post Office and the Auditor's Office. Some government buildings separated Black and white employees by screens and the bathrooms and lunch rooms were segregated. Blacks were appointed to menial positions in attempts to restrict them from Civil Service jobs. Candidates for Civil Service positions from 1914 on had to submit photographs. It is believed that this change was also used to eliminate Black applicants. President Woodrow Wilson had approved segregation plans and defended the official policy. Wilson believed that it would take a hundred years to eradicate prejudice. Many white and Black liberal groups protested Wilson's racist policies.

TRUE STORIES OF SEGREGATION

No Postmaster For Georgia

The late Williston Henry Lofton was my former professor at Howard University, Washington, D.C. The following true story is about his father, Isiah Henry Lofton, a graduate of Atlanta University, Georgia. He had served as superintendent of schools. Later he was appointed Postmaster of Hogansville, Georgia, by President McKinley on May 17, 1897. The whites believed that Lofton's job was a white man's job". Some whites burned down the post office and shot Isiah Lofton. In 1899, Lofton and his family moved to Washington, D.C.

Reflections of Employment, 1920'S

Thomas C. Fleming, former co-founder of the *Sun Reporter*, San Francisco, Black weekly in 1944 recently was reflecting on job discrimination in the 1920's. He recalled that the town of Chico, California had only 65 Black residents and there were no job opportunities for Blacks in 1926.

Fleming stated that one Black owned a farm, he was Hadwick Thompson and the only Black to farm rice in northern California. He lived in Willows West, Chico. There was also a Black who had the contract to collect the city trash. This example of minimal employment for Blacks in some northern and western small cities were numerous in the 1920's and 1930's.

Roosevelt's Fair Employment Practices Committee (FEPC), 1941

President Franklin Delano Roosevelt issued Executive Order 8802 on June 23, 1941 which said, "That there should be no discrimination in the employment of workers in defense industries or government because of race, creed, color or national origin"' Roosevelt established a five man FEPC committee on May 27, 1943 to enforce the executive order. The committee expired on June 28, 1946.

It should be understood that this FEPC did not just appear because the white majority thought it was necessary. Credit must be given to activist Blacks under the excellent leadership of A. Philip Randolph, President of the Brotherhood of Sleeping Car Porters who organized a March on Washington Movement. Roosevelt did not want the protest march to occur, especially during the war years. The behind the scenes advice and urging of the president's wife Eleanor Roosevelt helped F.D. Roosevelt decide to issue the Executive Order 8802. The March was then called off. Some significant highlights of the order were: there was to be no discrimination in the employment of workers in defense industries or government because of race. The clause was included in defense contracts. There were some

Blacks who were employed in some private industries, government navy yard, army ordinance plants, clerical and secretarial positions in federal agencies.

Racial Segregation Labor Unions, 1930's - 1940's

During the 1930's and 1940's there were some labor unions that excluded Blacks by using special clauses in their constitutions or rituals. There are many American citizens who believe today that we have corrected past job discrimination inequalities and exclusions within the past 35 years; therefore affirmative action is not needed. Black American in the majority cases were excluded from membership in the following professional unions and organizations: locomotive engineers, aeronautical workers, railway carmen, steamship clerks, trainmen, firemen, pilots, yardmaster, switchmen, railroad telegraphers, boilermakers and machinists.

There were some unions which had separate locals. They were rural letter carriers, motion picture operators, musicians, longshoremen, federal employees, textile workers, and tobacco workers. Some labor unions did prohibit racial discriminations. There were independent Black unions, pullman porters, redcaps, transport workers, postal employees, colored railway trainmen, plumbers, ship workers and sheet metal workers.

Breaking The Barriers In Journalism-Employment

The late journalist Ethel L. Payne, who died on May 28, 1991, was the first Black female commentator on network television. She had served as a columnist for the Chicago Defender and Afro American newspapers during the period 1952-1980. While covering news conferences at the White House, Ms. Payne would often ask questions on civil rights issues. At a conference in 1954, she asked about a possible executive order to end train segregation in interstate and bus travel. President Dwight Eisenhower responded in a somewhat tense mood and said, "What makes you think that I am going to give you special favoritism to special interests? I am the President of all people". That statement by Eisenhower adds some credence to the mental reasoning on that subject that was blowing in the wind and it was shared with the world when the President frankly said that he would do nothing about that issue at that time. Of course later it would take the Supreme Court to do some update "reinterpretation". This is another story demonstrating why people of all races today need to realize that as I continue to remind the reader, Black pleas for equal citizenship rights were not easily addressed.

Ms. Ethel Payne, the first lady of the Black Press was working as a journalist when many white institutions were not used to dealing with Black journalists on an equal basis. While working as an army club director in 1949, in Tokyo, Japan, Ms. Payne kept a journal of her observations about discrimination against Black servicemen. Ethel Payne covered news conferences in Bandung, Indonesia in 1956, when Black newspapers were not covering international leaders Chou En Lai, Haile Selassie and Idi Amin.

Civil Rights Law of 1964

The Civil Rights Law of 1964 outlawed discrimination based on race or sex of employees engaged in commerce. The act or law created the Federal Equal Opportunity Commission (EEOC) to investigate complaints of job discrimination. At this time the EEOC did not have the power to investigate complaints of job discrimination.

Segregated Unions 1960's

I wrote this information 26 years for my race relations classes. Whatever significant changes we have today in these figures did not come about by osmosis. I am sure that affirmative action played some part in present day integrations of American labor unions.

Justice Within the Unions

Boston, Massachusetts 1960

1,297 apprentices in building trades 15 Black, 1965, 2680 apprentices, Black.

Cleveland, Ohio 1966

Plumbers Union Local 1,428 licensed journey men 4 Black members, 1786 journeymen ironworkers, one Black ironworker apprentice.

"Institutional racism has been deeply embedded in American society. Slavery was an early practice. Political, economic, educational and religious policies cooperated with slave holders to sustain Blacks in their status quo of that period. Through the years Black Americans have experienced residential and employment discrimination. Second class citizenship became a social fact as well as a legal status. Overt institutional racism was practiced widely throughout American society. Today, we experience some practices of covert institutional racism."

"Segregation, Legacy Lingers On"

The following stories will illustrate how some forms of segregation and alleged discrimination are still present today in employment: University City, St. Louis, Missouri, some minority fire fighters were complaining about racial discrimination in 1997. It was necessary for Black fire fighters to organize and have their chapter of the Fire Fighters League for the Advancement of Minority Equalization (FLAME). There was an affirmative action plan in effect calling for a goal to obtain 50 representatives of Blacks and women in management positions. There were only a total of 15 in management or supervisory positions.

One can read in a newspaper in 1998 about a major airplane manufacturer in Seattle, Washington. Blacks are filing a law suit alleging discrimination and harassment at the company's facilities in Auburn and Everett, Washington. The complaints were that many Blacks have more seniority over Caucasian workers, but were not promoted. The supervisors responded that "they can promote whoever they want, and there were some Blacks who could not pass tests."

The Army Corps of Engineers in Memphis, Tennessee, announced in 1997 that it would pay Black deck hands of a Mississippi river discrimination complaint filed in 1996. The Engineer Corps agreed to pay 62,500 dollars to 16 deck hands who were restricted to seasonal work aboard the dredge Hurley. The last 68 years, since 1934, no Blacks were offered full time jobs aboard the Engineer Corps dredges in the six state Memphis district. The Department of Defense concluded that the Hurley did show indifference to Black employees that were degrading and demeaning. There were allegations that racial slurs were common and words such as "little Black sambo and nigger" were used. Ironically the current Chief of Engineers, U.S. Army is a Black Lieutenant General who graduated from a predominantly Black university and has achieved a prestigious military position, the first Black Chief of Engineers. When I was commissioned a second lieutenant in the Corps of Engineers in 1955, and was assigned to Fort Belvoir, Virginia, it was a rarity to see a Black Engineer officer in the rank of captain. Yes, the military has made progress in overcoming the spoils of the segregated past in American history. America has a long way to go before we reach some equitable progress in employment for African Americans and other minorities in a white dominated employment arena.

BUSINESS

Segregation In Wartime Industries
World War II

The United States entered World War II in 1941 and was again trying to make the world free for democracy. However, on American soil, the minority of Black skin color was experiencing discrimination and segregation in private war time industries who were receiving millions of dollars in government contracts.

Some of the companies who were adhering to the law segregation and exclusion were: The Wichita Sternman Aircraft Co., a division of Boeing Aircraft had received 5.9 million dollars in government contracts for plane orders. The total number of Blacks employed in two Boeing plants was three, two were porters and one was a cook.

A Westinghouse Manufacturing company had received government contracts totaling over 8 million dollars. There was a workforce of 800 in their Baltimore, Maryland plant. There were only three Black employees.

The Glenn L. Martin Company of Baltimore, Maryland, Colt Arms Company, of Hartford, Connecticut, Spartan Aircraft Company, Tulsa Oklahoma, and General Motors White Company, Cleveland, Ohio, all had received government contracts and employed no Blacks.

Black Americans throughout the years of segregation experienced barriers when some whites desired to assist them. A Tampa, Florida, shipbuilding Company, and Dry Dock Company had received some contracts from the Maritime Commission exceeding 17 million dollars. The company wanted to employ some Blacks. However, the International Boilermakers Union had a constitutional clause that restricted membership to members of the white race. Earlier Blacks had comprised 50 percent of the company's workforce and helped to organize the union, but they were left out when a closed shop agreement was made.

There was a Boeing Aircraft branch that agreed to accept Blacks if they were members of the Aeronautical Mechanics Union No. 757 with which the company had a contract. But the union had a clause that denied membership to Blacks.

An industry in Rochester, N.Y., employed 17,000 employees. This private firm was a large manufacturer of photographic equipment and supplies. The number of Black employed included one porter and nineteen construction workers.

There was a large insurance company in New York with many Black policy holders. The company did not have a single Black among its employees. A Sperry bombsight Company. refused to employ a single Black worker. A Southern California Aviation Company. had 12 Blacks among its workforce. The Wright Aeronautical Workers and Brewster Aircraft Company hired no Blacks. The Nashville branch of Vultee Aircraft Company. hired no Blacks. The Consolidated Aircraft Corporation of San Diego, California, hired no Blacks. The Metal trades industries in New York, at one time, would not employ Blacks.

in 1940, sometimes defense jobs on military bases were not available to Blacks. There was a construction project at Fort Dix, New Jersey, that would not hire skilled and unskilled Black workers. The only exceptions was the employment of three Black carpenters. There were 350 white carpenters working on the job.

The exclusion of Blacks from labor unions would prevent them from obtaining union jobs.

I believe that Blacks and other non whites today should be appreciative of the many opportunities that are available to them today in the labor market with attractive salaries, since some 50 years ago Blacks were denied equal employment and sometimes the Constitution was interpreted by judges to justify the exclusions. The District of Columbia Court of Appeals ruled in January, 1940, that "a labor union may limit the rights of its Negro members without trespassing upon their Constitutional rights."

Today Blacks purchase high price cars, especially the German models, if they have the finance and/or credit. During segregation few Blacks purchased Cadillacs from dealerships in New Orleans, Louisiana, because there was an unwritten policy of not selling to Blacks.

Beach Hotel

Mrs. Lyncia Pearl Bonner of Baltimore, Maryland, operated the Henry Hotel in Ocean City, Maryland during segregation. The hotel is located on the corners of Division Street and Baltimore Avenue and is a twenty room facility. It is located in walking distance of the beach homes and resorts. This hotel is the last surviving structure in Ocean City that catered to Blacks prior to desegregation. The hotel had celebrity guests such as Count Basie, Cab Calloway and Duke Ellington. There were times when Blacks could not walk on the board walk or stay in white hotels. Mrs. Bonner purchased the hotel 30 year ago and in recent years Whites have stayed there.

TRUE STORIES OF SEGREGATION

There has been an significant increase in the number of Black businesses today, and many of the owners are Black women. There is still a need for more businesses owned and operated by Black in the predominantly Black neighborhoods where many Asian merchants are operating the corner grocery stores that were under Jewish management when I was a child. Their economic successes were due to an organization known as the District Grocery Stores (DGS). They communicated in a friendly manner with the residents and when they closed their stores, they went up the stairs or in the back area to their family living quarters and not Maryland and Virginia as the Asians appear to do today.

SPORTS

Sports Break-through During Segregation

The late Minnesota Mayor, Senator and Vice President of the United States, Hubert A. Humphrey, was one of the concerned members of a 1948 committee that was instrumental in eradicating a provision of the International Bowling Congress Constitution. The provision had restricted its membership to individuals of the WHITE MALE SEX.

The Amateur Athletic Union located in our Nation's Capital, decided in 1948 to lift the ban on mixed race competition in boxing and track.

The current popular game of basketball had its outstanding stars of color forty-two years ago. The National Basketball Association welcomed Afro-Americans for the FIRST TIME in 1949. The New York Knickerbockers had Sweet Water Clifton, a center; the Washington Caps had Earl Lloyd from West Virginia State College, and Harold Hunter. The Boston Celtics had Chuck Cooper, a graduate of Duquesne University.

Horse Racing - An African American Horse Breeder

The late Basil A. Hall was one of the first known African American horse breeders and owner of race horses. Hall was born in 1885 in Maryland. As a young man he worked as a grave digger and in later years purchased raw furs (beaver, racoon, fox, and other small animal pelts) from farmers in Maryland and Pennsylvania.

Basil Hall decided to breed, train, and race horses in Canada and Cuba. In 1934, he entered six horses in races at the Charleston, West Virginia race track and was successful in winning thirty races. After some 59 years in horse breeding, training, and racing horses, Basil Hall was invited to join the all white (at that time) Maryland Horse Breeders Association. This association honored Hall on his 90th birthday with a party. Basil Hall was married to the late Alice Mitchell and they are the parents of Jacques, Basil Jr., and Annette Hall. Hall had lived on a 60-acre farm in Maryland. Basil Hall died in 1979.

A Basketball First

Charles Henry Cooper was born in Pittsburgh, Pennsylvania. He was a graduate of Duquesne University. He was the converse All-American, 1948 and All-American Basketball Choice, 1950. Cooper was the first African American to be drafted into a National Basketball Association team. He signed with the Boston Celtics in June 1950.

Jesse Owens Experiences in Segregation

Jesse Owens, the outstanding 1936 Olympic Sprinter, expressed in his book *Black Think* some of his experiences living in the segregated era of American history. He recalled traveling to Indianapolis, Indiana, in February, 1936, with his fellow colleagues, Black and white, in a car. When they stopped in Southern Indiana one morning to have breakfast, he and the other Black athletes had to wait in the car. They had to wait until their white teammates brought them some food. His other Black teammates were the track stars, Mel Walker and Ralph Metcalfe. While they were eating their breakfast in the car, the owner of the restaurant came to the car window near Jesse Owens and yelled "So this is what they wanted those extra orders for!" Ralph Metcalfe said, "You were paid, weren't you mister". The white owner then replied " I don't want money to feed no niggers". Then he reached in the car and grabbed the plates, and silverware and food was spilled everywhere. Jesse said that the three years he was at Ohio State, he never had eaten with the white athletes at the college or on the road trips. They had to eat their meals at the house where all the Negroes lived. If you did not take your meals there, you did not eat. This true story should be read and understood by Blacks, Whites and especially immigrants today. When we read about alleged instances of some big name chain restaurants discriminating against Blacks, some people do not believe it or think Blacks are too sensitive. I am sure that Jesse Owens and his Black teammates were not too sensitive 62 years ago in Southern Indiana. Just another nutritional reasoning or food for thought.

Jesse Owens included in his book some stories that he had heard and read about white brutality against Blacks during segregation. He wrote that before his family left Alabama he heard about a white mob lynching some Blacks in Georgia. They were lynched because someone in the town had murdered a white man, and the authorities never knew if the person was Black or white. When they were in doubt, they would just go ahead and murder some Blacks. Jesse also said that in World War II a colored soldier could be court-martialed for walking into a white USO (United Services Organization) club, and in Alexandria, Louisiana, in 1941, 24 Negroes were lined up and shot in cold blood by some racist white officers. Owens related that a young Black artist in the South without provocation was castrated by three white men. These stories are just a few of the many he recalled, and unfortunately such atrocities are not magnified and placed in a scenario of remembrance for the world as were the six million atrocities of German Nazi's.

Jesse revealed that his father never read the words of the Bible, because he actually believed that if he had laid a finger on a book, someone in the family would fall suddenly ill and possible die. This was possibly due to his father's parents and their parents not being allowed to own or read a book under the dehumanizing system of slavery.

The late Jesse Owens believed in race pride and carrying the torch of excellence for Black progress. He admired Joe Louis, the boxing champion especially for his accomplishment in 1935; becoming the first Black to win the Associated Press Athlete of the Year Award. Jesse was able to accomplish a celebrated feat in 1936. Another Black would not be selected until the middle fifties. He was the famous baseball player, Willie Mays. Jesse said until Jackie Robinson came along he and Joe Louis had to carry the Negro image of achievements in sports. I think that was a strong statement by Jesse Owens in 1970 because today with a great majority of Black athletes occupying the sports teams, their competition is mainly among other Blacks and not the majority of whites whom the lone Black athletes during segregation had as their competitors for the choice awards. More "nutritional reasoning".

Owens said Joe Louis made a difference in his life when he realized that Louis accomplished many things against the odds. He wrote that Louis was a great human being, fighter who never hurt anyone. Jesse said that Joe Louis came from a background of poverty, made fortunes for many people (Mike Jacobs also) and was a household name in Black and white houses. He said Joe was not dumb, but people had their own individual perceptions. Owens recalled that at one of Joe Louis' fights he overheard a white man say to his white date "That big dumb nigger might not be able to do any other thing, but he sure can fight".

Some people will deny the fact that in 1998, similar utterances can be heard openly justified as a slip of the tongue or politically incorrect. Yes, segregation, discrimination and stereotypes are an American legacy. I have selected Jesse

Owens' experiences about segregation and race because I will always cherish his experiences as a most creditable and truthful source.

Breaking Barriers, Youth Track Meet, Washington, D.C.

The Washington Evening Star newspaper conducted its first annual indoor track meet at the D.C. National Guard building January 3, 1947. Some 5,000 spectators observed Black and white young men compete for the first time in an interracial track meet in Washington, D.C.

Bench The Black Players

Dr. Charles F. West, a physician of Alexandria, Virginia, played football for Washington and Jefferson College. He played the position, half back, for four years, 1920-1924. When his team was scheduled to play Washington and Lee College, Virginia, the team refused to play unless West was benched. The courageous Washington and Jefferson College football teams refused and athletic relations between the two college were severed.

Georgia Tech requested that Brice Taylor, player for the University of California stay on the side lines during a 1929 Tournament of Roses. The University of California insisted that Brice Taylor would play, and he did.

When Syracuse University played the University of Maryland at College Park, the Black player Wilmer Sidat-Singh was benched. However when Maryland played Syracuse on their home grounds, Sidat-Singh played. A strange event of Southern Jim Crow.

Interracial Games, 1946-1947

During the era of segregation, when sports' barriers were broken, they were significant and newsworthy events. In 1946, A and T College of North Carolina played the New London Submarine Base team. It was reported as the first interracial football game in New York City. In 1947, Wilberforce State University played against Bergen College in New York City. Chester Pierce of Harvard University was the first Black player to play on a southern college campus when he played against the University of Virginia on the Charlottesville Campus in 1947.

Early Racism In Basketball

In 1998, a major magazine has a cover picture honoring Michael Jordan, star Chicago Bulls basketball player. One can observe many white institutions with basketball teams of five Black players. But in the 1930's Black players were not represented on the Big-Ten Colleges' teams. The late Dr. Ralph Bunche was represented as a player in the Pacific Conference games.

Passing as an Indian Oriole Player 1920's

A manager of the Baltimore Orioles in the 1920's, John McGraw, observed a mulatto playing in spring training camp in Hot Springs, Arkansas, McGraw liked his style and performance. The Black was Charlie Grant. McGraw asked Grant to pass as an Indian and use the name Tokohama. He practiced with the Orioles during spring training, playing first base. Some of Grant's Black friends had a party and the secret was known to others. Charles Comiskey, President of the White Sox learned about McGraw's scheme and Grant was dropped from the team.

The late Shirley Povich's Early Predictions

Shirley Povich, the outstanding sports writer, who recently died wrote in the *Washington Post*, April 7, 1939. "There's a couple of million dollars worth of baseball talent on the loose, ready for the big leagues, yet unsigned by any major league clubs. There are pitchers who would win 20 games this season for any big league club that offered them contracts and there are outfielders who could hit, 350, infielders who could win quick recognition as stars and there is at least one catcher who at this writing is probably superior to Bill Dickey. Only one thing is keeping them out of the big leagues, the pigmentation of their skin. They happen to be colored. That's their crime in the eyes of big league club owners".

Those were some powerful words in those days for a courageous sports writer to really tell it like it was in evaluating the true abilities and performances of some qualified Black baseball players who could have made it big in professional leagues in 1939. The words of Shirley Povich in 1939 are a tribute to his memory and perception when the majority of white sport writers were mute on the subject and their typewriters were silent on the subject of Negro competency on the baseball field.

Black American Tennis Association

The years of segregation created many all Black groups whose major purposes were to provide opportunities in the Black communities that were comparable to the all white sports groups. On November 30, 1916, the tennis pioneers, H.S. McCard, William Wright, B.M. Rhetta, Ralph V. Cook, Henry Freeman, John F.M. Wilkinson and Talley Holmes founded the American Tennis Association. Their major purpose was to develop the game of tennis among colored people of the United States, encouraging the formation of clubs, the building of courts and encouraging young girls and boys to have an interest in the sport of tennis. The first national championships were held in Baltimore in August, 1917, in Druid Hill Park under the auspices of the Monumental Tennis Club of Baltimore. In 1949, some 134 individual clubs were members of the Association. During the years 1917, 1928, and 1935, women's singles and doubles meets were organized.

Black Golfers During Segregation

The superb accomplishments of Tiger Woods on the golf courses in the last two years have aroused a great interest in golf among the Black community. However, many Blacks and non Blacks might not be aware of the interest in golf existed during segregation because their accomplishments were not reported by the sports writers of the major newspapers.

When writing about Tiger Woods, some white newspapers did acknowledge the fact that in the early 1900's there were two brothers of color who played golf. John Shippen was an instructor on golf courses in the eastern part of the country. His brother, Cyrus Shippen also played and served as an instructor. John was an instructor on the golf courses at the East Hampton Club, New York, the Merion, Philadelphia, and the Spring Lake Golf and Country Club. The brothers had professional privileges at some golf clubs in New jersey and played with famous white golfers. John was known for his good "driving" skills.

There were some Blacks in the South and North who were exposed to golf by serving as caddies. It was necessary for the majority of Black golf enthusiasts to form their own golf organization. The group was called "United Golf Association". Around 1926, they held National Tournaments annually, and it was necessary to use public links. There were a few private courses for Blacks. Some were located in Baltimore, Washington, D.C., Massachusetts, New Jersey; and Kankakee, Illinois; A few country clubs were owned and operated by Blacks, namely, the Shady Rest Country Club, Westerfield, New Jersey, the Sunset Hills Country Club, Kankakee, Illinois, and the Lincoln Country Club, Atlanta, Georgia. There were Black professional golfers among the Black golfers. Some of them were John Dendy,

Ashville, N.C., Solomon Hughes, Gadsen, Alabama; Pat Ball, Chicago, Illinois, Harry Jackson, Washington, D.C.; and Porter Washington, Boston, Massachusetts. The University of Michigan in 1930 demonstrated some racial tolerance when two Black players were invited to participate in their All Campus Golf Tournament. They were Crosby, who was a winner, and R.G. Robinson, a runner up. The Asheville Country Club of North Carolina invited four Blacks to play in an exhibition match in 1933. Tuskegee Institute, Alabama, was one of the first Black colleges to have intercollegiate golf in 1938. It is unfortunate that this information on golf experiences by Blacks in America has been concealed, since many Blacks as well as others believe that the golf interests of the Black community are something new.

Black women demonstrated an interest in golf during the 1930's. The only woman's golf club for Blacks at that time was the Wake Robin Club of Washington, D.C. Sara Smith and Esther Webb Terrell were two of their outstanding players. The Black women golfers were members of the United Golf Association and did participate in some annual meets.

Early Black Women Athletes

During segregation there were outstanding Black female athletes who performed not in just one sport but several. The presence of excellent female athletes of color in various sports today is just a magnification of their presence in sports. Their predecessors had to perform under segregated conditions that they do not face today. Current women athletes are able to become wealthy professionals, while enjoying a sport that they love. I suggest that they be appreciative of the equal opportunities available to them today because they are living in a time when their qualifications are known to their Black community and to the world.

Some of those early Black women athletes included Lula Haynes who scored first place in the 100 yard meter dash and the running broad jumps, as a member of Tuskegee Institute's Girls Track team in 1937. The team won records in the National Amateur Athletic Union Women's Track and field championship. The team was coached by Christine Perry who led the team to another championship title in 1938. A Washingtonian, Anita Gant, was an all-round athlete in basketball, tennis and swimming. She was captain of the local Y.W.C.A. basketball team and was victorious in the 1925, 1926 and 1933 National Mixed Doubles Championship Team. Anita Gant was a swimming sprint champion in an intercity meet in 1928. The New York Mercury Club had some successful track stars. They were Ivy Wilson, Romona Harris, Gertrude Johnson, Ida Byone, Pearl Edwards, Etta Tate and Esther Dennis.

Mistaken Identity At American Trapshooting Association's Tournament

Blacks participated in their own Rod and Gun Clubs during segregation. There were clubs in Baltimore, Maryland; Red Bank, New Jersey; St. Louis, Missouri; Washington, D.C.; Coatesville, Pennsylvania; Philadelphia, Pennsylvania; and Chicago, Illinois. Dr. Ernest B. Wetmore, a dentist, and his wife were very successful during the rod and gun sports competition. The climate of segregation could change; at times there was no outward segregation in trap shooting competition. However, in 1934, the "Official Rules of the Amateur Trapshooting Association Meeting in Vandalia, Ohio, in stipulating who may take part in a registered tournament, were amended to read, five or more persons, except those of Negroid extraction, may take part in registered competition, provided they first become members of the American Trapshooting Association. This change in rules followed the participation of Dr. Wetmore in the 12th Annual North and South Target Tournament at the Pinehurst, N.C. Gun Club, a generally white event in 1931. Dr. Wetmore participated in the tournament and was paired against W.E. Gladstone, a white man from Winston, Salem, N.C. They tied with 89 each. In the shoot off, Wetmore "broke 22 to 18 targets by Gladstone. His score for the event was 96 out of 100 targets". There was also a Black lady from Washington, D.C. who in the tournament officials did not recognize as Black. She was the dentist's wife Kay C. Hughes Wetmore. Just another true story of racism during the segregated years.

Colored Inter-Scholastic Athletic Association (CIAA)

During segregation 1906 it was necessary for Negroes to organize an Association of Colored Schools for athletic purposes. It was called the Inter-Scholastic Athletic Association of the Middle Atlantic States. The first members were Howard University, M Street (later Dunbar) High School, Armstrong High School, Douglass High School, Baltimore, and the Howard High School of Wilmington, Delaware.

Later in 1912 two college associations were begun. The first was the Colored Inter-Collegiate Athletic Association (ICAA) and the North Carolina Inter Collegiate Athletic Association which later merged with the CIAA.

Early Black Sports Officials

When you observe sports games today and see Blacks officiating, it really is no "big thing". Strange as it may sound, during segregation even Blacks believed that it was not possible for "a Negro official to be capable of officiating in games where all of the contestants and spectators were Black. Some of the leading educators and institutions would not risk the use of a colored umpire or referee". Eventually they were used, and even then, "it was contended their compensation should not be that of white men". An early organization of Black officials was formed in Washington, D.C. by some very competent and prominent citizens of color. They were Garnet C. Wilkinson, Benjamin Washington, A. Kiger Savoy, Edwin B. Henderson, Haley G. Douglass, Merton P. Robinson, W.H.J. Beckett, and John F. Wilkinson. As a young child I saw most of these men at one time or another in the Washington, D.C. 12th Street Y.M.C.A. This group later initiated the organization of the affiliated Board of Officials which comprised the Middle Atlantic, the Baltimore, the Piedmont, the West Virginia, the Eastern and the Virginia Boards. The affiliated board was recognized as spokesman for the group of local boards by the CIAA. During the 1930's and 1940's membership of the Eastern Board of officials consisted of local Washington, D.C. area director or teachers of physical educations, athletics and recreation. Their sports interests were football, baseball, softball, basketball, boxing, hand ball, swimming, track and field and tennis. My father, Arthur Alonzo Greene Sr. was a member of the Eastern Board of Officials.

"Blacks' and Sports Obsession"

The television, radio, news media, schools and individual Black families seem to have a strong obsession in relating a simple basketball to youth today. I have driven through predominantly Black neighborhoods with real estate ranging from 200,000 to 400,000 in prices. What did I observe besides beautiful homes with expensive cars parked in a drive way? I also observed outside basketball equipment with youngsters ranging from 7-17 years old trying to learn basketball. It is a mania or a real belief that one day they can be a member of the 5 Black players team of a billion dollar professional sports organization. Yes, I believe it is a magnificent obsession, with some false hopes, that is present among all social classes of many African Americans today. There is still a needed academic basket that some of these youngsters need to shoot for and do all the "dunking" in those books. The following articles that I wrote in 1997 will clearly depict that basketball has been around a long time for African Americans, and truly it is an integral part of our culture as other sports are. The article about my father shows that one can achieve excellence in sports and also in academic endeavors. I am very happy to see many Black athletes in 1998 receive million dollar contracts in sports because Blacks are long overdue in sharing the same wealth that Whites have shared for many years in the rich sports of boxing, basketball, track, baseball, and football. We must remember that during segregation, sports also played an important part in our togetherness, sound minds, and above all survival through the years of dehumanizing oppressive measures from a majority society whose skin color was not classified as Black, brown or high yellow.

I sincerely believe that many Blacks, youth and adults, do not have a historical awareness of the early presence of basketball and other sports in the Black community as early as the 1900's, 1910-1913. The late Dr. Edwin Bancroft Henderson, a physical educator teacher and author of the book *Negro In Sports,* wrote in 1939 that basketball had originated in 1891 at the Springfield, Massachusetts Young Men's Christian Association (YMCA) using two peach baskets. Henderson said that at first it was considered a "sissy game" as was tennis in the rugged days of football. He said that he learned basketball in his physical education classes in 1904 at Harvard University during summer school. When he returned to Washington, D.C., he taught it to the boys in the winter of 1904. Henderson said that by 1906, a league of teams had developed in Washington, D.C. and by 1911, every elementary school and high school in Washington, D.C. had basketball teams. Throughout the South, North, East and West basketball teams were organized in the Black communities in recreational centers, college and universities. Comments on the success of basketball and other sports by the Black coaches in 1912 were:

> The mentality shown on the courts is on par with the brainy work of many of the seniors. Passing, shooting, dribbling and in a measure signaling plays are mastered by elementary school players.

> Basketball has proved to be the most popular game among colored athletes of the north and has several strong organizations in existence.

I ask the question, if basketball teams could be organized in the separate public schools in Washington, D.C. and other cities in 1911 for people of color, why do we need to have young people playing basketball after midnight or earlier? Consider the facts that some 87 years ago basketball was a prime part-time sport, and many young people were organized into supervised leagues and they learned the skills, morals and fair sportsmanship. They did it so wonderfully, without the influence of weapons, and drugs and did not have to be organized by law enforcement personnel. I believe that those early players did not have an obsession for just basketball; they had other goals in mind.

I personally have a special interest in athletics because my father the late Arthur A. Greene Sr. believed in sports and loved the area as a profession. He was exposed to sports at a very young age in St. Louis, Missouri. As a child from a family of 12 children and the only one to graduate from high school and college, he was introduced to sports early, but it did not become an obsession that would preclude his upward mobility. *I am* privileged to possess my father's medals for the following triumphs in his sports career.

Golden Rule Athletic League Vandventer and

Laclede, St. Louis, Missouri, July-4, 1912
130 lb class 220 yard dash first place
130 lb class 100 yard dash - first place
130 lb class running high jump - first place

Sumner High School Athletic Association Second

Annual Meet, May 12, 1912
2rd place high Jump Middle weight
1st place shot put middle weight

St. Louis Public Schools' Field Day May 27, 1911
First prize Boys Unlimited weight class

Sumner High School, St. Louis Missouri
1912 100 yard dash First prize

Sumner High School Athletic Association
Third Annual Meet 1913 Middle Weight Champion
Fourth Annual Meet Open Champion, 1914
Howard University, Second Annual Track meet
1921
Broad Jump Collegiate First Place

Hampton Institute, Va, Track and Field Meet 1922
120 yard hurdle first place

Howard University Games, 1923
120 yard hurdle First place
220 yard hurdle First place

Arthur Greene was a student at Howard University in World War I. While a member of the University's Student Army Training Corps (SATC), he was federalized for six months as a private, Signal Corps. Greene graduated in 1923 with a LL.B in law. After working for a brief time as a special agent, Census Bureau, he decided to return to college and obtained a degree in physical education. In the early 1930's, he returned to his love, athletics, and accepted a position as physical education director at the 12th Street YMCA, Washington, D.C. He initiated an innovative program at the YMCA with a tumbling team, cross-country marathon team, volley ball, basketball and city wide horseshoe tournaments. Later he accepted a position with the St. Louis Pine Street, YMCA. A local newspaper, the *St. Louis Argus* wrote in an article, "Arthur A. Greene returns to St. Louis to accept a position with the St. Louis YMCA. He ran the 100 yard dash in ten (10) seconds flat and scored many points as a member of the Sumner Football Team."

My father never forgot his fondness for sports and chose a physical education career over a law career serving for 45 years, helping youth and leading them in the right direction.

Scholarly Black Sports Leadership During Segregation

Just fourteen years after America had announced the separate but equal doctrine, some professional, educated Blacks in Washington, D.C. were instrumental in establishing a network of efficient, competent and scholarly Blacks in physical education and recreation to establish guidelines, rules, procedures and organization of athletic clubs to guide Black youth, male and female in a positive direction in their participation in sports. I do not believe that these men and women had goals of personal rewards and political ambitions in their direction of sports leadership in those early years of 1910-1913 and later. Today we have some very "honorable and ambitious" people who have other intentions than the welfare of young people.

The historical legacy of these outstanding pioneers has been preserved in an official handbook that was published for them by the Spalding Athletic Library Series. The handbook contained records including pictures of the Interscholastic Athletic Association, the Colored Intercollegiate Athletic Association, The Washington Public Schools Athletic League, Colored School and Amateur Athletics and the North Carolina Intercollegiate Athletic Association. I have been fortunate to have in my private library, a copy of the 1913 edition, edited by Edwin B. Henderson and Garnett C. Wilkinson. I will include in the following discussions some major highlights and a summary of events in able to portray how sports were an essential part of young people's lives, and their involvement was structured and organized by individuals whose credentials in physical education and other academic areas provided the youth with a superb cadre of leadership. This leadership played an important part in a segregated Black community devoid of Whites, and emphasis was placed and directed on young people's morals, values and personal problems, if necessary. I believe that those leaders and coaches told their players in all the sports they played that "when the great scorer comes to write against your name, he writes not how you won but how you played the game".

This should be repeated at every game that is played by some of our Black athletes who have gone astray from the real morals and values of the Black sportsmen and sportswomen of the yesteryears.

The city of Washington, D.C. had a Public School's Athletic League that included elementary and high school boys. There was strict discipline rules without compromises and exceptions by "grass root community citizens who were promoting their individual causes." Some eligibility rules were: "attendance of at least twenty school days should be required of all pupils, maintain a scholarship grade which entitles them to promotion. Elementary school boys could represent their school and church teams, entry must be countersigned by respective principals, an elementary boy remains a novice until he has won a medal in the public schools athletic league games, and their conduct must be satisfactory.

William H.J. Beckett, physical director, Washington, YMCA, wrote about what participation in sports can offer besides just the satisfaction of playing a ball game and winning. Beckett said, "Sports present an excellent opportunity for organized athletics among young colored men. A higher standard of athleticism, a more scientific method of training, a greater intelligence in competition and athletic control will be disseminated among the growing generation. With the united efforts of all interested in racial improvement, much good can be accomplished in matters pertaining to health, right living and racial conservation".

These words were written 85 years ago. However today, I can pass a public basketball court with all Black youngsters playing ball in an unorganized setting. They are not only cursing among themselves but even calling the basketball a curse name. My former high school coach had some very high esteem for Black youths prior to my birth; and when he was in the gymnasium, he was still demonstrating his belief in 1949. But where are the principles of values and clean sportsmanship among some Black youth today, some of whom will curse the equipment they use in their play performance during a game. "Just nutritional reasoning".

Unity among African Americans was definitely present in the organized sports programs that were in many cities, states and institutions of higher learning. Some of those colleges, schools and private teams and clubs in the early 1900's were; football teams of colleges, West Virginia Colored Institute, Hampton Institute, Lincoln University (Pa.), Livingstone College, Tuskegee Institute, Florida Baptist Academy, Arkansas Baptist College, Howard University and Virginia Union baseball team, A and M College, Greensboro, N.C., baseball team, Biddle University, baseball team, Mary Potter School baseball team, Oxford, N.C., M Street High School, Washington, D.C., football team, Armstrong and Commercial high School football teams, Washington, D.C., Whittier Graded School Track team, Hampton, Va and Garrison School basketball team, Washington, D.C.

There were Girls basketball teams at West Virginia Colored Institute, Baltimore Colored High School, Maryland; Younger Set Basketball team, New York and Steele High School Dayton, Ohio. Some other sports clubs were Hilldale (Pa.) Baseball

Club, Cardinal-Hiawatha Basketball team, Alpha Physical Culture, basketball team, New York City, Wissahiskon School Club, basketball team; Philadelphia, Pa., Independent Pleasure Club, basket ball team; East Orange, N.J., St. Christopher's Club basketball team; New York and New Jersey, Smart Set Athletic Club, basketball team, Claver Catholic Club, basketball team; Philadelphia, Pa., Monticello basketball team, Pittsburgh, Pa.; Orion basketball team; Philadelphia, Pa.; and the YMCA Junior Basketball Team; Washington, D.C. Many of the schools and clubs had teams in track, tennis, golf and swimming.

Those sports participants, some 90 years ago, probably never dreamed in their lives that if segregation was no more, there would be Black youngsters who would in some cases receive scholarships and thousands of dollars to play professionally for financial gain sacrificing education beyond the 12th grade. If there were in a mystical way the "voices from the graves" could speak to these athletes, they would have special messages for some of our young athletes. Yes, sports will continue to have great significance in our Black culture in the American experience.

Segregation Off The Field

Simpson Younger was born in slavery on May 17, 1850, in Jackson County, Missouri. He was the son of a 20 year old mulatto slave named Elizabeth. He was the third mulatto child fathered by a wealthy white landowner. Simpson took the last name of his father, Charles Younger. Younger was the grandfather of the famed notorious outlaws, the Younger brothers. Charles Younger freed Elizabeth and her children in his will. Simpson Younger served in the 27th Colored U.S. Infantry during the Civil War. After the war, he studied at the Preparatory School, Oberlin, Ohio, and was a member of the college baseball team in 1867, known as the Penfield Club. In the 1880's, Simpson Younger refused to sit in the balcony of a Kansas City, Missouri theater that was reserved for Blacks. The case went to the Missouri Supreme Court, the case of Younger v. Judah. The court ruled that "such separation does not necessarily assert or imply inferiority on the part of one or the other. It does no more than work out natural laws and race peculiarities".

Sports Racism, Stanford University, 1920

Stanford University's Athletic Department had an unwritten policy in 1920 that prevented any direct contact with Negroes during sports' event. There was a Black member of the Pacific Coast Intercollegiate UCLA Boxing team. He was a lightweight boxing champion. The UCLA boxing team had a meet with the Stanford team on the UCLA campus. The Stanford coach said his lightweight boxer could not meet the Black boxer. Then the UCLA coach decided to substitute a white boxer for the Black champion. Unfortunately, for UCLA, their substitute white boxer lost

TRUE STORIES OF SEGREGATION

to the Stanford boxer and UCLA lost the match. Later the provost of UCLA issued a notice that there would be complete equality for all in the University irrespective of race or creed. Their boxing coach lost his job.

Military's Early Affirmative Action, 1957

When Secretary of Army, Wilbur Brucker, learned in September 1957, that the Black West Point Military Cadets would have segregated seats when the Academy's football team would play a scheduled game with Tulane University at their stadium in New Orleans, Louisiana initiated an affirmative action.

Brucker informed the University that the game would be transferred to the West Point Stadium because of Louisiana's segregation laws. A Louisiana law at that time forbade any athletic contest involving both Negroes and whites and provided for segregated seating at all sports events. There were no Black players on either team.

Sports Stereotypes

Scientists and laypersons have characterized some Black athletes as individuals who portray "angry facial expressions, wear earrings, flashy rings, walk in a weird manner, are basketball freaks and physical giants with anatomical differences. One study said that Blacks sprinting successes were due to their blood type "O" and differences in their buttocks, and that their muscles are longer and more powerful." Some people believe that Blacks have a "low vital capacity (amount of air a subject could exhale in a single effort). There have also been a stereotype that "it is harder for Blacks to master the art of pitching a ball because the are not as in control as Whites".

A popular sports magazine in 1994 interviewed the famous golfer Jack Nicklaus He was alleged to have said that Blacks "were anatomically unsuited for golf because they have different muscles that react in different ways".

During segregation and even today some Whites are presenting their findings and personal conclusions about the Black athletes so-called physical stamina and superiority in some sports and their inabilities to master other sports. The late Dr. W. Montague Cobb conducted comprehensive research attacking the myths of racial physical stereotypes. Who was Dr. Cobb?

Dr. Cobb was a native of Washington, D.C. and a graduate of Amherst College, Massachusetts. While studying at Amherst, he participated in sports and was the college's lightweight boxing champion in 1923 and the welterweight champion in

1924. Cobb was the ranking student in biology and was able to study at the Marine Biological Laboratory at Woods Hole, Massachusetts. He received a medical degree from Howard University in 1929 and a Ph.D from Western Reserve University in 1932. Dr. Cobb was a professor at Howard University College of Medicine for over 50 years. He taught more than 5,000 medical and dental students during his career. He was a distinguished physician, medical educator, scientific investigator, anatomist, physical anthropologist, historian and civic activist. He served as president of the Association of Physical Anthropologist, Associate editor of the American Journal of Physical Anthropology, secretary of the District of Columbia Anatomical Board, member of the Executive Committee, White House Conference on Health. Dr. Cobb had served as a member of the board of directors of the American Heart Association and also served as a member of the Gerontological Society and other scientific societies. This late distinguished physician and anthropologists' superb creditable and notable accomplishments nominate him as an expert to refute present day scientific inferences that support myths about the capabilities of Black athletes. Dr. Cobb, a man of color, addressed that subject many years ago with scientific proof.

In 1972, while serving as the Director of the U.S. Army Race Relations School in Germany, I read an article in a popular German magazine. The article stated that a 17 year old girl whose mother was white and father Black had achieved honors in swimming. The article said, however, the fans were confused because her achievements contradicted the legend that is called the biggest lie in sports by many. The writer of the article said the biggest lie was that it is often mentioned as a fact is that Negroes or Blacks could not achieve in water events Blacks have heavier bones which hinder the lifting in water, that Blacks have longer legs and arms which is a disadvantage; they also have less chest cavity which is detrimental to breathing and that they also have overly-long heel bones and less calf muscles, and both are not an advantage for swimmers. The article also stated that these facts have been challenged by the American professor of anthropology, Dr. Montague Cobb of Howard University, when he said, " In the anatomy of the Negro or Black person there is not a single mark or trait which all Blacks have in common. The author of the article was referring to some of the scientific research that Dr. Cobb had completed at Western Reserve University with Jesse Owens and white Olympic track star Frank Wycoff who also was a co-holder of the 9.4 second world record of 100 yard dash. Dr. Cobb examined and compared the skeletal and muscular systems and neuro muscular coordinations of Jesse Owens and compared them with similar measurements of white athletes. Cobb also had taken X-rays of Owen's heel bone and compared it with an average White of similar stature. Dr. Cobb concluded that Jesse Owens in particular revealed nothing to indicate that Negroid physical characteristics are anatomically significant with the dominance of Negro athletes in national competition in the short dashes and the broad jumps. He clearly stated that Jesse Owens, who had run faster and leaped than any human being at that time, does not have what is considered the Negroid type of calf, foot or heel bone.

Dr. Cobb also wrote that physical superiority in any line is the product of innate (born) capacities and training or conditioning. It has been found that a direct correlation exists between speed and the knee jerk reflex (patella tendon reflex). Running executes this in track participation, sprinters showing the shortest reflex and distance men the longest reflex. Cobb then said that in a sample of 82 Negroes and 82 white subjects, it was found that the Negroes showed no significantly shorter reflex time. Cobb asked the question, would this justify the conclusion that Negroes as a group were adapted for sprints and coaching them for the mile run, would be a waste of time? Obviously not, as the achievements of both white and Negro distance men, deny that. Yet such is the pattern of misleading thinking which conditions many popular attitudes about race and other matters. Dr. Cobb was stating that race is a biological reality and not a myth.

I read the German magazine article in 1972, twenty-six years ago, not in the United States, but in Munich, Germany, the home of the Bavarian Motor Works (BMW). As I tell my young college students that they must broaden their reading resources and be aware of the real world, and whether you like to hear or it not, listen and read what people in general will not tell you, I often tell my students that many things I tell them, they will read about or hear. Ironically before I could conclude this biograph, I read in a newspaper recently an article about Black aquatics instructors sink the assumption that African Americans cannot swim. It was interesting to read how the so-called expert of both races present their intellectual reasons such as lack of opportunity, training, and facilities. Facilities are expensive have no revenue producing appeal, and Blacks are attracted to other sports. My only response is that Blacks have been interested in several sports today and sometimes the other sports take a back seat. Contrary to many beliefs during the era of segregation, many Blacks were refused entry into white swimming facilities. However, in many cities the Black YMCA did offer swimming lessons to young boys and men. Today the pools are plentiful and available, I ask where is the interest, motivation and personal desire for some Black youngsters to engage in more than two sports. I was most proud of my late son Robert II because on his own he learned to swim; if I may say so he was a good swimmer and the day before he died seven years ago from the day I am writing, he had completed his evening duties the day before as a certified Red Cross life guard instructor. He probably never heard of the so-called myths and by the way he loved basketball and also calculus and physics.

POLITICS

Politics During Pre-Segregation

The Republican party in 1870's did not demonstrate its outward conservative view in considering the significance of the Black vote, especially in the House of Representatives in the state of Mississippi. When there was a contest for the Speaker of the Mississippi's House of Representatives during the reconstruction period, there were 77 whites and 38 Blacks in the House, all Republicans. The contest was not between white and colored, but between Democrats and Republicans. John Roy Lynch, a man of color was the choice for speaker by the Black members and a large majority of the white Republicans. Senator Alcorn had arrived from Washington, D.C. and took the leadership in ensuring a Republican victory for the speakers' seat. Some white Republicans members were apprehensive about voting for a Black man and they would not be able to defend these actions with their constituents. Senator Alcorn responded by saying "Could you have been elected without the votes of colored men? If you now vote against a colored man, who is in every way a fit and capable man for the position, simply because he is a colored man, would you expect those men to support you in the future? Can you then afford to offend the great mass of colored men that supported you in order to please an insignificantly small number of narrow-minded whites?" Senator Alcorn, a courageous white southerners of that day and time assured his white colleagues that they had nothing to fear as a result of their action in voting for Lynch. The final outcome was that John Roy Lynch was elected speaker with the vote of every Republican present and two Independents. Where is that liberal spirit today, Mr. Speaker of the U.S. House?

Mississippi Senator B.K. Bruce

Senator Ame's term as senator expired in March 4, 1875. The candidacy of B.K. Bruce for U.S. Senate was suggested by Ames who became Governor of Mississippi. Bruce refused to allow his name to be entered for Lt. Governor which could have resulted in making him governor; however, he wanted to become a senator. He was the choice of a large majority of Republican members of the legislature, white as well as colored. It was expected that he could be sent to the senate for long terms rather than filling out the unexpired term of Governor elect Ames. Senator Alcorn; disappointed at the outcome of his fight with Governor Ames was manifested when Senator Bruce was to be sworn in. He did not escort Bruce, his colleague, to the desk of the President of the Senate to be sworn in. As Bruce started to the desk unattended, Senator Roscoe Conkling of New York sitting nearby immediately rose, extended his arm and escorted him to the President's desk, standing by the new Senator's side until the oath had been administered. He extended his congratulations along with the other Republican Senators. Senator Alcorn decided to join later.

It is interesting to know that J. Roy Lynch believes that Mr. Alcorn's actions were political not racial. They were not assured in that day of such home made terms as politically correct or "race cards". Lynch said Alcorn was concerned that Bruce had opposed him and supported Governor Ames in the fight for Governor in 1873. Alcorn had assisted in the election of Bruce to the position of Sergeant of Arms of the State Senate. This helped him later to become elected Sheriff and Tax Collector in 1871. Senator Alcorn believed that when Bruce took sides against him in favor of Ames in 1873, that he was guilty of gross ingratitude. This is why he did not escort Mr. Bruce to Senate President's desk. It has been said that Bruce did not know Alcorn had strong ambition to become governor. Lynch remarked that when Mr. Pinchback from Louisiana was elected to the Senate and a contravention prevented him from being seated, Senator Alcorn spoke and voted for his admission whereas a staunch Republican Senator Edmund of Vermont opposed his admission. We must remember both were elected chiefly by votes of colored men.

Who was Alcorn? He represented his Coahoma county in the Secession Convention of 1861. He opposed Secession, but when he realized that it was inevitable, he signed the ordinance of Secession, joined the Confederate Army, raised troops and was promoted to Brigadier General. After the war, Alcorn supported the Andrew Johnson Plan of Reconstruction and was elected under that plan as a U.S. Senator. When the plan was rejected by the northern states, he was not seated. With the Congressional plan in effect, he decided to join the Republican Party in 1869. Then later he was elected governor.

When we view politics today to some major cities with a large number of Black votes potentially dominating the political arena, we see some non-whites using legal maneuvers to divide and diminish the power of those Black votes, we should flash back to the pre and post Reconstruction era and reflect on what Major Roy Lynch experienced in those days and the similarities between his times and the political atmosphere in 1998. There simply is a fear of Black political power when it is present in some communities. Roy Lynch discussed in his writings the subject of "Negro Domination". He gave specific examples of what it meant to him in reviewing the politics in local and national elections. He said some Whites believed that if the Black votes were not suppressed in all such states districts, and counties, Black men would be supported and elected to office because they were Black, and white men would be opposed and defeated because they were white. He used Mississippi as an illustration. Lynch was able to show that the unified Black vote was not a threat and that there was never any ground for the alleged apprehension of Black domination as a result of free, fair and honest election in any one of the southern or reconstructed states.

Lynch said Negro Domination was best defined by an Associate Justice of the Supreme Court of Mississippi. H.H. Chambers wrote an article in the *North American Review,* 1881. Chambers wrote that in order to have "Negro Domination" it does not necessarily mean that Negroes must be elected to office, but that in all elections in which white men may be divided, if the Negro vote should be sufficiently decisive to be determinative in the result, the white men who would be elected through the aid of the Black vote would represent "Negro Domination"., wherever the will of a majority of the whites would be defeated through the votes of colored men. Lynch's analyses of these statements caused him to say that if this is correct, then we are to have "Negro Domination" not only in all states, districts and counties even where they are few in number. If that is the correct definition of "Negro Domination" then the suppression of the Negro vote is not only necessary in states, districts and counties in which Negroes are in the majority but in every state, district, and county in the U.S. Lynch realized the colored vote had been significant in certain national elections; namely, the 1868 election of Republican candidate U.S. Grant, when he lost a major state, New York which would have resulted in his defeat if the southern states that took part in that election had all voted against him. The fact that they did not do so was attributed to the Black men's votes in those states, representing "Negro Domination".

In 1876, President Rutherford B. Hayes was elected President by a majority of one vote in the electoral college. This was made possible by the election result in the states of Louisiana, South Carolina and Florida, which there was a considerable dispute and controversy because Hayes was running against Tilden. The Hayes administration represented President James Garfield, Republican candidate for President in 1880 who was victorious in the State of New York with some 20,000 critical votes. If the Black men in New York State had voted against him, he would have lost the State and the Presidency. Again, the Garfield and Arthur administrations represented "Negro Domination".

In 1884, Grover Cleveland, a Democratic candidate, gained the State of New York by a narrow margin of 1,147 votes which resulted in his election. The number of Black that voted for Cleveland was far in excess of the plurality by which he carried the state. It has been stated that President Cleveland was unaware of the significance of the Black vote.

General Harrison, a Republican candidate in 1888, carried the State of New York by some 20,000 votes which resulted in his election. He would have lost but for the Black votes in the state. President Harrison's administration represented "Negro Domination".

TRUE STORIES OF SEGREGATION

To really understand what the concept of "Negro Domination" meant in the early 1870's and also today, ask yourself what effect did the Black man and Black woman's vote have on the elections of the late President John F. Kennedy, former Presidents Lyndon Johnson, and Jimmy Carter and our current President William Jefferson Clinton. One also must realize why it was necessary for some whites to find legal or illegal ways to suppress the Black vote. These reactions led the minority people of color, now called African Americans, to initiate measures to regain the Black vote.

"The Importance of Race and Intermarriage in Politics"

When President Grover Cleveland formed his first cabinet, he appointed a Mr. Lamar (D) from the State of Mississippi as his Secretary of the Interior. John Roy Lynch, then an ex-Congressman, visited Lamar in his office and was offered an appointment for his past support as a special agent of public lands. Lynch believed that Lamar could not as a member of the National Democrat Administration comfortably offer a position. He therefore refused it and suggested that the Secretary appoint some other qualified person to the available offices. He provided him with a list which included a Black physician and a white lawyer who had been appointed by Senator Bruce to a Clerkship in the Pension Bureau. When Secretary Lamar examined the list, he told Lynch that the name of everyone on the list will be retained except the colored physician and the white lawyer. His reason was that the physician was a colored man married to a white wife; and the lawyer, a white man was married to a Black wife and that he could not promise that they would retained, however capable and efficient they might be. Secretary Lamar presented his justifications for his decision by reasoning that he could not afford to antagonize public opinion in the State of Mississippi on the question of amalgamation because the white lawyer was from Mississippi where he was well known and his case is recent and fresh in the public mind. "I can see no escape for his selection," Adding, "It may be different for the Black doctor because he is not from my state and is not known in the state". The physician was able to remain in office during the whole of President Cleveland's first administration. Lynch made a strong appeal to Lamar to reconsider the white lawyer's appointment. He even gave him a lengthy lecture on his views of race mixing by saying, "The law against race intermarriage has a tendency to encourage and promote race intermixture rather than discourage and prevent it, because under existing circumstances local sentiment in our part of the country tolerates the intermixture provided that the white husband and father does not lead to the altar in honorable wedlock the woman he may have selected as the companion of his life and mother of his children". If, instead of prohibiting race intermarriage, the law would compel marriage in all cases of concubinage, such a law would have a tendency to discourage race intermixture because it is only when they are legally married that whites tend to be concerned.

Segregation During New Deal Era

President Franklin Delano Roosevelt had introduced his "New Deal Program" to solve many problems of the post depression years in the mid 1930's. However, there was blatant segregation in the New Deal programs. The Agricultural Adjustment Administration had a program to reduce acreage in order to increase crop prices. This action forced many Black farmers off the tenant lands they were working and lived on. The National Recovery Administration forced Blacks to accept lower pay or give their jobs to Whites. The Tennessee Valley Authority hired Blacks only as unskilled laborers. The Federal Housing Administration wrote restrictive convenants into each lease.

The late Robert C. Weaver, who died in New York City in 1997, was appointed as the first Black named to a presidential cabinet, and also served as President Roosevelt's race advisor. Weaver was appointed in the late 1930's as Secretary of Housing and Urban Development. In 1933, he had served as an aide to the Interior Secretary, Harold Ickes.

Prior to the 1940 election, President Roosevelt's Press Secretary, Stephen T. Early, had an embarrasing incident to occur that turned somewhat racial. Early had arrived at the Union Station, Washington, D.C. and lost his temper when a line of police officers blocked his path. Early then knocked one of the officers to the ground. The officer happened to be Black. This incident began to spread throughout the Washington Black community. Just as the president does today, dispatch his so-called hand picked Black leaders to the racial scene, Roosevelt did this in 1940. A White House advisor immediately called Robert Weaver in Washington, because the Democrats were concerned about losing the Black vote over the incident. The White House aide asked Mr. Weaver to find other Black advisors and prepare a speech for him which appeal to Blacks. Robert Weaver told the advisor that he doubted if he could find anyone in the middle of the night. ("It has been stated that when Weaver said this to the white aide, most of the "other advisors" were playing poker in his basement when the phone rang"). However, Robert Weaver told the aide he did not think that a speech would help the problem. Weaver said what we need right now is something so dramatic that it will make the Negro voters forget about Steve Early and the Black policeman. Now in those days, Blacks did not have ambitious media leaders and political activists as we have in 1998, those who make speeches suggest, and ask for things in the Black community that are seldom delivered. During segregation there were many well educated and efficient Black political appointees like Robert Weaver and Judge William Hastie who suggested direct action on their requests and received positive results, even though they knew it was "political appeasement". Evidently the White House aide convinced President Roosevelt to initiate something dramatic to appease the Black voters, because within 48 hours, the President announced the appointment of the first Black active duty Army General officer, the late Brigadier General Benjamin O. Davis Sr., a well qualified officer. He also announced the appointments of William Hastie as the first Black civilian aide to the Secretary of War and Colonel Campbell C. Johnson (he was a close friend of my father) as an assistant to the Director of the Selective Service, General Hershey. (another Black would not be appointed to that political position until 1997).

This true story should depict how the power of the Black vote during segregation was used to eradicate some discrimination and also to provide efficient and capable Blacks in high ranking positions in the government and military. These early leaders for some reason did not become involved in alleged scandals of impropriety while in office.

A Black Politician who Challenged The System

There have been in recent years numerous pioneer municipal politicians who have retired or died. The newspapers will highlight their careers, the good and bad, briefly; and the television will allow a few minutes of coverage of their careers. However the public sometimes is never informed of their accomplishments relating to racial matters and their experiences living and surviving the segregated years. I had heard over the years about Detroit's former mayor of twenty years, the late Coleman Young, but I did not really know who Coleman Young was as a politician, citizen and a civil rights activist over the years, even before he entered the political arena. This discussion will highlight some interesting information about a distinguished and possibly controversial politician who actually challenged the system during segregation and so-called integration.

The political accomplishments of Coleman Young are many. But there will be people who will remember him for these noteworthy achivements. While serving as Mayor of Detroit, Michigan, his leadership was able to develop a strong Black political machine, an integrated police department (in 1968, Black officers assigned to the old sixth precinct were not allowed to patrol in the all white neighborhoods), the Joe Louis Sports Arena, Cobb Renaissance Center, minority contracts for city projects, and the disbanding of an undercover police unit called "STRESS" (Stop The Robbers Enjoy Safe Streets). The unit was alleged to have been involved in the fatal shooting of 22 young men, mostly Black.

Now, I ask this question, how many Blacks, Whites, Asians Hispanics and European immigrants living in the Detroit Metropolitan and suburbs know the following about Young's segregated living experiences?

During World War II, Coleman Young was commissioned as a second lieutenant in the segregated U.S. Army Air Force and became a Tuskegee Airman. He was with some Black servicemen in Midland Texas who protested their eating arrangements. They were all considered instigators. Young was one of the sixty Black officers at Freeman Field, Indiana, who were arrested for refusing to leave an all white officers club in April, 1943.

Coleman Young later would join protests in his hometown Detroit, Michigan. He was with the picketers at a Detroit bank that would not employ Black tellers. He protested at the Ford Motor plants because of their hiring policies. He was an outspoken person who voiced his opinions if he believed they were needed, especially on racial matters. A white congressman from Georgia, Frank Tavenner was conducting an investigation on Communist influences in the labor unions in Detroit in 1952 for the House UnAmerican Activities Committee. Young decided during the meeting to inform the congressman on the correct pronunciation of a word. Young told the congressman "the word is Negro not niggra".

There is a story about Coleman Young's visit in 1970 to Washington, D.C. to keep an appointment with a top government official in the U.S. Department of Housing and Urban Development. It was said that when he arrived he was greeted by a Black undersecretary. Young then said to him, "I did not come here to see the House Nigger, get me the man". Today we can read about a magazine in Masschusetts that allegedly referred to a Black Harvard professor as the "Head Negro In Charge". I wonder if the writer and even the professor really understand the significance of that term that was used frequently not just in slavery but also for 40-50 years during segregation.

A quote from the late Mayor Coleman Young of Detroit could best explain his views on racism. "Racism is something like high blood pressure. The person who has it does not know he has it until he drops over with a stroke. The victim of racism is in a much better position to tell you whether or not you are a racist that, you are".

Young lived in a time when race was a dominant theme in one's life experiences, more than it is today. One could have been exposed to being hit over the head by a white police officer for no reason other than one's skin color. A Black student could have a fine academic record and then be denied admission to a high school and also prevented from securing a college scholarship. I am sure that Coleman Young knew about these acts of racism during segregation, and Blacks too need not to forget and also echo in 1998 "NEVER AGAIN".

White Texas Segregated Primaries

Thousands of immigrants over the years have passed through Ellis Island and other ports of entry into these democratic freedom loving United States. The immigrants have been representative of Europeans, Asians, Hispanics, Africans and Caribbeans or West Indians. Many had entered this country during segregation and later become naturalized citizen or are awaiting citizenship today. Once they become citizens, they enjoy one of the most precious and cherished rights, the right to freely vote in national and local primary elections. I want these immigrants today to just be aware of the five Texas Primary cases. Also I want Americans who were born in this country to know about the primary cases, because recalling of these political historical facts might in some way inform and reeducate someone to the fact that there has been a difference in the connotation of a minority forty-five years ago as well as today. I do not believe that the majority of the immigrants to America had to confront legal interpretations and denial tactics to prevent them from voting in a primary as was the case in Texas, defined and sanctioned by interpretative rulings of the U.S. Supreme Court from 1927-1953.

In Texas, the right to vote in a democratic society for people of African descent, called Negroes and Blacks, was predicated on the judicial system's interpretation of the 15th Amendment to the Constitution. In 1965, some jurists would reinterpret the Constitution and then ask the Congress to enforce the law. Prior to the famous 1965 Voting Rights Acts, the states rights judicial system of Texas had legally disenfranchised the Negro by 1915, through the poll tax and the white primary. The white primary had voters rather than conventions nominate candidates for public office. The southern states were dominated by one party, the present day "loving" party of many African Americans, the Democratic Party. Small groups of white men selected a small number of white candidates, who then were nominated by a small margin of voters and elected to office. This was an undemocratic primary because it excluded Black participation and the right to membership in these small clubs or groups. The result was Blacks could not vote, period.

An examination of these five legal cases by laypersons might help them to understand that someone had a sound idea that there was a need for new laws and some affirmative actions to correct wrongs, not only from slavery but also the actions of some citizens.

The <u>Texas Primary Cases</u> - represent an example of second class citizenship of Blacks in America prior to 1965. Blacks were given the right to vote in 1865. Plessy vs. Ferguson had some impact on denying Blacks the right to vote. Any laws passed by Congress must be enforced for its reality. Black leaders and citizens used the courts to fight for their right to vote and their cases were before U.S. Supreme Court 5 times, during the period 1927-1953. The cases were: <u>Nixon v.</u>

Herndon, 1932, ruled that Texas white Primary statutes of 1923, denying Blacks the right to vote were unconstitutional. Response - Texas passed a law giving political parties power to determine voter qualification. Nixon v Condon, 1932, Supreme Court ruled party regulations barred Blacks from voting. Response - Texas repealed its laws restricting membership, but left these matters to respective political parties. Response by concerned Blacks was to go back to the courts. Grovey v. Townsend, 1935, the Supreme Court agreed with the resolution of Texas State Convention that limited primary voting to whites. The resolution did not constitute state action. Smith v. Allwright, 1944, decision overruled Grovey v. Townsend. The Court voted "Privilege of membership in party may be no concern of a state, but when that privilege is qualification for voting in a Primary, the state makes the action of the party, action of the state." Texas response - requested restricted device to keep white primary by Democratic party, privately, and transferred the duties of the party to "Jaybird Association whose membership was limited to whites. The fifth and last case, Terry v. Adams, 1953, Supreme Court divided ruling that the voters could not be barred from voting in Jaybird election because there was state action involved, and the Jaybird group was an integral part of the election process that must conform with the command of the 15th amendment. Concerned white and Black Civil Rights Activist continued the legal efforts, protests and congressional and presidential lobbying to implement the 15th Amendment, finally resulting in the passage of Civil Rights Act and Voting Rights Acts of 1957, 1960, and 1965.

True Stories About Black Disenfranchisement In the South

I have selected some true stories about Black disenfranchisement in the segregated South from interviews by the late noted educator and statesman, Ralph Bunche and his assistants. The following biographical sketch of Ralph Bunche is included in my recent book, *Black Presence In World History.* This sketch will give the reader some unknown facts about one of America's outstanding statesman and peace negotiator.

I can recall sitting in a classroom many years ago in Banneker Junior High School, Washington, D.C. where one of my classmates was Joan Bunche, I only knew that her father was a professor at Howard University. A few years ago, when I arrived at my present college position, I shared an office with a colleague who had a large picture of Ralph Bunche on the wall; and at that time, I asked a question, "How many people today really know who Ralph Bunche was and of his many outstanding contributions to World peace, independence for African nations and his peace making efforts in the Israel - Arab conflict in the late 1940's?" I then proceeded to answer the question myself, because very few if any of the media would ever recall the efforts of Bunche in the United Nations peace making involvement in its early years. Therefore, I have accumulated these missing pages of facts about the life and times of Dr. Ralph Bunche, the first African American to be awarded the prestigious Nobel Peace Prize.

Dr. Ralph Bunche was born in Detroit, Michigan. His parents died when he was thirteen years old, and he was raised by an affectionate maternal grandmother, Mrs. Lucy Taylor, who provided Ralph with great wisdom. Bunche learned about prejudice and racism in his early years. When he graduated from high school in Los Angeles, California, the Honor Society of Jefferson High School refused to elect him to membership even though he was the class valedictorian. In later years, the West Side Tennis Club in Forest Hills would apologize for barring him and his son. Ralph Bunche had a goal to pursue excellence in education and his projected endeavors. He was a Phi Beta Kappa scholar, and Rosenwald scholar when he went to Europe and East Africa on a social science research council fellowship. Dr. Bunche earned his Doctor of Philosophy Degree in the discipline of government from Harvard.

While studying at the University of California at Los Angeles (UCLA), Ralph Bunche was a member of its championship basketball team for three years and its football team. He suffered an injury that caused him to stop playing the game and his years as a basketball star caused damage to the vascular system in his legs from which he would suffer in later years.

While serving as a professor in government at Howard University, Bunche used his talents of research in American government and International Relations and was instrumental in establishing a department of government and political science at Howard University. He also authored some interesting papers. He wrote on the *"Disenfranchisement of the Negro"* and a *Comparative Study of Togo.* Ralph Bunche made a significant contribution to the manuscript written by Gunnar Mydral in 1944, *An American Dilemma,* Gunnar acknowledged Bunche in the book when he wrote the Chapter on *Political Practices.* The data on southern politics in the chapter are for the most part taken from Ralph Bunche's seven volume study *"The Political Status of the Negro" an unpublished manuscript. His investigation assisted by several field workers is rich in material on the South.*

Ralph Bunche worked briefly as an acting chief of the United State Department's Division of Dependent Areas Affairs. During World War II, Bunche worked for the Office of Strategic Services, in the areas of Africa and North Africa. In 1945, Bunche participated in the Dunbarton Oaks Conference and the United Nations San Francisco Conferences. He also assisted in devising the trusteeship provisions of the United Nation's Charter. Later he was appointed to head the United Nations Division of Trusteeship and Non Governing Territories. He was promoted to the Under secretary of the United Nations for Special Political Affairs. He headed the

UN's team responsible for the decolonization of all the colonial protectorates, except Portugal, Rhodesia and the Republic of South Africa.

In 1948, the United Nation Secretary, General Trygve Lie appointed Bunche as the chief assistant to Count Folks Bernadotte of Sweden who was selected to be the UN mediator in Palestine. A seventy year old man secretariat was present in Palestine. On September 17, 1948, Bernadotte was assassinated in Jerusalem by an Israeli assassin. Bunche was selected to serve as acting mediator. The UN had ordered an immediate cease fire between the Arabs and Israeli forces.

Dr. Ralph Bunche invited the Israel and Arab representatives to meet in Rhodes, in the Dodecanese Islands, for negotiations. Bunche was required to establish dates, time, and hours of the cease fire, and he informed the Egyptian and Israeli governments to make arrangements for the Armistice meetings. It was necessary for him to meet with both sides separately and he requested the cooperation from both governments. Dr. Bunche was responsible for submitting proposals that would be acceptable for Israel and Syria. At one time, there was a deadlock for awhile and talks were suspended. Later Syria and Israel accepted a proposal and resumed the Armistice discussion. An Armistice agreement between Israel and Syria was concluded on July 20, 1949. Dr. Bunche was most successful in his mission as a United Nations mediator and above all as an American statesman of color. Bunche was recognized by President Harry S. Truman, the Foreign Minister of Israel, Moshe Shertor, and Egypt's Seyed Din, for his diplomatic achievements in the Middle East.

In the 1950's, he assisted Libya and other Black African nations in gaining independence. Bunche was responsible for having the countries involved in the League of Nations Mandate System to have their mandate transferred to the United Nations and trust territories. South Africa refused.

Ralph Bunche was responsible for a peace keeping force in 1956 to mediate disputes when the British, French and Israeli attempted an invasion of the Suez Canal area and Egypt. President Eisenhower had suggested United Nations intervention. The matter escalated when the Egyptian President Nasser demanded foreign withdrawal. Then Israel attacked Egypt and there has been no firm peace in that area in recent years.

When we read and hear about the civil strifes in the Congo and Rwanda Burundi areas or the country of Zaire. I still challenge the competent news media experts to reeducate the people about how some of the problems of today do have a relationship to what occurred 37 years ago in the former colonial protectorate of a country named Belgium. Ralph Bunche was diplomatically involved in the early independence matters in Zaire in 1960. Bunche was asked to visit the Congo and assist in having the Belgium government give the new government an opportunity to establish a democratic government and have their people return to Belgium. He also was interested in preventing any interference by Russia and give the United States an opportunity to assist the new government. While he was in the Congo he was arrested and almost shot because some Black Congolese soldiers mistook him for an un-tanned Belgian. In 1963, the UN troops left the country of Zaire or the Congo. It is quite possible that Bunche and the UN actions prevented Russian interferences and averted a possible war between Russia and the United States in the Congo region. The Russians did not pay their share of the Congo expense. France disagreed with the UN's actions and believed they were interfering in the internal affairs of Belgium. The British believed that the UN went too far in the Belgium Congo's situation. France refused to pay her costs of the UN's role in the Congo.

UN General Secretary U Thant sent Ralph Bunche to Cyprus. He was chief of the peace keeping operation on the island with 6,000 UN troops. The operation was assisting in the mediation process between the Turks and the Greeks.

Dr. Ralph Bunche died on December 9, 1971. He believed that the battle for peace can best be waged with patience and persistence. Today, the United Nations has its first African Secretary General. However, we must be reminded that an African American, Ralph Bunche is an image model for those of all colors to emulate for his diplomacy and peace making in the years to come.

Ralph Bunche documented the following accounts of racism and segregation during the 1930's and 1940's: I do not believe that present day documentaries and Hollywood's revisions of true Black historical events will present these stories to the public and including our newly welcomed immigrant minorities of 1998. These truths can set the mind free of ignorance and replace it with the truth of what really occurred prior to the civil rights movement. The interviews with southern white and Black individuals in 1940 was part of a comprehensive survey of the Negro in America conducted under the sponsorship of the Carnegie Corporation of New York. These interviews showed that the Negro and some Whites were denied the right to vote because of the economic and political structure of the South at that time. In some states, a few Blacks were permitted to vote on local and bond elections. But overall Blacks were confronted with measures to ensure that they would not vote in the all white primary elections. Some of the measures were: a requirement that Negroes have two or more white character witnesses to appear in person, literacy tests that required Negroes to demonstrate a reasonable interpretation of the Constitution, (such as asking the Black to explain what was meant by "non compos mentis" when it is applied to a citizen in legal jeopardy? Blacks were required to show their property tax receipts. If an applicant made an error in filling out registration blanks by not giving the correct age by the month, year or date, he was denied the chance to register. At times Black applicants would be told that their registration cards were invalid and that registration was closed after they had been waiting for a long time. In South Carolina, Blacks were required to have been enrolled in the Democratic clubs in order to vote clubs which in reality they excluded Blacks from membership. Blacks also faced the poll tax requirement, loss of jobs and physical violence if they tried to vote. A white treasurer - secretary of a Georgia Democratic county committee said in 1940, "Niggers have been ruled out; it is our private affair and we don't invite them in and that's that". A city manager of a South Carolina town said a Negro Baptist Minister tried to vote in the Democratic primary. The former mayor of the town asked him "What do you want nigger? and when the minister politely said that he wanted to vote, he was warned to leave and stay away if he knew what was good for him. There was a white member of the Board of Registrars of an Alabama County who said the registrars did not take anybody's signature for Negro applicants; normally, the signature of a prominent lawyer, business woman or one of the registrars was acceptable. He said a Negro could never sign for another Negro applicant. He also said that if the Negro can show that he is a good citizen, he would sign for him because he would not want anyone to think he was discriminating against them. Because he had been "doing business in a nigger town for the past 20 years and I have learned to tell between them".

There was a situation in Alabama where a Negro applicant was told to read the Constitution. The Negro decided to recite the Gettysburg address, and the white registrar said, "That's right; you can go ahead and register". That interview was taken from two Black physicians in Alabama on November 17, 1939. I found these stories very significant because while doing some research in 1970 on my book *Black Defenders of America 1775-1973*, I obtained the following information from a copy of the actual State of Tennessee's colored man's application for a pension of Leroy Jones, No. 120. In July of this year, the nation will be focusing on those brave Black union soldiers of the Civil War as a memorial will be unveiled in Washington, D.C. It is unfortunate that many Black citizens and non whites are not aware of the subservient and at times heroic combat roles that many illiterate Black body servants and cooks were forced to play in the Confederate Army. I completed over the years extensive documented research on the Black Confederate Body Servant and Soldier and even had the opportunity to become the first Black ever to give a lecture as the honored guest at the Winchester, Virginia, Rotary Club in 1971. But who was Leroy Jones? Leroy Jones was a body servant in Company I, Fourth Tennessee Regiment, Confederate Army during the War between the states. He was born in Shelby County, Tennessee, on March 9, 1838. His master was Wallis Jones from Germantown, Tennessee. Leroy stayed with his master until he died of typhoid fever in 1862 in Panola County, Mississippi. At this time Leroy Jones slipped through the federal lines and returned to his master's home where he remained until he was given his freedom. Jones was living in Tipton County,

Tennessee when he applied for a pension and was successful at the age of 91 years. In 1921, some white southerners would assist former Black body servants to obtain pensions by writing letters to support their known service to the Confederacy.

The Secretary of the Pension Board, Nashville, Tennessee, P.H. Green wrote the following: "In the fall of 1865, Leroy married one of Dr. John A. Greene's Negro girls. Rev. David H. Cummins, Pastor of the First Presbyterian church of Covington, performed the ceremony. From this time he lived with my grandfather and afterward my father for many years. He was what was known as a <u>white man's Negro</u> (emphasis added) and voted with us in every election, thus incurring the enmity of the leading Negroes, but old Leroy always told them he was going to stick to his white folks. . . . He has been loyal to his white people ever since the war, regardless of his freedom."

I believe seriously that there are some professional and non professional Blacks today who emulate some of Leroy Jones' political savvy but they are protected from the "enmity" of many Blacks because they use certain political terminology as their protective shield from racial ostracism by their Black peers. In simple terms Uncle Tom and Aunt Thomasina are not applicable to their character as it was to Leroy Jones during segregation. "Just another bit of nutritional reasoning".

A Black Congressman and Activist

There are Black congressmen and congresswomen today who are present in the halls of congress but sometimes their voices are silenced by political motives and other reasons. There are a few who show some activism related to their Black heritage and current problems affecting the Black community. I believe that it will be a long time before there will be another controversial but vocal race-concerned politician in the image of the late Congressman, Reverend Adam Clayton Powell Jr.

The late Congressman Adam Clayton Powell Jr. was from New York. He was investigated by the 89th Congress special subcommittee on House Administration. The special subcommittee members were concerned about Powell's expenditures for the Committee on Education and Labor. Powell was the chairman of the committee. The special subcommittee's report stated that certain illegal salary payments had been made to Powell's wife at his direction. The report concluded that Powell and certain staff employees had deceived the House authorities concerning travel expenses.

When the 90th Congress convened in January, 1967, Powell was asked to step aside while the oath was administered to other members elect. Later the Congress voted 364 to 64 to have the speaker to appoint a select committee to determine Powell's eligibility. On March 1, 1967, the House voted 307 to 116 to exclude him from the Ninetieth Congress. Powell won a special election on April 11, 1967 to fill the vacancy caused by his exclusion. He did not take his seat. Powell was reelected to Congress in November, 1968. The House of Representatives voted to deny him his seniority. He again declined to take his seat when the ninety-first Congress convened in January 1969.

The United States Supreme Court ruled on June 16, 1967 in the case of Adam Clayton Powell, Jr. and other petitioners. The Chief Justice Warren delivered the opinion of the court. The court said Powell was duly elected by his constituents from the 18th Congressional District of New York and it was error to dismiss the complaint and that petitioner Powell is entitled to a declaratory judgement that he was unlawfully excluded from the 90th Congress. Powell returned to his seat without his twenty years seniority. He was unsuccessful for renomination in the June 1970 primary, and he did not get on the ballot as an independent. Adam Clayton Powell was the Pastor of the Abyssinian Baptist Church in New York City. He was a graduate of Colgate University and Columbia University. Powell was a pioneer in civil right actions in New York and later in Congress. He led picket lines and mass meetings to improve conditions at Harlem Hospital. He established programs for food, clothing and jobs for the needy. He organized rent strikes. When he arrived in Washington, he challenged segregated practices in Capitol facilities reserved for members only but which had excluded Black representatives. As Chairman of the Committee on Education and Labor, Adam Clayton Powell accomplished the following: His committee "approved over fifty measures authorizing federal programs for minimum wage increases, education and training for the deaf, school lunches, vocational training, student loans and standards for wages and work hours, aid to elementary and secondary education and public libraries." Adam Clayton Powell retired as Pastor of the Abyssinian Baptist Church in 1971. A minister of the gospel, a civil rights activist and a powerful politician died in Miami, Florida, on April 4, 1972.

MEDICINE - HOSPITALS

Breaking The Barriers of Segregation In Medicine

During the years of segregation there were some courageous Black physicians, and surgeons who were instrumental in removing many barriers of segregation and discrimination in America prior to the 1960's. There were only a few Black doctors who were trained at all white medical schools. Many times the Black doctors had to supplement their incomes because most of their patients were receiving low wages. Black physicians worked for Black insurance companies, benevolent societies, real estate investments and owned drug stores and private hospitals. I am sure readers will say they had some unethical income means. As a historian, I will say some Black doctors did engage in illegal abortions and in many cases their patients were whites. However, I will not include those individuals as representative of the majority of Black physicians in the yesteryears. The Black physicians were denied membership in most county medical societies and professional scientific societies in the South and North. Their opportunities for internship and residencies were restricted in most white hospitals. Some of those physicians and surgeons who were pioneers in breaking the barriers were:

CHARLES BURLEIGH PURVIS was born in Philadelphia, PA in 1842. He graduated from Oberlin College in 1860. He received his M.D. degree from Western Reserve University Medical School. Dr. Purvis served as surgeon in charge, Freedmen's Hospital. He also was professor Emeritus of Obstetrics and Gynecology, Howard University School of Medicine. It has been stated that Dr. Purvis was one of the physicians who treated President Garfield when he was attacked by an assassin. Dr. Purvis was the first Black physician to serve on the District of Columbia's Board of Medical Examiners and he was the second Black to serve on the faculty of Howard University School of Medicine.

MYRA ADELE LOGAN is a native of Tuskegee, Alabama. She graduated from Atlanta University and received her M.D. degree from New York Medical College. She also received an MS degree from Columbia University. She has conducted research in aureomycin and antibiotics. Dr. Logan was the first African American woman surgeon to be elected a Fellow of the American College of Surgeons. Dr. Myra Logan was the first female surgeon to operate on the heart.

DOROTHY L. BROWN was born in 1919. She became an orphan at the age of five months. She lived in an orphanage until she was twelve years old. Brown and her foster parents lived in Troy, New York. She was able to receive a four year scholarship to Bennett College, North Carolina. She received it from the Troy Methodist Church's Women's Club. While she was studying at Bennett College, the officials were concerned about her future at the college. However, Brown was able to graduate second in her class. She received her M.D. degree from Meharry Medical College in 1944. She completed her internship at Harlem Hospital, New York, and her residency at Hubbard Hospital, Nashville, Tennessee. She served as Chief of Surgery at the Riverside Hospital, Nashville, Tennessee. She was a Fellow of the American College of Surgeons.

Dr. Brown was the first known African American woman surgeon to practice in the South. She was also the first Black woman to serve in the Tennessee State legislature. She was also the first single woman in the State of Tennessee to adopt a child. She was a recipient of the honorary Doctor of Science Degree from Russell Sage College, Troy, New York.

FREDERICK DOUGLASS STUBBS. was a barrier breaker in several areas. He graduated with honors from Dartmouth College, cum laude, and Phi Beta Kappa and also cum laude from Harvard Medical School in 1927 and 1931 respectively. Dr. Stubbs was the first known Black to become a member of the Harvard Chapter of Alpha Omega Alpha. He practiced medicine in Philadelphia, Pennsylvania and served as Chief of Surgery at Mercy and Douglass Hospitals. He was the first Black physician to be formally trained at Sea View Hospital, Staten island, New York, 1937-1939.

JANE COOKE WRIGHT is a graduate of Smith College, B.A. degree, 1942. She received her M.D. Degree from New York Medical College in 1945. She has served on the staff of Harlem Hospital and served as a Professor of Surgery at New York Medical College. Dr. Wright served on the President's commission on Heart Disease and Stroke in 1963. She made outstanding contributions in cancer chemotherapy or the use of chemicals in cancer treatment. Dr. Wright served as Dean of the New York Medical School. She is the daughter of noted physician, Dr. Louis T. Wright.

ARTHUR HOWELL JR. was born in Midland, North Carolina in 1926. He graduated valedictorian in 1943 from Logan High school, Concord, North Carolina. He graduated from Howard University with honors, cum laude with a B.S. in chemistry. After serving two years in the Navy, Howell entered Howard University's College of Medicine and received a M.D. Degree. Later he received a Doctor of Dental Science Degree (D.D.S.) from the Indiana University School of Dentistry, Indianapolis. In 1972, Dr. Howell became the first Black plastic surgeon in the United States to be certified by the American Board of Plastic and Reconstructive Surgery. Dr. Arthur Howell Jr. died January 26, 1991 at St. Luke's Hospital in Milwaukee, Wisconsin.

WILLIAM HARRY BARNES was born in Philadelphia, PA. He graduated from Central High School in Philadelphia. Dr. Barnes was the first Black to receive a four year scholarship to the University of Pennsylvania, where he attended their School of Medicine. He served on the medical staffs of Mercy and Douglass Hospitals. In 1918, he served as an acting assistant surgeon in the U.S. Public Health Services. Dr. Barnes was the first Black to be certified by an American Specialty Board in Otolaryngology in 1927. He was a President of the National Medical Association (NMA).

JAMES ROBERT GLADDEN was born in Charlotte, North Carolina in 1911. He received his B.S. Degree from Long Island College, New York and his M.D. Degree from Meharry Medical College in 1938. He was one of the first residents at

Freedmen's Hospital in orthopedic surgery. Dr. Gladden was the first Black certified by the American Board of Orthopedic Surgery in 1949.

Segregated Emergency Hospital Services

"In 1927, a Black child was injured in an automobile accident and was refused service at hospitals in Decatur, Alabama and other hospitals in Alabama. After he was finally admitted to a hospital in Huntsville, Alabama, he died of pneumonia caused by exposure and lack of medical care for several hours following the accident.

In November 1931, Miss Juliette Derricotte, former Dean of Women, Fisk University, Tennessee was injured in an accident at Dalton, Georgia. She was not admitted to the all white local hospital. Miss Derricotte died in an ambulance on the road to Chattanooga, Tennessee, fifty miles away.

The presence of all white hospitals were not just limited to southern cities. The North had its share. "On March 11, 1937, the wife of the noted composer, William C. Handy suffered a cerebral hemorrhage and was forced to wait in an ambulance outside the Knickerbocker Hospital, New York City, New York for fifty minutes while authorities argued whether they could admit Negroes to private rooms. Mrs. Handy died two hours later".

As late as the 1940's St. Louis University hospitals were segregated. There was a St. Mary's Infirmary for Blacks. One of the early integrated students at St. Louis University fell on some steps, she was transported across town to St. Mary's Infirmary whereas she could have been taken to the University Hospital several blocks away. That was the way it was in segregated medical facilities in St. Louis, Missouri.

A Black was critically injured in an auto accident on the way to Jacksonville, Florida in 1937. An ambulance arrived at the scene of the accident and the attendants observed that the injured person was Black and refused to carry him to the nearest hospital. When a second ambulance arrived to carry the man to a hospital that would accept Blacks, the injured man died later.

A Black lady in Washington, D. C. was suffering from high blood pressure and was bleeding from the nose. She lived on Sherman Avenue, NW near Fairmont Street. One block from her house was the all white Garfield Hospital. When the lady's physician arrived, he said I wish I could take you to Garfield Hospital right now, but there is no use. When the ambulance comes he will take you to Howard University's Freedman Hospital.

A very capable and efficient nurse worked at Hospital No. 2 in Anniston, Alabama. Number 2 was a section or wing of the white hospital that was provided for Blacks. Nurse Curry served sometimes as the Chief Nurse and also acting Doctor when the white physicians were busy. There were instances when a seriously injured Black patient would have to wait until the white Emergency Room doctor would finish with a minor case involving a white patient. This was a situation where the Blacks' pains lingered on and on.

Frederick Maryland's Memorial Hospital
Segregated Maternity Rooms, 1962

On April 14, 1962, a baby boy was born to a Army captain of color and his wife in Frederick Memorial Hospital, Frederick, Maryland. The Black Captain had made previous arrangements to reserve a private room for his wife and new baby. The room would cost him twenty-five dollars a day. When the captain arrived at the hospital to see his new baby and his wife, he took the elevator to the maternity floor and was proceeding towards the area of private rooms. When he entered the area, a nurse stopped him and told him that his wife and baby were in the ward down the hall. As he approached the ward area, he realized that it was the segregated Black area and that there was one private room that was reserved for Blacks. He had visited the hospital previously and knew where the private rooms were located, but he was not aware that the hospital had separate facilities for Blacks. The military in the 1960's was trying very hard not to have contracts with outside facilities that were still practicing segregation. When his family was ready to leave the hospital, he told the cashier that there would be no charge for the private room. The cashier said, No, your wife had a private room. He demanded to see the Hospital Administrator and asked for an explanation. The embarrassed administrator apologized and did not charge the Captain for the room. As he left the hospital he told his wife you had a little pain I know during the delivery of our son and I have a little pain now because of how they welcomed him into a still painful America that I serve so faithfully. This is another true story of the legacy of segregation.

An Emergency Treatment for High Blood Pressure In the 1940's
That's the Way We Were

Charles was the fifth child born to Ruth and Alonzo Durante. He was raised in a modest low middle class family. As a very young child at the age of nine years, he did not understand the medical term high blood pressure or hypertension. He only knew that his loving mother, Ruth, was a stout little lady that he loved so much who often experienced periods of being sick or recuperating from an illness.

He often remembered Christmas Eve when he was a little boy. Mother was busy cooking her favorite Christmas dishes and those sweet pastries that only she could bake, the fruit cakes, butter cakes, ginger bread, cookies and pies. She was also busy that Christmas Eve night wrapping gifts with the assistance of his three older sisters and one brother. Fortunately, his dad had arrived home early that night because around 10 o'clock Christmas Eve, mother had a serious attack of her blood pressure condition as they called it in those days. She felt faint and her head was like a pressure cooker, with tightness and feelings of a little pain and headaches. His father knew what was coming and he assisted her to a chair and immediately called our family doctor, said Charles as he retold this story years later. In those days, he said your physician would make house calls and without beepers, the telephone would still bring him to your home as soon as possible. They were very concerned and dedicated physicians, who had one specialty and that was providing the immediate cheerful and pleasant service to their patients with concern about payment later.

Charles' family doctor arrived very promptly. He said to his father, "Well Alonzo, it seems as though Ruth's pressure has hit the ceiling. We must get her upstairs to the bathroom immediately." Charles, quite upset and worried, watched quietly as his older brother, father and Doctor placed his stout mother in a chair and the three assisted in carrying her upstairs to the bathroom. Charles went upstairs, but he hid so he could not be seen as the doctor and his father worked with his mother in the bathroom. This young boy, of nine, saw the doctor induce bleeding from the nose of his mother and after filling the bath tub half full of water, he could observe the blood from his mother's nose dripping into the bath tub and the water now appearing as a bloody solution. Charles was seeing a possible crude but necessary procedure to lower a person's blood pressure immediately until other medical procedures could be administered. This was in the 1940's and that was the way it was on Christmas Eve for the Durante family.

Charles recalled that the doctor who had delivered all five children at home knew his mother's medical history and did not have to ponder or procrastinate as to what is the best approach for this emergency. Later, his mother was placed in bed and Charles said his mother remained in bed for some two weeks recuperating from a serious high blood pressure attack and gaining her strength back. Charles realized in later years that the medicines that we are fortunate to have for the treatment of high blood pressure today were not available for his mother in the 1940's.

At the age of 17 years when his sisters and brother were away at school, Charles was at home when his mother became seriously ill with high blood pressure again. Unfortunately, the family had moved to another city and a new young physician was treating his mother. When the doctor arrived Charles had just finished assisting his mother in a chair and dragging it to the bathroom. He was at home taking care of her but when the condition worsened, the doctor was called. He stood at his mother's bedside when he observed this competent physician examining his mother and then he took a seat, placed his hands over his face and was in deep thought for a few minutes. Then, he looked up at Charles and said, "Please call your father at work and also see if we can get a private ambulance to have your mother admitted immediately to St. Mary's Infirmary Hospital". St Mary's was the Black hospital for Blacks operated by the Catholic Church in the Midwestern city. The doctor told Charles after the ambulance had arrived, "I believe that your mother has had or is going into a cerebral hemorrhage, blood is going to the brain."

Charles' mother died a week later of a cerebral hemorrhage due to hypertension. Charles learned later that while his mother was dying in the hospital, a very distinguished physician and surgeon of color who lived in the community was being operated on for the same condition his mother had, but he died on the operating table. But Charles was wondering why is it his mother was not given the operation. He learned later that at that time it was a new surgical procedure that had not been perfected and that the doctor was taking the chance at that time.

Two years after his mother died, Charles learned that his mother's room mate had related the following story to a person who knew his family. She said that during the night prior to the morning of his mother's demise,. her roommate heard her say something for the first time since she was in the room. Charles' mother said, according to the lady, "Jesus, I am ready, and called two names Alonzo and Charles". These words have always been part of Charles' comfort and belief that his mother's victory unto Christ was won.

Charles' experiences with his mother's illness were a motivator for him to study medicine to help others. But living in that time and the way it was, he was not able to be accepted for medical school because of the strong competition to enter Howard or Meharry or those white schools that were accepting Blacks at that time. He selected another profession but he always remembers his early experiences about an early treatment for hypertension. That was the way we were with some rudimentary medical treatment in yesteryears.

A Physician's Views On Race Mortality, 1903

The late Dr. James Randall Wilder, a graduate of Howard University School of Medicine, Class of 1888, wrote a speech on the Negro's mortality in 1903. Some of the major highlights of his speech were: Dr Randall wrote that the occupations of the Negro tend to keep him in the background and to encourage a neglect on the part of the census enumerator to record accurately all of the Negroes in a certain locality. But the Negro dies faster than the white man and it is not my purpose to deny it, but to recite a few of the real causes of the disparity in the cities of the South and to show how the mortality is to be lessened.

Dr. Randall said American slavery with its unparalleled cruelty and bestiality has injured the Negro intellectually, physically and morally. It has been claimed that the admixture of the Negro with the Caucasian has given us a resulting mulatto, weaker physically than either of the parent stock. This belief is based upon hypothesis and is not true or borne out by the facts in the case. It is true, however that a resulting lowering of vitality has followed the admixture of kindred blood which was almost unavoidable during the days of slavery. This was the result of certain well known procreative practices that obtained on the part of the white master and on account of the itinerary state of the Negro, incident to his chattelism. Randall said that in those dark days it was hard enough for the Negro to recognize his near kin on his maternal side and it was infinitely impossible for him to trace the family tree from the paternal side. The evil effects of this admixture of similar blood cannot be denied and must bear a modicum (small amount) of responsibility for the excessive mortality of the Negro today.

You Do Not Know Me

A mid western physician of color who likes to dress in casual neat attire when not at work, wears a sweater, sport shirt and pants or even jeans. As we would say in the Black community, he does not dress or look like a doctor. He is a very personable and pleasant individual who is accepted and admired by many for his casual and down to earth manner with all classes of people. Just a few days ago, in May, 1996, he visited a jewelry store in his town, dressed casually and he told his wife when he arrived home that he was amazed how he was greeted and treated in the store. He was watched and the usual concern or sensitive surveillance by some merchants was prevalent. He stated at his age of over sixty years that it is still there. You are Black and you must realize that even if they do not know you, you are still that Black person, with potential to do something wrong.

Color Me Black

The Civil Rights Movement of the 1960's and earlier had very interesting stories and accounts of individual's dealing first with themselves and others. A Caucasian psychiatrist told me that he had an African American young lady patient who was a mulatto with very distinguishing so called Caucasian features to visit his office. Her parents were an upper middle class Boston, Massachusetts' family of color. The young lady's problem, said the physician, was coping with decisions to conceal her white looking physical descriptions and a desire to appear more Black like her peers at school. She tried very diligently to create a hair style of a bush or Afro and used some creams to darken her skin. That was the way it was for some young mulatto teenager yesterday.

True Human Interest Stories

These stories relate to some experiences of patients and physicians during segregation and after.

Early Black Views On Black Doctors

A former slave woman named Sarah Fitzpatrick, born and enslaved in Alabama, worked as a house servant. At the age of 90 years, she was interviewed in 1938 and said the following: Even since I have been grown, I had good health until a few years ago. When I was a child I had typhoid fever. They had good white doctors in those days. When the colored got sick, especially those who worked in the big house, the mistress gave them medicine and the colored mammies worked on them. Back then, we always had white doctors. I did not have a colored doctor put his hands on me until about seven years ago. (note - she was 83 years old at that time). I just thought a white doctor understood my constitution better than a colored doctor. I got a daughter living in Cleveland, Ohio, and she sent for me to come up there and spend some time with her. While I was there I got sick and they sent for a doctor to come in, and when I found out he was a colored doctor, I sure did feel funny with that colored doctor waiting on me. Then when I came back home I had a colored doctor again; so now I feel safe with him.

Do You Have Indian Genes?

An African American physician happened to ask her patient a question. She said it is interesting how you look so much like an Indian. Do you have Indian genes? The patient replied, "My mother is an Indian and my father is half Black and Indian. However, I have problems interacting with people if I say I am an Indian, and I just decided to be called a Black American.

This story was related to me in a conversation with a lady on July 13, 1993. When this lady was born that was the way she was genetically and over the years she was confronted with people who had a problem themselves in dealing with her mixed heritage. But through the years, I believe this lady has found peace with herself by being accepted as a Black.

Are you Going to Examine Me?

There are many true stories about the past involving the trials and tribulations that the Black physician and surgeons experienced some 35 years ago. I am sure that many of those doctors had dozens of stories to relate especially with Black and white relations in civilian and military life. Sometimes it is very difficult to tell college students of all ages and color how it really was prior to the 1970's when they were not living or if they were, they had no knowledge of some of the problems that Black physicians confronted in those yesteryears. I also believe many younger physicians of all colors today do not really realize the historical, psychological and residual effects that race has today on some peoples minds. They will use the popular term, it is an isolated incident or you are sensitive and you must believe that it is necessary for them to respond that way to a particular incident. In other words some of these energetic, and intellectual young medical specialists really need a course in the real facts of historical America and racism. They were not isolated incidents yesterday and today, I can recall that when I went on sick call in 1959 at the Fort Leavenworth, Kansas Army Hospital, I was seen by a young Black physician. It was a rarity at that time because there were only four or five Black junior officers, lieutenants and captains permanently assigned to the Army Garrison at Fort Leavenworth. I asked the doctor what was his specialty? He replied, I am a gynecologist and I was assigned here on that military occupational specialty (MOS) for a vacancy. However, when I arrived they decided to assign me as a general medical officer. Now without going into specific details, I told the doctor, I have received the message because you know we have some high ranking officers with their wives stationed here, and I can only speculate that was part of the decision not to assign you as the gynecologist.

In 1993, I went to the medical facility at a Maryland Air Force Base and was seen by an African contract doctor who worked for the military. Ironically, he shared with me that on several occasions, Whites would arrive at his office door and then would tactfully leave because they had recognized who would be examining them. I believe I have referred to this previously in the manuscript. However, I am stating it again to show that this is the real world. These are things that are not important to some people and the news media and especially those people who think this is a color blind society. As I said before my young friends and adults, I only tell true stories. The following is a true story that happened and it involved a very competent and outstanding physician and surgeon of color during the early days of his successful medical career.

This Black surgeon was on duty one evening at a U.S. Air Force Base Hospital some 35 years ago. He was preparing his patients for the next days surgery, mostly paper work for admittance and a brief examination. A white woman, the wife of a sergeant, entered his office and at her surprise, she was greeted by the Black doctor. She says, "Are you going to have to examine me?" The doctor replied, "Yes, from head to toe". The woman said " I would rather that you not examine me, you see, I am prejudiced and I think I'd better go outside and discuss this with my husband". The doctor then said "Take these medical records with you when you go to talk with your husband". The doctor handed her a folder containing all of her records. The lady took the folder and left. Since she was the doctor's last patient for the evening, he also left. As he was leaving, the nurse on duty said, "Doctor, you have not seen the patient sitting here". The doctor looked over to the waiting area and noticed that it was the same woman and her husband. The doctor replied to the nurse, "I am sorry, but she is prejudiced". The nurse was astonished and asked what the problem was. The doctor explained the situation to the nurse. He then said "Good night" and left. However, the next day the incident had spread all over the surgical department and eventually the whole hospital. The hospital commander as well as the other doctors were furious. The sergeant and his wife were informed that she would not have her surgery at that hospital. She was also informed that if she was to have the surgery, she would have to use a local civilian hospital and doctor which would cost her a great amount of money. The doctor said it was not known what she did. But one thing for sure, said the physician of color, she did not have surgery at that Air Force Base hospital.

Segregated Hospitals, Kansas City, Missouri, 1908

The city of Kansas City, Missouri operated segregated hospitals as early as 1908 and later. A new hospital was built at 23rd and Cherry Streets and was called General Hospital No. 1 for Whites and the old city hospital was called General hospital No. 2., for Blacks. It was not until 1911 that Black doctors joined the staff at Hospital No. 2., and in 1914, Blacks were given the responsibility of managing their segregated hospital. It is believed that it was the first public city hospital in the country to initiate that affirmative action of that day and time. General Hospital had several Black medical specialists. Some of the pioneer physicians on the staff were: Dr. J. Edward Perry and Dr. Thomas C. Unthank who had established the all Black Douglass Hospital in Kansas City, Kansas.

Medical Treatment For Southern Maryland Blacks, 1920-1930's

Black families in the Brandywine area of Southern Maryland had to travel to Freedmen's Hospital, Washington, D.C., for their medical treatment, or go to Baltimore, Maryland's City hospital or the University of Maryland's hospital, which had colored and white entrances.

Segregated Medical Facilities, Detroit, Michigan, 1920's

A Dr. Alexander Turner was the only Black physician who had staff privileges at a large Detroit general hospital. Other Black physicians had no facilities to provide care for their seriously ill patients. This segregated practice necessitated that some Black doctors open private hospitals. Dr. David Northcross opened a private hospital in the southeastern area of Detroit. It was called Mercy General hospital or Northcross Hospital. Later, some Black citizens incorporated the Dunbar hospital. Sometimes whites would make exceptions to include one Black in their segregated facilities. When the Detroit Receiving Hospital opened in 1915 and refused to admit Black interns or resident physicians despite protest by the NAACP, they did make one concession. They gave Dr. Chester Ames an internship as a special personal favor. He was the son of a Dr. J.W. Ames.

In 1950, there were four ratified board specialists practicing in Detroit. They were Drs. Harold Thornell and Robert Greenridge, X-Ray; Drs. A.B. Henderson, Medicine and Remus Robinson, Surgery.

Segregation in Veterans Hospitals

The practice of segregation varied throughout the country for some veteran medical facilities. In the South Blacks were treated in separate wards, and were excluded at some VA medical facilities. The majority of Blacks were treated at Tuskegee's VA Hospital. In 1947, Veteran Hospitals had separate wards and 19 VA Hospitals in the South did not admit Blacks. Blacks did protest about the government segregated facilities. Representative Adam Clayton Powell Jr. joined in the protest.

Admission of Black Staff Physicians

During the period, 1946-1948, some white hospitals began to admit Black staff physicians and interns to their staffs for the first time. I believe that it is necessary to revisit these actions of 50 years ago to see how Blacks had to demand, protest be patient and have faith that things would eventually improve in race relations. This information is not available in most public and private education curricula. The struggle to bring Black people thus far has not been a gift from the government or individuals.

The hospitals which opened their doors and the physicians who went in to integrate the facilities were: Newark, N.J. Hospital, Dr. E. Mae Carroll; Cook County Hospital, Chicago, Ill., Dr. Leonidas H. Berry; (he removed a 50 year tradition of excluding Black physicians) Sydenham Hospital, New York City, N.Y., Dr. Frank B. Adam; Winter Veterans Hospital, Topeka, Kansas, Dr. Rutherford B. Stevens, resident psychiatrist; Bronx Hospital, New York, staff appointments of Drs. T. Roosevelt Gathings and Arthur J. Sayers; Philadelphia General Hospital, Pa., Dr. Maurice Clifford internship; Queens General Hospital, Queens, N.Y., Dr. A.R. Tweed; Waverly Hills Unit, General Hospital, Louisville, Kentucky, Dr. John McPhaer, intern. There was a plan to admit one Negro intern each year. Would this be called a quota today? The Los Angeles, California Hospital appointed Dr. Oner B. Barker Jr. to a 3 year residency in internal medicine. The Gallinger Municipal Hospital, Washington, D.C. decided to admit Black resident physicians.

John E.T. Camper
A Physician and Civil Rights Activist

Teaching at a predominantly Black University can be very rewarding when you are able to communicate with young Black students and also read their personal thoughts on many subjects. I have learned that many students are not aware of some courageous men and women of color who years ago demonstrated their sincere and personal convictions to challenge the American system of legal segregation and ostracism of African Americans. I am sure that they have not heard or read about a physician who could take the time from his medical profession and pave the way for youth and adults today to have a better opportunity to achieve goals in a society that still struggles with the issues of civil rights.

The man who believed in standing up, marching, if necessary to protest continuing policies of discrimination in hiring practices in Baltimore City's white owned stores was John E. T. Camper, M.D. Dr. Camper, with the support of Baltimore's NAACP President, Juanita Jackson Mitchell, created a Citizen Committee for Justice. One of Camper's main tasks was to unite Baltimore's Black physicians to support the civil rights movement. His continual protest in the 1940's did bring some results. An internal legislative committee to study the problems of Baltimore Blacks was created, and Camper was appointed to the State Board that administered Crownville State Mental Institution and also to the governor's committee. Dr. Camper assisted in the voter registration drives.

A Layperson In The Operating Room

A man named Viven Thomas of Baltimore, Maryland, was for 30 years the Supervisor of the John Hopkins Surgical Research Laboratory. He was born in New Iberia, Louisiana. He attended Tennessee A and I University, Nashville, Tennessee. In 1930, he worked as a surgical assistant for Dr. Albert Blaylock, or Blalock, of

Vanderbilt University. Later, he accompanied Dr. Blaylock to Johns Hopkins University Baltimore, Maryland where Blaylock had been appointed as the Chief of Surgery in 1941. In 1944, Drs. Helen Taussig and Blaylock were recognized internationally for their "blue baby" operation on a fourteen month old girl. At this time, there was no recognition involvement of Thomas in the operation. It has been stated that the success of the procedure could not have been accomplished without Thomas' earlier and then current research. Vivien Thomas was advising the two doctors throughout the historic operation, because he had performed the same operation more than 300 times on dogs. He had worked with the doctors in the development of the surgical procedures for the operation. The condition of the patient was known as "Tetralogy of Fallot or blue-baby syndrome". The operation in future years saved thousands of children and corrected the lack of oxygen in their blood that causes the appearance of a pinkish blue color. Finally in 1969, some recognition was given to Vivien. A group of former John Hopkins surgical residents commissioned a portrait of Thomas that was presented to the Hospital and in 1976 he was awarded an honorary doctorate. This true story of Vivien Thomas is an example of how Blacks during segregation were denied credit and recognition for their outstanding achievements when working inside white institutions.

Segregated Provisions In the Hill - Burton Act, 1946

The Hill-Burton Act was passed in August, 1946. The act provided federal funds for the construction of hospitals. The legislation stipulated that "the hospitals must either accept Negro patients or give assurance that separate hospital facilities will be available to Negro patients in the area". Many hospitals were built in the south with federal assistance. However in 1962, there were 98 hospitals that would accept no Blacks. The others would provide separate areas for Negroes. Atlanta hospitals had a total of 4,000 available beds, and only 600 were reserved for Blacks. Some hospitals would place the beds for Black patients in the hospital's basements and services for obstetrics and pediatrics were not available. There was considerable segregation in private hospitals, thereby overcrowding the available public hospitals for Blacks.

The Importance of Family History In Patient Diagnosis

During segregation and even today many individuals of all ethnic groups look at Black people and their first glances register guarded emotions, if sufficient physical descriptive indicators are present, namely hair, nose, skin color, and eyes. In July 1947, the son of two Blacks was diagnosed at one month old as mongoloid; in a clinic at Washington, D.C.'s old Children's Hospital. (Today's term for this condition is Downs syndrome). When the mother was informed about her abnormal baby boy, she called her family physician. When he examined the child, he told the parents that the physician at the hospital could have been a little confused because of the baby's slant eyes which are a major visible symptom. The family physician said the doctor probably was not aware that his father was half Chinese and a mulatto. The next day, the mother called the doctor at Children's hospital and talked with him. He said "Oh, I did not know the baby's family background and do you have any baby pictures of you other children? She said, "Yes", She went to the hospital the next day and carried the pictures of her other children. A girl of 5 years and a boy 10 years and also had the children to accompany her. Ironically, their baby pictures showed no hair and their eyes were slanted, but not as much as the new born baby. The doctor decided to further examine the baby and noticed that he kept pushing out his tongue, which usually was a sign of retardation. The doctor told the mother, "since you have told me about your baby's background and knowing that he is of Mongolian descent, I would like to keep a constant check on him. Please bring him in every two weeks". Unfortunately, for the parents within several months, it was fully confirmed that he was a "Downs Syndrome child".

The mother in this case was a Black mulatto who genetically was the daughter of a Black mulatto mother and a father whose father was Jewish and whose mother was a brown skinned Egyptian. But remember during segregation and even in 1998, the characters in this story would still be classified as Black regardless of their heterogeneous genetic make ups. Only in our "America the Beautiful".

"Breast Feeding and The Brain"

There was a recent article published in the *Journal of Pediatrics* on the impact of breast feeding on a child's mental abilities. Researchers in New Zealand studied some one thousand children through their 18th birthday. Some of their findings were "the longer a child is breast fed, the more likely he or she is to have higher scores on tests of cognitive ability and on standardized tests of reading and mathematics. The study is most interesting when one reflects on child rearing during the time of slavery which could suggest another study. During slavery and even in the days of segregation, the mammy or Black nurse maid breast fed many white babies in the South. As late as 1995, a 51 years old white active duty colonel from Mississippi told me that he was breast fed, by a Black woman or his "mammy". I pose the question, What effect, if any, did the chemical substance of the Black woman's milk have on those white babies over hundreds of years?. Maybe her milk has contributed to the genius of some white scholars who have written about the inferiority of Black Americans. I am sure they did not consider this now controversial subject. Just another example of "nutritional reasoning".

LAW ENFORCEMENT

Blacks and the Justice System During Segregation

Many Blacks did not have confidence in the court system, they believed they could not find justice by the due process of the law. Police protection to Black communities in some cities was limited to patrol cars cruising on the main streets. Police departments were involved in city politics, and they would work in political campaigns often receiving promises of employment. A considerable number of Blacks became informers, spotters or "stool pigeons". Then some Blacks were arrested for drunkenness; they received harsher punishment than white men arrested for the same offense. There would be conductors on trains who were given police powers to enforce regulations of segregation. Some conductors were armed with guns used to threaten and intimidate Black passengers. A white man on February 18, 1936 in Raleigh, North Carolina, was executed for killing a Negro. This definitely was a rarity, probably the first recorded incident of this kind in the news media. Some poor Whites and Blacks were known to carry deadly weapons. They carried guns, knives and long pocket knives with sharp, 4 inch blades. They were called "crab apple switches".

Mob Action, Chicago, Illinois, 1940

A white family living in a suburbs of Chicago, Kenwood, invited some Blacks to their home for a party in December 1940. A group of lower class whites gathered outside of their home and broke the house windows. It was necessary for police to provide some protection and evacuate safely the party guests. The white owners of the home were shot by the mob.

"Permission Not Granted"

During the 1940's a white lady in Princeton, New Jersey, was planning a dinner party and some Blacks were to be invited. She was visited by a delegation of white leaders in the town who told her she could not invite the Blacks. This was not in Georgia, but in Princeton, New Jersey. Segregation had no geographical boundaries.

"What Blacks Want, Is Justice"

Langston Hughes, the late noted poet and writer wrote an essay in 1944 on "What the Negro Wants". In reference to law enforcement and justice, he was echoing what many Blacks were asking in the segregation era. Hughes wrote: We want a fair deal before the law. That means we desire Negroes on all jury panels, and that we be fairly called for jury service. We desire the right to elect judges, desire adequate legal representation". He also said that "Negroes desire police protection from police brutality, which is severe in Negro neighborhoods; we desire Negro policemen, and we desire equality before the law." These words were written 48 years ago and we still hear some of these "wants" today. Again, Black people have been asking America for things that other citizens enjoy from the first day they arrive in this country.

Police Color Obsession During Segregation

The Chief of Police of a Midwestern town's in the 1940's would raid any place where Negroes and Whites were associating as equals. The Chief and his officers would intimidate light colored women with dark skinned escorts, "beat up and shoot bad Niggers" in self defense and raid Black's homes without a warrant. In one town, the police would threaten to cancel the license of any Negro taxicab driver observed transporting a white passenger, and especially a white woman.

A Convincing Survival Speech

The late distinguished educator and founder of the Piney Woods Country Life School, Piney Woods, Mississippi, Laurence Clifton Jones, was born November 21, 1884 in St. Louis, Missouri. He was the son of John Q. and Lydia Foster Jones. He married Grace Morris Allen. They were the parents of Turner Harris Jones and Lawrence Clifton Jones Jr. Jones received the bachelor of Philosophy Degree from the University of Iowa in 1907, a certificate of accomplishment, 1947, and a Doctor of Humane Letters. He founded and built a school for boys and girls in Mississippi in 1909. He was 25 years old when he started the school without any funds. Today, this school is still open and has modern facilities. The following true story relates how Jones tactfully confronted and dealt with white people during those segregated days in Mississippi. An incident that occurred during World War II reflects his courage and tact.

Jones was addressing an audience of Black people at a revival. He told the people that they must fight against sin, ignorance, superstition, and poverty. Evidently some white racists were listening outside and misunderstood what Laurence Jones was saying. The whites believed that Jones was inciting his people to fight Whites. Suddenly the Whites formed a hate mob outside. They apprehended Jones and threw him on a pile of wood. The Whites stood near him with their weapons in hand, ready to fire. A member of the racist mob suggested that Jones make a speech. Considering that his life was in danger and also fearing what could happen to other Blacks, it is believed that Laurence Jones used superb tact, common sense and unique ways of calming the emotions of an enraged White mob of potential killers. Jones' remarks were able to convince the Whites that he was not talking about Blacks fighting Whites or starting a riot. The White mob released Jones. They were a little friendly toward Jones after almost lynching him.

Early Segregated Legislation

There was restrictive legislation passed by the District of Columbia Corporation in 1827. An act required the registration of all free colored people and their families to include proof of freedom. There was also an ordinance that prohibited free Color persons from going out on the streets after ten o'clock in the evening without special permission. The violation was a ten dollar fine. An act of 1836 forbade secret, private and religious meetings of colored people beyond 10:00 p.m. There was a five dollar fine. These laws were not repealed until 1862.

A Dr. Roderick Badger practiced dentistry in Atlanta, Georgia in 1905 and was a graduate of Howard University. When he arrived in Atlanta, the white citizens presented a petition to the city council stating that they could not tolerate a Black dentist in their community. The city council responded to their request by requiring all free persons of color who come to Atlanta to pay 200 hundred dollars to the clerk of the court, failure to do so would merit five days in jail.

Police Brutality, Raleigh N.C., 1920's

The late C.C. Spaulding who was the President of North Carolina Mutual Life Insurance Company which in 1920's was one of the largest Negro insurance companies in the world with a surety of more than 35 million dollars in force and employed 879 employees in the home and field forces to include 500 medical examiners, was arrested for purchasing a bottle of soda water. The newspaper account of the incident read: "Mr. Spaulding was visiting the Raleigh office of his company and went into a white cigar stand located in a building belonging to a Negro man and purchased a bottle of soda water, which he started to drink in the back of the store. The clerk ordered him out. Mr. Spaulding was assaulted, two of his teeth were knocked out and he was maltreated".

"Arrested, the assailant was put under a bond of only $25 and was let off with the maximum fine of $15. So deeply incensed were the Negro citizens that special policemen were called out for that beat. The better element of white citizens deplored the incident".

States' Rights - Not Outside Interference

The current efforts by the President's Race Relations Committee are to be commended. However if one examines the historical beliefs of white Americans over the years and really interprets the goals of Contract America, their aims have been addressed by leaders over the years, simply leaving local problems to the individual states. President Coolidge expressed these views in an address to congress in December, 1923. He said: "..Numbered among our population are some 12,000,000 colored people. Under our Constitution their rights are just as sacred as those of any other citizen. It is both a public and a private duty to protect those rights. . . . On account of the migration of large numbers into industrial centers, it has been proposed that a commission be created, composed of members from both races, to formulate a better policy for mutual understanding and confidence. Such an effort is to be commended. Everyone would rejoice in the accomplishment of the results which it seeks. <u>But it is well to recognize that these difficulties are to a large extent local problems which must be worked out by the mutual forbearance and human kindness of each community. Such a method gives much more promise of a real remedy than outside interference</u>".

Southerner Justice

In the 1930's, a man of color is pleading for a white farmer to obtain medical care for his dying father who was injured in an accident. The Black man's car accidentally ran into the farmer's fence. When the son, insisted that the white farmer call an ambulance, the farmer called the police and had the Black man arrested for possible manslaughter. Fortunately, two qualified Black lawyers went South to plead the Black man's case, and finally the charges were dropped. But somehow over the years and possibly even today that pain of racism lingers.

LEGAL INJUSTICE

A bulletin was issued to the all Black troops of the 92nd Division stationed at Camp Funston, Kansas, Several paragraphs of the bulletin stated in March 28, 1918. "It should be well known to all colored officers and men that no useful purpose is served by such acts as will cause the color question to be raised. It is not a question of legal rights, but a question of policy . . . . A sergeant entered a theater as he undoubtedly had a legal right to do, and precipitated trouble by making it possible to allege racial discrimination in the seat he was given. He is strictly within his legal right in the matter and the theater manager is legally wrong. Nevertheless, the sergeant is guilty of the greater wrong in doing anything, no matter how legally correct, that will provoke racial animosity.

Community and Police Relations

The YMCA in Washington had very good relations with the police department.

In September, 1942, the Washington, D.C. Twelfth Street YMCA hosted jujitsu classes conducted by Clifford Buck Smith. Prior to the 1980's and 1990's when many Americans became quite concerned about personal safety and protection against crime related street attacks and even at home, the YMCA was addressing these problems in 1942.

Clifford Buck Smith and his assistants presented a demonstration of jujitsu in hand to hand combat. The classes conducted at the YMCA were offered to the Black metropolitan police officers from the 13th Street Precinct on U Street near 8th Street, and District of Columbia citizens of color. Many of the classes were directed toward policemen and policewomen who were daily faced with the problems of disarming dangerous criminals and prisoners. The demonstrations and classes were also available for civilians especially women who wanted to know how to take care of themselves against potential criminals and predatory people.

Mr. Clifford Buck Smith was assisted by some women and auxiliary policemen during his demonstrations. They were Misses Lunabelle Wedlock and Bernice Thomas, and S. L. Jackson.

"Pull over Boy!"

The year was 1965 and Franz had just buried his father back East. He was returning to his military base in Alabama around 4 o'clock a.m. in the morning, when he was stopped by a city policeman near Pritchard, Alabama. Franz was a young captain in the United States Army and was stationed at Fort McClellan, Alabama. It was a normal thing for him to wear his uniform while traveling South, somehow he believed it was a badge of some protection or respect that he would receive while traveling through some still Confederate flag waving towns and counties in Alabama. He had a large brief case in the back area of his car and he was carrying about two hundred dollars cash in the brief case.

The tall stout white policeman stopped Franz when he was driving within the posted speed limit of 25 miles per hour. The officer said, "Get out of the car, show me your license and registration and also boy where is the liquor you are carrying", Well Franz was not carrying any liquor and after looking in the trunk of the car, the policeman was convinced that he did not have any liquor in the car. The policemen then looked in the back of the car and saw on the floor the briefcase. Franz was quite concerned because he had heard of actual situations where some white policeman would take all of a Black person's money.

Realizing that there were only two people standing near the car, a white policeman and himself, Franz was cautious, polite but somewhat stood his firm ground, when he said "Officer this is my personal briefcase and my military papers are in the briefcase." The officer paused and said, "Okay, you can go." Then Franz said, "Officer, I thank you very much", extended his hand and the white Alabama policeman who said, "I don't shake no nigger's hand." Well, that is the way it was in Alabama in 1965 and the way some of us were forced to experience life.

Ku Klux Klan During Segregation

The Ku Klux Klan (KKK) was organized after the end of the Civil War, 1865, in Pulaski, Tennessee by six confederate veterans. It is believed that they wanted to frighten the former slaves. The group used white sheets, ghost like attire and they developed titles such as "dragons, cyclops, titans, circle of spooks, KuKlos, Klan craft and the final name, Ku Klux Klan. They had ceremonies, passwords, codes, prayers, solemn oaths of secrecy and some religious rights. There were also hooded night raiders. The Klan was present in the southern states of Alabama, Georgia, and Mississippi by 1869. They were organized throughout the South within five years. Although the U.S. Congress passed laws in 1871 making it a federal offense to violate a citizens' civil rights, an all white jury would normally acquit whites in the state courts.

There was a rebirth of the Klan in 1915. When a best seller was released The Klansman; then a motion picture called, *the Birth of a Nation* was produced. I told the story of the stereotyped Blacks stressing their inferiorities. The Klans also held a ceremony on Georgia's Stone Mountain located near Atlanta, Georgia. The KKK stated their opposition and hatred of European immigrants, Catholics, Jews and Blacks. Their membership began to increase in the North and Midwest, especially in Pennsylvania, Maine, Oregon and Indiana. The Ku Klux Klan had their march down Washington, D.C.'s Pennsylvania Avenue in the 1920's. They were able to assist in the elections of 16 politicians to the U.S. Senate and eleven governors, mayors, sheriffs and city councilmen. They were in favor of the 1924 Immigration Restriction Act, which reduced the number of Mediterranean and Slavic immigrants to America. It was reported that in Chicago, Illinois, some 1500 college students made Klan robes and hoods their prom costumes. Some would sing the lyric "Daddy swiped the last clean sheet".

The KKK was alleged to have been involved in the bombing of a Birmingham, Alabama, church where four little Black girls were killed in 1963. Viola Liuzzo, a white Detroit, Michigan volunteer, was killed in a car in Alabama while transporting a Black youth during the 1965 Selma-Montgomery voting rights march. A Black man was kidnaped at random by two Klansmen who beat him to death with a tree limb, slit his throat and hanged him.

Proof of KKK Letter Writings of Black's Warnings

During the period of segregation, the Ku Klux Klan would notify Blacks of their intentions if they would not conform to their wishes. The late Thomas Sewell Inborden was an early educator of color in Arkansas, Georgia and North Carolina. He had attended Oberlin College and graduated from Fisk University. He was born in the Blue Ridge Mountains of Upperville, Virginia in 1865. It has been suggested that Inborden was possibly the son of General Robert E. Lee or some cultured southern white gentleman. The American Missionary Association in 1895 sent him to Enfield, North Carolina, to found the Joseph Keasbey Brick Normal School, where he was principal for many years. He knew several distinguished Black leaders, Frederick Douglass, Booker T. Washington and William Pickens. He was a community leader, the farmers' friend and advisor.

Many books and even movies have been made available to the public to learn about the Ku Klux Klan. One thing about a primary source is that its contents are factual and leaves no doubt as to its authenticity. On July 18, 1929, a letter was sent to Thomas Sewell Inborden at the Brick School. The letter read: "Professor Inborden, it is with regret that we find it necessary to call your attention to this matter and warn you thus. We find that for recent months you have been taking up considerable time and made a close associate of one Dr. M.E. Dubissette. After having given his record a thorough investigation, we find that his policies, principles and activities are very undesirable. He is a treacherous and dangerous character, one who is designed to create and cause trouble both in his own circles and among races. If you value your past record and standing in the community, your future, for yourself and family and the welfare of your people, we advise you here and now and urge that you put a stop in your association with or coming under the influence of Dr. Dubissette. Accept this warning and save further trouble in the future. Knights of the Ku Klux Klan".

The letter from the Ku Klux Klan definitely supports the fact that they were present in the area of Enfield, North Carolina in 1929. It is believed that Inborden continued his interest in the hospital project that was being planned by the Black citizens in the local communities.

Lynching

The NAACP and Tuskegee Institute (now University) should be given credit for their documentation over the years of lynching records of Blacks during the period 1882-1947. An analysis of some statistics revealed that out of a total of 4,717 lynchings of Whites and Negroes, that some 1,291 whites were lynched and some 3,426 Blacks during the stated period. When I lecture about lynching in my U.S. History classes in college, I tell the students that one must realize the importance of time by years and the political system reinterpretations of the Constitution through the years in order to arrive at decisions that will provide equal rights for all citizens and also eliminate gross injustices which represent a legal component of segregation. This as I continue to mention throughout this book is most essential for young people as well as others under the ages of 50 years, who in most cases have no understanding about lynching. Yes, this should also be known by our newly arrived immigrants, who are now hailed as a minority.

The following true stories depict some classic cases, occurring as late as the 1940's, that were instrumental in changing the minds of the Black robed defenders of the justice system to finally, after years of protest by Blacks and concerned Whites, pass anti-lynching legislation.

James Edward Person was a Black who was lynched in Danville, Illinois (not Georgia) in October, 1942. Four years later nine white farmers were tried for the offense in the U.S. District Court in Danville, Illinois. Their shrewd legal advice was to plead "nolo contendere". (This is when the defendant's pleading does not admit guilt, but subjects him to punishment as though he had pleaded guilty). The defendants were ordered to pay a fine of 300 dollars each and court costs. The plea was actually a compromise between the state and defendant.

There were some attempts by the White House and the Department of Justice to intervene after pressure and nation-wide attention by national groups who offered rewards. Some of the concerned American groups were the Civil Liberties Union, Civil Rights Congress, Southern Regional Council, NAACP, Baptist Ministers Conference of Chicago, Atlanta Defense Group, Ohio Negro Chamber of Commerce and the Elks. After numerous investigations and finally some Grand Juries were convened. However, let the following results speak for themselves:

Monroe, Georgia case. Two Black couples were killed on July 25, 1946 near the Watson County - Oconee County line in Georgia. The victims were Mr. and Mrs.

Roger Malcolm and Mr. and Mrs. George Dorsey. They worked as farm hands for two white farmers. Both couples were around 20 years of age.

It was alleged that Roger Malcolm had been arrested for stabbing the white farmer, Barney Hester, for whom he worked. Malcolm was upset over Hester's paying attention to his wife. However, Malcolm was released from jail under a bond of 600 dollars. His friend J. Loy Harrison supplied Malcolm's bail and the two couples left the jail in the direction of the farms. They were stopped by a white mob of twenty, ordered from the car, and shot to death. Governor Ellis Arnell of Georgia did offer a reward of 10,000 dollars for evidence leading to the identification of the lynchers. The FBI was also involved. A Federal Grand Jury was convened in Athens, Georgia and both Harrison and Hester were questioned as well as one hundred other witnesses. There were two Blacks present on the jury. After a three week hearing of the Grand Jury, no witness questioned could reveal the identity of any of the lynchers and no one was indicted. A year later, the U.S. Justice Department announced that it had closed its investigation of the case.

<u>Corporal John C. Jones case</u>. Corporal Jones, 28 years old was arrested and jailed on a charge of breaking and entering the house of a white woman. Later, he was released when the woman failed to press formal charges. Jones was accompanied by his 17 year old cousin, Albert Harris, when their car was stopped shortly after his release from jail. Two car loads of white men forced Jones into one car and his cousin another car. Albert Harris was beaten into unconsciousness by the mob and left for dead along the road side. The body of Corporal Jones, a veteran of World War II, was found defaced, burned and partially castrated. The corner believed that he had been beaten with a wide leather belt or a thick plank and that a blow torch had been used on his body. His cousin, Albert Harris, was found alive and fortunately hidden by NAACP officials and safety carried out of Minden, Louisiana, where the killing occurred, to New York City.

On October 18, 1946, a federal grand jury convened in Minden, Louisiana indicted six white men named by Albert Harris who had testified in Minden under the protection of FBI agents. The grand jury charged that the chief of police, B. Geary Gantt, Deputy Sheriff, Charles Edwards, and O.B. Haynes Jr. had deprived the Negroes of their constitutional rights by causing them to be released from jail and handed over to a mob which inflicted the beatings" resulting in the death of Jones. Samuel Madden Sr. H.E. Perry and W.D. Perkins were indicted for complicity in the crime. Prior to the trial, Police Chief Gantt was exonerated by the federal court on recommendations of United States Attorney LeFarge. The other five men went to trial in a federal court in Shreveport, Louisiana and all were exonerated by a trial jury of white persons. I would like to ask many Americans not of color who were so upset when a predominantly Black jury issued their verdict of acquittal in the famous O.J. Simpson trial and could not understand why some knowledgeable

Black Americans were jubilant over the decision in the 1990's if they know this legal history. I am quite sure that some of those concerned Whites have heard of lynching from reading a simple paragraph or two in their United States History textbooks. But I do believe that they have never read the detailed substances of these cases. Also I wish to state adamantly that the recent killing of a Black man in Texas allegedly by several white men again reflects my chosen book title, Segregation is beyond any doubt an American legacy in 1998. Just "nutritional reasoning".

There were some convictions for lynching, but overall the majority of the accused were set free. The long round for equal justice was evident when some hopes for an anti-lynching bill by Congress were dashed since in 1948 the bill did not reach the floor of the House or the Senate.

<u>Congressman Clifford P. Case</u>. Republican New Jersey and Congresswoman Helen Gahagan Douglas, Democrat, California, sponsored an anti-lynching bill. The bill provided heavy penalties for any persons connected with a lynching mob and penalties for state and local officials of the area in which the lynching occurred. The bill also broadened the definition of lynching to include any physical violence presumably aimed at punishing or correcting any one in the custody of the law. It also provided for civil damages to be awarded the victims or members of their families. The bill was introduced in 1947, but in 1948 the Senate Judiciary Subcommittee held hearings on a companion Senate bill which was introduced by Senator Robert F. Wagner, Democrat, New York, and Senator Wayne Morse, Republican, Oregon. The House Judiciary Committee approved the Case Bill by a 18-8 vote. In June, 1948, a watered-down Senate bill unacceptable to Blacks was reported favorably by the Senate Judiciary Committee, but as previously stated neither bill was submitted for a vote.

Highlights of Lynching

The late Walter White, former Executive Secretary of the NAACP, had investigated some 41 lynchings and eight race riots for the NAACP. He said that all of the lynchings and seven of the race riots occurred in rural or semi-rural communities, and the towns' population was one hundred to ten thousand. White's physical appearance helped him to pass as white while investigating the lynchings. He said on one occasion it almost cost him his life, it was during the Chicago race riots in 1919, when a Black shot at him, thinking White was a Caucasian.

In an essay, Walter White described some of his experiences in towns that he visited to investigate lynchings. Some of these true stories portray the realities of the horrors of lynching and how average citizens and politicians supported the lynchings and were sometimes involved in instigating the crimes.

White tells the story about nine men and a pregnant woman who were lynched in a small Georgia town in 1918. White engaged a store merchant in conversation about the recent lynching. The merchant was one of the leaders of the lynch mob. He told Walter White that the government could not do anything about the lynching because state rights would not permit Congress to intervene in lynchings. He also said the state government, governor, sheriff, police officers and the prosecutor all would not interfere, because we elected them to office and the "Niggers" are disenfranchised, said the merchant. White asked who was the white man who was killed by the Black? The merchant replied, oh, he never paid his debts to whites or Niggers and no one around here liked him. Then why did you lynch the nigger, asked White. The merchant said, "It's a matter of safety, we gotta show the Niggers that they must not touch a white man, no matter how low down he is.

The merchant told Walter White the two men were arguing over a crop settlement and that the accused Black, nine men and one woman were lynched because they were all viewed as uppity and talked back to white people. The merchant described to White how they lynched the pregnant woman after the nine Black men were lynched. He said "the woman had been protecting two of the lynched men at her house, and they had shot into the white mob as they approached her cabin". The merchant said that the mob displayed anger as they strung the Black woman by her feet to a tree; then they "ripped the baby from her body and burned the child and mother in a great bonfire". Walter White said that while the man was telling the story, he slapped his thigh and said "it was the best show mister I ever did see, and you ought to have heard the wench howl when we strung her up". Walter White said that he was able to obtain the names of the other participants. He was able to identify prosperous farmers, business men, bankers, newspaper reporters, editors and several law enforcement officers. Walter White made a powerful statement when he wrote 54 years ago (1944), "this crime called the "nigger bee" is one of the most brutal crimes ever uncovered in America or in Nazi Germany (my emphasis)." I wonder how many African Americans who have heard similar stories have said "NEVER AGAIN" and are still reminding the world about the brutal lynchings that occurred during segregation and were not stopped by the federal government until years after their holocaust condition. "Nutritional reasoning".

Walter White related a true story about how three Blacks were killed for a white man's crime. He said a white sheriff had been a candidate for reelection and a wealthy white man contributed greatly to his campaign fund and helped his reelection. The wealthy man had been intimate with a married woman. One night she had a quarrel with her husband and he charged his wife with infidelity. The married woman killed her husband while he was asleep with a butcher knife and carved him up. While bleeding profusely, the husband was able to drag himself to the steps of a neighbors home and died there. The sheriff came to the assistance of the wealthy contributor's mistress by never interrogating her. Three Negroes, two men and a woman were charged with the murder. They were convicted in a court with armed Klansmen present and sentenced to death. Their case was appealed to the State Supreme Court and the convictions were reversed, calling for a new trial. During the new trial one defendant was granted the motion to dismiss but was arrested on a trivial charge and sent back to jail. Later, a mob took the prisoners to the outskirts of town and told them to run. As they were running, they were shot in the back. Two died instantly and the woman was wounded. Then the mob shot her to death. White said that one of the mob members told him "we had to waste fifty bullets on the wench before one bullet stopped her howling." An investigation revealed that members of this lynch mob included the "sheriff, his deputies, jailers, three relatives of the governor of the state, business men and a member of the state legislature". This incident occurred in 1926; Black people today do not need to press for an apology for slavery, they do need to ask for an apology for these lynchings, because I am sure that some of the individuals involved in the lynching might have been pleased with greater longevity.

Black farmers who had entered into sharecropping and tenant agreements with Whites sometimes would protest against the Whites injustice toward them by telling the farmers that their bill for supplies exceeded their share of the crop and some Blacks would be lynched for their persistent demands for their rightful share of the crop.

A Lynching in 1934

Only 59 years ago the land of the free and home of the brave still allowed public lynching in some southern states respecting their congressional "states rights". During the autumn of 1934, a Claude Neal who had been detained for some possible crime was lynched in the State of Florida. Approximately 11 hours prior to the lynching, the nation's news media and radio announced that Neal had been taken from an Alabama jail and was scheduled to be lynched in Florida. The day of the lynching, 4,000 to 7,000 whites had gathered and among them were many small children. Unfortunately, no one was arrested for the citizen's lynching of Claude Neal. That was the way we were in 1934 when criminal justice was supposed to be our guardian of individual liberties and rights under a then so-called democratic and freedom loving government.

TRUE STORIES OF SEGREGATION

1948 Georgia Lynching

A Black insurance salesman was lynched in Lyons, Georgia in November, 1948. He was lynched because some southern whites did not like to see Blacks in attractive cars and clothing.

Assumed legality of Lynching

Lynching in the South was considered legal at times. The large crowds with men and young boys would gather to witness the lynching. Some people took pictures, collected souvenirs of the lynched man or woman's body parts, fingers and toes. Sometimes parts of the body were displayed.

Lynching Facts

There were 3,436 lynchings of Negroes between 1882 and 1950. During the period 1882-1933, thirty Blacks were lynched in the State of Maryland. A George Armwood was hanged and burned by a mob consisting of women and children in Princess Anne County, Maryland. In 1931, a Black person was lynched on the court house grounds in Salisbury, Maryland. Eight Blacks were lynched in a span of five days in Georgia.

There was a specific reference to Afro-Americans in the 1928 Republican Platform for President. The Republican candidate was Warren G. Harding, Ohio. The reference was "we urge Congress to consider the most effective means to end lynching in this country which continues to be a terrible blot on our American civilization." Note: (The Afro-Americans were affected in large numbers by lynching in the 1920's, approximately 50).

"Black Presence In Segregated Prisons"

The American Correctional Association produced a pictorial calendar for the years 1984-1985. The photographs depict the diverse population and its custom of prison segregation in the 1800's and 1930's. There was a rare photograph showing two Blacks in a head brace called "stocks" and a whipping post at the Joliet, Illinois prison in the 1800's. There was a picture of prisoners returning from work on Blackwell's Island, New York, 1876, showing the Inmates standing in line and two Blacks were visible in the integrated formation. Five Black women were shown in a picture with cleaning materials in the Joliet, Illinois prison. One photograph portrayed Black inmates in a segregated wagon in a North Carolina road camp.

Some guards were standing outside with a Black banjo player, Black cook and a Black man with hound dogs. A photograph showed the Black prisoners at a social event called "making do" at the Auburn, New York, prison. The white prisoners were standing on one side of the room and the Blacks on the other side. It appeared that some Black prisoners (male) were dancing together. There was a photograph that portrayed two Blacks with their arms outside of their cells playing checkers on Death Row in a Texas state prison.

When I visited the state prison at McAlester, Oklahoma in 1958, before we could enter the prison yards we had to enter through a large metal and iron bar door. There was a Black man sitting in a small cage, and he had to run a large wheel similar to a steering wheel to open the double doors. When I was shown the Black men's dormitory it definitely was inferior in construction, furniture and cleanliness to the white dormitory, I was in my military uniform and the Black inmates greeted me and it seemed that they were proud to see me, because my white associates and I were being escorted by the prison warden, and he personally asked me if I would like to visit the Black building. As I have previously mentioned in the book that I was there to see their electric chair facilities. There were many Black inmates and some were on a rodeo team.

Women's Part In Race Adjustment

A series of lectures was conducted on Race Relations at Fisk University in 1918. There was a lecture delivered in the University Memorial Chapel and the guest speaker was the late Mrs. Booker T. Washington. She spoke on "Women's Part in Adjustment". She told her audience that "public sentiment must be turned in the direction of the colored woman. It must be made to see that she is protected by the law. She can lay claim to no justice. She lives in a world where the white man may work his will on her without "let" or hindrance outside of the law, outside of social code and moral restraint which protects the white woman and should protect every woman. Equality of protection is imperative for the moral life and growth of the country." Mrs. Booker T. Washington's concern for the chastity and morals of the Black women was expressed some 80 years ago. Today the Black woman is playing an important part in the improvement and advancement in her community and the country as a whole. Black women have been crusading and providing at times their own leadership in the attainment of justice and equal rights in the United States.

First Prince George's County Black Sheriff

In the 1960's, the late Peter L. Moore, a staunch republican and first Black elected to the State of Maryland's Central Republican Committee was the first Black man appointed to a salaried deputy sheriff in Prince Georges County, Maryland.

Discrimination of Black Lawyers During Segregation

Black lawyers were practicing or had passed the bar in some Indiana cities and counties in the 1920's and 1930's. They were present in Gary, Michigan City, Richmond, South Bend and Indianapolis, Indiana. There were still attempts by Black lawyers to practice in other parts of Indiana, but some were prevented by white resistance. The Evansville Bar Association in 1920 filed a court action to block a Black lawyer, Ernest G. Tidrington, from becoming a member. The action would have precluded him from practicing law in Vanderburg County, Indiana. The Association claimed that Tidrington was a person of unsavory character. This claim was rejected by Judge Tracewell. His fight to practice in southern Indiana and the Judge's refusal to give in to local pressure was noted. But it was a "race victory". In spite of the difficulty Tidrington had faced in southern Indiana it was different in Southwestern, Indiana, since the late Arthur A. Greene Sr., a 1923 Howard University law graduate, was admitted to the bar in Brazil, Indiana, the seat of Clay County in 1925. (see the previous discussion on education for the details).

Discrimination, Los Angeles and California Bar Associations, 1927

Hugh Ellwood Macbeth Sr. was president of the Blackstone Club in California. This group in 1927 included Black and Jewish lawyers who were denied membership in the California Bar Association.

Segregated Lawyer's Bar Groups

During segregation there were numerous white bar groups that denied membership to Blacks and some other minorities. The American Bar Association was "organized in 1878 and in 1911, there were three Black members: William Henry Lewis, Buther Roland Wilson of Boston, Massachusetts, and William R. Morris of Minneapolis, Minnesota. When the southern lawyers learned of their membership, they said that the American Bar Association (ABA) was a social organization and it was unwise to admit colored lawyers and the three Blacks should be expelled, because they did not identify themselves as Blacks on their applications. The ABA Executive Committee decided to submit the question of their qualifications to the general membership's Annual Convention that was held in Milwaukee, Wisconsin, 1912. Attorney's Lewis and Wilson refused to resign, however Morris did so. In the future the Blacks were required to identify their race.

Americans today must realize that those predecessors of color long before the Civil Rights Movement Black lawyers were denied their opportunities and privileges to become members of the ABA. On August 26, 1943 at the 60th Annual meeting of the ABA, agreed to settle a problem of some 31 years. The ABA resolved that "it is the sense of this meeting that the membership in the ABA is not dependent upon race, creed or color."

Judges Francis Ellis River and Samuel Watson became the first Black lawyers admitted to the ABA in 31 years. White women have been denied numerous equal rights over the years. But they have been tolerated by some white males in many instances. They were admitted to membership in 1918. The Black women were not admitted in 1944. There was a National Association of Women Lawyers (NAWEL) that was founded in New York City in 1899. They followed the exclusion policy of the ABA and did not admit Black women lawyers until 1943. They admitted Attorney Sophia B. Boaz from Chicago, Illinois, at their 44th meeting in Chicago. They also admitted Georgia Ellis and Edith Sampson.

A Federal Bar Association (FBA) was founded in 1925 in Washington, D.C. Their first constitution restricted membership to any white person with good character. They finally admitted Black members in 1945. The National Lawyers Guild (NLG) was founded in 1937. This was a liberal lawyers' group whose membership was open to persons without regard to race. They assisted the National Bar Association in opposing discrimination in the military service.

I am sure that some Americans of all colors and ethnic groups do not understand why people of color have so many parallel organizations that are predominantly Black in membership. One major reason is that during the segregated years, it was necessary for the formation of these professional organizations. The first Black lawyers' group was an auxiliary of Booker T. Washington's National Negro Business League, founded in 1900. The National Bar Association (NBA) was founded at Des Moines, Iowa in August 1, 1925.

ORGANIZATIONS

American Red Cross and Segregation, World War I

The American Red Cross was responsible for providing a large number of nurses for disaster relief and emergency services. The Red Cross nurses were reserves for the Army Nurse Corp. In 1909, the National Association of Colored Graduate

Nurses (NACGN) was founded to help professional Black nurses to gain employment and to improve their professional training. A co-founder of the association, Mrs. Ada Thomas, urged Black nurses to enroll into the American Red Cross Nurse Reserves. The Red Cross rejected all Black applicants. They told Mrs. Thomas that their ability to accept Black nurses was conditional upon the acceptance of Blacks for service by the Surgeon General, and that they had not received this acceptance. They did encourage Blacks to register in the event the army would accept Black nurses. Two months prior to the signing of the Armistice, September, 1918, some Black nurses were accepted in the Army Nurse Corp. There was a need for them, because of an influenza epidemic that was worldwide and an estimated 22 million people throughout the world had died from the flu or related complications. Some 500,000 people died in the United States. Medical personnel, soldiers and civilians were affected. There was a shortage of military nurses. Therefore, the Army accepted 18 Black nurses in December, 1918, and assigned them to Camp Sherman, Ohio and Camp Grant, Illinois. These nurses lived in segregated quarters. They also had segregated recreational facilities. However, they worked during the day in an integrated environment serving both white and Black patients. The Black nurses were praised for their competent, professional service by the hospital commander.

North Carolina Negro Teachers Association

I read an article that was published in the Association's *North Carolina Teachers Record*, March, 1933. The article was written by the white superintendent and Director of Negro Education in North Carolina, Dr. N.C. Newbold. He mentioned his views on Blacks in an article "*Needed A True Picture of the Negro*". Newbold said there was a splendid article on health conditions among Negro children in a popular magazine with national circulation, however a teacher quoted in it was almost illiterate, note the following quotation: "yassum Miss _____, said the elder teacher, we teaches them what we thinks, they kin do. I reckon it aint all they need, but it helps a heap". Newbold said that this was the teacher speaking and she was sharing the "brer rabbit" sort of language with her students. Dr. Newbold said that when the article was published it was criticized by prominent Negroes in the country because it portrayed the dense illiteracy of the teachers and pupils.

Dr. Newbold asked why writers of books and articles on subjects dealing with Negroes and Negro life employ the rapidly passing and outworn dialects to express their ideas or to paint the mental pictures they wish their readers to see? What Mr. Newbold was writing about in 1933, is prevalent today in the movies, books and documentaries produced by Whites and Blacks, especially some who think it is cool to sing and joke about the dialect of ignorance.

Arlington, Virginia Change of Heart

The Arlington County, Virginia, Medical Society decided in 1950 to extend membership to Black physicians.

Early Black Organizations

A review of a "Guide to Black Organizations" has revealed that there are some 300 recognized Black organizations, professional, fraternal, sorority, religious and social. There were only 30 organizations founded prior to the 1950's. Where is that needed clearing house for all of the organizations today to come together for one major thrust, to share with each other and work as a unified body to combat the legacy of segregation and discrimination in America? Following is a list of organizations that existed during segregation.

Some early national Afro American organizations were formed to provide unity, awareness and professional guidance and networking for Blacks, when they were denied membership in white national organizations. Some of these national Negro organizations are:

Organization	Year Organized
National Medical Association	1895
American Teachers Association	1903
Colored Intercollegiate Athletic Association	1912
National Association of Colored Graduate Nurses	1908
National Negro Business League	1900
National Negro Insurance Association	1920
National Urban League	1911
National Dental Association	1913
Association For The Study of Negro Life and History	1915
National Association for Advancement of Colored People	1909
National Association of Collegiate Deans and Registrars in Negro Schools	1926
National Association of Colored Women	1922
National Association of Business and Professional Women's Clubs	1936
National Association of Dental Hygienists	1939
National Association of Negro Musicians	1923
National Bar Association	1925
National Congress of Parents and Teachers	1926

National Council of Negro Women	1935
National Student Health Association	1940
National Association of Accountants	1933
Midwestern Athletic Association	1931
Conference of Negro Land Grant Colleges	1923
John A. Andrew Clinical society	1912
National Conference on Adult Education and the Negro	1938
National Builders Association	1922
New Farmers of America	
National Technical Association	1929
Association of Social Science Teachers in Negro Schools	1935
Beta Kappa Chi Scientific Society	n.d.
Association of Colleges and Secondary Schools	1933
National Beauty Culturists League	n.d.
National Negro Bankers Association	n.d.

Daughters of the American Revolution (DAR) Affirmative Actions, 1984-85

I can clearly remember my family members discussing a newspaper article and looking at a picture of the distinguished late contralto opera singer, Marian Anderson singing on the steps of the Lincoln Memorial on Sunday, April 9, 1939. The article was in the former Washington, *Evening Star*. Howard University had sponsored a concert series and asked the Daughters of The American Revolution (DAR) to use Constitution Hall for Marian Anderson's scheduled concert. Constitution Hall's manager, Fred Hand, informed the concert series chairman, Charles Cohen, that the hall had been previously booked on the date requested for the National Symphony Orchestra. Ms. Anderson's manager, Sol Hurok, proposed some alternate dates for the concert. At this time, he was informed by the DAR that Marian Anderson could not appear at Constitution Hall because of a ruling of March 23, 1932 which excluded Blacks from appearing in the hall. Hurok submitted a request to waive the ruling for Ms. Anderson. The DAR's executive committee decided on February 1, 1934, by a vote of 39-1 to uphold their white artists only clause. It has been stated "Mrs. Henry M. Robert Jr., then the President of DAR had corresponded with Secretary of Interior, Ickes, and informed him that the DAR's position was not completely in compliance with the custom and procedures of segregation in Washington". There were some public and private facilities which would provide separate seating arrangements for Negroes. However, they did not exclude Blacks from performing. It has been learned that Ms. Anderson had performed at the Belasco Rialto Theatre, Washington, D.C. in 1930. This is the theatre where the noted physicist and scientist, spoke in German to an audience in 1921.

Constitution Hall had opened in 1929 with segregated seating for Blacks. After the denial of Marian Anderson to perform at Constitution Hall, there was another request for an outstanding artist to perform in 1945. The artist was Hazel Scott, pianist and wife of Congressman Adam Clayton Powell Jr. of New York. The DAR refused her request and said that it was conforming to its 1932 regulation. In April 1946, there was an announcement that "Tuskegee Institute, Alabama's Choir would perform in concert at Constitution Hall". This announcement generated a nationwide protest from Blacks because of the action that the President of Tuskegee, Dr. Frederick D. Patterson, decided to take. The choir would perform at the hall without cost because the proceeds would be given to the United Negro College Fund. The President of DAR at that time, Mrs. Julius Y. Talmadge of Atlanta, Georgia said "that granting of the hall to Tuskegee Institute was not in violation of the organization's white artists clause", because it was not being rented, but given free of charge. Mrs. Talmadge stated that her organization had an interest in the United Negro College Fund (UNCF). A great number of Black leaders condemned Dr. Patterson for asking to use the hall in view of the denial of its use for Marian Anderson and Hazel Scott. It was interesting how white people during segregation could justify their actions and in turn appease Blacks through financial assistance. The DAR justified permitting the Tuskegee choir to perform because they were helping the maintenance of separate colleges for Negroes. Dr. Frederick D. Patterson disagreed with those who had protested his actions and refused to cancel the engagement. In 1946 the Washington Branch of the UNCF refused to accept the money that was raised by the concert. They sent the money directly to UNCF National Headquarters in New York.

In 1960's, the DAR had no Black women members of their organization; however in December 1977, a Black woman from Detroit, Michigan, became DAR's first Black member. Karen Farmer had traced her ancestry to a white Revolutionary war soldier from Pennsylvania. The DAR requires its members be able to trace their ancestry to men and women who served in the American Revolution Military or Government. Mrs. Farmer said that "she learned that a maternal great grandmother, Jennie Weaver, was a white woman from Waterford, Pennsylvania who married a Black man from Cleveland, Ohio. Jennie Weaver's maiden name was Hood. Mrs. Farmer was able to locate an ancestor named William Hood who was a soldier in the Continental Army. Farmer said in a press interview that "she was warmly received and welcomed into the DAR". She also said that she joined the organization because "it was the logical conclusion to the line of research, and that the DAR was the kind of organization which could help someone interested in genealogical research and history". The DAR announced at that time through a statement by their president- general that "our organization is changing as are many of our national institutions. We want people to realize that we are not concerned with a prospective members' race or place of national origin", said Mrs. George Baylies.

When this announcement was made in 1977, I am sure that many Americans were not aware of the alleged racism that had characterized the image of the DAR. They probably did not know that President Harry S. Truman once said, the DAR's Whites only policy "could be compared with Nazism". Connecticut Congresswoman Clare Boothe Luce who was a member of DAR "pleaded nationwide in a radio broadcast for the elimination of DAR's anti-Black rule". There was a committee formed called "Committee Against Racial Discrimination". Rep. Luce told the DAR that "in your deep concern for white faces, you are paradoxically enough given our DAR a couple Black eyes". Rep. Luce decided, along with Rep Francis Bolton of Ohio, to resign from the DAR.

The Daughters of the American Revolution was founded in 1890; and in 1985, the organization had over 211,000 members organized in 3,155 chapters in all fifty states, the District of Columbia, England, France, Mexico and Canada. The DAR has had an active program with students nationwide to include Junior American Citizen Clubs, sponsored in schools through local DAR chapters. Some 70,000 student members participated in service and citizenship projects. Local chapters have awarded ROTC medals to graduating cadets. The DAR has awarded a sword to the outstanding graduate of the U.S. Naval Academy at Annapolis, Maryland and presented awards to honor graduates of five service academies and three other military schools.

The DAR's alleged racism resurfaced again in 1984 when the *Washington Post* newspaper published a front page article with its caption "Black Unable to Join Local DAR". A lady of color, Mrs. Lena Ferguson, a Catholic school administrative secretary, had tried for three years to have the DAR to recognize her legitimate eligibility for membership. A day after the publication of the article, "the late District of Columbia Council Chairman, David A. Clarke introduced legislation to remove the DAR's annual real estate tax exemption some 534,597 dollars". The bill died in committee at the end of the year. Two days after Clarke had introduced his proposed legislation, the *Washington Post* printed an editorial "Daughters of What? and concluded the editorial with "Someday the Mary Washington chapter might even grow up".

President General Sarah M. King, the president general at that time had remarked that "Mrs. Ferguson had been accepted as a member of the National DAR. Mrs. King also said that she would propose a DAR rule prohibiting local chapters from discriminating and would enforce the prohibition by appointing an ethics committee. She also stated that the DAR would launch "its own affirmative action plan, including a genealogist to assist Blacks and other applicants and establishing a system to monitor minorities membership progress. The DAR was attempting to incorporate revolutionary changes to increase Black membership.

I had read about the DAR controversy and Mrs. Ferguson in April 1984. I told my late son Robert II, that I was going to visit the DAR headquarters and see if I could talk to someone about a manuscript that I had written on the Black presence in the American Revolution. After I had entered the building, I met a gentleman who kindly asked me if he could help me and I replied yes. He was the DAR's, Public Affairs Director and was a retired Major General, U.S. Army. While sitting in his office talking, we were interrupted by a lady who came in and said General, excuse me, but I would like to see you later. The general used that opportunity to introduce me to Mrs. King, the President General. I was given the chance to brief her on my manuscript and my request to have the DAR to consider publishing it. She asked me a question about a former Black revolutionary soldier, Peter Jennings who later moved to Murfreesboro, Tennessee, which is her hometown. She told me that his grave was unmarked and abandoned, but it was now marked indicating that he was a patriot of the American Revolution. Fortunately, I had brought along my first publication *Black Defenders of America 1775-1973* that was published by Johnson Publishing Company, Chicago, Illinois, the publisher of *Jet* and *Ebony* Magazines. I looked at the chapter on the Revolution and to my surprise, I saw the name Peter Jennings. Mrs. King then said, you have Peter Jennings, Mr. Greene and then she told the general, "We will examine his book and I believe that the DAR will publish this manuscript". That was the birth of *Black Courage* and my future contact with the DAR. Later, I told Mrs. King directly that I knew that this book would help the DAR's image. (However, I could not forget my childhood experience in learning about the exclusion of Mrs. Marian Anderson). I also told her she would be publishing my book and I would be helping the organization. I was most appreciative and thankful when the DAR in 1985 gave me a first class "red carpet" reception and booking signing at their headquarters. Mrs. King also invited her Senator from Tennessee who later was elected the Vice President of the United States the Honorable Albert Gore of Tennessee. Later, Mrs. King would invite me to several social events at the DAR and during a Christmas season affair, I had the honor to meet the retiring Honorable Supreme Court Chief Justice Burger.

Mrs. King had sent invitations to the Black Caucus and the D.C. City Council. To my surprise and really not, no member of the Black Caucus and only one member of the D.C. Council appeared at the reception. I was most appreciative when Congressman Louis Stokes of Ohio sent a representative with an apology for his absence. I was able to meet him when I was attending a professional meeting in Cleveland, Ohio, later; and I personally thanked him.

I would have friends and people that I did not know to tell me their views on my having the DAR to publish my book in view of the Marian Anderson incident of 1939. The only response that I thought was appropriate was to balance the situation at that time. I told them consider the facts that Constitution Hall was being used as the auditorium for the graduating exercises for most of the practically all Black

District High Schools. I also reminded them that on several weekends in the month, promoters would schedule noted Black music artists to perform before a "foot stomping" emotional Black music lovers group who would sit in the hall. Some of them may never have heard of Marian Anderson.

In concluding this true story about the DAR controversy over the years, I have included some press releases that might portray their new image and also the literary impact it has had on my personal life. In 1991, I went to a large, competent and friendly printing company that had printed the book for the DAR. Since 1991, they have published my successive publications and the President of the company, Mr. William Grant, is an outstanding helpful and concerned businessman who has taken a personal interest in my publications by insuring that I receive a finished professional product.

These press releases will show the impact of *Black Courage* on the DAR during their racial challenge in 1984-1985.

New York Times, February 19, 1985. "Washington Talk of Black Courage".

"Lena Ferguson, a descendant of a white man who fought in the Revolutionary War, contended last year that she had been denied membership in the Washington Chapter of the Daughters of the American Revolution because she was Black. The case jarred the organization with internal dissension that subsided after Sarah M. King, the national president, acknowledged that Mrs. Ferguson's case had been handled "inappropriately" and called for a special investigation.

Mrs. King also promised that the organization would strive to give greater recognition "to the contributions of Black patriots in the American Revolution."

One step in that direction is the publication of a new book, *Black Courage: Documentation of Black Participation in the American Revolutionary War*," commissioned by the D.A.R. and written by Robert Ewell Greene. Historians have estimated that 5,000 Blacks, many of them slaves who went to battle as substitutes for their masters, fought in the War for Independence. General George Washington first issued an order barring states from recruiting Blacks for military duty. But he quickly reversed himself after learning that John Murray, 4th Earl of Dunmore and the Royal Governor of Virginia, had issued a Proclamation November 7, 1775, offering freedom to all slaves who were willing to join the British forces."

Jet Magazine, March 18, 1985. White History Group Backs Book On Black Soldiers

The President General of the National Society of the Daughters of the American Revolution (DAR) made a courageous move during the recent Black History Month celebration.

Head of an organization that long has been accused of racism and of denying Blacks their rightful due, DAR President Sarah M. King authorized the DAR's publication of a book by military historian Robert Ewell Greene about Black participation during the Revolutionary War entitled *Black Courage - The Documentation of Black Participation In The American Revolution.* Greene researched pension records and other documents in national and state archives to compile not only the names of long forgotten Black Revolutionary War soldiers but to uncover crucial information about their lives, social and economic background, length of war service, and their fortunes after the war."

BIACK AMERICAN PATRIOTS
HONORED IN DAR PUBLICATION

HON. BART GORDON
Of TENNESSEE
IN THE HOUSE OF REPRESENTATIVES
Tuesday, February 19, 1985

o Mr. GORDON. Mr. Speaker, it is my desire to bring to the attention of the 99th Congress the publication of a book which adds greatly to our understanding and appreciation of the contributions Black Americans made during the American struggle for independence.

The book, published by the National Society Daughters of the American Revolution, is entitled "Black Courage. 1775-1783: Documentation of Black Participation in the American Revolution." This book documents the courage and valor of Black Americans who struggled for freedom during the American Revolution.

The DAR has performed a great service by publishing this book. I intend to distribute copies of the publication to a number of public libraries and other such depositories in my congressional district so that this important story Is available to all those might benefit from it, be they scholars, schoolchildren, genealogists or amateur historians.

To help fully explain the benefit of this publication, I ask, Mr. Speaker, that the attached statement of Sarah M. King, president general of the National Society Daughters of the American Revolution, be made a part of the RECORD of the 99th Congress. Mrs. King made these statements upon the publication of the book. In her remarks, she singles out one Black patriot from her hometown, Murfreesboro, TN. Peter Jennings fought in many important battles during the revolution and later settled in Murfreesboro, which is also my hometown. His grave, once unmarked and abandoned, is now a symbol of Black participation in the American Revolution and is marked due to the efforts of Mrs. King and the DAR. In a similar but more symbolic effort, the DAR's publication of this book lights forever what was once an unmarked record of service rendered by these brave men.

Following are Mrs. King's remarks:
EXCERPTED STATEMENT OF Sarah M. King

On the eve of Black History Month, which is also American History Month, it is both appropriate and a privilege for the DAR to formally announce the publication of "Black Courage: Documentation of Black Participation in the American Revolution," by Robert Ewell Greene.

As you may know, the National Society Daughters of the American Revolution is dedicated to the perpetuation of the memory and spirit of those brave and visionary men and women who fought to secure American Independence. Some names are familiar to us

TRUE STORIES OF SEGREGATION

all-George Washington, Nathan Hale, the Marquis de Lafayette. But these celebrated patriots were by no means the only great carriers of the torch of Liberty.

Foot-soldiers, militiamen, medics, porters and countless others fought the battles. weathered the storm and, in many instances, gave their lives so that their neighbors and children might live free. These patriots were no less great, no less important, than the celebrated men who led them. They came from all walks of life and they were of varied ethnic and religious backgrounds. But they were joined by a spirit, and, driven by a strength, that built the greatest nation in the world.

Our history books pay tribute to many of these Revolutionary War heroes. Our history books, however, are far from complete. Some groups have not received the recognition they deserve. So it is with the nearly 5,000 Revolutionary soldiers and militiamen who were Black. It is time to honor those courageous Black Americans.

The National Society Daughters of the American Revolution is committed to doing just that. "Black Courage" was sponsored and published by the National Society. We believe it to be an important contribution to our nation's historical record.

"Black Courage" is the result of Mr. Greene's meticulous research of pension records and other documents in national and state archives. Most of his sources were original manuscripts. From those documents. Mr. Greene compiled more than just the names of Black Revolutionary soldiers: he uncovered crucial information about their lives, their social and economic back. grounds, their length of service and their fortunes after the war. In short, Mr. Greene has brought elements of the Massasoit Guards, the "Bucks of America", the Rhode Island Black Regiment, and many others, to life.

In so doing Mr. Greene has accomplished something else that is important to the DAR: he has increased the sum of genealogical data which other Americans can use to trace their families back to the American Revolution and beyond. It is our sincere hope that Mr. Greene, and others like him who have taken the time to expand modern recognition of Black patriots, will inspire the living descendants of those patriots to discover their eligibility and join the DAR. Just as our young nation needed their forefather, to join in the fight for liberty. We need them to contribute to our work in the fields of history, education and patriotism.

Now, before I introduce the author of "Black Courage" to you today, I would like to add one personal note. I was pleased to see that one of the patriots listed in "Black Courage" settled in my home town of Murfreesboro, Tennessee. Peter Jennings enlisted in the army in Providence, Rhode Island, in 1776. He served in several companies. including Colonel Edward Olney's 5th Regiment of Artillery for Blacks, and he fought in the battles of Trenton, Princeton, Brandywine, and Germantown, and right to the end at Yorktown.

After the war, Mr. Jennings moved to Murfreesboro, where he was a baker. He was given a pension In 1832, when he was eighty years-old. He died ten years later. More than ten years ago in 1974 - while searching the old city cemetery for the grave of my own maternal grandfather six generations removed. My DAR chapter and I found that Peter Jennings had been buried there in an unmarked grave. We applied to the General Services Administration for grave-stones, and then marked both graves with stones bearing their names and their titles as Revolutionary War Soldiers. Those headstones were placed side-by-side. "Now, who says genealogy isn't exciting?*

MUSIC

Confrontations With Racism

There were some musicians, composers, actors and actresses who experienced or contributed to segregation during the early years.

Ku Klux Klan and Paul Robeson

The world renowned Paul Robeson, actor, Phi Beta Kappa and activist had performed in "All God's Chillum Got Wings" and "Had To Kiss His Wife" starring a white actress. The Ku Klux Klan did not appreciate that and some Klan members sent Paul Robeson death threats.

Paul Robeson Retained His Dignity

Paul Robeson was able to demand and receive the right for final approval of his scheduled films. He was the first Black in the film industry to refuse work under segregated conditions. Robeson stipulated in his contracts that he would not work in the South. He dignified his African culture and essential African awareness in the screen. Paul Robeson once said, "In my music, my plays, and my films, I want to always carry this central idea, to be African because multitudes of men have died for less worthy ideas, it is even more eminently worth living for."

A Change Of Name To Fight Racism

Prior to 1917, Blacks in America were welcomed into the white dominated musical world as singers of spirituals, minstrel tunes and the blues. In later years, there would be a small number of Black classical artists emerging. These artists were paving the way for present day classical opera singers. One of those talented artists was the late Lillian Evans Tibbs, who later changed her name to Lillian Evanti. It was necessary for her to travel to Europe to be accepted as an opera singer. She made her professional debut in Nice, France as the lead singer in "Delives Opera Lakme". She then earned a contract for three seasons of performances with the Paris Opera Company and performed in the countries of France, Italy and Germany. Lillian Evanti became the first Black American to perform with an organized European company. When Ms. Evanti returned to the United States, she was not invited to join any American opera company. She had to perform at local theatres and churches. However in 1934, Evanti was invited by

Mrs. Eleanor Roosevelt to perform at the White House. Later Ms. Evanti gave performance at the White House for Presidents Truman and Eisenhower.

Lillian Evanti was instrumental in establishing the Negro National Opera Company in 1942 in Philadelphia, Pennsylvania. A Ms. Dawson was responsible for the management of the company and also assisted in its formation. Ms. Evanti at times was responsible for the opera company's artistic direction. While she was with the company, she wrote the Libretto and sang the lead role of Videtta. Evanti was appointed as a goodwill ambassador by the Roosevelt administration. She traveled extensively through South America with Toscanini's orchestra. During a visit, endorsed by the State Department, Evanti served as chairman of the Inter-American Relations. She assisted in a program to promote knowledge of the Afro American culture in Latin America. Evanti assisted in a campaign to donote libraries to Latin American governments. When the African country of Ghana celebrated its independence, Ms. Evanti was commissioned by the Voice of America to present her composition, "Salute to Ghana".

Evanti received awards from the governments of Haiti and Liberia. She received Haiti's high culture award "Chevalier de L'Honier et Mercie". Lillian Evanti M. composed the presidential candidate's campaign song "There's a Better Day a Coming". Congress requested Evanti to testify on the need to establish a national culture center, a movement which eventually established the Kennedy Center for the Performing Arts. Lillian Evanti died in 1967 at the age of 77 years. During the period of segregation, Lillian Evanti was a pioneer in the world of opera.

Lena Horne and Segregation

Lena Horne performed for the soldiers at Fort Riley Kansas. The Whites would position themselves alongside the prisoners of war to hear Lena Horne sing, while the Black soldiers were standing in the back of the rooms.

Porgy and Bess and Some Racist Images

The popular musical "Porgy and Bess" was a fictional love story about a disabled man and a promiscuous woman in Charleston, South Carolina's "Catfish Row". The musical score was George Gershwins'. The musical played in theaters and opera houses. Later movies and television versions would be made. The musical was actually based on novel, Porgy, written by Dubose Heyward, a southern writer who had read a story about a legless beggar. The novel did reflect some southern stereotypes of Blacks in that day and time. The early performances included the late Todd Duncan as Porgy and Anne Brown as Bess. This musical gave Blacks an opportunity to perform an opera. It was a stage play then introduced to Broadway in 1935. In later years, the actor and actress were Leontyne Price and William Warfield.

There was definitely some opposition by Blacks to Porgy and Bess musical. One renowned Black musician said, "the times are here to debunk Gershwin's lamp Black Negroisms". A question was posed "Is there a creation of white creators stealing and mangling Black culture?" Heyward once said that he "saw the Negro as the inheritor of a source of delight that I would have given much to possess". Gershwin also remarked, "I choose to combine folk, operatic and jazz idioms. I suppose it's a distinct breed, an American urge". There were some Blacks who did not want to see Black characters in the drug dealing sporting life. Some opponents to the musical said that it was socially embarrassing, simply "white put downs".

Anne Brown graduated from Baltimore's Frederick Douglass High School which was the only Black high school. She wanted to pursue her musical education at Baltimore's Peabody Conservatory. They refused to admit her because she was Black. She was accepted at Juillard School of Music. When she was selected to try out for the role of Bess in the musical, Gershwin asked if she could sing a Negro Spiritual. Ms. Brown said to Gershwin "Why is it that you people always expect Black singers to sing spirituals? She realized that Gershwin understood her resentment of the stereotype. In reality she wanted to sing a spiritual because her mother had sung them and she loved them too. Therefore she sang "A City Called Heaven" with which Gershwin was pleased saying "Wherever you go you must sing that spiritual; it is the most beautiful one I have ever heard". He then decided to give her the role of Bess. Ms. Brown was the daughter of Harry Francis Brown, a physician and Mary Allen Wiggins who had studied voice and piano in New York. In later years Anne Brown moved to Europe and in 1948 she married living in Norway with her Norwegian husband and two children.

An Unusual Composer

John Newton, a white man, was born in 1725. As a youngster he learned to read the Bible and received religious guidance from his mother who was a devout Christian. His mother died when he was seven years old. After receiving two years of education he joined his father at sea. Newton sailed the sea for eighteen years. six of these years, he performed duties as the Captain of a slave ship. Even though Newton had his Bible with him at sea and studied in the cabin, his attitude towards slavery was not affected. He had prayers with the members of his crew as the cargo lay chained and cramped under inhuman conditions. Newton delivered one cargo of slaves to Charleston, South Carolina. To him they were chattel.

John Newton experienced a spiritual awakening at the age of twenty-three years while aboard ship. He was steering his ship through a gale or strong current of wind when he was about to lose control of the ship. Newton began to pray and asked God to see them through this ordeal.

Later, Newton decided to return to Liverpool, England where he worked for nine years in an office and studied for the ministry. Newton was ordained as curate of a church in Olney in 1764. He remained there for sixteen years. During the period 1780 to 1807, Newton served as Rector of St. Mary Woolworth, London. When he was eighty years of age, he became feeble and his eye sight began to decline. He was unable to read the text and had to resign from his preaching duties. It appeared that Newton's past life was not forgotten in his memories. When he was told he should retire, he said *"What! Shall the old African blasphemer (one who abuses others) stop while he can speak!!!* While preaching at Olney, Newton developed a close friendship with William Cowpers, the noted poet. One of the outstanding contributions of the Eighteenth Century was the development of the English hymnody (hymn writing). There was a collection of hymns during this time that included three hundred and forty-eight hymns. Cowper wrote sixty-eight and Newton wrote two-hundred and eighty.

John Newton composed his epitaph by himself:

"John Newton, Clerk, once an infidel and Libertine (one who is unrestrained in Morality and religious matters) was by the rich mercy Of Our Lord and Savior & Jesus Christ preserved, restored and pardoned, and appointed to preach the faith he had long labored to destroy near 16 years at Olney in Buck's and years in the church."

I have often sat in a church and attended programs where I heard the beautiful lyrics of a song being sung slowly, and sweetly. I always think of this particular song as one that reflects our slavery past and the dehumanizing process of our ancestors during those days of injustice. However they were the times of the American experience that our great grandparents and other relatives lived. But somehow the comfort received, and the meditation of smoothness and contentment is present where these words are being sung:

"Amazing grace, how sweet the sound that saved a wretch like me. I once was lost, but now I'm found, was blind, but now I see".

I know that this song has been sung for many years by African Americans and is still a part of our music selection today. But in our American experience we live so many amazing moments. Yes, during my research I was amazed that this beautiful song that some churches of color include in their song books of Zion was composed by an Englishman who at one time was a Captain of a slave ship, the late Reverend John Newton who died in 1807. This is another revelation of living experiences of African Americans in America. I wonder if the descendants of those slaves Newton left in Charleston, South Carolina, ever sing the lyrics of *Amazing Grace.* I conclude by saying, as I read the words of the song, I feel that John Newton lived the rest of his life asking our Lord Jesus for forgiveness and it is ironic that these beautiful verses would be sung slowly and freely, with feeling, by the descendants of those Africans he once saw as just chattel in the hold of his ship at sea.

CHAPTER 3

BLACK CULTURE - GENETIC DIVERSITY

The previous chapters have been a discussion of true stories related to segregation and discrimination in America over some 100 years. During my teaching career, especially on the college level and during outside lectures, I assume a position and character, that I am the "man from Mars". I simply want my students, especially my white students, to view and listen to me as a person discussing the subject of race and related matters as an unbiased individual, just a person analyzing and commenting, developing inferences about very controversial subjects, people and cultures. I often tell my audiences that I might be literally "stepping on some toes, not to offend but to explain both sides."

Therefore during this in-depth discussion of the real Black minority, the child, man and woman, I will reveal these true stories that I have experienced and researched, not giving my opinions but saying what millions of people might think but never say. I will be discussing topics that many people, especially Blacks go to the grave and never talk about it. I believe that this frank scholarly evaluation of the diverse Black society, culture and genetic heterogeneity will actually reveal to the uninformed and miseducated person, some things about people who have been called many different names in the American experience.

Therefore this discussion will be presented by the mystical man from Mars who takes no sides Black or white, as he discusses the good and the bad of the Black cultural history in America during the past 100 years. Remember the man from mars sees only the composite situation without any preferences in the revelation of the facts as they have occurred and are continuing to be manifested in what is called Black culture and a diverse genetical being. Sociologists will define caste or class systems as the feelings, consciousness of individuals in unity and an enjoyment of their privileges. There is also a presence of the family background, wealth, national origin, and religion, in the respective classes. Some characteristics of caste are social distance, differences in physical descriptions, restrictions and a class system.

The African American community during segregation and even after segregation has maintained some aspects of a low, middle and upper class, along with sub classes. Today, we see a closer union with all classes in the Black community than was present during segregation. The three classes did live side by side in their residential areas and respect was shown between all neighbors of various class distinction imposed upon them. I believe that there was more assistance provided to the lower and middle class by the upper classes at times. But there was a distinction, color.

This discussion will examine some true stories and facts about the three classes, their religions, Black leadership, white involvement among the classes, and racial etiquette that was dictated and enforced by white society on all three classes.

The Black Lower Class

There were some domestic workers to include maids, servants, cooks, butlers and gardeners who would love to serve as the eyes, ears and informers in the Black community for the Whites. They would gossip about the conditions in the community, church and lodge meetings, and what the Black politicians, were doing. There were also some Black leaders who had lower class workers to provide them information about the Whites.

These descriptive characteristics will depict some lower class Blacks during segregation and how they were perceived by whites and some Blacks who had moved out of a lower class status. The lower class Blacks were renters, unskilled and skilled workers, domestics, laborers and migrant farmers in many southern areas. A large number of Blacks were dependent on relief or welfare. Many were described by Whites as part of a typical folk culture that included "pimps, prostitutes, gamblers, good entertainers, superb athletes, super spiritual, good domestics, love flashy clothes and jewelry, lazy, inefficient, non ambitious, low self concept, insulting, use vulgar language, used street slang, and possessed a negative criminal behavior." There were some members of a Black sub class who would portray their frustrations by using phrases that somehow reinforced their complacency and low self concept. One could hear these sayings exchanged between some Blacks, to include entertainers and comedians:

> "nigger ain't nothing
> nigger ain't got a thing
> he cannot win
> no hope for us, so what
> we have no guts
> lack of culture"

There were Whites who used insulting terms to describe Blacks. Some of these terms were:

"Jade and blue Black, coffee-colored, high yellow, chocolate brown, nigger, nigra, smooth yellow, darkey, jade and blue Black, pickaninny, coal Black or Black as the shoe, octoroon and quadroon, and zigaboo (sometimes used by Blacks)." A typical menu that was prepared by the lower class and also the middle and upper classes some times were: "chicken, hog maws, neck bones, pig feet, navy, pinto and red beans, string beans, greens, potatoes, white and sweet, corn bread chitterlings, water melon cobblers, pound cake, pies, fish, Black eye peas, gravy and bread, scrapple, eggs, bacon, clabber milk, cakes, home made ice cream, rice, biscuits, ice box rolls, sausage, fat back, pancakes, potato cakes, turnips, ham, turkey, beets, peas, onions, tomatoes, grits, bread pudding, ginger bread, fruit cakes, seafood, and fowl. This menu was enjoyed by many whites who employed Black cooks.

Upper and Middle Class Blacks

Some distinctive characteristics of the Black upper and middle class during segregation were: they established goals for upward mobility and considered their family backgrounds, morals, values, education and positive traditions. There were some dark skin Blacks who would receive a good education and they would marry light skin women. This was mostly common among the male. The upper class did not condone illegitimacy (all classes) and they would avoid lower class Blacks who demonstrated characteristics of being boisterous, dirty, loud, bad manners and morals and sexual obsessed. The upper class would worship in the Christian churches such as Catholic, Episcopal, Lutheran, Baptist, Methodist, Presbyterian and Congregational whose pastors were educated. Many upper class Blacks were conservative, wealthy and powerful in the Black community.

Some upper class Blacks would provide standards of values and aspirations for the other classes. They even had an effective net work through businesses, churches and the schools.

The large middle class would strive for a higher class level and living standards. They wanted more economic gains and a college education. Their family life was more stable, but there were some in both classes (upper) who would engage in extra marital relations, but mostly in extreme secrecy, not as open as it is today.

The upper and middle class manners in public differed greatly from some lower class Blacks. One would seldom see them yawning in public, blowing bubbles in people's faces, not turning their heads when coughing, using abusive language and other negative mannerism. Many upper and middle class Blacks would emulate white culture at times.

Some middle and upper class Blacks would communicate with the lower class in their dialect and slang in order to retain their prestige among lower class Blacks. The upper classes would shop in their own neighborhoods and support the Black businesses.

The middle class Blacks were responsible individuals. Many were professional, unskilled and semi skilled workers, hair dressers, barbers, social workers, policemen, firemen, waiters, housekeepers, porters, cab drivers, postal employees, some ministers, and low level government workers. They would maintain steady employment and also were homeowners. Normally some middle class Blacks would accept segregation, but others would show their outward personal resentments.

There were some Black radical leaders in southern communities who spoke out against segregation and many Blacks in the town would avoid them. Some whites would personally inform the radicals to stop their aggressive actions or leave town. Some middle and upper class Blacks would avoid their segregated status and problems by refusing to buy and read Black newspapers, magazines and books. They made sure that they were away from the common Black. The students at the Black colleges were sheltered from segregation on the campuses. They were away from the white and Negro masses. They were busy with their college studies and student activities.

There were some upper class Blacks who would work with lower class Blacks in political campaigns, since some lower class Blacks served as precinct captains and bosses.

It was necessary for all classes of Blacks to visit "for colored only" beaches and resorts during segregation. Some of them were Carrs, Sparrows and Highland Beaches and resorts areas in Annapolis, Maryland.

Religion

I must say that religion has played an integral part in Black society and the class systems. I do believe that the church has been the most essential influence and continual leadership in the Black community during segregation. The church has been the cornerstone of our faith and the mortar board beacon for our education. The Black churches regardless of their numerous branches from the major Christian churches in America have been able to carry on the torch of needed faith and survival. I believe the Black church has been the most unifying force in a divided people.

Although there are some imperfections in several denominations today and still a continuance of uneducated individuals occupying the pulpits and delivering messages of ignorance and misinformation, the Black churches will still survive and provide the Christian and lay leadership to the Black community. When one reexamine the Black church during segregation we can see some of the trials and tribulations they faced.

When there was an absence of upper class leadership in the South, the Black ministers assumed a responsible role in communicating with the white leaders in their respective communities. There were some Black ministers who would preach from the pulpit that " too much education was not needed". This was stated by many uneducated ministers. The Negro Church in the south provided fraternal and burial lodges for their membership and even constructed cemeteries next to their churches. Many Blacks would criticize some lower class Black ministers by calling them "jack leg preachers, uncouth, illiterate, promiscuous, self interest pastors and false prophets of the gospel".

During segregation, a majority of Black worshipers preferred Baptist and Methodist Congregations. A small number of upper class and middle class Blacks attended Episcopalian, Congregational, Presbyterian and Catholic churches. The news media, writers, educators, historians, television producers, film directors, and lay persons have characterized Black church members during segregation and even today as worshipers who are very "emotional, foot stompers, players of percussion type musical in their services, baptizers by different means, rivers, creeks, hog wallowers, and users of fire hoses". Some people perceive Black churches as a magnetic force to invite members and potential elders, deacons, evangelists and ministers to their membership who carry "a heavy baggage" of an unfortunate non Christian idealistic past. It was during segregation that the down trodden Black sinner who had cursed, brutalized people, had a criminal record, used drugs, gambled, disbanded their family and engaged in overall deviant behavioral acts, were attracted to the church. Yesterday and today some Black churches are attracting a large number of new preachers who have the similar profiles.

Many Black churches today have revived some traditions that were present in worship services for many years and especially during segregation. During the 1930's and 1940's, some churches requested their members to shake hands and embrace each other; then they would move around the pews or in front of the church along with their pastors and church officers. They would begin to sing, cry, dance and stomp their feet, sometimes in unison. There were some churches where the members would begin to laugh and the pastors would generate the laughter during his preaching and collecting the money.

I can remember as a little boy that my friends and I would be walking down Seventh Street near Georgia Avenue NW, and we would stop and look at the church people in Daddy Grace's church. The doors were wide open and you could hear the music and shouting a half block away. During segregation the majority of the real emotional and praise services were present in the Apostolic, Holiness, Pentecostal and Church of God denominations. I believe my paternal grandfather attended the Holiness church and today my second cousin prides herself on attendance in the Pentecostal faith for some 80 years. She was raised in the church and her mother was a faithful member until her demise at 100 years. I often tell my college students, regardless of the differing views about the Black church and regardless of an individuals own class selection, if he was born and called Black in America, then the spiritual gift of their culture will never leave their presence. It might be dominant or stay recessive for years, but somewhere between the Alpha and Omega, a great number of African Americans are called to their heritage of spirituality either as a church member, officer or minister of the Gospel.

There are some Black churches today which have started their services in tents and later moved to inside facilities and some today are located in shopping areas where former business stores were located. They must be complimented for their initiative and efforts to carry the gospel to their people. I personally am aware of a small congregation that was started by a born-again pastor who possibly have used some of his personal funds to organize and house a congregation with attractive church furniture within a year. I am able to recall when I visited my late uncle and aunt, Joseph and Hazel Bass Greene in Brazil, Indiana, at the age of twelve years, Aunt Hazel's mother was affectionately called "Grandma Beecham". She invited me along with the rest of her immediate family to attend Sunday services with her small congregation at her home. There were some Blacks from the town and our family who filled two rooms with chairs arranged everywhere and she would preach and play a large antique organ. Yes, Black Americans have come a long way in the faith as one observes throughout the country many 3-5 million dollar Black churches.

We see many Black ministers today incorporate new community outreach programs in their churches. The public should be aware that they are reviving some past customs and traditions of the church that were present during segregation. The Black preachers in the 1920's, 1930's, and 1940's were performing duties as leaders and idealists who supported Black businesses and offered education, social services and recreation facilities at their churches. The Black ministers in the South, North, West and East were members of a select class of leaders and spiritual advisers for Blacks. Many Black churches and their leadership during segregation would urge their membership to abstain from bad habits of smoking, pre marital sex, drugs, drinking, snuff dipping and smoking, gambling, card playing, vulgar language, dancing and minor vices. The churches were using preventive actions, rather than waiting for their members to come to church after committing the negative deeds.

When I visit Christian churches of all faiths today, I am comfortable appreciating the doctrines and beliefs of the different faiths. I can understand and place in a historical perspective their form of worship and the innovative emotional praise in many Black churches today. I observed a revival and adjustment of the "real old time religion". I have observed the following in many Black churches of all faiths in recent years and even in 1998.

Some members engage in excessive handclapping, there are elders, deacons and deaconesses who would engage in very long prayers, even in one church with a membership of over 3,000. The assistant pastors and evangelists have the opportunity to make remarks, or pray, taking almost one hour. Then the order of service would start, lasting a total service of 3 hours. I have seen and heard pastors repeat several phrases from scriptures some 12 times and possibly used this repetition to arouse his members emotionally. I have observed some ministers in their healing process attempting to perform supernatural and natural healing. There are many Black church members who are very attentive followers and will respond in a rap style and never have really understood the scripture that they were told to read. These characteristics are often the legacy of many low class and uneducated ministers in the South who were trying to do the best they could. Many of them have no formal diploma supporting their requirements for ordination. They say that they were "called" to the pulpit. In 1998, many faiths of churches operate outstanding theological schools and also some of our private institutions. In respect to the Black church, we cannot forget that during Reconstruction and after, a great number of historically Black colleges were founded by Black churches. They had a major responsibility to educate Black ministers. Today, however there are some Black self proclaimed ministers and there are those who are ordained by friends after they have attended in some instances non accredited religious schools. They also assume the prefix title "Doctor or Dr". I am not in anyway critizing these ministers. I am telling the facts that millions of people know, but its insignificance to them might be the reason why they are not as vocal as I am. As I stated before, I accept their personal actions and respect them for the efforts to preach the gospel. I also can relate their current status to many Black pastors during the era of segregation. I see it as another legacy of segregation that has not been obliterated. These remarks are just "nutritional reasoning". A professional Black citizen that was high on the list was the minister. The minister would be solicited or appointed to serve as school principals, college presidents, member of interracial councils and Black spokesmen. In the South, some Whites believed that their character would represent a sober, sane, educated, restrained and temperate good Negro for the job. They also viewed them as a Black they could trust, loyal and able to control racial problems within the college and surrounding Black community. They also saw them as guardians of the segregated caste system. Many of the principals and college presidents would remain in their positions for 25 years or more, as long as they were pleasing the white majority and had some support from Blacks who agreed with their leadership of tolerance and patient during those years of segregation. This did not include all Black leaders, because there were many who believed that Blacks could overcome their tribulations one day.

The upper and middle class Blacks who attended Black schools in the South which were founded by the American Missionary Association, would receive a well-rounded education to include a religious fervor that would be supported with the teachings of positive morals, values and self concept. There would also be some Blacks who had attended other schools such as public colleges, private universities, Black or predominantly white. Many would be introduced to the Catholic, Lutheran, Episcopal Congregational and Presberyterian faiths if they were not already members. But a great majority of Blacks would be members of the Baptist, Methodist and Pentecostal Churches that would in most cases provide services and ministry compatible to their respective cultural class and ideals.

During segregation white southerners and northerners would depend on Black ministers low, middle, and upper class, to be their available resource persons and an available pool for political and civil appointments within their communities and even nationally.

Black Culture

The Black class systems in America have been affected by the beliefs and ideals of the majority American white people to insure enforcement of segregation laws and establish a visible and invisible color line. This invisible line did have a serious impact on the minds and thinking processes of millions of African Americans during segregation. There was a common term that was used in the South and even the North "keep Negroes in their designated place in society". This also reinforced the beliefs of inferiority among Black Americans. There were many innocent Black citizens and innocent white citizens who really believed that whites are superior beings. The white southerners expected all classes of Blacks to realize that they were to be subservient to Whites and were not to be their equal. Some Whites would be vocal about their impressions of Blacks and even Jewish people. Whites would make statements such as "The Negro in his place is really an assistant in the South. The Lord intended him to be the servant of the people. We could not get along without him, and the cotton belt needs the Negro labor. Our attitude is that the white man is superior and the colored are looked upon as servants".

A wealthy Norfolk, Virginia socialite once remarked that "Blacks should be free, but more capable of the domestic arts than fine arts". A manager of a machine shop said a mule is made to work, horse is made for beauty and the Negro is made to be the working man of the South. A man in Georgia said that he observed a white foreman with the colored workers doing all the carpentry work and the foreman was doing nothing but cursing the workers. Many whites would justify why they resented Black people. A South Carolina attorney said, "respect is not what you should feel but what you do feel and the white man does not respect the colored woman. I would find it difficult to trust the Negro with the same courtesy, because it would be embarrassing to me".

There was a White who said they would help an old woman to cross the street, but I would cut off my hand before I would offer that courtesy to a younger colored woman. He also said that he would not tip his hat to a Black lady, because it would hurt me in the estimate of people I care more about. I also do not like to see a white woman sitting beside a servant.

A white Virginia lawyer said that he could not call Blacks Mr. and Mrs. because doing it was a recognition of the Blacks social status,

The major rules and customs of segregation that were enforced in the society were: Blacks should not marry Whites, dance, eat and play games with them. Whites should never use "Mr. and Mrs. when addressing Blacks. Blacks were not to enter the front door of white homes, only the rear door. When walking on the sidewalks, Blacks were to give the Whites the right of way. a Negro man was expected to take off his hat in banks, and stores. Whites did not have to conform. Blacks were required at one time to say "yes sir, yes Ma'm" when addressing Whites. Blacks could not try on hats and shoes in department stores and they had to sit in a segregated area in the court rooms.

There were situations where upper class Blacks would experience some race related situations. These true stories are examples. The late George Washington Carver, noted scientist, had to adjust to southern customs when he arrived at Tuskegee, Alabama to teach at Tuskegee Institute. He had to realize that the following expectations of the Negroes' respect for whites were the law of the land. Carver was traveling in the town where the Blacks did not walk to the right on the side walk, but on the gutter side, right or left so that he could be shoved off quickly, where he belonged. Blacks could not be on the streets after dark. In this Alabama town, Blacks were expected to stand with hat off while talking to a white man, whether he were a college president or the low income tenant. In Alabama, the towns people seldom called Booker T. Washington by his surname. They would call him "Booker or Professor".

When the late William Pickens, educator and NAACP official, gave a speech at a white college, after his speech, a young white man said "I would like what he said if he was a white man, but I hate to have niggers get such publicity. They won't keep their proper place if this goes on".

During segregation, some non Blacks were considered inferior by some whites. A white mother decided to send her daughter to a private boarding school because she could not stand having her daughter in a northern high school where she was attending a class with "five dagoes (Italians) pollacks (Polish) and a darkie (Black)". The mother said "and do you know one of those dagoes was head of the class and the darkie actually played on the hockey team. I insist that Mary be brought up a real American".

There were some caring white people who would show their respect to upper class Blacks at times. A true story was printed about two Black women sitting in a tea room in the North. After a long wait, one of them made an effort to get the attention of the waiter. He came to their table and said "I don't wait on no Niggers".
At the next table sat two members of Smith College faculty. One of them, a lady, took over to the Black ladies tea and cake which had just been served to them, remarking, "Won't you let us offer you ours? It is such a pleasure to wait on Mrs. Paul Laurence Dunbar". (Alice Dunbar was the wife of the distinguished poet of color).

The late Mrs. Mary McCleod Bethune, an educator, said that when she was a small child and entered the classroom of her mission school in a small church near Maysville, Sumter, South Carolina, that she met her teacher, Miss Emma Wilson. Mrs. Bethune said later that Ms. Wilson was the first Negro she ever heard called "Miss" and the fairest skin colored person she ever had seen.

Today, there are some Blacks who are debating the subject, "segregation vs. integration". The late Governor and Judge, William Hastie stated in a speech to the 62nd Annual NAACP Convention Minneapolis, Minn. on July 7, 1971, that "some Negroes have tended uncritically to adopt and encourage racial separatism in our country as a desirable and potentially rewarding pattern of American life. This trend must be halted and reversed for it can lead only to greater bitterness and frustration and to even more inferior status Black Americans now experience. Where are we today? Whites for over 100 years succeeded in imposing racial separation in our political, economic and social life, why return to it?" These words spoken 17 years ago should be nutritional reasoning for some Blacks, in 1998.

"Upper Class Assistance to the Lower Class"

When Thomas Sewell Inborden founded Brick school for the AMA in 1895, one of his major goals was to become the farmer's friend and advisor. In 1900, T.S. held his first farmer's meeting on the school campus at Enfield, North Carolina. He was interested in how they used different farm equipment and their farming methods. He conducted successive meetings throught the years and also visited many farmers and offered advice, both technical and administrative. Inborden attempted to assist the farmers with their personal economic and financial problems. He also was able to assess the overall situation that affected the Black farmers and their relations with white farmers, white businessmen and bankers. Evidently, Inborden was quite perturbed when he wrote his personal beliefs, views and observations of the North Carolina Black farmers' problems in the 1930's shortly after the Great Depression. He expressed his thoughts in correspondence with a friend, W.G. Jackson on February 21, 1932. Inborden wrote that he had canned himself 400 quarts of fruit and tomatoes and later he gave them freely to some people in the community. He said that he is receiving daily lamentations from various sources relative to the way some landlords are treating the tenants. He said a man brought mules several years ago and tried to pay for them together with other furnishings for two years and all he has made has gone into the landlord's pocket. A few days ago, the landlord came to his house and took everything in sight that was of any value. T.S. stated that the tenant is absolutely stranded. The tenant had to beg among his friends and the last report T.S. received was that he was planning to go to the county seat for support. T.S. wrote about a land lady who was quite wealthy and had taken every mule, cow, horse, chicken and pig from her tenants. Many whites wrote Inborden, obtained their wealth from the Negroes and the confiscation of their farms. T.S. said he went to this wealthy white land lady for a small contribution for the school. But she told T. S. she could not help because she had to pay her taxes. T. S. wrote about a Black farmer who was paying taxes on more than 50,000 dollars worth of property. For seven years the farmer had found it impossible to pay his bills. The prices of the crop fell lower and lower and the interest on his loans higher and higher. T.S. went to Durham with the farmer to see if some of his Black friends in the business world would help the farmer. But the men told T.S. they had the money but were not allowed to use it on real estate. Eventually the farmer's property was advertised and sold. T.S. said that he had heard from another source that his house was taken by the landlords. He had ten children and was trying to educate them. The past summer when he should have been canning fruit, he was growing many crops with which to clear his debts, but he was getting further in debt. Inborden had to give this farmer 20 quarts of fruit. The farmer had to pay rent on his house and his barns if he remained on the farm.

An Upper Class Black's Views on Race Relations, 1932

Thomas Sewell Inborden expressed his views on Whites and his southern experiences in correspondence to his friends in 1932. He wrote: "that he had travelled far and wide, all over the country and had contact with white people in every part of this country. T. S. said that he had studied with white boys and girls, slept in their homes, eaten at their tables, spoken with them in their churches and halls. Their refinement and great culture is absolutely beyond measure of description. However, how some white people can do the things they do without absolutely any compunctions of conscience is beyond my conception. inborden continued by saying that he was born in the South, lived in the South all my life, all of my traditions are southern all of my best friends are in the South all my relatives on both sides of the race line are southern. Yet, this race complex puzzles me more than any expression I can make. I get on the train anywhere I wish so long as they know I am White, but soon as they see I am colored I am prescribed to every inconvenience. Inborden stated that prohibition is counted a failure because it began at the wrong end, with the law instead of with the cradle, in theSunday school and in the pulpit. If race prejudice is ever rooted out as it never will, it must begin with the cradle and in the home about the fire side, in the Sunday school and churches. Respect must begin with human personality. Graduations are formed by natural aptitudes. The one solvent is Christianity. T.S. closed his letter to Jackson by writing, If we cannot solve the problem of our generation, our philosophy is wrong and we would do well to analyze the whole situation, ourselves and change our philosophy.

On February 28, 1932, Inborden wrote a letter to Lawyer Andrews. T.S. discussed an article in a newspaper on *The Carpet baggers, Negro and the Constitution of North Carolina.* Inborden stated that when one reads the white man's history, he gets the idea that Negroes did nothing that was good in the reconstruction days. The truth will leak out here and there. Forty years ago the Negroes were counted as a factor to be recognized more than he is now. T.S. said our position today is one of complacency, we are jim crowed in every way because we accept it and have no power. Inborden wrote how some white people calling themselves superior can do the things that most of them do is beyond my comprehension. We meet in conferences, farm meetings and various other gatherings to hear a lot of what I call purely palaver. We are asked to meet them halfway in settling race relations, when we have always met them two-thirds and three fourths of the way. We must let them dole out what they want us to have in the way of social matters and public places of influence. T.S. told Attorney Andrews that he is an eminent lawyer, but he can get all the law that Blackstone ever knew or be as great as the greatest lawyer in the country, you need not ever expect to be a judge in the South or a solicitor. Inborden said that he was in the Supreme Court of North Carolina in Raleigh recently, and he was blessed if he could not make a better speech than some of those men and reason better. T.S. said that at the next meeting of the state relations committee, they should have some of the Black lawyers to include Lewis and Rich to draw up an indictment against our complacency and I might say against the complacency of the whole race relations committee for not developing a more radical program for absolute human rights. T.S. wrote that he with all his education and background of achievement for the past forty years had no more rights than his mother who was born in a low environment reared under the conditions of human slavery though not a slave herself. Our school teachers are on less salary and other semi school officials are on less than white people would receive doing less than the same work. Our complacency gives an assent to it. I move about among farm people almost daily and it would interest you to know how perfectly subjected they are to conditions imposed on them by their "superior whites". T.S. said he was making inquiries to Washington, D.C. to see how this class of Negro will be handled in the newly organized Reconstruction Finance Corporation (RFC). If left solely to the southern white man's administration and especially the small county banks and landlords, it simply means a better tool with which to exploit the Negro and poor white man. Inborden stated that he went to a bank and they knew nothing about the RFC. It is to their advantage to keep the Negro in all the ignorance they can. I am going to get all the information I can and will use every opportunity to give this information to the Negro farmers. T.S. remarked how he was attending a meeting at Chapel Hill, N.C. Only at noon an announcement was made as to the time and place for lunch. We were advised after some little excitement and my inquiry that we would have to go down to a certain street and in a specific building, and the YMCA secretary would tell us where to go and the cook might give us a handout. There was to have been another meeting after lunch. We found our car and went to Hall's Hotel in Raleigh. When we got to our car, we found a red tag saying call at Police headquarters. We went to Police headquarters and waited but no official was to be found. I learned the officials were having court and I went over there to where I found an officer, to whom I explained my predicament. We had gone to the university on a special invitation and had parked on the school campus near the building where the meeting was held along with other parked cars. The officer was nice, after seeing that we were completely at his mercy. He advised us that since we were out of town to forget it. The point was not that I was doing all the talking and I took all the responsibility for the situation but that he thought I was a white man. I have been caught in that sort of mesh before. I do not think the angels in heaven can be nicer than some white people I have met as I move about from place to place. They seem to be the embodiment of everything fine, culture, refinement, education, religion, free from every semblance of race prejudice. Yet one does not have to go very far in any direction without their showing the cloven feet. There are only a few whites one can meet and talk to as one man should talk to another. He shows intuitively his superior complex and most of us Blacks feel that we ought to take off our hat and put it under our left arm while we talk to them. I never go into a court house, said T.S. where there are Negroes but that I have to tell them to keep their hats on in the halls and lobbies unless white men have theirs off. The background for this tradition is bad and is still the common white man takes as humility in his presence. He thinks it is obeyance to him.

The President Emeritus former Principal Thomas Sewell Inborden in 1932 was very sincere and adamant about his observations and experiences of the Black status in the southern states and the power-ruling dominance by white people in subjugating Blacks to an inferior status, politically, economically and socially. Inborden was not a politician or known Black leader giving speeches without any direct results. He was a man who understood his people, the common Black man and woman and their children. He knew poverty, ignorance and the continuing imposition the Whites placed upon Blacks. He was displeased with a so-called North Carolina Race Relations Committee. In 1932, T.S. Inborden wrote his friends and expressed so eloquently the situation and some possible solutions. I sincerely believe Inborden was quite conscious of the race problems in America.

"A White Supporter's Wife Desires Recognition For Him"

The Black upper class in the 1930's received support from some white politicians, pacifists, suffrage leaders for Black rights and the educational opportunities. Sometimes the Black leaders would decide who they should recognize and show public recognition for their contributions and generous support for Black American. I found in the T.S. Inborden papers a letter he received from the wife of a great supporter of the NAACP and some Black colleges. There was an article about T.S.' school in the *New York Times* and it was read by Mrs. Milholland, whose husband was a distinguished attorney and suffragist leader for Negro rights. He was John E. Milholland. He founded the Republican state party in New York and he was a pacifist. He also played an integral role in the founding of the NAACP. Later he served as treasurer, Executive Committee and served as a member of the Board of Directors. He was also interested in Women's rights, prison reforms, and federal and state education.

There were times when Milholland and W.E.B. Dubois did not agree with some of the philosophies of Booker T. Washington of Tuskegee, Institute, Alabama. However, he did assist Tuskegee Institute on numerous occasions. Inborden received a letter from Jean Milholland of Meadowmount, Lodge Waltham, New York in August, 1931. After reading the letter, T.S. realized that some of the contents referred to Tuskegee Institute and he decided to write a letter to his friend, Dr. R.R. Moton, President of Tuskegee. He told Moton that he had received the letter and that the original was in Mrs. Milholland's own hand and he was copying it and sending it as a suggestion and possibly Moton would know how to handle it to his advantage. Inborden said he was copying only the part with reference to Tuskegee. The letter to Dr. Moton read:

My Dear Professor, In reading about your wonderful work in the New York Sunday Tribune, August 23, 1931, 1 immediately began to recall the days when John E. Milholland and Booker T. Washington were so friendly and regret so much that Tuskegee, the one of Mr. Milholland's favorite schools seems to be the only one among all those he delighted so to help, has no reminder there of him. Howard University and the NAACP's crisis in New York have busts, but somehow there was never any effort made at Tuskegee. Some time you might ask Emmett Scott (former secretary for Booker T. Washington) about Mr. Milholland and what he did for them. I should like so much to have that school above all others see that his bust was there.

Frederick Douglass' Second Marriage

Frederick Douglass, the outstanding abolitionist, and statesman in later years of his life married a white lady, Helen Pitts, the daughter of a white abolitionist. Two couples, close friends of the Douglass' were Senator and Mrs. B.K. Bruce and Rev. Francis J. and Mrs. Grimke. There were some Blacks who did not approve of the marriage, especially that Douglass was marrying a white woman. Some Blacks remarked that Douglass was showing "contempt for the women of his race and that he had married a common poor white". This was not true because Ms. Pitts was a college graduate and from a highly respectable family. The historical Frederick Douglass' home in Washington, D.C. was preserved due to her efforts to save the Cedar Hill Home from being sold. There were also some other people who strongly objected to the marriage.

The Rev. Grimke had received a letter from a white southerner who thought Grimke was a white person. The southerner wrote "any white minister who would marry a Negro to a white woman ought to be tarred and feathered".

"Just Speak From The Hip"

There have been times during segregation when white leaders have requested Black educators and professional to deviate from normal presentations protocol and asked them to speak from the "hip or off handed". Thomas Sewell Inborden, an early educator, experienced this when he was asked to speak at the American Missionary Association's (AMA) Forty-Eighth Annual meeting at the First Congregational church, Lowell, Massachusetts in October, 1894. Inborden wrote that "I prepared a paper to be read on the subject as requested by Dr. Beard. Just before I went to sit upon the platform with all the speakers both of these men, one at a time came to me and told me that they wanted me to speak off handed. All the other speakers spoke from their papers, even Dr. Beard and President Cravath, who preceded me and so did I. I am Inborden North and South. But I have in consolation that I made a big hit. The house applauded me three times and President Gates came to his feet almost and emphasized a certain point in my paper and that part he read again. I received high congratulations from men whose judgement means something. Dr. Woodbury took my paper as soon as I was seated to have it published."

"A Legacy of Segregation, KKK"

A North Carolina newspaper the *News and Observer* published an article on June 30, 1993 about a Black senior citizen of Edgecombe who recalled some experiences of segregation. This senior citizen said that "he does not like to remember when he had to play music for the white family who owned the farm where he was raised. He said that he would play the guitar for the family's yard parties near Bishopville, North Carolina in 1930's. Sometimes the party guests would call him "nigger:, said the senior citizen".

A former student at Brick School, Enfield, N.C. remembers one day when the Ku Klux Klan burned a cross in the front yard on the school campus. She said that she was in the school's Ingraham Chapel on Easter Sunday when the charred cross was brought into the service. I am sure that this story would be insignificant to those officials who will reinterpret the constitution and state it is within the law to issue a march permit for a Ku Klux Klan group to have a scheduled march down Pennsylvania Avenue, Washington, D.C. in 1998. Just more "nutritional reasoning".

"Why Don't They Stay Where They Belong"

The current discussion on defacto segregated schools in 1998 in major cities and counties in the United States does raise many questions as to whether there will ever be welcome mat for Blacks to integrate all white city public schools. In 1954, just after the May 17 school decision, resistance was present everywhere. The Baltimore Western High School in Maryland was an example, not necessarily from the administration, but from some individual teachers. A Black young lady said that her white English teacher told her class "I don't know why some people don't stay where they are wanted and where they belong". Just another true story of resisting segregation in the yesteryears.

"Something to Really Rap About 1919 and 1998

Many young Black youngsters listen to popular "rap" songs that tend to explain their past hardships and denial of opportunities in life, and sometimes these youngsters feel comfortable listening to the lyrics because they appear to equate the rap stories with their personal lives. However, I believe that if they could learn about what real poverty and hardships were all about during segregation, they might be able to see that their present living conditions are greatly improved over those persons who once lived under the majority society's dictates and exclusions for people of color. The Thomas S. Inborden papers revealed to me how a family of color elevated their caste status or class level upward. In March, 1998, I was given an opportunity to say a few words at the memorial services for the late Mrs. Jesse Bullock Thornton who died at the age of 98 years. She was the last immediate survivor of the Bullock family of Brick (Enfield), N.C. Inborden (T.S.) was quite fascinated by the achievements of this family and wrote an article *"Does It Pay"*. Some of the highlights of the article were: Mr. an Mrs. George Bullock were the parents of four boys and four girls. All of the children attended school at Brick Normal. Inborden said that the children had to walk eight miles to school prior to the family moving on the farm. Some of Bullock's friends, told him that it would be impossible to feed and cloth his children, run a farm and at the same time give them an education. T.S. said the Bullocks met every discouragement but they kept their children in school. Inborden stated that all of Bullock's possessions were under a mortgage for rations, farm implements and supplies. However, under the Brick School system, Bullock was able to pay off the mortgage and afterwards buy his provisions in cash and as the opportunity came he purchased a farm with 83 acres. Inborden discussed in the article how the Bullock children were successful in their chosen endeavors. A son Benjamin, graduated from the University of Minnesota with honors; a son, Joseph was a training teacher in an Episcopal school in Charlotte, North Carolina and later became a dentist. The oldest daughter studied at Brick and later married a minister of one of the largest Baptist churches in the state, Reverend A.S. Croom of Salisbury, N.C. A daughter married a merchant in Salisbury, N.C. She had finished Brick with a major in sewing and became a dressmaker. A daughter Lula was a graduate of Brick and Fisk University. Another daughter, Jessie was a Brick graduate and also a graduate of Howard University. She became a teacher in home economics and the wife of the late Dr. Robert A. Thornton, a distinguished physicist and master teacher who had studied with Albert Einstein, the noted physicist. Inborden raised the question, Does It Pay? because he had observed that the Bullock boys came home one summer and built a house for their parents. They drew up the plans and worked out every detail in the construction of the house. The house cost about 2,000 dollars. The only cost outlay was the material. T.S. said that the house was not only built well, but was furnished largely by the boys themselves and was constructed on their own farm. Inborden said it does pay to do the challenging things. T.S. said their experiences were a transition from the small cabin, but the mother was a woman of natural endowment and she knew how to take care of such a house. While it is three miles from town, it was lighted with electric lights within a year. He replied by saying that if success is to be measured by the accumulation of a beautiful home with 80 acres surrounding it and sufficient horses to work the farm with implements and other necessities for farm life, it pays. T.S. said the success does not stop here. There are the boys with mechanical skill, agricultural knowledge and academic training which have given them eminent success in life. The girls of the family have accomplished in their spheres. T.S. concluded his article by saying the process of the Bullock's family training has given them an ethical concept that is invaluable in any community in which they may live.

The Bullock story portrays how many Black families in the South, especially North Carolina, were able to survive, receive an education and obtain monumental attainments in life in their respective professions. They were faced with the walls of oppression and forced segregation, but it did pay off for them through faith, and belief in God. I ask the question why cannot more young people of today have the self discipline, inspiration, motivation and initiative to achieve excellence in their endeavors. The Bullocks did it so well. There are some descendants of the Bullocks today who have made outstanding contributions in their professions. As T.S. would say, it has paid off for them, the descendants of the Bullocks of Brick, North Carolina.

Black Social Problems, 1916

Thomas Sewell Inborden would clearly express his personal thoughts and analysis of Blacks, their conditions of poverty, education and oppression. Inborden wrote in a published article March, 1916, that *"many things are stated about the Negro and every phase of his life has been exploited in public address, in literature and upon the stage. So much has been said against him that the name suggests the worst features of the race. He has been caricatured in every conceivable way. We should learn to discriminate between the worth and worthless of all races and to condemn any classification that includes the good with the bad; it is unjust. You missionaries who go South are good people and worthy of all praise but often they come home and inadvertently leave a sad picture. They do not mean to do so but they do. They tell you about the one room log hut where the family of ten cook, eat and sleep and that room without a window; they tell you about the crude way in which everything is done; they tell you about the quack lawyers, doctors, preachers, and teachers. There are log huts in the South by the thousands, quacks in every profession and apparently few change in the methods of doing things. If I were supporting education work in the South or anywhere else and had only the saddest pictures presented to me as rewards of my philanthropy, I would get discouraged as doubtless some of you have done. I want to show you a brighter side. Take for example, Fisk University organized nearly 50 years ago. Her graduates have gone out into the world and created public sentiment, changed the conditions of life, established schools, preached the gospel instead of a merely emotional religion. They are teachers of a very high order in every part of the South. Instead of one room huts, they are building cottages with rooms ranging from 4 to 12. What is true of one school is equally true of many of the other AMA schools. These schools have a purpose of the moral and intellectual advancement of the*

Negro. One cannot get the knowledge of the progress made in the South by riding through the country on trains and know nothing about the masses of Negroes. You must know the plantation and home quarters, real conditions. A ride through the country will give you an external view of the log cabins and a sight of a crowd of children with appearance of poverty. Many of these Negroes are discouraged but still some have the highest form of chastity and virtue. There are three difficulties encountered in the educational problems of the Negro. one is discouragement. Some Negroes feel they are only intended for cotton fields and house servants.

Another difficulty is the popular prejudice on the part of a great many white people against Negro education, whatever nature. It is only intensified. The third difficulty we have is a financial one. The system of land tenure in the South makes it hard for the poor man colored or white to rise far above the obsolete necessities of life because of problems, especially for Blacks, discriminatory laws and juries. Negro intellect is as active and capable of high attainments as that of any other nationality in the world. The lower the scale of general intelligence of the masses, the higher should be the attainment of the leaders in intelligence morality, temperance, virtue, loyalty, truth and patriotism."

It is interesting to study history some 94 years ago and learn that some Blacks had life styles that can be found today in some Black communities. Educator Thomas S. Inborden wrote "an article on the *Facts On Joseph K. Brick Agricultural and Normal School in 1904*. He stated where the school was located and gave some descriptive characteristics of the community and people. He said a minister told him that he never encouraged his congregation to purchase a home and to educate their children for those who did so would not support the gospel. Inborden wrote that some Black graduates from the best schools of the South do not support them as they should, not from lack of loyalty but because they too are trying to get comfortable homes. T.S. said most educated <u>Negroes</u> tried to get a home and have better things.

"Do Not Tell Them Your First Name"

During segregation some upper class Blacks would advise their children, to demand respect if possible or prevent attempts to discredit them. Mrs. Sarah J. Inborden informed her children at an early age. She wrote her daughter Julia a letter in June, 1917 and said: "I am sending you in this letter a check for 15 *dollars I hope you will have no trouble in getting it cashed. I have* written the check addressed to Miss J.E. Inborden, because in dealing *with those people especially the white people, do* not tell *them that your name is Julia. They will be calling you by your first name instead of Miss Inborden which is due you. If there is need to use more than the term Miss, I tell them my name is S.J. Inborden, therefore you tell them you name is J.E. Inborden. If they persist in trying to find out more, then tell* the *white people or other people that is what you are* to all but your most intimate friends.

Now the majority of the lower class southern Blacks would conform to southern traditions and respond to whites when called by their first name or other titles.

"I Know Where I Am Going"

There was an occasion where Sarah Jane Inborden and her children were returning from Oberlin, Ohio. When they arrived in Richmond, Virginia, they changed trains for North Carolina. Mrs. Inborden approached the Jim Crow car for colored and was about to enter the doorway when the conductor said, "lady, you getting on the wrong car". Mrs. Inborden replied, *I know where I am going, to this car.* The conductor let her proceed. She was not trying to pass for white.

"Black Culture and African Awareness"

Today there are characteristics of Black culture that somewhat minimize the knowledge and historical facts of Black Americans in the building of the United States in its economic, political and military areas. Many Blacks of all class levels, have made considerable efforts toward educating themselves about a part of their Afriican heritage. Some have adopted different dress and hair styles, mainly from West Africa. Also some in the past twenty years have named their children with "home made" and actual African names which unfortunately some young children cannot correctly pronounce. Black professionals of all ages have changed their given American names to African names and when in certain public situations, they will then use both names, instead of just using their new name. There are some middle and upper class Blacks who will don African dress occasionally if it will assist and promote their political, economic and professional image when among some low class and middle class Blacks. Their desired African awareness has almost created another subculture within the different subcultures of the overall Black community. Many Blacks have been able to have the Post Office issue a stamp for a an annual celebration that possibly millions of Blacks have accepted. There are many Black scholars and laypersons who spend a considerable amount of time debating slavery along with some Whites instead of concentrating and reexamining the 80 years of legal segregation against people of color in America or placing a reminder daily as the Jewish Americans do in relation to the Holocaust. I strongly support the academic and layperson's emphasis on reeducating our community about Africa. Since African history was one of my minors in graduate school, I believe that I have a thorough background in the scholarly studies of African history. I do become concerned when some Black leaders, teachers and community workers conduct classes and programs with some myth and untruths about African history. Many of them cannot present the real academic background, but they become so-call experts in song, dance and the drums. Many of them cannot discuss the other geographical areas of the African continent from which some Black slaves came. This is part of my analysis and observations as the "man from Mars". I have stated some facts that can be debated but millions of Black Americans could say the same thing. The news media and some pollsters will give the world an image that these characteristics of a new subculture are representative of many African Americans of all three class levels.

I often tell my college students, that when the "Million Man March" was held, there were some "honorable, innocent, intelligent" Black ministers who instructed their congregations not to attend the march, because of its Islamic influence. Now I would present a "nutritional reasoning". I would tell the students that many Black ministers who possibly delivered the message to their congregation would be appearing in very colorful, beautiful African robes in their pulpits. I am sure that there were some who had no knowledge whatsoever that the original or copy African robe could very well be material or design from one of the many African nations that today have a large population of Islamic followers. between 40 to 90 percent.

Immigrant Africans' Perceptions of Blacks

What class of society in the Black community today generates characteristics that are perceived and believed by some of their African sisters and brothers who have immigrated to America recently. Some African immigrants have established their cultural barriers with African Americans in the 1990's.

A successful African businessman from Nigeria said, "Half of them still have the slave mentality. They get reliant on welfare and food stamps. We have always had problems with them". A young African female student studying in Boston, stated that "the African student organization and the Black American student organization on campus never interested her". A Liberian said, "African Americans are people from a different culture, an American culture".

Some Africans believe that even African Americans who are well educated have a bias against Africa and show lack of interest in Africa's problems of disease, famine, war and corruption. There are some African Americans today who are showing a great interest in Africa. Now there are some Africans who listen to the media stereotypes of Blacks and have little respect for their culture, said an Ethiopian in Washington, D.C.

There have been some Africans who believe that Black Americans are inferior to them and very violent. These Africans interact different with American whites; they receive different treatments. An Ethiopian shared a true story with me some six years ago about some whites' perceptions of Black and reminded the Ethiopian who he was not. The young Ethiopian was invited to a social affair at an Ethiopian-Italian family friend. She was married to a high level northern Virginia police officer who is white. During a conversation with the lady's husband, while having their drinks, the white police official told the Ethiopian, "Young man, we have some problems at times with those Blacks, you know, but we take care of them, arrest them in a minute". That is literally what he told me. My friend said he immediately responded and said you know I am Black. The white man replied, "Oh no, you are an Ethiopian".

I often tell students that history can be so interesting especially when one recalls facts and parallels. When I was a child, I used to hear the "old folks" say "You know those Ethiopians are considered white. Well in respect to this true story I really believe that the police official could never classify his Italian appearing wife as having any drop of Black blood, because remember he said, "She is an Ethiopian". "Nutritional reasoning".

Interracial Marriages

A Diplomatic Family Affair

The *Time magazine* of September 29, 1967 with its cover picture of an interracial couple, called it "a marriage of Enlightenment". The parents of the bride called the wedding arrangements a family affair and it would be handled that way. The bride had attended integrated public schools in Washington, D.C., when many of her father's colleagues and friends sent their children to private schools. She was enrolled at Wilson High School in 1965. Ironically, the bridegroom, the son of a civilian analyst at the Pentagon and whose mother was a counselor and teacher in the District of Columbia Public Schools, attended private schools. Living in an integrated Washington Northeast neighborhood, he was enrolled in the Georgetown Day School and was one of the 30 Black children out of a student body of 100. In the ninth grade he was elected class president and to the student council. He had earned straight A's. Later he was enrolled at the progressive private school, Hawthorne. He was very fond of horses and rode in horse shows in Rock Creek Park, Washington, D.C., where he met his wife; she was then 14 years old. This couple would be married later in a very prestigious and yet controversial wedding ceremony at Stanford's University's Memorial Church. Now who were the parents of this bride? Peggy was the lovely daughter of the United States Secretary of

State, a native of Cherokee County, Georgia and grandson of two confederate soldiers; he was the late Honorable Dean Rush.

Dean Rush's family members did not attend and Clarence and Artenia Smith's family members were not present; however, Mrs. Virginia Rush, a native of Seattle, Washington, had some of her family members at the wedding. It has been said that Dean Rush had always exhibited his liberal concern about race; during World War II while serving as an Army Captain, he severed the color line when he invited an OSS officer to dinner. The OSS officer of color was Ralph Bunche.

"Rush's hometown of 26,000 people, Cherokee County, Georgia showed some negative reactions toward the marriage and his cousin, a business man said "I would rather people marry somebody of their own race, but that is their business".

The reactions to this marriage were expressed openly by some family members of the couple, historians, journalist and they even relived history by referring to previous interracial marriage of some notable individuals.

The people in 1967 had a very strong racial dialogue and commentaries when they openly expressed the following stories: "In 1948, it would have been impossible for the marriage to take place in California because it would have been a criminal offense in the state". There was a rumor that Dean Rush was prepared to resign if President Lyndon Johnson thought it would be necessary after he revealed to him the plan. Another cousin of Dean Rush said that she believed that Rush should have done something about it and not let it go that far. He should have prevented it" Many Georgians believed that Dean Rush did a bad thing when he walked down the aisle and gave her away and that it sounds as if it was all done with his knowledge.

The State department received some vile letters and calls from bigots. Some of them wrote and said, "I would probably kill any of my children before I would let them do such a thing. "If I were Rush I would be inclined to shoot the guy". "It will serve the old goat right to have nigger grand babies."

There were also some Blacks who objected to the wedding. However, most Black leaders preferred to see the marriage as a personal affair. Some militant Blacks would say "Tokenism again". She only married one Negro. There were some favorable responses. James Meredith said, "The event is a favorable way to look at race relations today". John H. Johnson, publisher, Ebony and Jet said "The marriage is a measure of America's maturity and it might help us in the eyes of the world."

The marriage of Margaret Rush and Guy Smith in 1967 was a historical and significant event because their wedding caused many Americans both Black and white to express their inner feeling about a most powerful subject that even people today might say with those wonderful senior citizens of yesteryears. "There are things folks don't talk about".

"Bald Heads and Stocking Caps"

Today some Black men have adopted the fad of shaving their heads and wearing the "bald head" style. During the segregation years, bald heads were not considered a popular hair style or model image of one's favorite sports figures. I can recall playing in my neighborhood at 9 years old, and the kids would remark, "Mr. Jones is back home and he is wearing the "jail bird style hair cut; look at baldy, Mr. Jones" The prison system in those days would shave all of the hair off the inmates head creating the bald head hair style.

I also remember when boys and men would wear stocking caps (obtain old stockings from their mother or sisters) to press down their hair. However no one in their right mind would wear one outside in the streets or in public places. The only exception would be when a person had ring worms and they would become the target of ridicule and embarrassment.

Styles and fads will change throughout the years, but a knowledge of their significance years ago and their cultural meanings and acceptance could preclude the adoption of old stereotypes in 1998. Well, sometimes "ignorance is bliss". just another true story of the way we were during segregation and another nutritional thought!

DIVERSITY OF AFRICAN AMERICANS

GENETIC DIVERSITY

"What Would Daddy Think"

A Story of Color Obsession

John William Henry Clark was born in 1863. He enlisted on April 26, 1863 at Chicago, Illinois. The official records listed him as five feet, six inches, and dark complexion, Black hair and Black eyes. Clark was present for duty on Morris Island, South Carolina on August 15, 1863 where he was injured while on a detail unloading large loads of timber piles, boxes of ammunition and shells. Clark fell with a heavy timber on his shoulder and was badly injured. Clark married Francis M. Woods on March 30, 1871. They were married by the Reverend William Jones. John H.W. Clark worked at Hook and Ladder Company Volunteer, No. 6. John H.W. Clark was admitted to the Central Branch National Home for Disabled Veterans Soldier (DVS), Columbus, Ohio in July 1893. He died at the home on October 11, 1893.

Clark's widow, Frances M. Woods, requested a widow's pension. Her pension was rejected because she could not establish sufficient evidence to show that her first husband, Granville W. Demarest, was deceased.

These comments by a special examiner of the Bureau of Pensions in 1890 were common in many instances when they were confronted with the problem of that time, the *color problem,* especially miscegenation or race-mixing. The examiner wrote his summation of the interview with Clark's widow and his personal views. They were: The claimant is a white woman of very, fair complexion with not a drop of Negro blood in her veins. Furthermore, she is fairly intelligent and a good talker and shows evidence of having had some refinement. If her own story is true, she is of good ancestry, her father having been a practicing physician in New York City. She has now hanging in her front room of her house two old paintings of (she says) her father and mother. They are very old paintings. The man in the painting is represented with an old *fashioned standing collar and beach stock and behind him on a little shelf are painted some large volumes labeled "Practice of Medicine".*

The elements of racism were quite evident in the special examiner's character when he wrote in his report the following: *In the room where those pictures hang, claimant (Frances Clark) now, has a male colored roomer. If the departed spirit of claimant's father could look down through the painted eyes of that old picture of himself and see his daughter's Negro consorts and the depths to which she has descended, what would he think? Miscegenation (race mixing) between whites and Negroes, in Ohio, is legal and* common.

"Black Body Problem"

The late Dr. Robert A. Thornton, master teacher, scholar, physicist and humanist was discussing a physics problem with Albert Einstein during one of his meeting with him. Thornton said that Einstein misunderstood a phrase that Thornton used and the response by Einstein was quite humorous. Dr. Thornton and Dr. Albert Einstein, the noted physicist, believed that Thornton being Black and Einstein Jewish helped their relationship tremendously. The following quote is from my book the *Master Teacher, Robert Thornton*. "During a visit to Einstein's laboratory I told him that I had been working on a 'black body' problem in Physics. When referring to the 'black body' and its emission of wave lengths in a spectrum scientists describe the numbers and their relationship in three different basic ways: tables, graphs and equations. You have two numbers associated therefore you can represent them in three different ways. One way is to just draw a graph and use two sides. If one of the values is called X, and one is Y, what is the equation that relates to the two. This was the problem I had. (reference the equation). When I arrived at the laboratory I stated to Einstein that I was having trouble with my Black Body problem. Einstein evidently misunderstood me and replied: I certainly have sympathy for all of your people on this problem. We had quite a laugh about this misunderstanding."

DIVERSITY OF AFRICAN AMERICANS

I delivered a speech to a high level government agency in 1995. This speech will provide some information about the differences among Black Americans.

"I sincerely believe that the residuals effects of America's dehumanizing system of slavery and its many years of covert and overt forms of racism. especially institutional racism have taken their toll in the education and miseducation of many Americans of all ethnic groups. Today, 1995, people of all ethnic and racial groups have the stereotypical visions of African Americans, visions portrayed through the news media, television and the mind tranquilizer of humor and laughter that actually omit the serious and scholarly representation of a diverse or different people.

Today, I would like to address some very significant facts and thoughts for you to consider about the Diversity of African Americans, a diversity that is quite profound in biological, social, economic and political perspectives. These diversities should reflect that African Americans, Blacks, Negroes, Afro Americans, colored, Africa, Ethiopians, slaves, free people and the infamous words nigger and darkey all have been used to describe Black people. Biological diversity represents the race mixing of the African slave during slavery with European, Indian, and in some cases Asian genes. This occurred over a period of at least 250 years. Original slaves and mixed slaves reproduced among themselves; therefore, we have many Blacks who are representative of their dominant African genetic heritage. However, in 1995 the African American whether they agree, reject, or care less, are still representative of genes of other races. There was one group of Blacks during slavery that were given different names because of their visible resemblance of a half mixture other than African with European. They were assigned the names of octoroons, quadroons, mustie, mulattoes, high yellows and chestnuts. Unfortunately, the biological genetic diversity and genetic offsprings of an African or half African and a white person created a problem for the slave and master. This was beginning of a dilution among African peoples of their beautiful ebony skin color who in some instances had already been divided by some groups or tribal groups. Many of the mulattoes were born free or later freed by their biological white father or purchased their own freedom as some other slaves did. They created their own community when freed, and this was the beginning of a mulatto class within the divided Black community. This was also the start of disunity among African peoples in America based on the degree of lightness of the skin and certain physical characteristics Some mulattos developed a self concept, individual pride and superiority a sense that they were different from other Blacks. They developed the life styles and a new culture based on the majority white culture. In later years, the U.S. Census in 1860 and 1870 would identify the family as mulatto. There were also some Blacks prior to the 1860's who owned slaves. Yes, skin color is an obsession in America today, possibly a residual effect of yesterday. This early social division among Blacks did have an effect on the unity of Blacks. This social division was portrayed in community activities to include burial societies, churches and clubs among Blacks, and later some colleges would reflect the color problem. In South Carolina, in the 1870's there was a Brown Men's Society for lighter skin Blacks. Episcopal churches in Charleston for Blacks would reflect the color difference. This was a beginning of segregation within a segregated society, perpetuated by Blacks. The point is simply that Black people over the years in culture, values, folkways, morals, speech and religious beliefs have been quite different from other ethnic groups in America. I am saying historically and realistically that Blacks do not think the same or act the same in spite of the ways they may be presented on the evening news.

There are many majority members and even some Black representatives of all classes of society, managers, government leaders and military leaders, who honestly believe that the so-called street Blacks and a few other Blacks who act out antics on weekly humor shows including popular talk shows, actually indicate how most African Americans really are.

Economically and politically Blacks are diverse and the residual effects of segregation and exclusion over the years have contributed to some conditions of poverty, ignorance, illiteracy and low performance. But these problems are not based on any physical or mental differences rather on political, social and educational inequities. Politically, one must realize that most Blacks had been denied the right to vote for many years prior to the relatively recent Civil Rights thrust. Some did vote and many in the South were led to the polls by their masters or former masters. There were many Blacks after the Civil War with no where to go who remained with some former masters or other majority member as share croppers. There were white sharecroppers but they were eventually able to realize upward mobility void of an inferior segregated life style. One must realize that prior to 1954, there was only one major minority in America subject to enforced separation, the Blacks, both men and women. The Civil Rights Movement of 1960 gave long overdue consideration to American Blacks. Prior to 1954 and especially

World War II, there were two categories of race in the U.S. Army, Navy, Marines, and Air Force, Negro and White, everyone else who was not Negro or Black was considered White. Since the dehumanizing slavery system Blacks have been considered by non Blacks as inferior. There are so many variables to the problems of African Americans today and it is not really easy to understand the diversity of Blacks and their long historical road toward equality.

I do not have the solutions to any problems. However, as a concerned American of color, I have some inferences, suggestions and logical thoughts and crucial facts to be considered. First, the intent of Brown vs Board of Education 1954 has not been met. We do have a polarized society, yes, still based on living patterns, cultures, churches and most aspects of life to include schools. How can people communicate, erase the fears of others and reject stereotypes. The educational system does not assist in solving the problem. Why? Because the standard curriculum of public textbooks is oriented toward a 98% focus on the history of the majority group in America. When one pursues an education whether in a Black or majority school system, the history is not complete. There is definitely a need for all youth and adults to be reeducated about the achievements of African Americans in America's society. There is a necessity for all Americans and foreigners, especially, to be reeducated about the history of African Americans, their past and their present. They cannot be compared with other Americans including people of color from the West Indies and Africa. This is a distinct and different American of color. African Americans over the years have been confronted with difficult problems, situations and legal inequities in America. I repeat, 35 years cannot correct those past injustices and denials. The trials and frustrations and states of low self esteem and thoughts of inferiority were accepted by many Blacks when they could not overcome these challenges. Many survived, some did not. There were separated families and recurring illegitimacy during slavery as well as the denial of an education and the right to enjoy the better things of life.

Let us not forget that Americans have constructed monuments, museums and elaborate memorials to remind the world of their past inhumane treatment and injustices. Yet, people of all races fail to study and discuss the challenging human drama of African American. African Americans and other groups must be reeducated. Many Black youth today are not aware that a baby born years ago at home or in the separate wings of segregated hospitals in the North and South began his first month of growth and development in a restricted neighborhood across the railroad tracks. Of course, his physician was probably white because there were few Black doctors in the town.

On Sunday, church worship was separate. Some Catholic churches reserved a section in the rear for Blacks. When school age was reached, youngsters started school in an inferior classroom setting to include buildings, textbooks and sometimes state approved low quality teachers. When children would go to the grocery stores on the corner, friendly Jewish merchants had a writing pad to give them credit before the emergence of the credit card. These grocers did not take the flight to the suburbs when they closed shop. They went upstairs to their living quarters. They did not need plastic and bullet proof glass to protect them against belligerent Blacks. Their security force was their Black customers who shared a sense of mutual respect, communication, trust and loyalty and not fear. That was the way things were.

When the young Black child reached maturity, he was aware that the laws of the land sanctioned the segregation in ice cream parlors, restaurants, skating rinks, bowling alleys, theaters, Griffith Stadium, (home of the Redskins) barber shops, and hair dressers. (But in the 1950's a fair skinned Black lady who lived in the Black community would prefer to pass as white to have her hair done at a white salon on Connecticut Avenue). Some Blacks would "pass", as their physical descriptions dictated, as Spanish, Indian or other to go to white theaters in Washington, D.C. One would see white municipal judges, firemen, store clerks, insurance agents (most white insurance companies wrote only term insurance for Blacks). There were no Black parole officers, prison guards, milkmen, or secretaries. Black youth must wake up and smell the real coffee because he or she is living in a new time period and opportunities are available, some facilities are open, and people of all races are willing to assist them in thinking positively and striving for excellence in the pursuit of education. Even though covert institutional racism is still present in the community, private business and government, one can overcome them with education, faith, strong self concept, high self respect and morals. Now, I am not naive, they cannot do this alone because residual effects of the past still have clouds on Black progress. Some people still believe that Blacks are outstanding in entertainment, sports, and music because they all have rhythm, song and dance skills, are religious and emotional and loud. I believe the most diverse and different race of people in the world is the African American in the U.S. Why do I stress this because the nonBlack youth especially white needs to learn about why and how some Black people think the way they do. Blacks continue to see injustices in America and possibly betrayal in the legal actions of some lawyers, judges and juries against affirmative action before it has completed its job.

There are many Whites and even Blacks who will say the past is fine but remember that other people have the same problems. I tell them if I drive a Volkswagen and you a Mercedes and we leave our starting points at different times, (you leave one hour ahead of me) there is no way for me to catch up with you unless someone does something miraculous to cause that to occur. I call the positive accomplishments of Blacks under all the conditions of yesteryears and even today miraculous. When Blacks first realized the truth of the situation and they still accomplished these wonders against great odds.

Dr. Martin Luther King had a dream and the fact that the dream has not been fulfilled even though there is not a closed door, a whip, nor a chain. There are the legal reinterpretations of congressional and Supreme Court decisions, which are now being altered because of reverse discrimination". Yes, there are discussions today about affirmative action and quotas. I must say that our government along with the business world has a history in resisting equal employment for Blacks. Case in point, in 1969, our largest civil service employer the Department of Defense had only 6 Blacks on the GS-15 grade level. In the past 30 years, many Blacks have moved from the status of messenger and custodians to clerks, laborers, technicians, computer specialists, analysts, typists and a few higher positions. Many Blacks today still appear on a curve between GS-5 and GS-12.

There are many leather chairs still not filled with people of color in the upper level positions. But let us examine the situation. With the tables turned, and it's not racism, if there was a Black dominated government in the work place and Blacks were in charge, they would hire many Blacks in all positions just as whites have done over the years. But there is one difference, the Blacks would have had a four hundred year history of being legally dominated means by the majority population; there is a difference. All must be reeducated about what happened and the residual effects that exist today that have caused the problems we are now experiencing.

In view of all the complexities of racial polarization in America, I must state emphatically that there is a need for managers and employees to listen to each other and learn something about each other's differences. Stop stereotyping each others. Use tact. The minority employee must maintain self esteem, be prepared, qualified and ten times better and then, stand at the door and trust that concerned managers will open it without any reservations. If agencies throughout government would take actions immediately and avoid practices of long mitigations and extenuations giving qualified loyal employees an opportunity based on their performances then we can move toward a color blind society, including the work place. After 300 years of toils and struggle, I believe America still has the faith and desire to survive and achieve. But the majority view of superiority, power and control must stop. Let us be frank and realize that in today's civil service system, "fully qualified" or "satisfactory" is not the means toward rapid upward mobility for promotion; most outstanding is the mark of the day and someone is more likely to accept you if you are highly qualified. The employee must possess the qualification and the employer must be considerate. The military has been somewhat successful in using these approaches.

Ladies and gentlemen, sometimes I realize that future in the African American advances appears bleak and doomed. However, I am not a pessimist but an optimist, and I sincerely believe like Dr. Martin Luther King that there are some people of all backgrounds who really would like to see an equitable American society. The day is coming when there will be a Black president. I deeply believe that the continual closed door policy will not prevail forever. I ask, what race of people have accomplished so much in a span of 130 years since removal from slavery? This is a proud and sustaining thought that gives me the assurance that there will be better tomorrows for people of color even if barriers are present today. I also believe that (maybe not my tomorrows) one tomorrow some day, America will really extend to all peoples a feeling of love and welcome. It is in the future and it must come if we all expect to survive together here in America the Beautiful.

"An American Legacy of Color Designation"

Some historians have stated that during the Colonial Period, offsprings of Black and white unions were not recognized as Black or white, and were referred to as mulattoes, quadroons and octoroons. But after the Civil War mulattoes were being recognized and referred to as Black.

The U.S. Census during the periods 1820-1880 used different classifications to identify and call people of color various names. I do not think they ever asked the majority of these ethnic groups what they would like to be called. The late Mrs. Miller who lived for almost one hundred years, lacking two months and 28 days, had been called many names to identify her race, but at her death she was still a "colored" lady and even in death she looked as white as she did in life. During her life time, they were still debating an appropriate name. Whites solved the problem easily between 1829-1970, because the designations were white, mulatto and slaves. In 1870, race was used for the first time with sub categories of White and Black. In later years, these terms used would be "colored, Negro, Chinese, Indian, Japanese, Mexican, Filipino, Hindu, Korean and American Indian.

The U.S. Census Bureau in 1940 held that a person of mixed white and Negro blood should be classified as a Negro, no matter how small the percentage of Negro blood. An Indian and a Negro mixture was still a Negro". They also said that a mixture of non white races should be reported according to the race of the father, except that the Negro-Indian relationship is still a Negro.

The 21st century will be highlighted by the second millenium census, in 2000. The Office of Management and Budget (OMB) will be responsible for the revised classification of federal data on race and ethnicity, the agency directly responsible is the Office of Information and Regulatory Affairs. This Census revision has been stated in the 1998 Statistical Policy Directive No. 15 "Race and Ethnic Standards For Federal Statistics and Administrative Reporting". There are two noticeable modifications, the Asian or Pacific Islanders category will be separated into two categories, Asian and Native Hawaiian or other Pacific Islands. The other is Hispanics will be changed to Hispanic, or Latino."

These revised standards will have five minimum categories on race. They are "American Indian or Alaska Native, Asian, Black or African American, Native American or other Pacific Islanders". There will be two categories to identify ethnicity. They are "Hispanic, or Latino and not Hispanic".

The government uses data on race and ethnicity to monitor equal access in housing, employment and education. This information is crucial for populations that historically have experienced discrimination and differential treatment because of their race or ethnicity. This information is also used in surveys on administrative forms, school registration, mortgage lending applications, and medical research. It is interesting how these new regulations state that "the data will be designed on a 'construct' and no data will be collected on race and there will be no basis for anthropological or scientifically significance to race or ethnic group".

The persons responsible for this revision have stated clearly "that race and ethnicity may be thought in terms of social and cultural characteristics as well as ancestry. But the OMB racial and ethnic categories set forth in the standards should not be interpreted as being primarily, biological or genetic".

Americans, including Blacks themselves, perceive Black people in America by sight and cultural characteristics. However, the Native American and even the "untouchable or Dalit Indians from India can be darker in skin color than many Black Americans, but because of other features including hair texture these groups will definitely be classified immediately as their OMB designated racial group. Yet, an African American "white as white" will still be a Black person in American society. "Nutritional reasoning".

During the revisions of the new census standards on race and ethnicity several questions were debated. There were concerns about how to collect data on persons who identify themselves as multiracial? Do you combine race and Hispanic origin in one question? Should there be separate questions on race and Hispanic origin? Do you combine concepts of race, ethnicity, and ancestry? And should terminology be changed or added? Some of the final recommendations were: There should be self identification, (Blacks do not have options), no multiracial category; a person can select more than one of the racial categories in Directive No. 15 and he can report multiple races. There was an agreement to change Black to "Black or African American". It is interesting to see how the OMB agreed to define categories in detail. "The Asians or Pacific Islanders are in two categories, one Asian and native American or Pacific Islanders. The Native Hawaiian will include persons having origins among any of the original peoples, namely Guam, Samoa, Native Hawaiians, Guamanians, Samoans (this category would include Pacific Islands groups reported in the 1990 Census), Carolinian, Fijian, Kosraean, Porropean (Pohpelan), Polynesian, Solomon Islands, Tahitian, Tarawa Islands, Tokelauan, Trukese (Chuukee), and Yapese".

The Asian category will be defined as a "person having origins in any of the original peoples of the Far East, Southeast Asia, or the Indian Subcontinent including for example Cambodia, China, India, Japan, Korea, Malaysia, Pakistan, Philippine Islands, Thailand and Vietnam".

OMB developed some interesting terminology for Hispanic or Latino because of the original usage of the terms differs in the eastern portion of the US, (Hispanic), and in the western portion (Latino). The Cape Verdians who some people regard as Black and not Portuguese wanted a separate category. However OMB said "that another category should not be added to the ethnic data. A decision was made to have Central and South American Indians classified as American Indian. The American Indian or Alaska Native category should be modified to include the original peoples from Central and South America. The name of the Black category should be changed to Black or African American. The category definition should remain unchanged. Haitian or Negro can be used if desired. The fact that should be considered is that since 1870, the definition of a Black American remains unchanged and people of African, European, Asian and Indian descent who comprise a multiracial hybrid are still considered "Black, African American or Negro" without any recognition of their biological or genetic diversity. I believe no other group of racially mixed genes in the world has been classified for 128 years as one basic color for their racial category regardless of the variance of deposits melanin ranging from "jet Black to high yellow". When examining the more in-depth meanings of Hispanic or Latino, OMB defines Hispanic or Latino as a person of "Cuban, Mexican, Puerto Rican, South or Central American or other Spanish culture or origin regardless of race. The term Spanish origin can be used in addition to Hispanic or Latino. The key points are "Spanish culture origin, regardless of race". What countries would the majority of these people represent? Let us examine the geographical missing material that shadows the real Hispanics in America. One should also consider beyond any doubt that a great majority of the peoples from the following countries lived at one time in America and even became American citizens, classified as whites. Also many have individually changed their classification to Hispanic in order to enjoy the privileges of a new minority since the 1960's. A geographical reality is that the new Hispanic, or Latino in the year 2000 will be classified on the basic of their origins in the following countries: "South America, Ecuador, Peru, Bolivia, Paraguay, Chile, Argentina, Uruguay, Central America and the Caribbean, Mexico, Guatemala, Honduras, El Salvador, Nicaragua, Costa Rico, Cuba, Dominican Republic, Puerto Rico, Venezuela,

Columbia, Guam, and Panama. Now members from these countries who immigrate to America can be easily designated as Spanish people.

After reviewing the new designation for peoples from the South Pacific Islands, I have decided to include an article from my recent book *"Black Presence in World History"*. This article should offer some interesting facts and inferences to show how genetic diversity involving possible "Black genes" is not a desired household subject or research theme for many people. Again, as the "old folk" used to say, "We don't talk about these things".

"The Genetic Black Presence In The South Pacific Islands"

I have used the term "genetic Black presence" because I am sure that some historians anthropologists, scientists and laypersons will not in most instances acknowledge the presence of Black skin and other African physical features in a variety of peoples who have been placed in different geographically inspired groupings.

The following ethnic groups inhabiting these areas could very possibly have African genes dominant and recessive, but have been classified otherwise because they have straight black hair.

Micronesians	Melanesians	Polynesians
Marianas	New Guinea	New Zealand
Carolines	Bismarck Archipelago	Hawaii
Marshalls	Admiralty Islands	Somoa
Gilberts	Solomons	Tonga (small Islands)
Oceania	New Caledonia	
	Loyalties	
	New Hebrides	
	Fiju	

When the Portuguese and Dutch observed the Australian Aborigines, the Twi, in 1769-7 they recorded in their journals that the physical description of the people was: "dark skinned wide nose, low brows, wavy hair and clearly distinct from African Negroes, the primitive ancestors from Asia. Without the sophisticated knowledge of present day molecular biology, these early observers had already reached a conclusion that these people were in no way related to Black Africans. I recently observed some pictures of Black youngsters in a 1990 newspaper subjects of a medical anthropologist studying some children from Gorke, New Guinea. The anthropologist was conducting research on the T-cells and possible relations to the leukemia virus. The physical descriptions of the children as I observed the picture were: wooly hair, Negroid nasal areas and brown skin color. Now if those children were dressed in American clothes, latest styles and fashion, and did not utter a word, in America, they would be considered Black, Negro or African American beyond a doubt.

In a 1995 newspaper article about Pope John Paul II's visit to Papua, New Guinea in the South Pacific, there were also pictures showing the people dancing in a welcome ceremony for the Pope. The people's physical description was definitely Negroid. Dressed in American attire they would be mistaken for Black people.

The realistic view is that over the years the cultural anthropologists and others have called the New Guinea populations an ethnic composition of Negroid, Micronesians, and Polynesians. They clearly state that these peoples speak some 715 indigenous languages to include pidgin, English and Notu.

In September, 1996, a popular magazine showed some New Guinea inhabitants, along the coasts being pushed by traffic jams more than one thousand aboriginal farther into the interior. The article said their ancient rituals survive and the highland clan engages in mock battle, practices like the real thing. Their weapons have been used since the domestication of plants and animals some 6,000 years ago. Their tribal wars were fought over pigs, land and women. The pictures clearly show people of Negroid characteristics resplendent in physical descriptions much like those whom we call Blacks, Negroes or Afro Americans.

A recent newspaper article featured an aboriginal tribe that inhabit the Uluru National Park. The article said the people consider the caves of Ayers Rock, which contain carvings and paintings, to be sacred. The Uluru is a sacred site for the nomads. The cervices and caves in the rock are regarded by the Aborigines as verses of scripture. The people believe in a dream time as the beginning of all life, a time they feel is still with them. The park was created in 1950. The people believe in a God, Kuniya.

Previously the government deeded the land to the local aborigines and as agreed they leased it back as the Uluru National Park. Ironically the picture in the magazine showed some people with visible Negroid features brown to dark skin and hair from curly straight to mild woolly.

Nutritional Reasoning or Food For Thought

I decided to refer to my Webster's New Collegiate Dictionary for some definitions. The word "Negro" is defined as "a member of the Black race distinguished from members of other races by usual inherited physical and physiological characteristics (inherited reception of genetic "qualities by transmission from parent to offspring, physiological - function and activities of life or living matter such as organs and tissues). Without regard to language or culture especially members of the Black race belonging to the African branch." Negroid - a person of Negro descent. Negrito - "a group of Negroid peoples of small stature that live in Oceania the southeastern part of Asia." Papuan - "members of any of the Negroid native peoples of New Guinea and adjacent areas of Melanesia." Fijian a member of the Melanesian people of the Fiji Islands and their language is the Austronesian language, (language spoken from the Malay peninsula, Madagascar area, Easter Island and most all native languages of the Pacific Islands with the exception of the Australian, Papuan and Negrito languages).

"Australoid - "relating to an ethnic group including the Australian Aborigines and other peoples of southern Asia and Pacific islands sometimes including the Ainu (a member of an indigenous Caucasoid people of Japan)."

Filipino - "a native of the Philippine islands". There was no mention in the dictionary's definition of the Filipino's early ancestors. However, I decided to refer to an Almanac and World Atlas. The Almanac stated that the ethnic groups were "91.5 Christian Malay and the Philippines were anciently settled by various Malayan peoples in several waves of migration from Southeast Asia. The Spanish conquered the island in 1521." The World Atlas stated that most Filipinos are of Malay Polynesian origin and there are some people of Pygmy (definition from Webster dictionary - "any of a small people of equatorial Africa ranging under five feet in height)," European and mixed descent".

Malay - "a member of a people of the Malay Peninsula, eastern Sumatra, parts of Borneo and some ancient islands". One historian wrote in a book many years ago that the Melanesians physical descriptive features were Negroid type, dark to Black skin color, crisp curly hair, flat nose and thick lips.

Now in consideration of this discussion and realizing that people in 1998 could possibly care less what color or race ancestral or aboriginal peoples were years ago and the fact that they are who they are called today and in no way identify with any genetic trace of Black genes in their ancestral line, especially those in the United States. I do not present any argument based on these facts. Logic may lead us to some interesting insights.

Therefore, when one considers the definitions of words discussed above and considers how a person's ancestral heritage can be defined over thousand of years Then the question could arise who is a Black person out of Africa who has mixed genetically over many years with various populations including their captors? One of course must understand that when the ethnic mixtures occurred among the groups, the distinctive original dominant African genes could have become recessive. But somehow as I often tell my college students, exposure to the sun did not sustain the amount of melanin in their bodies to reveal to an observer Black skin color.

A year ago, I learned some interesting facts from a female native of the Philippines who happens to be married to a retired army veteran of color. Both are the parents of mixed children. She overheard me talking to someone about genetic diversity among people. She told me that when she attended school in the Philippines some years ago she had to study about an ancestral tribal group of people who lived on the Philippine Islands years ago possibly prior to the arrival of the Malays and Spanish conquerors. She said those tribal ancestors were the first inhabitants of the area and that their descendants still live on the island. Some can be seen visiting the mainland of the Philippines. She described them as Negroid people, with dark skins somewhat flat noses, pygmy-like people with wooly hair. This Filipino lady said they were called Negritos. Now I have never read any of this information about the Negritos in an American textbook or reference book. She was very sincere about the validity of her story. I did ask my Filipino barber about the Negritos and he did acknowledge that they had Negroid characteristics. I am in no way saying anything about Black ancestry of the Filipino people. I am presenting some food for thought about the early Black presence on the Philippine Islands hundreds of years ago and the fact that some of the original Negritos descendants are present today. Some authors have chosen to use the simple term pygmies as part of the ethnic composition of the Philippines today.

When I write about the Black presence in the South Pacific Islands and the Philippines, the reader can use simple logic and realize why people do have a color obsession and consciousness in the world today. Recently, a popular American weekly magazine featured an article on an outstanding young professional golfer of color. The author of the article indicated color awareness or obsession by stating that the golf pro is "one eighth African American, one quarter white, one quarter Chinese and one-quarter Thai. (Remember some Almanac states that the Thai people are descendants of people who migrated from China after 1,000 A.D. and later came under the influences of people from the Indian civilization from adjacent states of Burma and the Khmer empire). Now if that professional golfer wants to declare his valid ancestral genetic blood line, what is the problem? America's problem is quite similar. A few weeks ago, I attended the funeral of a gracious lady whose physical description was white without any visible Negroid features. She lived 99 years and two months as a "colored person" and would tell you without any hesitation that she was colored. Her ancestral lineage was Irish, African and Indian. She was probably the illegitimate grand daughter of General Robert E. Lee or some southern white gentleman. But she never desired to be a descendant of Robert E. Lee. Just as she desired to cherish her Blackness, there are many other people in America who have similar feelings and genetic structure. Today they are characterized with politically designed terms such as biracial, mixed race and multiracial. Also what about African Americans in general? Where are the pure genes of African descent that would make them half African as the name African American denotes.

In view of millions of African Americans who in 1998 are comfortable with their given name category, I often question how many are aware of the controversial discussions during segregation based on the word "Negro". Even a special legal officer of the NAACP in 1946 expressed his views on the capitalization of the word Negro. The late Colonel Marcus Ray had received a letter concerning a Black soldier, Corporal A. Smithey, who protested a directive issued at Camp Lee, Virginia with four instances of the word Negro not capitalized though it was used in the position of a proper noun to designate a particular group of people according to some philologist, the word "Negro" is capitalized though it was used as a proper noun to designate a particular group of people. When Smithey protested he was being considered for a court martial. Colonel Ray reviewed the complaint which was sent to him from the NAACP legal counsel Franklin H. Williams. Ray made a final decision and presented his recommendations to the Secretary of the Army who directed that a War Department memorandum be sent to Smithey's commanding officer informing him that the word "Negro" is to be capitalized.

In 1998, when some political and news media asked certain Black civil rights leaders for their recommendations for census use, several leading Black organizations showed strong objections to any multiracial category. Their possible justifications were that the multiracial category would add to racial tensions because Blacks are a most diverse, multiracial group. Also this would affect Blacks status for federal programs, affirmative action initiatives, housing, education, health care assistance or any programs whose financial allocations are based on census data. These leaders said that African American gains would be diluted if individuals were given an opportunity to have many choices. They also stated that the Black count is necessary for the creation of minority voting districts. The "old folk" would possibly have said that Black leaders are unrealistic in their identification of a Black group and that individuals should continue to be regarded a homogeneous group, not a genetically mixed one.

The Cape Verdians

Some descendants of the original Africans who came to America from Portugal's Cape Verdes Islands, off the West African Coast live today in the New England areas of Pawtucket, East Providence, Newport, Rhode Island, and Cape Cod,

Massachusetts. Today, the descendants are called Cape Verdians and many are immigrants. They are racially or genetically mixed with Portuguese and African genes. Their physical features suggest the genetic structure of their two backgrounds. It has been stated that "some Cape Verdians tend to claim Portuguese identity and some accept the American identification Black.

The Louisiana Cajuns

The Cajuns have been defined as white descendants of French speaking Catholics (Acadians) who left Canada in the late 1700's and came to Southwestern Louisiana. It has been stated that there has been a fusion of Acadian culture with American Indians, African slaves, Spaniards, Germans, Irish, English, Caribbean Islanders and some Latino American cultures. Today, there is a group of people who live in Southwestern Louisiana that have some white Acadian genes and Black genes; they are called "Creoles".

In 1997, the Louisiana Cajuns were increasing an awareness of their presence through different marketing schemes. They have labeled landmarks as Cajuns and continue to preserve their music and culture. A Bayou, non-Cajun group consisting of Creoles want recognition of their non Cajun Creole culture. This heritage group is asking for equal recognition of their culture of selected foods, "rice, sea food, pork, hot spices, gumbo, shrimp and crawfish". Some Creoles in southwestern Louisiana believe that their music and Acadian music have some similarities. Cajun music has some elements of "country" music and the Creole's Zydeco music has some similar Cajun sounds, but it is more "rhythm and soul". It is quite obvious that the Cajuns consider themselves as white regardless of any past genetic exposures of racial groups. The University of Southeastern Louisiana at one time had a mascot "Cajun" with a drawing representing a white man riding a crawfish.

Triracial Groups

There are some groups of people whose genetic make up is white, Black, and Indian. They have been referred to as "Triracial isolates". These groups or clans can be found in numerous states and have been identified with various names. In 1971, some 80,000 triracials were present in the U.S. They were living in the following states: Tennessee, the Melungeons; Delaware, the Moors; South Carolina, the Turks; North Carolina, the Cubana; New Jersey and New York, the Jackson whites; Florida, the Dominickers; and Rhode Island, the Narragansetts.

In the early 18th century, the genesis of a triracial group occurred in the State of Maryland. Intermarriage was occurring between white indentured servants, free mulattoes, free Blacks and Native Americans in Southern Maryland. Through the years, the descending offsprings would intermarry within their closed groups, and in later years the State would have a law on the books permitting marriages of cousins. The physical characteristics of the group members would vary, but the majority's features were and are straight hair, some Indian features, white skin, and some curly hair. During the segregated years, they were required to attend Negro schools, although some in the Brandywine area tried to organize their separate schools. They were not successful. Their major occupations have been farming, hunting, guiding, fishing, blacksmithing, truck driving, machine operating, mechanics, domestic work, skilled and clerical jobs and school teachers. Sociologists have identified sixteen families names among the Maryland group. There have been members of the group who have denied any trace of Black blood. Their major religion is Roman Catholic.

COLOR OBSESSION

I have included this discussion on color obsession in this book because I believe that some of the articles and research that I have completed over the years will enable the reader to think about other views on this volatile subject In our present ever increasing polarized society. I first realized in the early years of my research in American, African and European history that many of the so-called people of color were racially mixed and often referred to as of African descent, mulattoes, mixed, quadroon, mustie, and zambo, creole; but never did I see "multiracial", biracial, half white, half Black and other popular terms used today. I must state very clearly that I am sure that many of the personalities that I discuss in this book lived and died as white even though they were aware of the presence of their Black genes.

Color obsession seems obvious when in 1993-1995 and 1996 several American magazines published articles on a multiracial society. A magazine in 1993 discussed how immigrants came to America many years ago and talked about the slaves who came from Africa. Yes, the subject of slavery is the starting point to address designated and assigned culture to Americans of African descent. They were also introduced to a naming system that would continue through the 1990's, assigning names such as slave, darkey, nigger, coon, colored, colored American, Negroes, Afro Americans, Blacks and African Americans. We must remember that there was no intention or considerations to assess the apparent biological changes in physical description of the original African slave who arrived in America in the early years. Biological diversity that occurred during slavery with the European, Indian, and in some cases the Asian was insignificant to the census takers in 1860 I say 1860 because when I was researching my book, *Thomas Sewell Inborden An*

Early Educator of Color, the Virginia census for Loudoun county, 1869, listed the family of Levi and Hannah Proctor as mulattoes. His wife was formerly Hannah Rector who was related to one of the distinguished first families of the local area. Thomas S. Inborden's mother was Harriet Proctor Smith, daughter of Hannah and Levi. I was able to locate several letters where T.S. Inborden did mention about his genetic inheritance. In a letter written to his daughter, Dorothy, T.S stated: "I am Indian for a large part. I have some French and Dutch extraction. These inherent qualities have given me tenacity and personality that has made one more than anything else except perhaps my environment. In all my life, I have never cared for the cheap and trashy element of people. I have had to mix with a great many of them. I have always tried to put myself with those who were looking upward and onward, especially those who wanted to be somebody. When I come into a bad environment and can not remake it, get out of it. The one thing to consider is whether one course will lead us to wealth or woe ".

"I have never said anything about my father. He died not an old man, but with Brights Disease. (Kidney disease). I have seen him on several occasions when he came to my mother's house. He was one of the cleanest and finest dressed man I ever saw. He was a typical southern gentleman. He was well educated and has the finest cultural bearing. He had one son who clerked in Conrad's store in Upperville where we all traded. I was too young to understand it but all of this was the tragedy of the old days for which none of us seemed responsible".

I researched the papers and self biographies of Thomas Sewell Inborden for eight years. At first, I did not understand his views on race and how he felt since he could pass as a white man day or night because of his obvious Caucasian physical features. However as I studied his papers, I realize that Thomas S. Inborden lived and died as a proud man who was sensitive to his Blackness, aware of it and proud and also respectful of his other genetic racial characters as stated above. He once wrote "It is fine to speak to people who have a sympathetic spirit especially when you have a feeling that you have an unpopular subject. My racial identity was not clear in the mind of a gentleman who introduced me. He said something like this: Professor Steiner of the University of California said somewhere that if he had to be born again, he would like to be born a colored man, so that he might be able to study the colored problem from the inside. We have with us today a gentleman who understands the colored problem, and who was not born colored either". These may not be the exact words, but it is the thought. The first thing that I had to do was to dispel the audience of the fact or statement just made, that I did not have to be born a colored man, and that I wanted them to know that the traditions of our country and the laws in many, if not all the states, had said that any man is colored who has one iota of Negro blood in his veins. I am glad to have the honor to address you as a colored man." If this occurred in 1920 and I read in a newspaper an article written by a popular news correspondent or columnist about an outstanding young golfer who prides himself on his genetic diversity, then can we really say we are color blind today? Just as Inborden had distinctive white features in 1920 and chose to live as a man of color, aware of his white genes, can the young golfer and other people of color who have mixed genes voice their own self awareness without people expressing their rightful, personal opinions sometimes expressed without the historical awareness.

Population biologists have developed an approach to explain race by analyzing genetic marks in selected populations. They have learned that there are more genetic differences within one race than there are between that race and another. Some of these genetic differences are difficult to explain. An example would be, if one would select at random any two Black Americans and an analysis is conducted on their 23 pairs of chromosomes, the results could show that their genes have less in common than do the genes of one of them with that of a randomly selected white person. This research adds some support to my simple statement that African Americans not Africans are probably the most diverse individuals on this planet as biological group.

One drop of blood theory: Historically this theory has had many variations or exceptions. In the 1800's, the state of Virginia would accept a person with less than one-fourth Black genes as white, and later defined white as having less than one sixteenth Black genes. Many states, especially in the South began to enact laws to prohibit whites from marrying any Black person. The legal significance was present in American society in 1986 when the U.S. Supreme Court ruled that a lower court could force a Louisiana woman with negligible African ancestry to be legally defined as Black.

Early Anthropological Investigation of the Mulatto Type

Caroline Bond was a 1919 graduate of Radcliffe College. She was a mulatto with a genetic profile of half Negro and half white genes. In her senior year at Radcliffe, she decided to collect genealogical, sociological, photographic and anthropometric (measurements of different body parts such as shoulder and arm, chest, leg, head, face, nose, cephalic index, and skin color) to determine racial differences and records of a number of families. The study would also determine the exact blood proportion of the family members who were or genetically mixed. Bond was able to complete her research in 1927 after obtaining assistance from the Bureau of International Research of Harvard University and Radcliffe College. A grant made it possible for her to study "346 Black families. Her results were completed with the assistance of Mr. Richard A. Post who was a graduate student in physical anthropology. A manuscript highlighting her work was published in 1932, *Negro-White Families in the United States.* The book was published by the Peabody Museum of Harvard University.

Bond's research presented an early background on scholarly thought and inferences on the miscegenation of Blacks and Whites and the so-called identification based on skin color, and physical descriptions, to include hair texture. Her study on Negro-white families in America presented results which will be relevant in understanding from a genetic, biological and cultural perspective the mulatto, light skin or high yellow person of color in the American experience, especially the Black family's daily usage of skin color, description namely as: "yellow, medium color, fair skin, pinkish white, pale yellow, brown, brunette white, light brown, golden yellow, olive tone, white skin, copper, light creamy, white with freckles, ivory, medium red brown, and dark brown." She also used these descriptions:

Race. Negro, Indian, quadroon, and mulatto, Negroid type, coarse hair, dark Spanish type, dominant mulatto, Mediterranean European.

Hair. crinkly, straight, frizzly, soft, low wavy, curly frizzly, silky, dark hair, medium brown, finer, true blond, straight Black, fine, deep waves, curved hair, pronounced wavy hair, light, golden, bushy, woolly.

Lips. Thickened membranous, thick medium thickness, heavy low lip, thin, integumental lip thickness, full lips, thickening of nasal tip.

Eyes. gray green, brown, hazel, gray-brown, heavy eyebrows (Dravidian type) blue, yellow-gray.

Nose. straight narrow, thin, narrow nasal rook, high and low bridged long, low or broad, elevated Pseudo Semetic or high budge jutting.

Face. broad, heavy.

Features. medium, moderately heavy, sharp, small, regular, European, Australian.

Head. long, general bony structure, brachycephaly form.

Mouth. wide.

Racial Combinations - Mixtures

octoroon - mulatto
mulatto - Negro Indian Quadroon
white - mulatto
quadroon - mulatto
mulatto of (English, Dutch, Negro) and Mulatto of (Half breed Indian and Negro)

white - quadroon
quadroon - quadroon
quadroon - mulatto

The general conclusion of Mrs. Day's study was "that there is nothing mysterious or unnatural in the mixture of races and nothing very extraordinary in the physical results of such mixtures. Within a group of set proportion of white and Negro genes, features are so combined in some individuals as to create approximations respectively to white and Negro types together with a majority of intermediate." She also stated in 1932, that "one doubts the existence of any large number of pure Negroes in the United States today (1932). The superiority, inferiority or mediocrity of the offspring is probably dependent upon the individual contribution of the various parental strains. That was the way a student of anthropology viewed the color obsession in 1932, because that was the way some of us were thinking.

In July 1932, the *American Journal of Sociology* published an article on "Children In Black and Mulatto Families". The article was written by the late distinguished sociologist of color, Dr. E. Franklin Frazier. He stated in the article that in the 1860's, there were Caucasian medical researchers who believed that mulattoes did not live as long as Negroes of unmixed blood or genes. The pure African should be chosen in preference to the mulatto because the Blacks were better. However, in a study by Dr. Frazier, he found that the higher proportioned of children in mulatto population have had a higher survival rate. A Caucasian physician, Dr. John Stainback, M.S., wrote an article on the "Peculiarities and Diseases of Negroes". The article was published in the *American Cotton Planter and Soil of the South Magazine,* 1860. Dr. Stainback wrote that the jet Black, shiny unadulterated greasy skinned strong Negro is the best even after he has been in the country long enough to undergo proper training to get rid of some of his native African notions." The perception or medical opinion of Dr. Stainback 133 years ago was an example of the early obsessions with skin color and labeling of a person. Ironically a Caucasian physician and geneticist, who is a professor at the University of Wisconsin, told me during a telephone conversation in 1992 that there has been some research completed with a conclusion that the average American Black probably has 20-25 percent of mixed genes, European or white. One could postulate from this statement that the more a person is racially mixed the more white genes they would have and again support the biological fact and reality that African Americans are of a diverse genetic structure. However, American people only see Black and white in labeling people who they are and do not address the biological significance, because that is the way we were and probably will always be in a society obsessed with skin color and physical features.

"3/32 Black in Louisiana Is Not White"

An Appeals Court in the State of Louisiana ruled that a lady must accept a legal designation of Black. She looked like a white person and lived as white all her life, and her children were classified as white including grand children. Her parents lived and died as white people. When she was applying for a passport, the state observed that her birth certificate listed her as Black. The lady then turned to the legal system to help her retain her white status. However, the court ruled that she was 3/32 Black under Louisiana law and that 1/32 Black was not white.

"They Were Called White Once"

Prior to 1940, Mexicans living in America were classified as non white, then the Census Bureau reclassified them as white. They would fight in World War II along with the white soldiers while Blacks and Asians were in separate units.

"The Name Game"

Prior to the 1860's and even during segregation Blacks have been designated by many names of ethnic identity, such as slave, darkey, coon, nigger, Black, Afro American, Negro, colored, mustie, octroon, quadroon, mulatto, high yellow, African America, Black leaders, lay persons and theologians have debated the "name game" over the years. Many Blacks would oppose the word Negro by stating "the title Negro is too narrow and exclusive to comprehend a race. It is certain that all Africans are not Negroes nor are all who are Negroes, Africans." Some leaders in the past years have made some logical statements when they said, "why should the race name of millions of Blacks be derived from color only? No such rule is applied to any other of the great races, the Caucasian, Indian, Asian and Arabian tell us only origin of those to whom these names apply". The writer of the above quote preferred "Afro American". W.E.B. Dubois wrote in the *Crisis Magazine* in 1928, "Negro is a fine word, etymologically and phonetically it is much better and more logical than 'African or colored' or any of the various hyphenated circumlocutions. Of course, it is not historically accurate."

"I Prefer Colored"

There were some middle and upper class Blacks in 1997 who openly voiced their opinions on "What's In a Name". A distinguished newspaper sports writer said in an interview with a Washington, D.C. newspaper, "I do not like the idea of Black or

African American. . . . All our ancestors did not come from Africa. Some came from Israel, Russia and the West Indies. Black is not right because I can not conceive of everyone in our ethnic group with all the various shades of complexion being called Black. My preference of course, is 'colored' because that covers the entire new situation".

"She Used Colored 99 Years"

The late Mrs. Dorothy Inborden Miller, former college professor and high school principal, used the term "colored" throughout her life time, even though she could have passed for white. In our conversations she used "colored" and I would reciprocate by also using the word 'colored'".

I Like The Word Black

A noted civil rights activist and leader while speaking to the National Press Club, Washington, D.C. in June 1998 said, "I am old enough to have been a Negro and I have been a colored person. Then a meeting was held (and it was announced and I was not asked to attend the meeting) that I had become an African American. I like the word Black. It sums up everything and it is just one syllable. . ."

Well, that leader's remarks are similar to mine because I have been called many names by a few "so called Black leaders" who possibly were appointed by a few Blacks, the white news media and while political leaders, national and local. I am sure at least some 30 million, Blacks did not know about those meetings.

What Is An Egyptian In America?

In 1997, a dark skinned Egyptian immigrant filed a law suit in the Detroit courts to request that the Federal Government change his racial classification from white to Black. The 46 year old man stated that his classification of white has prevented him from obtaining jobs, grants, scholarships and loans as a member of a minority group. This Egyptian is descended from an ancestry that goes back to the ancient Kingdom of Nubia, now a geographical part of Egypt and Sudan. There is a directive No. 15, U.S. Office of Management and Budget (OMB) that defines Blacks as "having an origin with Black racial groups of Africa and Whites as having origins with original peoples from Europe, Middle East, North Africa and Egypt. This Egyptian man is a naturalized U.S. citizen and his descriptive physical features have been said to include "kinky hair, and dark skin".

This true story aroused my interest because in 1992, I published in my book *They Did Not Tell Me True Facts...* an article about the Smithsonian's exhibit on Africa in the 1990's and a challenge they received as to the racial identity of Egyptians. I have included this article.

Confronting the Smithsonian Institution

An African American, Jacques Hall of Washington, D.C. had visited Egypt in 1988. He was able to observe the descriptive physical characteristic of the Egyptians and was convinced not only by their appearance but also from other knowledge about Egypt that Egyptians were Black people. One day in 1989, Jacques Hall happened to be visiting the Smithsonian National Museum of Natural History when he noticed an exhibit on Egyptians. The Human Origin and Variation section exhibit read mainly Caucasoid (Egyptian) African. Realizing that he had observed Egyptians having skin color ranging from jet Black to brown, he questioned the Smithsonian's rationale. Hall wrote a letter on July 15, 1989 and asked the Director of the National Museum of Natural History for their rationale?

On August 9, 1989, A Public Information Specialist from the Department of Anthropology answered Jacques Hall's letter by stating: "Egyptians as well as other people who inhabit the Mediterranean coast of North Africa are characterized by dark brown skin color, with good tanning capacity, that does not differ much from the skin color in Southern Europe. The range in skin color among the people of Egypt reflects the mobility of population over time. For instance, migrations from south of the Sahara and the prospensity to intermarry has created a mingling of characteristics that overlap between adjoining and even distant populations. This may help explain why it is difficult today to assign individuals to one and only one race. Such designations more often reflect cultural or ethnic identity rather than physical characteristics. The exhibit information " therefore is correct in stating that Egyptians as Africans are mainly caucasoid."

Jacques Hall did not accept this reply as the answer to his initial question. Therefore he wrote another letter to the Director of the National Museum of Natural History on February 27, 1990. Hall wrote "In order to inject an element of perspective, we note that pure blooded Caucasoid (Europeans) have a skin color that's generally considered to be white. Pure blooded Negroids have both Black and brown skin. Below the Sahara (in Africa) there are many brown people, as well as Black people. Are they mainly Caucasoid? Of course not. Right here in the U.S.A., there are many Black and brown people. Are they mainly Caucasoid? Of course not. And yet we claim that the Black and brown people of Egypt are mainly Caucasoid."

"I seem to recall that when I was a youngster, before World War II, that there was a branch of the caucasoids called the Mediterranean Race. It contained Middle Easterners and extended all the way into India. All of these people were supposed to be white, even the Black Ethiopians, and of course the Black and brown Egyptians as well. But what happened to the good old Mediterranean Race? Well, it seems to have just sort of faded away. Probably because now we realize that we can no longer obscure the unpleasant truth that most of these folks are simply a mixture of Black and white. Thus some of these people are mostly Black and some are mostly white. Some of them that are truly 'mainly Caucasoid, as the Greeks, the Italians and Spanish."

"Now for what purpose do we display this 'mainly Caucasoid' sign? Is it to inform the public as to the peoples of the globe that are 'mainly Caucasoid'? If this is so, then such is a worthwhile objective. But then, why are the Egyptians singled out7 Where are the signs that proclaim that the Greeks, Italians and Spanish are mostly caucasoids?

The big barrier between white Europe and Black Africa is not the Mediterranean sea but the Sahara Desert. Nature provides an excellent highway via the Nile River from Black Africa to Egypt. it is undoubtedly because of this link that other North Africans tend to be more white than the Egyptians. Such being the case, why don't we have signs proclaiming that the Moroccans; the Algerians, and the Tunisians are mostly caucasoids. Could it be because they have no outstanding civilization'? And again, why are the Egyptians singled out? And where, oh where is the sign that say that the Black Ethiopians are mainly caucasoids?

"European civilization has been dominant and has led the world for the past several centuries. Thus, it is little more than human nature that many would develop the feeling that the Europeans are simply special people. But then it develops that the ancient Egyptians a most magnificent civilization millennia before the awakening of the Europeans, and that a great deal of this early Egyptian culture and civilization was absorbed into the beginnings of the European civilization. This throws a monkey wrench into things as it tends to cast doubt upon the idea that Europeans are special. Is this why we, in decades gone by, have declared the Egyptians to be white? Could it be that today we still suffer from this hangover of the past now that it is obvious that the Egyptians are not white? Have we fallen back to the position that they are mainly Caucasoid simply because of their past magnificent civilizations? Is this simply a case where wishful thinking causes us to continue to try to horn in on the credit of their marvelous ancient culture? Are we simply creating "facts" and rationalizations to support our predetermined conclusions? Or are there indeed valid reasons why the Egyptians are deemed to be mainly Caucasoid? Reasons of which I am not yet unaware."

"They say that if it looks like a duck, walks like a duck, and goes quack, quack, quack, then its a duck. If the Egyptians are Black and brown, and they most certainly are, then the thought strikes me that this at least opens up the possibility that they just could be mainly Negroid."

"I am sure that the Smithsonian is as interested as am I in the unvarnished truth. Therefore, I again respectfully ask "What is the Smithsonian's rationale for the idea that the Egyptians are 'mainly caucasoid'? Your response would be greatly appreciated." Three months later, June 1990, Hall had not received a reply to his letter from the Smithsonian.

He then decided to contact the Black Caucus realizing that three Black congressmen were on the House Appropriations Committee. He was also aware that the Smithsonian Institution is partially funded by the U.S. Government. Hall discussed the matter with the Black Caucus staff. They in turn contacted the Smithsonian by phone in July. Hall received a call from the Black Caucus and they told him that the Smithsonian was going to effect necessary changes. Realizing that he had nothing in writing, Hall sent a telegram to the Director of the National Museum of Natural History. The telegram read "Sent you a letter dated February 27, no answer, very surprised and disappointed."

The Director of the National Museum of Natural History wrote Hall a letter, dated July 12, 1990. It read "[The Public Information Specialist] regrets the typographical error, and the confusion it caused, in her letter to you regarding the racial characteristics of the Egyptian people. She intended to say that the exhibit label was incorrect in describing Egyptians as "mainly Caucasoid." This was confirmed with the accompanying material she sent you. Our Human Origin and Variation Hall was installed in 1952 and reflects the biases, attitudes, and state of knowledge at that time. We are aware that the exhibit contains some material that is outdated or, by today's standards, occasionally inappropriate or insensitive. We have begun making changes to the hall to bring it more in line with current thinking. In fact the hall is scheduled to be dismantled and replaced with a new hall on Human Origins. However, given the time required to design and raise funds for the project of this scale, we do not anticipate a new exhibit before 1995 at least. Early works on race identified European sub-races (Nordic, Mediterranean, and Alpine) generally by stature, head and nose shape, and hair color. When these categories did not surface, other sub races were constructed. Alice M. Bruer does an excellent job in discussing this and other issues your letter mentions in her book, People *and Faces*". Jacques Hall was very appreciative of the response that he had received from the museum director, He wrote a letter to the Director on July 24, 1990, to address some issues that he believed were significant. Hall wrote "There are many things obviously wrong with your exhibit entitled, 'The Negroid Racial Stock Arose

In Africa'. So much so that it is my view that this exhibit in total does considerable violence to the Smithsonian's high standards of integrity and creditability."

"I do not think that I go too far in saying that this exhibit is an insult to the Negroid people of the world. It attempts to surreptitiously deny Negroid credit for the magnificent civilization of ancient Egypt by claiming that the Ancient Egyptians were, and that the present day Egyptians are predominantly white. The exhibit contains two photos of full figured Africans. Both are of horribly grotesque looking women. Regardless of intent, the impression that is given is that these two photos represent typical examples of Negroid peoples.

"It is very disturbing to realize that this offensive exhibit has existed since 1952, a period of 38 years. Thirty-eight years of distorted information. Distortions that 38 years have been negatively inaccurate and thus harmful to Blacks."

"I am delighted to read that you realize the need of change and that you do plan to thusly proceed. But in 1995? Five years from now? This exhibit for 38 long years has short changed some 30 million of our Black citizens. Everyday that this biased exhibit stands represents still another day of injustice to these 30 million Black American taxpayers. Somehow to me, there seems to be something wrong here.

In your letter to me you spoke favorably of Alice Bruer, People *and* Races. I happen to be familiar with this book. On page 285, Ms. Bruer states that the ancient Egyptians were archetypal (same type, model or origin) caucasoids. I fail to understand the apparent contradictions here. In your letter you indicate that the Egyptians are not mainly Caucasoid while at the same time you suggest her book that states just the opposite. This seem somewhat confusing,, however I would suggest that the Black African, Dr. Cheikh Anta Diop, in his book *The African Origin of Civilization* dispels decades and decades of this type of confusion. He says how can the Black and brown Egyptians be white, and that they are simply members of the Negroid race as are the rest of the Black and brown peoples of Africa. Dr. Diop, a former Dean at the University of Paris, and of impeccable credentials, devotes nearly half of his book to an analysis of this strange phenomenon whereby caucasoids continually dream up creative reasons to explain why the Black and brown Egyptians are white. The motive, of course, is obvious attempts to back off with the credit for the Ancient Egyptian civilization. Dr. Diop, himself a historian and an Egyptologist, sets the records straight as he debunks one after another of these sometimes very clever rationalization. Nevertheless, this myth has been with us for so long that still many, many sincere, well meaning people continue to believe it. It is my view that Ms. Bruer's statement here represents an excellent example of the type of wishful thinking anthropology that Diop so successfully exposes."

"Could it be without being confrontational or perhaps even a trouble maker, that I may respectfully make several suggestions as follows:

1. Please dismantle and remove this offensive exhibit as soon as possible.

2. From your vast annual funding, please fund the relatively small amount necessary to complete and install (within perhaps a year) an honest replacement exhibit.

3. In preparing the new exhibit, please seek, and accept counsel from qualified Blacks. Howard University as a source is suggested.

4. And last of all, I would respectively request that you please be kind enough to answer this letter."

Hall sent copies of this letter to the Executive Director, Congressional Black Caucus; Secretary of the Smithsonian; President, Charles Wesley Branch, Association for Study of Afro American Life and History; Assistant Secretaries of Public Service and Institutional Initiatives, Smithsonian Institution.

As a result of Jacques Hall's letter of July 24, 1990, the Smithsonian Institution invited Hall to come in for consultation. He had an opportunity to express his honest views and specifically told them that the entire exhibit was biased, which included several rooms, and that the exhibit should be immediately removed. Hall simply said no information is better then wrong information. The Smithsonian Institution listened and heard the message Hall brought to them in person. The whole entire exhibit was almost immediately dismantled.

The thought that still remains is where were our African American Anthropologists, Egyptologists, Historians, and Museum curators, with and without doctorates. Where were they while Hall, whose orientation is business, had to step forth and correct a serious and offensive error that had been in place for 38 years.

I personally applaud Jacques Hall for his initiative and successful actions in challenging the Smithsonian Institute to correct an inaccuracy of historical and biological information. I challenge African American and European, Asian and Hispanic scholars in this subject and related disciplines to use Jacques Hall's approach to correct many inaccuracies in the history of African Americans and Africans and to reeducate young Black, European, Asian and Hispanic youngsters about the truth by including African American History in their school curricula.

Amalgamation Georgia Style

The State of Georgia, as late as 1963, had some white only laws on the books. A Black soldier had received orders to report to a Georgia military base. He inquired about his white wife and four mixed children who would be accompanying him and he wanted to know how they would be treated in Georgia. The State Attorney General informed him that he could not properly answer the question, because the State does enforce their laws. The laws would vary depending on the locality. The Attorney General also told the soldier that "a Georgia law states that it shall be unlawful for a white person to marry anyone except a white person and that white persons included only persons of the white race (Caucasian)," that they must have no ascertainable trace of either Asiatic Indian, Mongolian, Japanese or Chinese, blood in their veins.

Color Blind?

The late Ralph Bunche, noted political scientist, educator and Nobel Peace Prize recipient studied at Cambridge University, England. He was given a letter of introduction to present to a Cambridge book store owner in order to receive a discount on his book purchases. The letter was written by an American book store owner. The Cambridge book store owner was nearsighted and wore heavy lensed glasses. He looked at the letter and said to Ralph Bunche, sure I will give you a job. Now Bunche did not go to the book store to obtain a job, but he decided to accept the job. Several weeks working on the job, the owner called Bunche aside and said "Ralph are you a Negro? Bunche replied "yes, I am", being surprised the store owner did not know it. The owner then told Bunche, "I can not see too well and if I had known this orginally, I would not have hired you". The owner decided to permit Bunche to continue to work at the store.

A Caucasian Definition of an African American

A Webster's Ninth Collegiate Dictionary dated 1989, does have a definition for African American. However, it defines African American as an American of African and especially of Negro descent. The word Negro is defined in the dictionary as a member of the Black race of mankind distinguished from members of other races by usually inherited physical and physiological characteristics without regard to language or culture; a member of a people belonging to the African branch of the Black race. A person of Negro descent. The dictionary defines the word mulatto as the first generation offspring of Negro and white; a person of mixed Negro and Caucasian ancestry. The term quadroon is defined as a person of one-quarter Negro ancestry. An octoroon is defined as a person with one-eighth Negro ancestry.

Some states in America have defined their state laws on race and color explaining what determines a Black or Negro person. Alabama said the word 'Negro' includes mulatto, or a person of mixed blood descended on the part of the father or mother from Negro ancestors without reference to or limit of time or number of generations removed. Arkansas simply stated a Negro is a person of the Negro race and any person who has in his or her veins any Negro blood whatever. Florida defined Negro, colored, mulatto, person of color to include every person having one-eighth or more of African or Negro blood. It is interesting to note that the Florida law of 1927 did not address the 1/4 of Negro descent or quadroon. Now how many persons of color have passed as white in Florida over the years when they were actually Black according to the historical definition and accepted meanings by both white and Black Americans today. The State of Georgia said all Negroes, mulattoes, mestizos (a person of mixed European and American Indian ancestry), West Indians or with Asiatic Indian blood in their veins and all descendants of any person having either Negro or African, West Indian, or Asiatic Indian blood in his or her veins shall be known in the State as a persons of color. The law said a white person shall include only persons of the Caucasian race who have no ascertainable trace of either blood of Negro, African, Asiatic Indian, Mongolian, Japanese, or Chinese blood in their veins. The State of Kentucky said colored children are all children wholly or in part of Negro blood in having any appreciable and mixture thereof and a child having one-sixteenth Negro blood may not attend a school for white children. Louisiana defined colored persons as all persons with any appreciable mixture of Negro blood. The State of Mississippi addressed the color problem by saying the word white means a member of the Caucasian race and the word colored includes not only Negroes but persons of mixed blood having any appreciable amount of Negro blood.

The State of Oklahoma said Negroes are persons of African descent. Texas said the term 'colored race" and "Negro" inlcude a person of mixed blood descended from Negro ancestry from the third generation inclusive, though one ancestor of each generation may have been a white person. Tennessee said the word "Negro" includes mulattoes, mestizos and their descendants having any blood of the African race in their veins. They shall also be defined as persons of color. The State of Virginia said every person in whom there is ascertainable any Negro blood shall be deemed and taken to be a colored person.

The author of An *American Dilemma,* Gunnar Myrdal defined the term "Negro" differently from most white Americans in 1944. Myrdal wrote that the definition of the Negro race is a social and conventional and not a biological concept. The Black is defined in America by Caucasians and in terms of percentage. Therefore, anyone having any known trace of Black blood or genes, regardless of how far back is still considered to be a Black or Negro.

Gunnar Myrdal discussed in his book instances of Blacks passing or crossing the line. I personally know of several individuals who told me some years ago that they passed to their advantages at times even though they were Black at birth and will die in America as a Black person. One lady in Washington, D.C. said (and this was prior to the permanent hair preparation) that she would go biweekly to a white hairdresser on Connecticut Avenue who would never admit a known Black person. There was a Black college professor who told me that his mulatto grandmother would take him downtown, Washington, D.C., to the segregated Loew's Theatre in the 1940's. They would pass as Spaniards or Mexicans in order to be admitted.

Students at some high schools are surprised when mulatto faculty members that they see everyday and believe to be white are revealed to be proud African Americans.

I know of a personal incident when I escorted a senior citizen to the old Greyhound bus station that was located at 11th and H Street, N.E., Washington, D.C. The kind white bus driver would make an available seat near him for her. He had done this on several occasions. However, it was on a midnight trip to Ohio when the majority of people in the waiting line to board the bus were Black including the very mulatto senior citizen, who then and still looks white. I asked her why she was so fortunate to obtain a special seat up front especially when the bus was crowded. She replied, I really think those nice white bus drivers think I am a white lady."

There are many stories similar to ones discussed that many African Americans can relate. However, these stories support the validity of statements made by the author, Gunnar Myrdal in 1944. He said, passing must have been going on in America for many years. The passing may occur only for occupational or recreational purposes or it may be complete. There are also instances where it may be voluntary and involuntary (reference some of the true stories stated in other discussions). It may be with knowledge on the part of the passer or without his knowledge, and it may be collective or individual. He said "passing" involves a greater change in an individuals social definition than it does in his biological classification. Myrdal stated that some dark skinned Blacks would pass by pretending to be Filipinos, Spaniards, Italians, or Mexicans. There was a true situation involving three professional Blacks returning from a weekend at Highland Beach in Maryland many years ago. One Black was a school teacher and his racial identity was a mixture of Chinese and mulatto Black. His features were dominantly Chinese to include black straight hair; complexion was dark brown. The other Black was a mulatto who appeared quite white and he was a physician at Howard-University's, Freedmen's Hospital. The third Black was a very dark person with so-called visible Negro features. He was also a physician at Howard University's Freedman's Hospital. The story was told that as the three Black men were approaching the District line from Maryland, a white motorcycle policeman stopped them and asked for their credentials. In those days, some white state policeman were very unfair when stopping Black people. The three passengers realized this and they decided to do the following: As the state trooper approached the car, the Black Chinese teacher was driving and the mulatto physician was sitting up front and the dark skinned physician who was sitting in the back seat had laid himself on the seat with a beach towel over him. The mulatto physican told the white trooper that they were speeding because this Nigger in the back was injured and we are rushing him to Freedman's, the colored hospital. The state trooper said, "I see doctor, well I will give you a personal escort to the hospital." The state trooper led them into the hospitals emergency drive way and when a young Black intern approached the car, he quickly recognized the physician in the back. The mulatto physician gestured to him to be quiet as they thanked the white state trooper for the escort service to the hospital. The doctors and teacher did not receive a ticket and the policeman was deceived because he believed, that there was only one Black in the car and the use of the word Nigger by the mulatto physican assisted in the scheme.

I sincerely believe that in all of the instances discussed, those persons of color knew that they were Black in mind and soul. They lived in their own time and they survived by any means that might have been necessary at those moments and times. There are many African Americans today who will ask why has this manuscript discussed in detail the color question. I can only respond as the author that because we as Americans regardless of color cannot truthfully say we are color blind, because all of us describe ourselves first by the terms "Black" or "White". The police, firemen, nurses, doctors, employment offices, military, businesses and almost all aspects of American society will talk and write about people's, race and skin color. When the policeman must give a description of a criminal or offender of the law, he will record and say Black male, or white male. The physician's medical chart will reflect, 20-year old Black female, etc. I did not create these scenarios, they are all American and have been for centuries and will possibly continue for many more.

We do have a magnificent obsession with color and sometimes its variables have negative effects on African Americans. Recent cases of people lying about being assaulted by a Black person or some white people becoming fearful when a Black person approaches are common. Many view television and see the recurring crimes involving Blacks, develop fears about Blacks from news coverage. During the recent Los Angeles riot, television and newspapers reported many Blacks as looters, burning buildings and assaulting Whites. The predominantly white television crew and newspaper reporters did not portray and write about the Asians, Hispanics, and Caucasians who were also looting and burning properties in Los Angeles.

Soldiers Descriptive Complexions or Genetic Diversity

The African slave was imported to America for economic reasons in an institution called slavery as early as 1619. Many documents, pamphlets and textbooks in the disciplines of American and Social History, Psychology and Medical History have tended to minimize and even omit the realistic genetic diversity that was produced among the descendants of the early African who came to America as slaves and suffered, in that dehumanizing social class system. It was very convenient, and possibly necessary, for the ruling majority class or white population to segregate, classify and name this new genetic hybrid a different racial group. The classification system was devised with names such *as Afric, Africano, Afro American, Colored, Negro* and still other names. The civil rights and Black revolutions of the 1960's was a positive experience. The residual effects were an improved pride in being Black and in their Motherland, *Africa.* These necessary changes of self awareness and cultural identity did not address the hidden agenda of who are we genetically? Of course, this would not be expected because of the past classification of Americans as Black or white regardless of genetic diversity.

I examined the descriptive characteristics for skin color of the soldiers of the Fifty-Fourth Massachusetts Regiment who enlisted some 126 years ago, and who were born on an average, 150 years ago. My hypothesis or thesis, or even inference, is that the representative genetic diversity of mother Africa's descendants 150 years ago definitely supports the biological fact that African Americans are quite diversified in their genetic heritage, that the continual sterotypic visions of them should and can be challenged by these facts. The fertile seeds of Afro Americans or African Americans were sowed in their Motherland Africa, Europe and North America. Somehow the elements of the universal created an admixture of the fertile cells of these continents. The significant result was the Black American whose African genetic splendor did remain dominant and whose prophetic faith and courage did sustain them through the tragic experiences of the dehumanizing institution of slavery.

I believe that a triangular model can represent Africa as the base, Europe and North America as the sides. This triangle can explain from a biological perspective that the following descriptions of complexions or skin color of the soldiers of the Fifty-Fourth Massachusetts Regiment 130-150 years ago supports the genetic and reproductive reality that African Americans are representative of a genetic diversity as well as a cultural diversity.

My hypothesis, inference, or supporting belief is that over the years Mother Africa's fertile genetic seed has always been dominant in its hybrids. The presence of many recessive genes of other races has resulted in a proud and determined African

American whose accomplishments and survivals have been due to a multiracial, diverse genetic heritage.

Regardless of their so-called descriptive complexions or known genetic heritage, those brave Black men of the Fifty-Fourth Massachusetts lived and fought together as brothers under the skin and probably would say, *Die Farbe ist Egal or the skin color makes no difference.*

Their so-called complexions, or possible amounts of melanin represented, were described as *Black, dark, brown, colored, light or mulatto, white, chestnut, copper and light brown.*

Color White - The Obsession of Color

What is an obsession of color? Is it something that just occurs naturally with people; are they programmed through their early period of maturation to observe and label people by their skin color? Is this an American or international obsession? Why do I use the term obsession? Only because over the hundreds of years since the founding of this country, the designation of one's color is part of the American vocabulary and mentality of many people. Over a period of twenty-five years, I have studied, researched and collected material that addresses color obsession and how it becomes a significant part of the vocabulary and experiences basic to identifying people.

True Narratives and Incidents Depicting the Color Obsession

During my twenty years of active military service and some thirty seven years of studying, researching and writing about African American experiences, I have collected many true stories from oral tradition, primary sources, secondary sources, and personal interviews. The following narratives and true incidents will reveal many realities of African and white Americans as they have interacted with one another over the years and even today as they attempt to confront the color problem. May these truths awaken and reeducate all Americans about the obsession of color today within our multi-ethnic society.

"Where is the Colored Man",

A group of three American Missionary Association ministers had made reservations at a small hotel in a Midwestern city in the 1930's. They had wired ahead that one of the ministers was a Negro. When they arrived at the hotel, the mulatto Afro American, the son of a white southern father and a Black mother was prepared for his separate quarters. The desk clerk greeted the three ministers and said "Oh, I see the colored man did not come with you."

"I ain't no kin to her"

Sixty years ago in a one-room school house in eastern Virginia sat several Black youngsters of different skin colors. However, they all were considered Black. There was a little boy who was a mulatto or commonly referred to in those days as "high yellow." There was a little girl in the class who possessed a very dark skin color that was referred to as "dark, jet Black or blue Black". Ironically, the two youngsters had the same last name, but were of no known relations. The teacher asked the little boy whose last name was Manderson, what was his name? The little girl, Janie Manderson was sitting a few seats from him when he answered, "My name is John Manderson and I ain't no kin to Janie Manderson".

My Identity Is Black

President William Howard Taft had requested Captain Walter H. Loving and the Philippine Constabulary band in 1908 "to escort him from the White House to the Capitol where he would take his oath of office The following incident occurred: "Just before the parade, some of the senior officers tried to prevail on him to pass himself off as a Cuban officer attached to the U.S. Army. This should have been very convenient since Taft had earlier served as Provisional Governor of Cuba, but Loving would have none of it. He replied, 'No, I cannot, and will not hide my identity Captain Loving, a man of color was born in Virginia and attended Public schools in Washington, D.C.

A Platonic Interracial Relationship

Wilma had left home to attend a college in the City of Decatur, Illinois. Her first year at Millikin was quite productive, and she was able to develop a cordial friendship with a classmate named Cynthia Lou Herald. Cynthia Lou was a Caucasian young lady around 20 years of age and a native of Decatur, Illinois. Her parents were residents in Decatur for many years and had developed firm thoughts about people of color. Wilma invited her brother from St. Louis to come to Decatur for a weekend visit. When he arrived he was introduced to Cynthia Lou and the next day the two had sparks in their eyes and a feeling in their hearts for each other. No, it was not love at first sight but a very close developing relationship that never went beyond a platonic friendship. Wilma's brother Fred invited Cynthia Lou to visit St.

Louis and be the guest of his older sister for the weekend. She was somewhat hesitant because she had a brother who lived in St. Louis and he would be quite upset if he knew that she was attempting to develop a relationship with a Black.

Cynthia Lou decided to visit St. Louis and spend the weekend as the guest of Fred's sister Cecelia. A visit to the park, a picnic and a ride on the local city bus was an experience for both. The red head, freckled face Cynthia Lou assured Fred that there was no need to be sensitive about their togetherness from either Blacks or Whites whose eyes were gazing from all angles toward the couple. A week later, after a weekend of talking, petting and some very serious kissing, the two of them believed that they had crossed the line of demarcation between love and infatuation. So Fred, who did not have a car, paid a friend eighty dollars to drive him to Decatur, Illinois, to see his so-called new white heart beat. When he arrived, they were so happy to see each other that she invited him and his sister Wilma to her house. She told him that if her parents would come in and see them together, she did not know what they would do. The three of them spent only a brief time at her house.

After an enjoyable weekend and time spent together, still retaining a platonic relationship, Fred returned to St. Louis, Missouri. He made several more visits to Decatur, and Cynthia Lou made another visit to St. Louis. She wrote Fred several letters. The letters were very deep in substance, and she told him that she had gone to confession and told her priest of her interracial courtship. The Catholic priest in her Decatur, Illinois, parish advised her to break up the relationship and forgave her for any sins that could have been committed in the light of her dating. She also wrote Fred that if their relationship developed and marriage was a possibility she would become very concerned about children, of mixed blood. Her letters became memories of the past; her platonic relationship became memories of a sincere colorblind person whose heart at first had no color obsession. That was the way it was for a white young lady named Cynthia Lou and a Black young man named Fred, forty-one years ago.

"Passing In the Society Column of a White Newspaper, 1959"

When a young African American was preparing for his wedding in a Midwestern city in 1959, he was quite aware that the city's most popular white daily newspaper, the Kansas City Star, did not include the pictures or announcements of African American potential brides. Starting off as a humorous suggestion after seeing the bride to be's photograph, a Jewish friend of the young groom of color came up with a suggestion. He told his friend that he knew a person who worked in the society section of the Kansas City Star newspaper. His plan was to take the picture and announcement of wedding plans to his friend in the society section. The racial identity of the bride was debatable because to many African Americans, the bride's hair and facial features, except for her blue-greenish eyes and very light mulatto skin would reveal that she was an Afro American. However, to many Whites and some Blacks she could appear to be a white person. Ironically, someone in the society section was concerned about the picture because they observed the address of the prospective groom and located a phone number and called his residence. The future groom happened to be home when the person who was calling asked, Does a person by the name written in the article live there? He abruptly told them that they had the wrong number. Whether it was the picture or address in a predominantly Black neighborhood in Kansas City, Missouri that aroused the society section's curiosity, the next Sunday's Society section carried the announcement with the future bride's picture. The picture was placed between pictures of future brides, all white.

The Jewish friend and the future groom joked about their accomplishment of possibly fooling the newspaper. But the newspaper was literally "up against the wall" and went ahead and published the announcement and picture of an African American mulatto who appears definitely as a Black person to her family, friends and others. When the bride and groom obtained their marriage license, the recorder had to be reminded that there was an error because her race should reflect Black Negro or colored and not white. Ironically, an East African lady saw the bride in question in 1989 and couldn't believe that she was Black. This is another true story of how we as multiracial Americans have become obsessed with color and sometimes our first impression from sight or observation incorrectly labels people what they are not. That was the way we were and in many instances still are today.

What's In A Name

A deposition dated 1910 revealed that a Maryland woman of color was married in 1868. She stated that she was an illegitimate child and took the name of her mother who was also illegitimate. This lady said her father was her white master prior to the Civil War. She also stated that it was a custom for illegitimate children to have the name of their mother. However, the Catholic church in Charles County, Maryland at the Baptism or Christening of illegitimate children, would always "place the child's name as that of its father". She said that is the reason she had the last name of her white father on the Baptismal Record.

Do Not Forget Payday

Sometimes Majority Members or Caucasians have a tendency to categorize Blacks upon sight. Twenty years ago the military services had few Black officers on active duty. One day a General officer inspected a company of soldiers at a military base in Alabama. The company was commanded by a Black Officer, commissioned in the rank of Captain. The General was addressing the 150 men and thanked them for their cooperation and also personally thanked the Company Commander. The General said, "Thank you very much for a wonderful tour of the company, Sergeant, and keep up the good work, Sergeant. When the General realized his error, he said, "I am sorry Captain". The Captain replied and said, "That is all right General, just do not forget it on payday".

You were not my kind

In a small Pennsylvania town a family of mulatto Afro Americans resided there for many years. There were two ebony colored cousins who lived to the ripe age of ninety years. When the last cousin died, she left an estate of a house and a bank account of approximately $40,000. A member of the mulatto family decided to become friendly with the surviving cousin a few years prior to her death. Previously the cousin was ignored and considered a distant family member of little significance. A lawyer requested the mulatto cousin to come in and hear the will; she became very upset when the lawyer said your cousin left you one dollar and her two neighbors, one white and one Black, the house and bank balance".

Remember The Children

The same mulatto family was quite conscious of their color legacy. One of the members was introduced to a very successful college graduate whose skin color was of a dark hue, with hair texture, somewhat curly. The daughter informed her parents of her desire to come engaged and the mother was quite upset and attempted to show her reasons why she should not marry this young man. After several family discussions, this obsession of color was minimized and the family accepted their daughter's decision to become engaged. The family had consented to the marriage after learning that this Afro American of a darker pigment possessed a doctor of philosophy degree, from a prestigious Midwestern university. Later, the couple was divorced. Today her brother and sister are passing as white Americans.

I Do Not See Your Color

The year was 1957, place - the land of the morning calm, Korea. A company of Engineer Troops were assigned along the demilitarized zone or (DMZ). An Infantry. Division Commanding General decided that the Engineer Lieutenant should be replaced by an Infantry Captain as Company Commander. The Engineer Lieutenant had received the news and was talking to the only Black lieutenant or officer in a battalion of some 40 or 50 officers. The two lieutenants were very close friends and respected each other. The white lieutenant remarked that "an Infantry Captain will be arriving soon and I hear that he is airborne, tough regular Army all the way. You know he will be working all of us like a bunch of niggers in a cotton field". The lieutenant immediately realized his slip of the tongue and said to his fellow lieutenant "I am sorry but you know I feel that you are just another white officer. I really do not see your color".

This is One Colored Passenger

A cultured mulatto Afro American was returning from a Christmas holiday in the South in the late 1930's. When she arrived at the train station, she decided that the line for "colored passengers to buy tickets was too long". She was tired and just wanted to return to Washington. This lady obtained her ticket at the white passenger ticket window and immediately went to her Pullman room. Later she decided to go to the ladies powder room. While she was waiting in the foyer, several white women were discussing the large number of Black passengers returning North. One white lady said, "I just do not understand why all of these niggers are returning to Washington today". Another white lady said, "Well they are going back after the holiday". Then a white lady said, "Well, I am glad we do not have any of them riding with us. At this moment the mulatto Afro American replied very strongly, "Well this is one colored that you have riding with you".

Who Am I?

A white soldier had received a lecture on miscegenation or race mixing in a race relations instructor's course. The lecture was given by a Black officer. The soldier decided to visit the instructor's office after class. He explained to the instructor that he was very confused and would like to know what race he was. The soldier said his family was of Polish descent and lived in a small Pennsylvania coal mining community. He also stated that he had one brother who did not like Black people and was upset because he was attending the race relation course. The white soldier told the instructor that often his Asian wife would question privately the racial origin of his mother. The soldier said, "My mother told me a few years ago that she was the child of a Polish woman and a mulatto man. She said years ago her mother met this nice colored man and they were friends for many years. The confused soldier then asked the officer - am I white or colored. The officer replied "You are white, because you are now part of your white community and never forget it, you are white."

Almost An Aggie Alumnus

During World War I, a St. Louis, Missouri Sumner High School graduate was accepted in the Student Army Training Corp (SATC). This student's physical description was; medium stature, reddish brown complexion, and curly mixed straight hair. When he departed St. Louis, he was given instructions to report to College Station, Texas, Texas A&M College. Upon his arrival it was quite obvious that a mistake had been made. This grandson of an Irish Alabama planter and African Indian slave woman stayed a month at Texas A&M. He was given a job of working around the Military Commander's house until he could be sent to Howard University, Washington, D.C.

Color Me White

A former slave of Lancaster District, South Carolina, adopted his master's name and enlisted on March 27, 1865, at Raleigh, North Carolina, as a Private in Company E 135th Regiment, U.S. Colored Infantry, Volunteers. His description was listed as 5 feet, 5 inches, complexion Black. After the Civil War, he married and had a mulatto daughter born March 13, 1875. During an interview with this veteran's late granddaughter, I learned that she was named after her father's mulatto sister. She stated that her Aunt appeared quite white and could easily be mistaken for white. Her aunt was quite fond of her niece and her brother and sister-in-law. She asked if she could take her niece to another city. The niece had a very light complexion and also could have passed as white. The parents refused the request and the aunt left Washington. It is believed that she became one of the many Blacks who used their white skin color to cross the color line and assume a white identity.

Graduations of Color

Porter Banks was born in Kentucky. He was the slave of a Dr. William Banks, who was commissioned an assistant surgeon, Confederate States Army (C.S.A.) Porter remained with a Dr. Banks until he was paroled at Greensboro, North Carolina, in May, 1865. From 1862 to 1865, Porter Banks was the cook for the Surgeons medical brigade. When Banks requested a colored man's pension, a letter written for him described Porter Banks as "a light copper color, weight about 180 or 200 pounds and about 30 or 40 years old." That was the way some Whites expressed their preoccupation with color among Blacks.

Mistaken Identity

Monroe was a faithful old servant and slave of his master, James F. Steward. When Steward was enlisted in the Confederate Army in 1862, Monroe accompanied his master. Monroe was wearing his master's cadet uniform. Monroe was taken prisoner and mistaken for a Confederate white officer. The union authorities eventually exchanged Monroe for two "Yankee Dutchmen" or Union soldiers.

White or Mulatto

The problem of the color line or race problem became one for the Pension Bureau's special examiner when he was reviewing a special claim for a Civil War Veteran's widow in 1921. Special Examiner J.H. Hines wrote: This woman is of good character and reputation. She claims to have Negro blood and she is very dark. she has the features of an Indian rather than a Negro. Two of her husbands were white men. I am told that there is no law against the marriage of a white person with a Negro in Michigan. Miscegenation (race mixing) apparently has no concern for the legislature of this state. However, one of the marriage records shows her as white another as mulatto".

Governor John Andrews of Massachusetts had recommended Sergeant Stephen Swails to accept a commission of second lieutenant in the Fifty-fourth Massachusetts Regiment. Secretary of War Stanton was procrastinating over Andrews' decision. When Stanton visited Hilton Head, South Carolina on January 15, 1865, General J.G. Foster attempted to assist Andrews in his decision to appoint Swails. He told Stanton: "Sergeant Swails is so nearly white that it would be difficult to discover any trace of his African blood. He is so intelligent and of such good character that after a fair trial I now recommend his being allowed to serve as a commissioned officer."

Swails was commissioned as a lieutenant even though some civilian and military authorities were having a color obsession problem in 1865, almost 130 years ago. That was the way we were 130 years ago. How far have we come with the color obsession? A recent article in the Johnson publication, *Jet,* dated July 12, 1993, concerned an African American Physician and Surgeon, Major M.P. Ketchens who experienced a color problem with his white peers when they saw his fianceé, a beautiful lady of color. The whites asked him, "Dr. Ketchens what are you doing?" He replied, "What do you mean?" They answered, "She's Black". "What do you mean", he said, "So am I". I still repeat it and say it loudly that in the later years of this 20th Century some white Americans still have a problem when dealing with people of color. But one must understand, that was the way we were in yesteryears and possibly in the years to come.

Marry and Get A Job

In 1913, a young African American named Robert Ambrose Thornton graduated from the Houston, Texas High School. Robert's mulatto high school principal told him, "Robert your parents are laborers and you are dark; you will not be able to go far in life. Why don't you marry and settle for a job in our local post office". Ironically, this young man did not take his principal's advice and in later years he became a master teacher, physicist, and scholar. He visited Princeton, New Jersey, and had seven meetings with the renowned Albert Einstein. That was the way it was for Robert Thornton.

Color Change In 1950

In 1981, I wrote a historical summary of a very distinguished African American sorority. A picture really is more than a thousand words. The photographs I included in my book actually reflect the presence of many light, light brown or mulatto members with a few members of dark complexion. A picture was taken in 1914 of a chapter in Washington, D.C. showing a majority of light or mulatto color members. The same chapter for 1931 continued its membership of mostly mulatto members. Their pledge club for 1931 was mostly mulatto ladies. In 1946, there was a beginning of color change and also 1950-1979 picture portrayed that the sorority had reached a color blind spot with beautiful skin complexions representative of our rainbow skin colors as African Americans. That was the way that sorority was some years ago.

White As Anyone

Cain Smith was born in 1845 in White Sulphur Springs, Fauquier County, Virginia. When he filed for a claim from the Southern Claims Commission for damages to his property by the Union Soldiers he stated in his deposition that: "I was a slave until 1863. Then I left home and went to Alexandria, Virginia and stayed until the end of the war. I then returned to Fauquier County. I was owned by Lewis Porter as a slave. I purchased a house from Absalom Rowe of Fredricksburg, Virginia. My occupation was a butcher and I hired out my time and paid my master. I married before the war and had a house and family at my mother-in-law's place with a few acres where I raised crops. My mother was a slave but I am as white as anyone else and my hair is light and straight, I could not read or write. My wife was colored".

"Thomas Inborden's Observations on Race"

Some Look Like Blacks

"The problem of racial identity is a complex one in this country. I saw Mexicans who looked all the world like Negroes, and Negroes who looked all the world like Mexicans. Their language was the only distinguishing feature, and in many cases the Negroes were better clad and better groomed. Negroes spoke the unadulterated English language. Their Alabama, Mississippi, Georgia, Louisiana or Texas previous environment may have given them more of the Southern brogue. The Mexicans have clung to their Spanish tongue or some broken dialect. Japanese, Chinese, Filipinos, Porto Ricans and others form another group. Then there is another group from northern Europe and southern Europe belonging to the white races, and all these people speak a language of their own and follow largely the customs of their country. I wondered who was fit and who could qualify under "The Restrictions."

An Illegitimate Carroll of Maryland

William Becroft was born at Carrollton in Maryland. His mother was a free woman of color and the housekeeper at the estate. William's father was a Caucasian, Charles Carroll who was a signer of the Declaration of Independence. William Becroft went to Georgetown as a young man and became a steward at the Union hotel. William Becroft's daughter, Marie Becroft established a school for girls in Georgetown. At the age of 22 years, she joined the Oblate Catholic Sisters of Providence, Baltimore, Maryland. Sister Aloyons died at 28 years of age in 1833. That was the way we were.

No Rights As A Citizen

Samuel Hord was born in Fauquier County, Virginia, in 1834. He was the son of a white physician, Dr. Hord, a wealthy man who owned a hundred slaves at one time. His mother was a woman of color, Polly Mann. Samuel was born free and saw his father frequently. He said his white father was a secessionist of the deepest degree. Dr. Hord did assist Polly Mann a great deal, said Samuel. His mother had 25 acres of land but never had ownership or the legal title to the land. Samuel Hord said he had no rights of citizenship because of his colored blood in his veins. He sued in Court but the court did not decide in his favor.

I Was One Sixteenth White

Prince Ponder stated in a sworn testimony, "I was a colored man 1/16 of Black blood and looked more like a white man than colored. I was white predominantly. That was the way it was for Prince Ponder during slavery and post war days. He probably used his color to his advantage to be a businessman in a white dominated society in Georgia.

Mulatto Dominates The Cotillion

In the mid 1950's a young man in his teens was invited to escort a young lady from an upper middle class family to the young people's cotillion dance and reception. This young lady was the daughter of a father who was of French, African and European origin and a mother who was half Negro mulatto and Pennsylvania Dutch European descent. Ironically, this young lady lives today as a Black passing for White. When the young man arrived at the affair, he was surprised to observe only three Blacks of brown color; himself, a young man and a young lady from a distinguished Philadelphia family of color who owned a bank and a weekly newspaper. That was the way we were.

I Hope He will Be Light

A very attractive brown skinned young lady, educated at the University of Chicago married a German from Bavaria. She is presently living in Germany with her husband and two children. While discussing the anticipated birth of her first child, she confided in some friends. I hope he will be of light skin. Another example of the obsession of skin color.

Not Even If Painted With Gold

A mulatto lady, 85 years at the time, told me that her father was Black as coal. However, when he married her stepmother, he told someone I will always have the whitest Black woman I can find, because I would not marry a Black skin woman if she was painted with gold. That was the way that a Black man from South Carolina expressed his obsession with skin color.

Not Completely Senile

There was a lady in the late 1980's who was very ill in Howard University Hospital suffering from Alzheimer Disease. Her sister would visit this mulatto lady daily and she would only smile, not talk. Her sister had observed that when an African resident physician would attend her, she would turn her head or never smile. One day while her sister was visiting, a mulatto resident doctor was at her beside and to the sister's surprise she was smiling as the doctor was examining her. While attending the repast at her demise, I listened while some of her classmates were talking about yesteryears. To my surprise, one lady said, "You know she had a hang up about skin color and so did her husband who was half white. You know they would remark about the dark skin color of their nieces and nephews, because the two of them just did not like dark skin people. That was the way some of us were.

No Time For Darkness

A half white Black lady was married to a light brown skin man who evidently had strong dominant white genes. They were the parents of children who could pass for white. Even though the family lived as Black people, the mother always maintained her superiority. She did not have any time for Black people though she was Black. That was the way she was for 98 years.

An Unfortunate Visit To The Dentist

A lady named Jennifer Jackson was born during the separate but equal period in America, seventy years ago. Her mother, Carrie Jackson was an African American, raised in Birmingham, Alabama. When Carrie was a teenager, she had to visit a white dentist's office to receive dental treatment. The rear entrance was used by Blacks as they walked into the "Colored Only" waiting room. On a visit to the white dentist one evening Carrie happened to be his last patient for the day. After sedating her for the treatment, he began to fondle Carrie and eventually he overcame her resistance and had sexual intercourse with her in the dental chair. Carrie became pregnant and a child was born who was named Jennifer Jackson, a very light skin mulatto child. Jennifer grew up and received good home training from her mother and stepfather who was aware of Carrie's ordeal prior to their marriage. Jennifer Jackson had one son who was also a mulatto and had inherited some mulatto genes from his grandmother. He showed some resemblance to his grandmother's half white brother who was living in Birmingham, Alabama. That was the way it was for Carrie Jackson and her mulatto daughter, Jennifer.

TRUE STORIES OF SEGREGATION

I Am A Black

An African American health specialist happened to ask her patient a question. She said, "It is interesting how you look so much like an Indian. Do you have Indian genes?" The patient replied, "My mother is an Indian and my father is half Indian and half Black. Of course, I could pass for an Indian even with my light complexion, however, I have problems in interacting with people if I say I am an Indian and I just decided to be called a Black American." This story was related to me in a conversation as late as July 13, 1993. When the patient was born that was the way she was genetically and over the years she probably was confronted with people who had a problem themselves in dealing with her identify. But through the years, I believe this lady has been at peace with herself by accepting her status as a Black. This is a story of the residual effects of color obsession in our society, 1998.

An Afro and Skin Cream Might Make A Difference

The Civil Rights Movement of the 1960's and earlier had very interesting stories and accounts of individuals dealing first with themselves and others. A Caucasian psychiatrist told me that he had an African American young lady who was a mulatto with very distinguishing Caucasian features. Her parents were an upper middle class Boston, Massachusetts, family of color. The young lady's problem said the physician was coping with decisions to conceal her white appearance and a desire to appear more Black like her peers at school. She tried very diligently to create a bush or Afro hair style and used cream to darken her skin. That was the way it was for a young mulatto teenager yesterday.

These true stories have actually reflected and depicted an obsession with color that is still prevalent today. I trust that someday all people will be able to look at individuals for their personal character and self-esteem and be more like a former physics student at Brandeis University some years ago. Even though this young lady was blind, she actually was not obsessed by skin color. The first African American Professor of Physics at Brandeis University, the late Dr. Robert Ambrose Thornton, a master teacher, physicist and scholar, was the former teacher of this young lady. During a reception in the Science Building at Brandeis, Ms. Susan Brandeis, the daughter of the late Supreme Court Justice Louis D. Brandeis was discussing with some students how highly regarded the head of the physics department at Brandeis University was and that he was considered one of the top Negro scientists in the country. The young lady turned to Susan Brandeis' husband and said, "I have been attending Dr. Thornton's classes for a month and all the students talk about him. This is the first time I heard he was a Negro!" That was the way it was for Dr. Thornton at Brandeis University in the 1950's.

It Must Be Faith

While in Massachusetts in 1894, Inborden met Frederick Douglass, the distinguished abolitionist, orator and statesman. T.S. spoke from the same platform with Douglass. While Frederick Douglass was speaking, T. S overheard a white man say *Faith, if a half Negro can make such a speech when one or a whole Negro can not.* That was probably the stereotype or mental thought of some white people as early as 1894 and in the New England so called liberal states.

His Features Were Similar To Longfellow's

Wilson Bruce Evans served during the Civil War. He volunteered at the age of 40 years in Ohio Volunteer Units and was assigned to Company D, 178th Ohio Volunteer Infantry as a private September 1, 1864. Evans served with the Post Commissary, Tullahoma, Tennessee. He was discharged on June 29, 1865 and received a bounty of one hundred dollars. W.B. Evans was a tall well-built man with white hair, hazel eyes and mulatto complexion. He was often asked by photographers and artists to pose for pictures. It has been said that his features resembled Longfellow. W.B. Evans was also a direct descendant of General Nathaniel Greene of Revolutionary War fame. Evans was a deacon of the Second Church in Oberlin, Ohio. W.B. Evans built his home, a hip roofed brick house (Italian style) at 33 Vine Street (in 1856, Old Mill Street) . The home has been placed on the National Register of Historic Places by the United States Department of the Interior, Family Home of Wilson Bruce Evans.

He Could Still Be A Colored Man

When the Executive Secretary of the AMA, Mr. Beard was visiting Brick School, North Carolina, a mistaken identity occurred when he was talking with a white man. Beard was sitting in a room with one of the teachers, Miss Dowell, and Mark Battle's son, Cullen Battle. During the conversation between Mr. Beard and Cullen Battle, Beard was talking to him as though he believed he was talking to a Black person. Miss Dowell became concerned and told Beard that he was talking to a white person. Dr. Beard said, "Yes, yes, I understand, but he could be a colored man and still be Mr. Mark Battle's son. This was quite an observation in 1895 because the statement by Mr. Beard was quite a realistic one.

Passing As Whites

Johnson Publishing Company's former magazine the *Negro Digest* published an article in March 1946 stating that it was estimated that "one third of a million people passed over the color line and there are some ten million Negroes with some white blood, and one million Negroes having as much as white as Negro blood". The *Collier's Magazine* published an article in August, 1946 that said "5-8 million people in the US have Negro blood and are known as white and 15-30,000 Negroes pass over to the white side each year".

The *Ebony Magazine's* April 1952 edition had an article on "White by Day - Negro By Night". Some significant highlights of the article were that approximately five million mulatto Black have passed into the "white world" in the last 20 years. There were also some mulattoes who would pass as white on their jobs, but would return at night to their Black neighborhoods. Surprisingly both Blacks and Whites have found it difficult at times to identify Blacks who were passing as Whites. It was learned that Blacks who have passed as Whites were able to assimilate into white society unnoticeable and their Black past became invisible in the white world. Some Blacks who have passed as whites were able to find employment in department stores, offices, government jobs, and they were able to attend white entertainment activities and enjoy the right to use all white public facilities. Many Negroes would not turn in those Blacks who were passing as white. Some Blacks would try to pass for Indians and Spanish people.

They Never Knew She was Black

The late Mrs. Dorothy Inborden Miller told me that after her mother graduated from Oberlin College in 1890, the American Missionary Association (AMA) offered her a position in the South. She sent her application with a picture and was accepted to teach at a school for poor white children in South Carolina. She taught there for one year and it is believed that they never knew she was a Black lady.

She Passed As White At Times

A lady named Daisy Fox was from Middleburg, Virginia. She lived in New York City during her adult years. Daisy's physical description was blue eyes, course straight hair, mulatto skin complexion and quite stout. At times, Daisy Fox would pass as white when traveling on a train or bus, especially when traveling in Virginia or the South. Sometimes she would wear a veil over her face. Daisy Fox left New York City one day to visit her relatives in Upperville, Virginia. When she arrived in Washington, D.C. she changed buses. She boarded the bus for Upperville and found a seat next to a white man from Upperville named Jim Kenslow. He did not recognize her. Daisy and Jim carried on a conversation and he assumed she was a white lady riding in the section of the bus reserved for Whites. Kenslow offered Daisy some chocolate candy from his box of chocolates. She practically ate all of his candy by the time the bus reached Upperville. When Daisy disembarked from the bus, she told the gentleman goodbye and walked swiftly toward her family's house. Mr. Kenslow never recognized her as Daisy Fox. This was an example of creative "passing".

What Is Your Race

The late physical education scholar, civil activist and teacher, E.B. Henderson appeared before the Virginia State Legislature to testify at a hearing on Civil Rights. A member of the legislative committee asked Henderson "What is your race". E.B. Henderson remarked, "This calls for some consideration. One of my great grandfathers was an Indian. My father's father was Portuguese and my mother's father's father was a highly respected white citizen in Williamsburg, Virginia. Her mother was the gentleman's slave. Now which race do you suggest that I subcumb to? There was silence within the court room and it was said that no further questions were asked Mr. E.B. Henderson.

Rev. Leiper's Genetic Surprise

The AMA had a group of missionary trained observers who traveled in foreign countries and in the southern states. They were called Members of the Deputations who came under the supervision of Secretary Cady. One of the trained observers was Reverend Henry S. Leiper. He had lived in Tennessee and North Carolina and had seen progress in Negro education. Leiper was very impressed by reports from a Mr. Newbold, Superintendent of Negro Education in North Carolina. He wrote in his report to the AMA that the kind of educational work the AMA is engaged in in the South produced profound faith in the mental, moral, and spiritual qualities of leadership in the colored race exemplified by such a man as Principal Inborden at Enfield, N.C. Leiper said Inborden revealed himself in a brief visit as a man of amazing resources, unfailing energy, transparent honesty and a degree of unselfishness rarely met anywhere. The effect of his personality upon the community was everywhere manifest. Leiper stated that T.S.'s energy and skill in managing a large enterprise was evidenced by the discipline, neatness and efficiency to be seen on the campus. The outreach of his life as invested in that school was manifest when we visited the homes of people who had come in contact with him who had come to appreciate the value of education for their children. Leiper wrote that after the children had received their training under Principal

Inborden, they went out into the world to make a success of their lives in broad fields of human endeavor. Rev. Leiper as an outsider was able to observe those magnificent qualities of T.S. Inborden as an educator and manager who gave the kind of leadership which others could compare. Leiper wrote that Principal Inborden was an outstanding example of the kind of leadership provided by such leaders as Booker T. Washington, Dr. Moten, Dr. Proctor, Dr. Garner and Dr. Lawless who also worked effectively among the colored people. I was quite surprised to read Rev. Leiper's remarks on biological genetic diversity in 1924 when he wrote about his views on the mingling of white and Negro heredity in the South. Leiper said he had seen government statistics showing that "one fourth of the Negroes in America today (1924) have some white blood in their veins". Rev. Leiper's observations in 1924 were interesting, because he went on to write that it never "came home to him" that numbers of Negroes had white blood in their veins until he visited the Black schools, sat and counted a room full of 150 to 200 students where very few could by any stretch of the imagination be considered pure Negro. Leiper said he saw a moral obligation of his white race toward the Negro race when he considered two and half million of sons and daughters or grandchildren of Black mothers and white fathers in our land. Rev. Leiper was discussing the phenomenon of the residual effects of racial mixing during and after slavery. It seems that his visits to the classrooms of Brick Normal School had a profound effect on him.

Worldwide Color Obsession

The American Black has traveled throughout the world as a performing artist and lecturer, guest theologian, visitor, and soldier. The countries they visited had an opportunity develop various opinions and impressions of the Black American, unvarinished by literature and recurring media accounts. These encounters allowed for fresh perceptions of Black Ameriicans. I read that a Yugoslavian young lady had told a Black American "You are my love because you are very black! Are you angry? You are very Black". This is just another true story of the residual effects of segregation as a world legacy.

AFRICAN AMERICAN'S OBSESSION OF COLOR

The victims were Black,

They did not report their race, they must be white.

He thinks he is white.

Is he a very dark skin person?

They are Black people.

Most Blacks live in that apartment.

Guess what, our new boss is colored.

You know her, she is that high yellow girl.

Mary is a Black Puerto Rican.

Did you see those real dark or Black skin Indians from India?

They look just like us, Black.

My doctor is Black.

Jane is married to a white man.

You know it was a Black person.

Have you seen Joseph? That fellow who is very light with his hair wrapped in a rag?

She tries to talk like a white person.

I only go to a white physician. You know how some of us Blacks are.

Carol hopes her baby will have good hair like hers.

Their father is very dark but their mother was a mulatto.

My white boss cannot stand those light skin Blacks.

He is married to an Ethiopian woman who is mixed with Italian, but he says she is not Black.

I will never forget those high flirting Black society clubs with all of those high yellow looking white people.

That funeral home used to bury the high yellows.

Kenneth said Remember Carrs and Sparrows Beaches, that's where dark Blacks use to go, not with those mulattos and a few of who made it at Highland Beach.

TRUE STORIES OF SEGREGATION

"I can remember" said Sinclair," when Bennett College Talledega, Morehouse, Spelman, Howard University and Fisk had the majority of the light and mulatto enrolled as students.

There are too many Blacks there, let's go somewhere else.

She wears that Kinte Cloth and Afro Bush but still doesn't conceal her white looking skin and mind.

He's too white and cannot relate to us Blacks of darker skin.

"Did you attend Dunbar High School asked Jim, "no man, I was too jet black"

SEPARATE LIFE STYLES

Black Churches.

Black predominantly Public Schools and Colleges

Barber and Beauty Shops, Restaurants

Newspapers, Magazines, Night Clubs and Bars

Cemeteries.

Predominantly Black Hospitals.

Movie Theaters.

Housing Areas Apartments.

Neighborhood Subdivisions

Fraternities and Sororities.

Social Clubs.

Golf Courses.

Recreational Societies.

Predominantly Black YMCA and YWCA.

In some cities Teacher's union.

Medical and Dental Schools.

Medical, Dental and Pharmacy Association.

Government Workers Group.

Political Group.

Radio Stations.

Banks.

SAYINGS RELATED TO COLOR

"Heave away! Heave away! I would rather catch a yellow gal, than work for Henry Clay A yellow girl I wish to go"

A Black minister, the Reverend Dean Babbitt, Rector Church of Epiphany, New York, said in 1903: "Who turned the Black man and woman yellow? Who is also mother, daughter and sweetheart though all under a Black skin."

The renowned physician, writer and activist, Franz Fanon said: "The mulatto went from a class of slaves to that class of his masters; joining the white world."

Frederick Douglass, noted Abolitionist, orator and statesman wrote in his autobiography, *My Bondage and Freedom:*
"Men do not love those who remind them of their sins unless they have a mind to repent and the mulatto child's face is a standing accusation against him who is master and father to the child"

D.H. 'Turner, a white man from Camden, Alabama, Reporter, Fourth Judicial circuit said: "The mulattoes were smarter than Blacks as a rule. However, some of the pure Blacks showed remarkable aptitude."

A mulatto educator once wrote: It means very much to any human life to be born with the correct heritage; blood will always count in the evolution of any plant or animal that grows because without the correct heritage, one has a hard road to travel.

BLACK FAMILIES, TRUE SHADES OF COLOR

The descendants of these families have been able to preserve their genetic heritage. These families lived during segregation. They also represent true "Shades of Color".

The Hudnall and Mann Families

Prior to the Civil War and earlier the freed mulattoes would either remain in the South or go North to live. Some Virginia mulattoes remained on or in the areas of the plantations where they were born. In Warrenton, Virginia, Fauquier County, there were three mulatto families that descended from three slave women and several Caucasian slave owners. There is a rich genealogical history of a family in Fauquier County called The Hudnalls. My research revealed that the following persons:

Joseph Hudnall	William Hudnall
Elizabeth Hudnall	Polly Hudnall
Nancy Hudnall	John Hudnall
Molly Hudnall	Alexander Hudnall
Thomas Hudnall	James Hudnall

were living in the county during the period from 1759 to the 1879. In 1745, Joseph Hudnall owned slaves. A will in the Fauquier County Courthouse revealed that Frances Hudnall made a will dated February 18, 1829. She bequeathed her possessions to William Hudnall, James Hudnall, Albert Hudnall, Joseph Hudnall, Alexander Hudnall and Nancy Hudnall. The land had been in her possession since 1787, a total of 42 years. She also gave to William Hudnall "said Negro man Sam and to Nancy she gave her bed and other furniture. The 1830 and 1840 census showed that Albert, James and William Hudnall owned slaves. A census for 1850 showed that there was a white Alexander Hudnall who was a school teacher. His family consisted of his wife Sarah, 37 years of age and their children John W., 14 yrs, William H. 13, Harriet 12 years, Athelia 10 years, James 9 years, Greenwood 7 years and Joseph Hudnall 2 years. There is a great possibility that this Alexander Hudnall is the Alexander listed in Francis Hudnall's will, especially in view of the fact that his children's names appear as William and James.

On February 8, 1850, Albert Hudnall made a will. It read "I now in the name of Almighty God do with a sound mind and sound body make this my last will. It is the first will that after my death that all just debts be paid and then the remainder of my property be sold and the money be given to Eliza Mann and the said Eliza to have a support out of it for life. It is for my will that her three youngest children, Drayton, Susanna and Ludwell have a thousand dollars a piece and the balance be equally divided among the rest as witness my hand and seal. Albert Hudnall".

When Albert Hudnall died in 1851, and the will was entered in probate court by Eliza Mann, a woman of color, it was resisted by three white men John Downing, the brother-in-law of James Downing who had married Ann Hudnall, Richard Hudnall and William Hudnall. A court summons was given on August 16, 1851 for Jordan W. Saunders, Richard Cooper, John C. Beale Jr., James Hudnall, and William Hudnall to appear before the justices of the County Court of Fauquier County to testify or to speak on behalf of Eliza Mann. The court eventually made William Hudnall administrator of the will and ruled the will valid.

The brother James Hudnall also had a woman of color as his mistress. Her name was Sophia Mann. James was the father of Sophia's children: Wilfred, Westwood, John, Thomas, Rush, Edward, Elizabeth and Mildred, all mulattoes. When James Hudnall died, a will was presented to the court for execution on January 26, 1850. "James Hudnall willed Sophie: 25-30 acres of land, $100, bureau, table and chair, choice of cow and one calf. She is to keep boy (nephew), Henry Clay. He is to be given his freedom also, but only limitation upon his liberty is that he shall be bound by indenture until 18 years to some respectable house or carpenter. The sum of $100 the interest on which direct to be paid yearly to the said Henry Clay until he shall attain the age of 21 years then the principal sum to be paid over to him and (Sophie's child Arthur Carter).

"He shall contribute toward the erection of some suitable site on the farm for Sophia and Henry Clay a comfortable log house and her children, and supply Sophia and the children above named Arthur Carter and Henry Clay with sufficient quantity of pork and corn. The residue of my estate seal and personals I give and devise to "Thomas Mann, Wilfred Mann, Westwood Mann, John Mann, Rush Mann, Edward Mann and Mildred Mann to be equally divided among them. When Mildred, the youngest shall be of legal age and until that time I wish that they remain together sharing equally the profits of the property which I shall direct shall be under the control and management of Thomas Mann the eldest brother who is hereby directed to attend to his mother having a maintenance for life to I give to the above named Thomas, Wilfred, Westwood, John and Rush Mann 100 dollars each to be given to them within 12 months after my decease". I also give to Alexander Hudnall for the benefit of his children, my Negro man Ben and land in the possession of William Hudnall one hundred dollars. I give to my three sisters Ann Downing, Elizabeth

Thompson and Fanny Hudnall one hundred dollars each for their attendance during my sickness in 1841.

An order from the Fauquier County Court dated November 1865, read as directed "the division and allocation of land of James Hudnall deceased and seven equal parts according to plot, Lot. No. I to West Mann, Lot No. 2 to Wilford Mann, and Mildred Mann, Lot No. 3 to John Mann, and Elizabeth Mann Lot No. 4 to Thomas Mann. The Woodlands near Old Mill Road.

It appears that William Hudnall was the white father of Eliza or Elizabeth Mann's children, Drayton, Francis, Mildred, Ludwell, William H. Tucker, Elizabeth and Blucher Mann. When William Hudnall died he left a will. His will read: "He give and grant unto William Tucker as I always call him the son of Eliza Mann a free woman of color who now lives on my land the following property as follows: land, Negroes, perishable property 2,000 acres with all stock, cattle, hogs wagons carts, plow harrow, dwelling house, poultry and stables.

I give again to him my three pet boys Daniel Webster, Don Pedro and David for to be free to all intents and purpose at 20 years old but they are not to be hired to anybody or to be liable in shape for any debt that I may contract. It is my desire that they be with Tucker under his own eyes to make them work, feed them well, cloth them and at the proper time liberate them and let them scuffle for themselves. Daniel Webster born 1840, Don Pedro, 1842, David Crock born 1845. It is my desire if the law of Virginia will at that time let them be free or they shall be hired out to raise something to take time to take them to one of the free states or limiting so as for them not to become subject to the laws of Virginia.

I give to William Tucker, my Negro man Charles to help him to take care of himself and the 3 boys and also his own little brother and sister's mother. To Tucker's mother, Eliza Mann, I give the land and house she lives in and for her life time use. To be a home for her little children and family. Her oldest daughter, Francis, if she should die to keep and take care of Drayton, Susanna and Ludwell and Mildred.

I give to Francis Tucker's oldest sister. My Negro girl Maria to keep to take care of her children so that she may be crafted to make clothes for my little boys with a fair profit of what I leave to Blucher, Julius, Drayton, my Negro man Fielding, free him in 14 years. Also give him Moses. Balance of my Negroes I give to Blucher, Drayton, Julius, Ludwell and Susanna.

The family of Sophia and Elizabeth Mann was the genesis of a mulatto group in the area of Warrenton, Virginia, Fauquier County, whose roots would extend over the years where court records could be found with names of the Mann and Hudnall peoples of color as late as the 1930's.

A review and examination of the census, marriage and death records have shown that these families intermarried and thereby were able to in many instances maintain their mulatto complexions in their offsprings. John Malvin, the son of James Hudnall and Sophia Mann Malvin married two sisters, first Mildred Mann and after her death, Elizabeth Mann, the daughter of William Hudnall and Elizabeth Mann. The children of Francis and John Mann Malvin were: Rosabel, Zeph Turner, Catherine (Kitty), Solomon, Roberta, Laura, John W. and Dorsey.

The 1860 census showed the household of Elizabeth Mann, age 59 years and those present were Edward, a farmer, Thomas a carpenter; Westford, Elizabeth, a seamstress; and Mildred. They were all described as mulattoes. Tucker Hudnall, known as William Hudnall, was listed in the 1860 census with a family of Kitty, 36 years, Columbia, 17 years; Sophia, 14 years and Richard, 12 years. They were all mulattoes.

I also examined the wills in the county court house and was able to ascertain that the continuity of these families was carried on by the execution of wills and leaving estates of some kind to their children or descendants. There were wills filed for William Tucker, Elizabeth Mann, and John Hudnall.

The obsession, frustrations and desire to maintain their status and mulatto skin color were present in their sworn statements or actions.

I observed in the marriage records that the page recording the names of Ludwell and Lillie Saunders had the word "white" written over the word "colored" which was first inscribed on September 29, 1875.

John Malvin said that when the Civil War was over, he took the amnesty oath at liberty. He went on his own accord when others were doing so. He stated that he was threatened with being taken behind Confederate lines and put into Confederate service. The conscript officers came after him six or seven times. Malvin hid or concealed himself in the pines when they were around. " I stayed in the pines a great deal and my wife would give a signal when they were gone," said John Malvin. Malvin said he was born free and not considered a white man. However, a white man once wrote in describing Malvin, "This man has no traces of African blood. His hair is perfect straight, eyes blue and skin white and his children are the same.

A Romulus Hudnall once wrote "I had no right to vote although I am white as any man and all my family. I was denied my rights as a citizen. I sued for them in the courts and provided myself 7/8 white but never had a vote until after the War". Blucher Hudnall said in an 1873 statement: "My mother was a colored woman and I was not entitled to the privileges of a white man".

One can draw many inferences and conclusions from this true story about the mulatto families of Fauquier County, Virginia. However, the main conclusion is that these families lived in a world of two colors and their experiences were repeated by many of the mulatto free families in the United States prior to and after the war. That was the way it was for the those ladies of color, Polly, Elizabeth and Sophia Mann, their mulatto families and descendants.

Inborden Family
Including
Robert E. Lee's Possible Illegitimate Children

Thomas Sewell Inborden (referred to as T.S. Inborden) did not admit knowing about his Caucasian father. To maintain historical accuracy an analysis of primary and secondary sources including oral tradition, I have decided to present the known available facts about the possible identification of T.S. Inborden's paternal heritage. The following will include some inferences and researched accounts from letters and interviews. In June, 1985, Dorothy Inborden Miller, daughter of T.S. Inborden, stated in an interview that she was attending a family reunion in Middleburg, Virginia, and decided to ask her first cousin who her grandfather was. She asked Nellie V. Corie Smith Young, the daughter of T.S.' brother, Ashton. Nellie replied without hesitation, "He is the son of Robert E. Lee" and was surprised that Dorothy Inborden Miller did not know. Mrs. Dorothy I. Miller informed me that it was not her desire to have Robert E. Lee as her grandfather. I decided to pursue this information, as far as possible. I made numerous visits to county court houses, towns of Middleburg, Upperville and Paris, Virginia. I also interviewed several people who believed General Robert E. Lee of Confederate fame was indirectly related to them. I have developed some inferences and a scenario that will reveal that Robert E. Lee possibly was involved in some intimate relations with some females of color, especially a family that has some direct relationship to T.S. Inborden. After some 15 years of researching this information, I sincerely believe that Robert E. Lee was not T.S. Inborden's father. However, there is a great possibility that Robert E. Lee's sons or Lee had himself intimate relations with a female closely related to Inborden. I will present some evidence that will show that T.S. Inborden possibly knew the identity of his father. I was not able to ascertain where the name Inborden originated. There was a Confederate officer named General John Imboden. There were present in Inborden's personal library some books written on the subjects of Robert E. Lee, and the Civil War. Several books had their pages folded and some pencil marks reference paragraphs pertaining to General Imboden. These books had T.S.' name stamped inside the front covers. These manuscripts are: *Treason of Major General Charles Lee, 1858, Robert E. Lee a Biography, 4 Volumes, 1936, Recollections and Letters of General Robert E. Lee,*

1904 and Jeb Stuart 1934. T.S. Inborden had clipped a picture from a newspaper, *The News and Observer*, Raleigh North Carolina, January 17, 1937. The picture was of Robert E. Lee on his horse, Traveler, and the caption read: "Tuesday, January 19, marks the 130th anniversary of the birth of that great Southern gentleman and leader in the Confederacy, Robert E. Lee. I have posed the question to Dorothy I. Miller several times: Why would her father have a personal interest in books on Robert E. Lee and the Civil War?

In November 1993, I had an interview with, Ashton E. Smith, the husband of a great granddaughter. He stated that there were discussions in the family that they could be related to Robert E. Lee. He also told me about a lady living in Chatham, Canada, whose family was also related to Robert E. Lee. I made a telephone call to a Mrs. Connie Travis and she informed me that her family was related to Robert E. Lee. She sent me a letter dated November 10, 1993, and later sent a book on the history of the early Black community in Canada after the Civil War. After reading the contents of the letter and the book, I was able to learn the following facts about her alleged relationship to General Robert E. Lee. Mrs. Connie Travis said that the story has passed down to family members through the years by oral tradition from her father, and mother, Martha Watts, daughter of Horace Black; her grandmother, Julia Black, and her Aunt Julia Black Chase. There was a young girl named Martha who worked, as a slave on the Kentucky plantation of Asher (or Ashton) Lee, a cousin of Robert E. Lee. She worked in the kitchen of the plantation house. General Robert E. Lee was apparently visiting his cousin Asher's plantation and as a southern custom, Martha was offered to Robert E. Lee to satisfy his sexual desires. This intimate relationship was possibly the biological conception of a baby who was named, Horace Lee. Horace was sent from Paris, Kentucky, as a substitute for his master's son during the Civil War and served in the Union Army. After his discharge from the army and receipt of his freedom, Horace Lee changed his last name to Black. Horace Black decided to travel to Canada and purchase some land. He purchased crown land in Raleigh Plains, Kent County, located near the Elgin Settlement where some former slaves found freedom prior to the Civil War. Horace's name appeared on the assessment rolls of Raleigh township as early as 1874 as the owner of 100 acres of land. Horace Black was married twice. His first wife was Maria Poindexter, a hair dresser from Detroit, Michigan. Their children were William Herbert Black, Cleveland, Ohio; George Poindexter Black, Allentown, California; Horace Greely Black, Canada. Horace's second wife was Julia Watts, and their children were Edith Ella Smead; Arnold Black, Omaha, Nebraska; Charles Black, Detroit, Michigan; Stanley Black, Cleveland, Ohio; Gladys Riddle, Ann Arbor, Michigan; Sidney Black, Canada, Julia Louis and Gordon Black, Canada. Mrs. Connie Travis said Horace received a bullet wound in the thigh while in military service and a pension. His widow received forty-two dollars a month until her demise in 1932. Mrs Travis also stated that some photos of Horace Black did resemble pictures of Robert E. Lee. The information that I received from Mrs. Connie Travis about Robert E. Lee enhanced the possibilities that Lee did have intimate relationships with women of color. I called a very gracious lady around the age of 80 years in 1993 to discuss Robert E. Lee. Ironically, during our discussion, I learned that my late aunt's husband was this lady's brother-in-law. I felt quite relaxed and received very warm and helpful responses from her during our telephone interviews. She lives in the area of Upperville - Middlleburg, Virginia. She stated that there was a lady named Hebie Fisher who married a Waynefield Fox. It is believed, through the oral tradition, that her father was Robert E. Lee. Hebie was born around 1840 and lived to be 103, dying in 1943. When Hebie Fisher was twelve years old, she worked for a Colonel Delaney in the Upperville area. Her physical description was: blue eyes, straight hair and a mulatto complexion or white appearing skin. The known children of Hebie Fisher and Waynefield Fox were Henry, Curtis, George, Lillie, Waynefield, Daisy, Hebie, Leslie and Roal. Waynefield Fox had a sister, Lillie who married Al Spinney, Caroline Fox another sister, married Oscar Sanford and they had a daughter, Alcinda. There are some relatives of color of Hebie and Waynefield Fox that live in Middleburg, Virginia, today. One of the daughters of Hebie and Waynefield Fox was Daisy Fox. She lived in New York City during her adult years. Daisy's physical description was blue eyes, coarse straight hair, mulatto skin complexion and quite stout. I learned from her niece that when she visited her Aunt Daisy in New York many years ago, she heard her say, "I am related to Robert E. Lee, he is my grandfather and sometimes I am mean like him."

Adams Family

When I was a youngster, I would visit my father's office at the 12th Street YMCA, Washington, D.C. Frequently, I would see my father's secretary. Her mother and my mother were close friends. Several years ago, I located the secretary's phone number. In 1997, I attended her late husband's funeral and I was able to meet her for the first time in 51 years.

She told me during a conversation that her grandmother had shared a true story with the family and said that her fifth generation grandfather was the late distinguished American, John Quincy Adams. Therefore my father's former secretary's seventh generation relative would have been John Quincy Adams.

Smalls Family

I had heard about Robert Smalls prior to 1978; but I never had the opportunity to write about this distinguished gentleman or have the opportunity, to meet one of his relatives. I was fortunate to meet the great grand daughter of Robert Smalls in 1978. In June, 1998, I had a chance to talk to her for the first time in 20 years. Following is the author's Preface to a booklet published in 1980: *"The Planter: A brief Sketch of the Civil War Steamer and its Pilot Robert Smalls.* It reads, "On Saturday, July 22, 1978, I arrived at one of the oldest seashore resorts on the Atlantic Coast, Cape May, New Jersey. I entered the office of the quaint, beautiful Planter Motel, located at 810 Lafayette Street, and asked the personable lady who greeted me, was she Mrs. Planter. She replied that she was the great grand daughter, of Ship Pilot Robert Smalls who made a daring flight to freedom using the confederate steamer planter during the Civil War. Even though I came to Cape May to relax, I found myself enjoying the weak-end but deeply involved in a historical quest for knowledge of the Planter and Robert Smalls. A personal interview with Robert Small's great grand daughter and former owner of the Planter Hotel provided me with rich knowledge of the real Robert Smalls as she related personal family memoirs of the distinguished ship pilot."

While standing on the boardwalk at Cape May one Saturday night in 1978, I gazed out into the ocean and wondered how many visitors over the years have passed through this prestigious resort area and viewed the sign "Planter Motel". I also wondered how many school children and even college students have heard about the intriguing and daring attempts of escapes to freedom throughout the world by men and women. But really, I thought, how many have heard of the Planter and Robert Smalls? I will resurrect this question in 1998 as I update some interesting information on Robert Smalls and the steamer Planter.

Robert Smalls was born on April 5, 1839, in Beaufort County, South Carolina, the son of a Jewish father and a Black mother, Lydia. His father was a sailmaker and rigger of sloops and other ships. Smalls learned the sailmakers trade at any early age and later became a master rigger. He helped his father in delivering boats to their owners on plantations and in towns and large cities, and from this experience gained valuable knowledge of the shoals and currents of the waters in the Charleston area. An interview with Robert Smalls' great grand daughter revealed some interesting accounts of the true Robert Smalls. Smalls was born on a special day in Beaufort; there was a hanging on his birthday. This event in later years was made known to him and may have inspired him to work diligently for freedom of other Blacks.

Smalls became a slave of Henry McKee in 1851 and was hired out there, where he resided until the start of the Civil War. Near the end of the Civil War, Henry McKee needed additional money and sent Robert Smalls to Charleston to make money for him. Ironically, after the Civil War, when Smalls became a prosperous freeman, he purchased McKee's house in Beaufort. He also befriended and waited on the senile Mrs. McKee. She never realized that her former slave was free and now the master-owner of her former home.

According to family oral tradition, Robert Smalls' daughter was sent to the West Newton Academy in Massachusetts and in later years she served as her father's secretary in Washington, D.C. helping him to read and write. Robert Smalls owned considerable property at one time in South Beaufort, South Carolina. Robert Smalls was elected a member of the Constitutional Convention of South Carolina in 1868, to the State Senate in 1872 and to the Congress of the United States in 1876, 1878, 1880 and 1882. He served longer in the Congress of the United States than any other Black member during that time. Smalls was a member of the South Carolina National Guard and attained the rank of Major General in 1873. Smalls enjoyed the distinction of being a member of two Constitutional Conventions, one in 1868 and the other in 1895. Robert Smalls died in 1915.

The Planter

Since my writing about Robert Smalls and the ship Planter in 1978, I have been very fortunate to obtain some additional facts about the vessel, and its wartime mission. I received a telephone call from a gentleman in Greenville, South Carolina, in February, 1998. He was inquiring about my booklet, *The Planter* because he wanted to obtain a copy. I was very pleased to meet Mr. Edward D. Sloan Jr. over the phone because he provided me with some historical information and a nexus. Mr. Sloan's wife is the great grand daughter of the late John Ferguson of Charleston, South Carolina. Ferguson was born in 1826 in Nova Scotia and operated a shipping business at Accommodation Wharf with a William Holmes in the 1860's. He was also involved in the blockade runners, Celt, Chesterfield, Fanny and Jenny during the Civil War. Mr. Sloan told me that John Ferguson was the owner and master of the Planter that was stolen from the Confederate service by Robert Smalls and his slave crew. Ironically, Robert Smalls' great grand daughter, Mrs. Janet Nash, lives in Beaufort, S.C. today. I suggested to Mr. Sloan and Mrs. Nash, that it would really be nice if the great grand daughter of John Ferguson, and the great grand daughter of Robert Smalls could meet each other some day.

I believe a great majority of people including some scholarly historians, do not really have a full view of the Robert Smalls and Planter story, because hundreds of books and articles written about the event do not address the details about the Planter. I was amazed to learn from the information provided to me by Mr. Sloan, how Smalls was able to accomplish his objective of taking the Planter to Union lines. I was also intrigued by the fact that a former slave with limited education was given the responsibility to pilot this distinctive Civil War steamer called the Planter.

The Planter was classified as a side-wheeler coastal steamer, built in 1860 in Charleston, S.C. The ship's hull was of a yellow color on pine and red cedar lumber, with a live oak frame. The Planter had "two oscillating steam engines, each driving side paddle wheels; the cylinders were 20" x 6" stroke and a 9" stroke." The ship also had four furnaces that burned wood, two boilers on the main deck (freight) and the ship was 147' long and 30 ft. wide. The Planter's machinery was protected from gunfire by a timber buckhead and was armed with "a 32 pounder model 1841 pivot mounted on the bow and a 24 pounder howitzer on the fan tail". These guns could have been seized by the Confederacy from the U.S. Arsenal in Charleston.

The mission of the Planter was to serve the Tidewater planters, and the ship could carry 1500 bales of cotton. The ship was rented to the Confederate States during the Civil War. Its primary mission was to be an armed dispatch boat and general transport for the Engineer's department. On May 13, 1882, the Planter had a mission to move some weapons to a new fortification because General Pemberton had issued orders to abandon the Confederate fortifications on an island which guarded the stone approach to Charleston, S.C. On the night of May 12, 1862, the white officers and white mates of the Planter spent the night in Charleston, S.C. for recreation, as was the habit once or twice a week.

Robert Smalls decided to pilot the Planter to Union Lines, early in the morning., May 13, 1882. He brought aboard his family and the families of some of his fellow slave crew members. When the ship departed from the Charleston Harbor, there were "eight men, five women and two children" aboard the Planter. The slave crew lit the fires under the boilers and the ship moved quietly down the harbor. When Smalls approached Fort Sumter, he gave the usual signal in order to pass through the Confederate Lines. He made "two long pulls and a jerk at the whistle as the boat passed the guards". It is believed that the duty officer of the day thought the Planter was a guard boat and allowed it to pass. Once Smalls was out of the range of confederate guns, he raised a "white bed sheet on the pole and headed directly for the Union blockade ships. He was greeted by the ships "Augusta and Onward", of the U.S. Navy blockade fleet. Robert Smalls and his crew reported to a Commodore Dupont, and their families were given assistance by General Stevens' command union troops. Smalls was able to provide the union forces with some valuable intelligence information. He reported "the abandonment of Cole Island, which it was a serious breach of Confederate Security: Smalls and his crew were normally paid two dollars a month by the Confederate service and their owners also received some money. However, it has been said that Smalls did receive some money from the union forces for bringing the Planter through Confederate Lines.

The U.S. Navy decided to transfer the Planter to the Army Quartermaster, September 10, 1862, because the Navy's fuel supply was coal and they did not use wood in their fleet.

While the Union military was celebrating the "prize victory" of obtaining the Planter, in Charleston, South Carolina, the Confederate States were conducting investigations and an assessment of their loss.

The Confederate Military decided to conduct a court martial for the white officers and crew mates who had left the Planter on the night of May 12, 1862 to go into town for recreation. A General Order 41 was issued by the Confederate Headquarters Departments of South Carolina and Georgia. There were charges against Captain C.J. Relyea. They read, "Captain C.J. Relyea, Captain of the steamer Planter in the employ of the Confederate states of America did on the night of May 12 and morning of May 13, 1862 absent himself without permission from his steamer lying at Southern Wharf in the City of Charleston in direct violation of General Orders No. 5 from Headquarters (HQ) of the Second Military District, South Carolina, dated at Charleston, February 17, 1862".

The material aboard the ship was ordnance for fortifications at Charleston Harbor. The charges also stated that Relyea had absented himself and allowed the steamer to be taken on the morning, May 13, 1862 to the blockading fleet of Charleston Harbor causing detriment to the service of the Confederate States. Relyea, a civilian, was not in the military service of the Confederacy, and therefore was not subject to the rules and articles of war and was not subject to court martial jurisdiction. He was found not guilty of the charges and specifications and the court agreed to sentence him to three months imprisonment and a fine of $500 dollars. The court also cited Relyea for failing to obey an order and neglect of duty. A white ship-mate, Samuel S. Hancock, was fined one hundred dollars and given one month imprisonment. The ship's engineer, S.Z. Pitcher, was charged with disobedience of orders and neglect of duty. However due to insufficient charges, the court dismissed them. The Confederate General, Major General Pemberton, was the reviewing officer for the charges. He concluded his review and wrote: "It is not clearly shown that General Orders No. 5 referred to in the specifications to the charges had ever been properly commissioned to Captain Relyea or Hancock the mate, nor do any measures appear to have been taken by their superiors to enforce as habitual, compliance with the requirement of the orders. Pemberton also concluded "that Captain Ferguson, owner of the Planter and principal agent of the government in its connection with her, seemed to have been entirely indifferent as to the deportment of his subordinates in that particular". Therefore, I do not "consider that the public service will be benefited by the punishment of Captain Relyea and Hancock, the mate. The sentences are therefore remitted and they will be released from confinement. The proceedings of the General Court Martial of Pitcher are confirmed and he will be released". It has been stated that William Ferguson had told Relyea to state that he had not received orders that they could not leave the ship.

The Union Army had Robert Smalls to take the Planter to Philadelphia, Pennsylvania for repairs in June, 1864. The repairs consisted of "new armament, a new aft on the wheel house, two boilers and repair to the engines". The repair work was completed by the National Iron and Ship Builders, Philadelphia, Pennsylvania. While the ship was being repaired, Smalls was the subject of several, newspaper articles for his involvement in racial discussions on "Trams".

The Union army utilized the competent services of Robert Smalls during the war. On December 1, 1863, Smalls was detailed as a pilot for the Army and successfully carried the ship through Folly Island to Philadelphia. He was involved in the Battle of the Keokuk which was fought in the harbor at Charleston, S.C. on April 7, 1863. The Keokuk was struck ninety-five times and sank to the bottom of the sea. During the battle, Robert Smalls enjoyed a distinction that had never been bestowed upon any Black at that time in America. Smalls was able to be among those pilots who were present with their ships during the entire fight. Smalls remained until the Keokuk went down.

In September, 1866, Robert Smalls signed a contract for "victualing and manning the U.S. Steamer Planter". His appointment as ship master gave him the responsibility of supervising and paying the crew. His crew consisted of "a captain, 2 mates, steward, a cook, waiter and seaman, two quartermasters, 1 engineer, 4 firemen, and 3 coal passers". The identification of Robert Smalls as a captain, possibly in the naval service has been somewhat confused because of his relationship with the Civil War vessel Planter. Throughout the Civil War, Smalls served as civilian pilot and master. Smalls outstanding knowledge of the waters and his superb abilities to pilot ships were essential in his travel through the waterways of Folly Island, Stone River to Kiawah River, Cape Hatteras, Hampton Roads, Delaware Bay and Chesapeake Bay.

On September 30, 1865, the Army gave the Planter to the Treasury Department to be sold after it had been in service for the Freedmen's Bureau during the Reconstruction era. The original owner of the Planter, John Ferguson, attempted to purchase the ship. He had a northern man, Charley H. Campbell, to try to purchase it, but the government refused. In 1867, the Planter was sold to a Mr. Mordecai, who later sold it to John Ferguson. After 1867, the Planter was owned by J. Randolph, John T. Foster, James and David Marsh, William Ravenel and Adelaide Ferguson. On May 25, 1876, the Planter was providing assistance to a ship ashore when she sprung a leak and was eventually wrecked causing the loss of a famous ship that once was a Confederate steamer and later the Union prize.

The story of the Smalls family is another example of how people of color accomplished many historical feats that have never been recorded correctly in our history books. Robert Smalls represented the genetic talents of an African slave woman and a free Jewish man. Another true story of genetic diversity and shades of color in the African American experience in "America The Beautiful".

The Wall Family

A slave owner named Colonel Stephen Wall had a plantation in Richmond County, North Carolina in the 1800's. He had a slave mistress named Rody. Stephen Wall was the father of her children. They were Albert and John Wall. Stephen Wall was also a member of the North Carolina State Legislature. It was stated that he was not married. However, he enjoyed the forced comfort of his slave mistress. He also fathered children by another slave mistress, Priscilla Ely. Her children were Napoleon, Orindatus Simon Bolivar, Sarah, Benjamin F. and Caroline. Six weeks prior to Wall's death on August 28, 1845, he wrote in his will that all of the property that he owned in Ohio was to be left to his (illegitimate) children and that each be given 1,000 dollars. This concerned slave master and father had sent these children to Ohio prior to his death and awarded them their freedom. They were sent to a Quaker school at Harrisburg, Ohio to receive an education. The daughter of Stephen Walls and Priscilla Ely, Caroline was able to receive an education at Oberlin College, Ohio. She graduated in the Class of 1856. Caroline married a distinguished Black lawyer and later the first Black congressman from the State of Virginia, John Mercer Langston. They were married on October 15, 1854. Albert Wall, the son of Stephen and Rody served in the Union Army during the Civil War.

The following sketch of Albert Wall's adult life was obtained during my research on my 1990 manuscript, *Swamp Angels: A biographical Study of the 54th Massachusetts' Regiment*. Albert Wall was enlisted by R.P. Hallowell in the Fifty-Fourth Massachusetts Regiment on May 12, 1863 at Readville for a term of three years The official record listed his description as 25 years, five feet, eleven inches, light or mulatto complexion, dark eyes and dark hair. His civilian occupation was a student and laborer. Albert had studied at Oberlin College's Preparatory Department in the 1860's. Wall and his brother, John, along with eighteen other young men from Oberlin, were recruited by the distinguished lecturer, lawyer and former Congressman, John Mercer Langston. During a rest period from training at Camp Meigs, Readville, Massachusetts on May 27, 1863, Albert decided to demonstrate his known skills of wrestling when he engaged in a match with a fellow camp mate named Joe or Joseph Stills. Unfortunately, Albert injured his knee and it was described as an injury involving a dislocation in the area of the patella bone and thickness occurring of the semilunar cartilage and compound fracture of the leg's tibia and fibula bones. Wall was given light duty for a period of time and the opportunity to remain on active duty. In 1864, Wall's injury worsened and the regimental surgeon recommended that he receive a disability discharge. Albert was discharged on May 21, 1864.

After his discharge, Albert returned to Oberlin, Ohio and enrolled again in the Oberlin College's Preparatory Department. Three years later he married Ella P. Fidler on June 27, 1867. They were married by a Rev. Norton at Chillicothe, Ohio. Ella had a brother named Abram Fidler who was a successful stable owner in Chillicothe. He had married Sarah Kelley Wall, Albert's half sister. Sarah graduated from Oberlin College in 1856 and was a teacher in the Colored Public Schools of Chillicothe. Abram and Sarah Fidler were the parents of two children.

Wall received a veteran's disability pension for his injured leg in 1892. He died on May 31, 1897 at the age of 54 years. The cause of his death was due to *chronic interstitial nephritis and acute uremia.* Albert Wall died at Freedmen's Hospital (Howard University Hospital). His attending physician was Dr. W.A. Warfield. He was buried in Arlington National Cemetery.

John Wall, the son of Stephen Wall and his slave mistress Rody, enlisted on April 14, 1863 and was assigned to Company G. 54th Massachusetts, Regiment. This brief sketch of his adult life is also included in *Swamp Angels.* John Wall was born in Richmond County, North Carolina, in 1842. John was the brother of Albert Wall. The official record lists his description as five feet, ten inch, light complexion, dark eyes, and dark hair. His civilian occupation was painter. Wall married Mary Fannie Shanks on February 6, 1879, at Oberlin, Ohio. The ceremony was performed by an Oberlin college professor, the Rev. Judson Smith. Mary F. Shanks was the daughter of Willis, H and Anna Brown Shanks, both born in Virginia. William H. Shanks served in Company C, 5th United States Colored Troops (USCT) during the Civil War. He enlisted on June 23, 1863. Shanks was discharged as a sergeant, and received a veteran disability pension for his wounds. The Shanks lived at 223 South Pleasant Street, Oberlin, Ohio. Their children were George, a tinsmith and their daughter, Mary Fannie Wall. At the age of 102 years, William Shanks died on July 26, 1938 in Denver, Colorado while living with a grand daughter. His remains were returned to Oberlin where he is buried in Westwood Cemetery.

John Wall and Mary F. Wall were the parents of seven children. They were Sarah, born July 16, 1881; Hugh, born on August 15, 1883; Horton, born October 17, 1885; Barbara, born July 18, 1889; John, born July 4, 1894; Albert, born October 28, 1896; and George, born December 31, 1901. Wall received a veterans disability pension for his injuries received during the Civil War. He signed a deposition that read: *While carrying timber to build stockades at DeVores Neck, South Carolina in December 1864, I received a hernia on* my right side. After a forced march, I bled a great *deal and could hardly make it back to camp when we started to march again. I could not continue and was ordered to stay behind. Fearing that I could be found by the enemy who was known to kill all the sick they caught in the area, I decided to march on. My wound, worsened as I was marching.*

Fielding Brown, late First Sergeant, Company C, 54th Mass. Regiment. wrote the pension examiner a letter in support of John's claim. In the letter Brown expressed his personal views on the subject of promotion and race in the army. He wrote: *John Wall received his disability in December, 1864. I had to take care of a green (young or new) lieutenant and the company; therefore I did not have much time to look after the disabled. Wall was promoted for gallantry in one of our fights in the South from the* ranks to a sergeant. If he had been a white man be would have been made a captain. A medical letter in support of John's pension claim was written by Dr. William Bunce of Oberlin, Ohio. He said, *"I was well-acquainted with John Wall prior to his enlistment in 1873. I knew he was free from a hernia after making a careful physical examination at the time of his enlistment. The exam was requested by recruiting officer John Mercer Langston.*

Oberlin College sent a letter to the Director of Pensions, Veterans Bureau, Washington, D.C. certifying that John Wall was a former student who was enrolled during 1860-1861. Wall tried to work at various trades even though he was disabled. He worked as a painter, plasterer, and as a shoemaker. John Wall died on March 24, 1912 at his residence, 85 Main Street, Oberlin, Ohio. Mary F. Wall requested a widow's pension and received it. She moved to Denver, Colorado, to live with her family. Mary Fannie Wall died April 7, 1934 in Denver. Her remains were brought back to Oberlin, Ohio, and she is buried in Westwood Cemetery with her husband. Her son, John W. Wall, Jr., residing at 85 South Main Street, Oberlin, Ohio on April 23, 1934 wrote a letter to Department of Pensions, Veterans Administration, Washington, D.C. He wanted to know if the government would provide some money toward burial expenses for a Civil War veteran's widow. He also mentioned in the letter that he was a World War I veteran and a member of the American Legion. John Wall was a regimental color bearer of the 54th Mass. Regiment. who did not stop at the parapet on July 18, 1863, at Fort Wagner, Morris Island, South Carolina.

Holland Family

Milton and William Holland served during the Civil War and were the sons of a distinguished white man and a slave woman. The two brothers achieved excellence in their chosen careers after the war. Their father was Captain Bird or Byrd Holland, who was a former governor of Texas. Prior to the Civil War, Captain Holland freed his sons, Milton, William and James, and sent them to Ohio to receive an education. The three brothers were recruited for the Union Army by John Mercer Langston. Milton and James enlisted in the 5th USCT (United States Colored Troops) and William enlisted in the 16th USCT in Nashville, Tennessee. After the war William Holland entered Post Reconstruction politics and was elected to the Texas State Legislature. William introduced a bill that created present day Prairie View University in Prairie View, Texas. Milton Holland was promoted to Sergeant Major and was awarded the Congressional Medal of Honor for valor when he assumed command of his company due to the loss of the white commanding officer and led the company into battle. After the war Milton enrolled at Howard University's School of Law and graduated in the class of 1872, receiving an L.L.B. Degree. His classmate was Albert Wall's half brother Orindatus S.B. Wall, a former recruiting officer for Black troops. Milton Holland is buried in Arlington National Cemetery.

The Monde Family

Aristide Monde was born in New Orleans, Louisiana on February 22, 1835, He enlisted on September 15, 1863 and was discharged on August 1, 1865. The official records listed his description as five feet, four inches, mulatto complexion, brown eyes *and crisp hair.* Monde was never a slave. He was the son of a white man, Peter P. Monde and an Afro American woman named, Nina Horne. He became ill on October 1, 1863 and after being treated he was sent to Morris Island, South Carolina on November 10, 1863. He was suffering rheumatism and typhoid malarial fever.

Aristide Monde was married to Louisa Smith on July 18, 1865 by the Reverend John More, Pastor of St. Patrick's Catholic Church in Charleston, South Carolina. They were the parents of two children. Joe and Octave. On April 6, 1869, he married Marsaline Monde. They were married by the Reverend Claudian B. Northrop, Pastor of St. Mary's Catholic Church, Charleston, South Carolina. In 1885, Monde married his third wife, Georgie Anna Williams, daughter of Elizabeth Norris. They were married on May 2, 1885, by the Reverend Foote, The witnesses present were John and Amanda Polite. They, were married in New Orleans, Louisiana.

Prior to his enlistment in the Civil War, Monde had served in the United States Navy. In June, 1862, he was serving aboard the Cayuga, Farraguts Squadron, under Captain N.B. Harrison. After the Civil War, he enlisted in the Navy and served on the following vessels: U.S. Revenue Cutter Wihdermens as cabin steward under Lieutenant Cary, October to December 31, 1867; steward on the U.S. Revenue Cutter Ela, John Brown, Commander, January 1868 to April 1868 at New Orleans Station; Cabin Steward on U.S. Racer, John W. Jones, Commander, April 1, 1868 to August 31, 1868 at the Charleston, South Carolina station from 1868 to December 5, 1874 to June 30, 1875; Wardroom steward on USRC Steavena, John Bauer, Commander, June 1, 1877 to November 9, 1877 at the New Bern, North Carolina, Wardroom Steward on the USRC Mocuran, George Moore, Commander, May 1, 1878 to March 1, 1879; Wardroom Steward on the U.S. New Hampshire, James Juitt, Commander from November 1879 to September 1880 at Port Royal, South Carolina and on the U.S. Wyoming as Wardroom Steward, James Juitt, Commander from September 1880 to December 1880 at Port Royal, South Carolina.

Aristide Monde was employed by the Illinois Central Railroad Company as a Porter for the General Manager's private car during the period 1880-1881. Monde was a devout Catholic and when he died he was buried from the Most Pure Heart of Mary's Colored Catholic Church in New Orleans. He was buried in St. Vincent de Paul's Cemetery on Louisa Street, New Orleans. His half-brother Octave Johnson who lived at 2725 Perdedo St. and was a former member of Company C, 99th United States Colored (USC) Infantry, Corporal, brought Aristide's body home from Mobile, Alabama, and held a wake in his house.

Tapscott Family

While conducting some research in the National Archives in Washington, D.C. in 1979, I was able to obtain a copy of the will of a man of color named, Telam Poor. He was from Warrenton, Fauquier County, Virginia and had died in 1863. He was survived by his wife, Elizabeth Tapscott Poor. Their children were Mack, Robert, Virginia, Telam, Nancy, George, Randolph, Mary Francis, Maggie, Elizabeth and William. His widow died in 1865. There was a sworn statement attached to the will which was the testimony of a son, Robert. He said that his mother was a white woman and when their father died, all the children assumed her maiden name Tapscott. In 1980, I was visiting a church in Washington, D.C. and met a man named Tapscott and asked him did he have any known relatives living in Warrenton, Virginia and he replied, yes. This is another true story of "shades of color".

Falkner Family

The literary world celebrated the 100 anniversary of the birth of a distinguished writer, and Nobel Peace Prize recipient, the late William Faulkner on September 25, 1997. He was born in New Albany, Mississippi, but had a home, Rowan Oaks in Oxford, Mississippi, a segregated town. His surname at birth was "Falkner", and he changed it to "Faulkner" in 1919. His grandfather was a Mexican War and Civil War veteran, Colonel William C. Falkner, who lived in Lafayette, Mississippi and was a slave owner. Faulkner, a recipient of two Pulitzer Prizes commenced writing in the 1930's and some of his noted publications are *"A Fable, The Hamlet, Asbalom, Absalom, As I lay Dying, Big Woods' The Hunting Stories, Go Down Moses, Soldier's Pay,* and *The Sound and the Fury*. Some of his writings addressed the subjects of racism and miscegenation, namely, *Sound and the Fury, Absalom, Absalom,* and *Go Down Moses.* Faulkner wrote in his book *Go Down Moses* about a character, a white slave owner who was guilty of miscegenation, because he had "impregnated" the daughter of a slave woman, who later committed suicide. It is interesting how Faulkner wrote on these subjects because the following true story is known today to the descendants of his late grandfather, Colonel Falkner. Court documents in

Mississippi have shown that Colonel Falkner owned a slave woman, Emeline and her children. She and her children were "a collateral on a $900 loan he made to a white man. Benjamin Harris in 1858. During the period 1864-1866, Colonel Falkner fathered the child of his slave; Emeline, and she gave birth to a girl, who was named Fannie. It is believed that her first name was from the Colonel's sister, Francis: and her middle name, Forrest was for his admired General of the Civil War, Nathan Bedford Forrest.

The Family descent of:

Fannie Forest Falkner
Colonel William Falkner - Emeline
Fannie - daughter
Fannie marries Matthew Dogan
Blanche - daughter
Blanche marries W.A.C. Hughes Jr.
Daughters
Alfreda, Faulkner, Miriam

Blanche's father was a President of Wiley College, Marshall, Texas. She married a native of Baltimore, Maryland, the late Attorney William Alfred Carroll Hughes Jr., who was the son of the late Bishop W.A.C. Hughes Sr. W.A.C. Hughes was an outstanding civil rights lawyer who served as a legal counsel for the Baltimore NAACP Branch and was instrumental in some successful civil rights cases during segregation. In 1938, W.A.C. Hughes Jr. was appointed by Governor Henry Nice of Maryland to serve as a member of the first Maryland commission to assist in the negotiations to transfer Morgan State College (now University) from the Methodist Church to the State of Maryland. When I park my car next to Hughes Stadium at Morgan State University, Baltimore, Maryland, I am aware that the stadium was named in honor of the father-in-law of Blanche Dogan Hughes, the granddaughter of William C. Falkner. William Faulkner died in July 1962; however the Colonel's grand daughter, Mrs. Blanche Dogan Hughes, was living in 1997. This is just another true story of the shades of color.

The Lum Family

A Chinese man, Charlie Lum arrived in Charleston, South Carolina, from China in 1900. He worked with a friend, Hop Sing, who was one of the first Chinese to operate a Chinese laundry in Charleston. Charlie Lum also worked briefly for Yee Lee. In 1908, Lum opened his laundry and lived briefly in Manning, South Carolina He was married to a mulatto lady of color, Mamie Lum. They were the parents of ten children: Lem Yu Wing, Lem Yu Ching, Lem Yu Sing, Lem Gong Slem, (Ethel) Lem

Yu Chung, Lem Yu Fung (Ernest), Lem Yu Hong, (Herman), Lem Yu Len (Lillie), Louis Lum, and Benny Lum.

Charlie Lum died in 1927. His widow and children were living in a beautiful home on Mary Street in Charleston, South Carolina in 1928. The Lum children attended a private school, Catholic Immaculate Conception School (Avery Institute). Mamie Lum attended a Black church, Centenary United Methodist Church. One of the Lum children decided to live and pass as a Chinese in 1947. He had married a mulatto lady who was able to pass as white. Their children appeared more white in physical description than either Chinese or Black. This son was Chung or Lem Yu Chung. He separated himself from his mother and other family members by attempting to associate and assimilate into the white society. He and his family attended the white Catholic Church in Charleston, Our Lady of Mercy. He even changed his name from Lum to Lem ("this was a variation of his original name in Cantonese Chinese"). It has been said that "he served as a Chinese interpreter for the Chinese Consulate and Chinese visitors who frequented the Charleston area. In September, 1947, two of his children were admitted to a white public school, Courtney School in Charleston. Unfortunately for Chung, someone called the school and said that "the Lem children were Chinese and Black". Therefore in April, 1948, the children were not permitted to attend Courtney school. The other children of Charlie and Mamie Lum lived their lives as people of color, even though some of them could have passed as white.

A son, Ernest Lum, lived in Washington, D.C. He was an outstanding aircraft mechanic and later a teacher for many years in a vocational school in Washington, D.C. He married Maria A. Conway Lum, who also taught in the Washington Public School System. They were the parents of the late Ernest Lum, Charles Lum and Ewella (Cookie) Lum Williams. This is another true story of a family of color who lived during segregation and of their descendants.

Ing-Jones-Boone - Pittman Families

There were some white masters who became intimate with their slave women and would have them as mistresses living in their homes. This is a true story about Jacob Ing, who followed this pattern. Jacob Ing was a wealthy white North Carolina farmer who was born in 1786 in Edgecombe County, N.C. He died in 1869 in Battlesboro, N.C. His interest in politics was evident when he became a delegate for District 43, Nash County, N.C. to the Constitutional Convention, Raleigh, N.C. 14 January - 7 March 1862 for the revision of the State Constitution. Ing also served as Constable and Justice of the Peace for Nash County. In 1849, Jacob Ing posted bond "to become the legal guardian of Benjamin A., Charlotte T., Julius and Martha Susan Dozier, orphans of Thomas Dozier. The Census records 1820-1850 have revealed that Ing had some free colored persons living in his household. The 1850 Census revealed the following:

Name	Age	Sex	Color	Occupation
Jacob Ing	64	M	white	farmer
Esther Jones	55	F	mulatto	
John Jones	20	M	mulatto	miller
Dolly Jones	21	F	mulatto	
Matthew Jones	18	M	mulatto	
Lucy Jones	16	F	mulatto	

Court records have shown that John C. Jones was granted his freedom in 1856. A certificate of freedom was granted by Governor Thomas Bragg, Raleigh, N.C. on 14 November, 1856. An affidavit of Jacob Ing signed in Nash County read: "I am acquainted with the said John C. Jones from infancy. He was born December 17, 1830, at my house and lived as one of the family until he arrived to 21 years. His mother was one Esther Jones (who is dead). I was acquainted with the said Esther Jones, I believe about 40 years. During this time, she was always reported to be a free woman of color and I never heard it doubted."

John C. Jones, his sisters, Sally, Sarah Jones Reynolds and his brother, Matthew Jones decided to leave North Carolina and move to Ohio. John and Matthew purchased 100 acres on Musselman Road in Concord Township, Ross County, Ohio. The sisters purchased a small farm near Sulpher Lick Springs. Matthew was a veteran of the Civil War. John was married to Dolly Boone from Halifax Co. N.C. They married on December 20, 1849. Their children were Lewis H., George W. and Sydney F. Jones. The Jones family lived in Cleveland, Ohio at one time. John C. Jones was a fruit farmer and grocer in Ross County. He had membership in the Second Baptist Church, Roxabel, Ohio, and once attended the Dunkard Church, Frankfurt, Ohio. Jones had a brother and some sisters who remained in the South. His sister, Elizabeth, wrote him a letter from North Carolina on June 12, 1872. Jones had a grandchild who stated that "my grandfather said his father was a white man. "Ironically, John C. Jones died August 22, 1912 at the age of 81 years, 8 months and 5 days. It has been stated that the death certificates of John C. Jones and Sarah Sally Jones Reynolds listed "Jacob Ing as their fathers. Since the State of North Carolina did not require death certificates until 1913" those who remained in North Carolina and died prior to 1913, had no official record of their deaths. It is possible that Jacob Ing was the father of some other children whose mother was Esther Jones according to the last will and testament of Jacob Ing.

TRUE STORIES OF SEGREGATION

While living in Nash County, N.C., Jacob Ing wrote a will in 1867 and later added a "codicil" on April 30, 1869 that a house servant should continue to live at his home in Battlesboro, Edgecombe County, N.C. during her natural life. The will was probated on January 18, 1870 in Edgecombe County, North Carolina. Jacob Ing's will read as follows: "I give and bequeath to Mary Reynolds, wife of Benjamin Reynolds, Elizabeth Boon, wife of Jesse Boon, Selah, wife of James White, Sally Reynolds, wife of William Reynolds, William Jones, Matthew Jones, also old Chaney, freedwoman, formerly my house servant. Also Lucinda Artis (dead) to her children if any surviving (all colored) to be equally divided in nine parts and distributed as directed. In case any of the above named persons died before the execution of the will leaving children; in that event, the child or children will take the parents or share to them, and their heirs for ever carried forward. 8 April 1867".

The said Elizabeth Boon named in the will and sister of John C. Jones lineage descent was as follows:

Jacob Ing (White)   and   Esther Jones (Mulatto Colored)
Elizabeth   John
Elizabeth and Jesse Boone
Octavius
Octavius and Laura Sandlin Boone
Viola   Almyra
Almyra and Carey Pittman

Olivia, Winton, Carey, Ozette, Geraldine, Gerald, Almyra, William, Viola, Doris, Selda

Elizabeth (Betsy) Jones and Jesse Boone were married on December 14, 1849, Nash County, North Carolina. (It should be noted that the surname of Boone has been written without the "e" "Boon" on some court documents. In successive years, the descendants use Boon with the letter "e". Octavius Boone married Laura Sandlin Boone, and they were the parents of Viola and Almyra. Almyra married Carey Pittman and they were the parents of eleven children. The eleven children of Almyra and Carey Pittman are "Olivia Elizabeth Pittman, Winton V. Pittman, Carey Pittman Jr., Ozette Pittman Bell, Geraldine Pittman Clark, Gerald S. Pittman, Almyra Pittman Wills, William J. Pittman, Viola Pittman Boone, Doris Pittman, and Selda Pittman McWilliams."

Carey Pittman's daughter, Almyra Pittman Wills said that "her father ran away from home when his stepfather gave him a beating". Then he was able to meet Mr. Thomas Sewell Inborden, Principal, Bricks Normal School. Mr. Inborden gave him an opportunity to obtain an education at Bricks. Later Carey Pittman became a teacher, insurance agent and contractor. Prior to his marriage, Carey built a home for his wife in front of his mother's home.

The late Julius Rosenwald, former President of Sears and Roebuck Company and philanthropist provided funds for the construction of some Black schools throughout the South. Rosenwald established a fund in 1917 to build schools in some 15 southern states. There were 633 schools constructed in Mississippi, 527 in Texas, and numerous schools constructed in North Carolina. The outstanding craftmanship abilities of Carey Pittman were instrumental in the construction of 30 or more Rosenwald schools in Halifax County, North Carolina. Recently, the historic Allen-Grove Rosenwald School that was constructed by Carey Pittman during the period of segregation, was relocated to the Halifax County 4-H Rural Life Center, where it is a county tourist attraction. The school had been used for Black students during the period, 1922-1959.

This true story of the Ing-Jones-Boone-Pittman families is another example of how people of color have survived and accomplished in the past 143 years and how the descendants in North Carolina in 1998 know from whence they came.

"A Human Interest Story"

He Made It Out Of The Inner City

I was reading an article in the *Kansas City Call* newspaper recently, and I observed the picture of a native Kansas Citian who had just retired in a midwestern city: After reading the article, I strongly believed it was a young man whom I knew when he was 17 years of age. Fortunately, I was able to obtain his phone number and I called him and my suspicion was true. After I identified myself as the son of the late Executive Director of the George Washington Carver Neighborhood Center and recalled that he had lived directly across the street from the Center, he was very receptive to succeeding conversations. I reminded him that I could recall when he would come to the Center to practice on our piano; he would sing and sometimes he would find a sanctuary to study his high school homework assignments.

This young man lived in a house with eleven children, including himself, and his two parents. The home was not large enough for 13 people, however they did the best they could. His environment at home was not conducive to studying. Even some of his siblings would tease and agitate him about being so studious and self confident that he could achieve greatness beyond his present status. I told him during our recent phone conversation that every minority youngster today who thinks he or she has a problem of surviving and a desire to eventually leave and improve living conditions should have lived some 40 years earlier. Then they would have some real problems to rap, sing, and dance about.

My late father, stepmother, and I always believed that this aggressive, determined and above average young man would succeed and accomplish notable things. I told him that our prophecy has been fulfilled and that what I was able to read from the article attests to his accomplishments. This native of Kansas City who now lives elsewhere was able to work his way through college, overcome many obstacles, leave an uncomfortable environment and prove to himself first, then others that he could overcome.

He served for 32 years as a public speech/language pathologist. After completing high school in Kansas City, Missouri, he graduated from Northeast Missouri State University, B.S., M.S. degree from Western Michigan University and completed post graduate work at Eastern Washington University, Central Missouri State University, Western Illinois University, Marycrest College, Kirkwood Community College and the University Of Iowa. The Academy of American Educators in America in 1973-1978 selected him as an outstanding American educator. This gentleman has used his talent as a singer, and his attainments are praise-worthy. He has presented recitals in Iowa, Kansas City and Illinois. He also has studied under some prestigious voice instructors and attended several symposiums at the Julliard School of Music, N.Y.

He has presented speech and language work shops in Hawaii, Alaska and Tennessee.

This story is about a man who achieved against the odds and it was during the segregation era when he did not have the financial assistance and other equal opportunity grants and scholarships that may be available to minority students today. I am sure that many young people today do not realize that they are living in a better time and a more integrated society, that they can participate in the financial, personal, and economic rewards if they are qualified, just as this young man was able to do. He was able to break the chains of exclusions that were present in the so-called separate but equal society.

"From India To Harlem"

On August 22, 1998, while autographing some books at Bolling Air Force Base, Washington, DC, I met a very articulate college student. He was interested in purchasing my book, *Physicians and Surgeons of Color*. He told me that he was from Harlem, New York: I asked him was one of his parents of Indian descent after observing his distinct Indian features including his straight black hair. His skin was of a dark ebony hue. He shared with me that his biological parents were Indians and that he was adopted by a black American diplomat at a very young age and had been raised in a middle-upper Class family. His ambition is to study medicine.

This young man also told me that some darker skin Indians (referred to as "Untouchables", Dalits or Dravidians) would approach him and start to speak in their dialect. He said some, desired not to associate with Black Americans or be mistaken for a person of Negroid descent in America.

CHAPTER 4

MILITARY

Recollections Of The Houston Riot of 1917

I was able to interview a retired white colonel, John McDonald, a native of Louisville, Kentucky, who was living in Northern Virginia in April, 1978. He shared with me some of his early experiences in civilian and military life. McDonald was a graduate of the University of Kentucky and during World War I was a member of the Student Army Training Corp (SATC). He entered on active duty in June, 1916 and was assigned near the Texas border. McDonald said that his company, an active National Guard unit was called back to Kentucky because the governor of the state needed protection for a prisoner. He told me that "a Negro named Braddock was scheduled to be lynched without a fair trial".

The newspapers throughout the country carried the news about the 24th Infantry Battalion who were involved in a riot in Houston, Texas and some of the men were court martialed. However in the 1970's, their sentences were remitted. Colonel McDonald at the time of the riot was assigned to Camp Columbus, New Mexico, 12th U.S. Corps. He said that he was not an eye witness but was responsible for arranging the transportation for the all Black 24th Infantry battalion to travel back and forth from Houston, Texas to Columbus, New Mexico. McDonald said that he received some information from third and fourth parties about the riot. Colonel McDonald told me the following story: "I was responsible for supervising the loading of the train to send the 24th Infantry Battalion to go to Houston, Texas. According to the newspapers, this Black battalion were recognized as the national heroes with Pershing expedition in Mexico against Pancho Villa and his insurgents. The 24th Infantry Battalion had been stationed for several months at Colonia Dublan and were treated very well by the Mexicans. When the Pershing expedition was withdrawn from Mexico, they went to Columbus, New Mexico. However, they were insulted by the inhabitants of the city, signs were on saloons 'dogs and Nigras not allowed here". The people would do things that could cause men to revolt. One night, the first Sergeant of Company A, 24th Infantry (Inf.) Battalion (Bn.) decided that he would not stand for the insults anymore and would go back to Mexico. The sergeant and a group of men went down to the city of Houston on their way to Mexico, and everywhere they saw a light they opened fire and in some cases killed or wounded people sitting in lighted rooms. The sheriff of Houston ordered the men to disperse and go back to their camp. They killed the sheriff and proceeded to shoot, eventually killing some 12 people. The First Sergeant said, "Come on let's go to Mexico. However, some of the men began to wonder what to do? The soldiers said they were not going to Mexico. Then the First Sergeant sat down on the railroad track and argued with the men. Finally, he said 'I will be hung for what I have done.".

He then placed his rifle in his mouth and shot his head off. The rest of the men decided to return to the Houston, Texas, Training Camp. There the 65th Infantry Bn placed the men under arrest".

Colonel McDonald said that the men were loaded on a train and shipped back to Columbus, New Mexico, and were housed in a large warehouse that his men had prepared. McDonald said that there were 139 men who were implicated in the riot. When the men were ordered back to Houston for their court martial, McDonald was responsible for furnishing the train. There were 12 men sentenced to death, and the rest were sent back to Columbus.

McDonald related to me a story about a white Lieutenant James who had commanded the 24th Inf. Bn's Companies. Lt. James was quite perturbed about the incident. He considered himself disgraced. Colonel McDonald told me that James lived in the same officers quarters where he did. He said that the night after the riot, Lt. James committed suicide rather than face the disgrace of his company's actions. McDonald said James was concerned about taking his men back to Columbus. adding that all members of the court martial board were white. Colonel John McDonald was assigned during his military career as a historian in the historical section of the Army War College, Fort McNair, Washington, D.C., I thanked Colonel McDonald 20 years ago for his earnest contribution to the oral collection of the Black experience in America.

Where Is The Color Line? 1944

An African American War Correspondent in World War II, Max Johnson, had some interesting observations while covering the troops in Italy, July, 1944. He wrote that a large group of high salaried soldiers arrived to join the Allied Forces. They were speaking the Portuguese language and many of the officers spoke English. Johnson stated that he saw many men who ranged from "fair-skinned men with kinky hair to whites. He said he did not observe a color line as was present with the American segregated military in World War II.

A Distinguished War Correspondent

As a youngster, I heard my father often speak about an Afro American newspaper reporter and writer who later became a noted Black war correspondent in Europe during World War II. He was the late Ollie Stewart. When President Franklin Delano Roosevelt was present at the famous Casablanca Conference in Morocco, January 1943. Ollie Stewart was present along with Walter Logan, United Press Correspondent, and Sam Schulman, INS photographer and other newsmen to interview the President. Prime Minister Winston Churchill of Great Britain and General deGaulle of France were also present at the conference. Stewart wrote that he observed the President's personal valet always at his side, a Black Navy man from Baltimore, Maryland, Arthur Prettyman. Stewart said that there was a company of Black soldiers who lined the roadway as the President arrived for the meeting. Ironically in 1965 while visiting Paris, France, I had the unique opportunity of meeting Ollie Stewart who had been living in France. He recalled knowing my father and he found the time to show me some historic places in Paris. For me it was a most memorable visit, especially with the distinguished Ollie Stewart.

Rarity of Black Officers

Ollie Stewart observed in North Africa few line or combat officers of color. He said there were some who had served in the regiments and occupied the same quarters with white officers with "no noticeable friction". However, there were separate recreational facilities such as movies and service clubs. He also saw the first Red Cross Club in North Africa to be staffed by Blacks in Casablanca. They were Sidney Williams, Donald Wyatt, Mae Moore and Geraldine Dyson.

Military Quotas, 1945

The Secretary of War appointed a board of officers headed by Lt. General A.G. Gillen Jr. to prepare a broad policy for the future utilization of Negro manpower in the military establishments in October 1945. After several months of study, the Gillem Board issued a report in April 1946 for postwar policies and it provided that "one tenth of the Army strength shall be Negro (In plain English this was a quota) and Negro units will be smaller, groupings of Negro and white units in composite organizations will be accepted policy. Qualified Negro officers will replace white officers in Negro units" Unfortunately, these policies did not reach actual fruition until the end of the Korean was 1954 and it required continuous revisions of policies to the mid 1975's to effect Korean War equitable climate in the military services.

Military Quotas, 1948

I am sure that there are many laypersons, politicians and authors who discuss, write and campaign in 1998 against civil rights, equal opportunity and affirmative action legislation and programs, who mention the word "quotas". It would be interesting to know how many of those persons are under the age of 50 years and if they are aware that during segregation the "quota" concept was considered constitutionally sound? As the man from Mars, I ask today, "Why is it constitutionally right to ban quotas. The following true story will show that quotas were the law of the land in 1948 but the term "percentage" was used to describe them

In 1948, the Department of the Army strengths for both Black and white personnel were; "a total of 63,000 Black troops and 987 officers. The white strength consisted of 564,000 troops and 72,000 officers". The breakdown of officer ranks among Blacks was "General-1, Colonel-2, Lt. Colonel-10, Major-28, Captain-241, 1st Lt.-538, and 2nd Lt.-114, total commissioned officers 934 and 43 warrant officers. The total number of Negro women was 77.

Do Not Exclude Blacks and Jews, 1950

Representative Joe D. Waggoner Jr., Democrat, Louisiana, requested information from the Air Force concerning their assignment policies. It had been alleged that "There was a policy to not assign Jewish and Black personnel to certain countries. The Air Force informed the Congressman that they would investigate the allegations.

The Progress Is Too Slow

The Black community had their efficient and courageous Black leaders during segregation who were less vocal but more persistent in their actions. There was an Urban League leader, Lester Granger who was appointed in the 1950's as a special consultant to the U.S. Navy on racial problems. Granger wrote the Secretary of the Navy, Thomas, and told him that he believed the Navy had initiated some steps in removing racial segregation, but he believed also that they were moving too slow. Therefore, he submitted his resignation. He stated in his letter to the Navy Secretary that "Three-fourths of all Negroes in the Navy were in the Steward Branch which is 100 percent Negro except for a few Filipinos." Again as we see the outstanding progress of the U.S. Navy on race relations today, we still must not forget that no one woke up one morning and said, "Well, let's integrate the Navy." Just more "nutritional reasoning".

1955 Legal Quotas

Today many "so-called" school-trained experts on race relations like to brief with statistical books and research papers. I suggest that they revisit 43 years ago and examine hard cold facts to learn what progress might have been achieved for African Americans in recent years, progress requiring constant verbal protests from Black leaders before any definitive actions were considered. A great leader who would remind the Congress and the nation about the Black disparity in the military services was Congressman Adam C. Powell. Powell stated in 1955: "Negroes comprise one tenth of one percent of the officers in both the Navy and Marine Corps and this is definitely not integration". "The Negro civilians are being discriminated against by the Pentagon". Congressman Powell also said that in U.S. Army, Europe, with over 1,250 civilians assigned, <u>only 12 were Negroes</u> (my emphasis). He said the Special Services of Europe are under the command of LTC Bernice Hughes and she had only <u>one</u> Black employee. Again, I repeat, how do people think that there can be a level playing field in 1998, when it has taken at least 50 years for some affirmative actions to be visible on the field.

The Military Responds To The Order: Integrate Schools, 1954

May 17, 1954, the Supreme Court of the United States issued the monumental ruling Brown vs. Board of Education. July, 1998, America is returning to the reverse intentions of that famous ruling with a current presence of defacto segregated schools in major American urban areas. The United States Military were the heroic pace setters to conform with the ruling in a most expeditious manner and not "deliberate", because 44 years ago complete racial integration occurred at Fort Belvoir, Virginia, in September, 1954, when the Post opened its own elementary educational system. It is interesting to note that the school system that has been lauded by the politicians and the Race Relations Commission as the example of "one America" had no intentions what-so-ever to comply with the 1954 Supreme Court decision in an expeditious manner. I say to those who are 45 years of age and younger; "Yes, it was a Black and white confrontation, a different scenario from today.

Prior to the 1954 School Decision, Fort Belvoir, Virginia's 18,000 military and civilian population had to depend on the Fairfax County School System to educate the Post children. Fairfax County had leased two school buildings on the Post; one was constructed in 1934 and the other in 1953. The County provided the teachers, books and maintenance of the schools to accommodate 715 white students (not Hispanics, Asians, Vietnamese, Iranians, Latin Americans and others). If they were included, we must assume they were classified as white. This is a fact of which some people today have no memory.

Now where did the Blacks on Post go to school? Well, the 56 Black students at Belvoir in 1954 had to travel by bus (that is an interesting word in 1998) to Fairfax County's segregated all Black Drew Smith School in Gum Springs, Virginia. With integration at Fort Belvoir in 1954, the 56 students were able to attend the integrated military operated schools (elementary) on post. There were 120 white high school students who were able to attend an offpost high school, Mount Vernon High School. There goes the bus again the thirty Black students had to attend the Manassa Regional High School which served the Black students from Alexandria, Fairfax and Prince William Counties.

The progressive and upper-middle class Fairfax County of 1998, said what they meant in 1954, when the Fairfax County Board on February 2, 1954 decided to end its association with Fort Belvoir in June. The Board clearly stated that "it had no alternative since the Virginia State Constitution forbids mixing white and colored children in the same school". (Remember it did not say Hispanics, Asians or other immigrants, and ironically Africans). "Nutritional reasoning". They did not call it affirmative action in 1954, but it really was because the U.S. military services were establishing an example for the country to follow.

The public school at Fort Myer was also opened on a non-segregated basis in September, 1954. When the new school on Ft. Myer was opened in May 1953, Arlington County wanted to operate it for white children only. Once Ft. Myer integrated its elementary school, there were only seven Black students in an enrollment of 322 students in the first six grades of school. Recognition should be given to the Archdiocese of Northern Virginia because the parochial schools, St. Thomas More, St. Charles, and St. Michaels admitted Black students for the first time. Just another true story of segregation, an American legacy.

A Plea To Integrate The National Guard 1955

I believe that it is essential for young people to know the truth, and the truth is that during segregation, it was necessary for Black leaders and their supporters to literally plead for integration. In 1955, there was a House Armed Forces Subcommittee Hearings on the Military Reserves. A non-segregation amendment to a major bill was proposed by a representative from New York, Adam Clayton Powell. The amendment would ban the training of reservists in National Guard units which are racially segregated. The late Clarence Mitchell, Director of the Washington Bureau of the NAACP, testified before the subcommittee that "President Eisenhower was willing to settle for racial segregation in the National Guard units in the South by indicating that he would accept a revised Military Reserves Bill". Mitchell emphasized that the President would accept the revised bill rather than have the entire reserve program defeated in Congress. The NAACP's difference with the bill was that the President was willing to settle for using all white manpower in the National Guard Units of cities like Charleston, South Carolina; Birmingham, Alabama; and Atlanta, Georgia. In 1998, I remind some young people of all colors of the need to know that the progress made in American race relations or civil rights came from persistent lobbying, protests and use of the courts to obtain some greatly needed relief.

TRUE STORIES OF SEGREGATION

A Military Affirmative Action, 1956

The Department of the Army abolished segregated off-duty courses conducted on Southern Military Installations under contract between the Army and private and public educational institutions. An Army directive specifically said that all civilians schools on Army posts must be open to all military personnel meeting entrance requirements. Senator Herbert H. Lehman's interest in the new policies played an important role in integrating of classes. He had learned that "colored airmen at Donaldson Air Force Base were denied courses offered by the University of South Carolina. There were also some restrictions for Black soldiers at Fort Jackson, Columbia, S.C. On May 31, 1956, civilian high school classes on the Fort Gordon Post, conducted by the Richmond County Public School System on a segregated basis, were terminated.

Escort Officer's Change In Orders, 1959

I had made plans to attend my Alma Mater's homecoming game in Jefferson City, Missouri, on October 24, 1959. My plans were placed on hold when I was instructed to report to a Lt. Colonel Lippincott at Fort Leavenworth, Kansas Headquarters. He informed me that I was detailed as escort for one of the six general officers scheduled to attend a two week course in nuclear weapons employment at the post's Command and General Staff College. I immediately told the Colonel that I would like to be excused from that detail because I had made my plans several weeks ago to go to the game. He told me that since there were few junior grade officers assigned to the post, that it was a problem because he needed six escort officers for the generals. He wanted the escort officer to personally greet and welcome the general at the airport, then upon arrival at Fort Leavenworth, escort them to their billets, and offer to assist them further if needed. The colonel was very understanding and I also realized his problem in finding six lieutenants to serve as escorts. We reached a compromise when he permitted me to attend the homecoming game and return immediately after the game to meet my general officer at the Kansas City, Missouri Airport, Delta Airlines gate with a sedan and driver at 11:00 p.m., October 14, 1959. I thanked the nice colonel and proceeded to Jefferson City, Missouri.

Just prior to half time, I was paged over the loudspeaker to report to the nearest phone because I had an emergency call from the Officer of the Day, Fort Leavenworth, Kansas. The Officer of the Day instructed me to return immediately to my residence in Kansas City and that a colonel would meet me to give my escort folder and other instructions relating to meeting my general officer. He only said that there seemed to be a problem in protocol. That statement concerned me as I was driving back to Kansas City, because Col. Lippincott and Major Ruth F. Taylor,

Acting Assistant Post Adjutant General, knew beyond any doubt the name of my designated general officer, and if there was any protocol problem that they had, it could have been easily resolved by permitting me to go to Jefferson City without any commitment to the escort detail.

The year was 1991, when I was attending an official reception for some Desert Shield, Desert Storm Veterans who were being treated at Walter Reed Medical Center, but they were the honored guests along with President Bush at this function. As I was moving through the crowd, I observed the general that I was detailed to escort 32 years ago. Since he was alone, I decided to go over and introduce myself, and he was most cordial. I then told him that in 1959, I was to be his escort officer and suddenly I was removed from the detail. He then in a most gracious manner replied "I would have been glad to have had you to serve as my escort officer. He then reached in his pocket and gave me one of his key chains that I presume he gives to people. As a historian, I was very pleased to meet this distinguished gentleman, because I have always said, sometimes your idealogy might change and even your political beliefs, especially when it involves America's continuing problem of Civil Rights. I end this true story by revealing the name of the General I was to meet. I met later the celebrated and distinguished member of the U.S. Senate and South Carolina's own, Senator Strom Thurmond, the general and the Senator. Just another true story from the days of segregation.

Have They Integrated the Blood Banks, 1965

While serving as the Company Commander, 12th Chemical Maintenance Company 1st Bn. 100th Chemical Group, Fort McClellan, Alabama, in July 1965, I was responsible for encouraging my men to participate in the postwide blood mobile campaign. Because I was aware of the fact that the Red Cross Centers, especially in southern states separated Black blood from white blood, I had a decision to make. Would I participate myself and suggest that others participate in a segregated program? I contacted the Post Red Cross Field Director, Mr. Andrew Tomasi and I was told that the policy was no longer in effect. Since my major goal as a company commander was to have the best company in the chemical group, it was necessary for me to obtain at least eighty to ninety percent participation in the volunteer blood program. The blood donation competition included all units in the group and other units assigned to Fort McClellan including the Women's Army Training Center and School. I had a serious talk with every man assigned to my company and expressed to them, while in company formation, the importance of volunteering to give blood to help some sick person in need. I was always proud of my men because they would always follow me when we had to achieve our mission and goals. I marched my company to the Red Cross Collection Center, and I was the first to give blood. They followed in turn. The 12th Company's participation in the blood program assured our eventual selection as the best Chemical Company in the 100th Chemical Group since the Post Commander presented me the Red Cross Blood Mobile Trophy for 86% unit participation in the blood drive.

The Black Confederate Combatant

A beautiful Sunday afternoon, my family and I drove to Winchester, Virginia. The nice trip was interrupted when I decided to stop and visit the General Stonewall Jackson House which had displayed near the front door, a Confederate flag. I was greeted by a gentleman who asked if he could help me. I told him that I have been doing some research on the Black Confederate body servant. During our conversation, I learned that I was talking to the President of the Winchester Historical Society, a businessman and a member of the Rotary Club. Prior to my departure, he had an invitation for me to speak at a Rotary Club meeting. I accepted the invitation and in November 1971, I was greeted by the Winchester Rotary Club President, Dr. John P. Arthur. I talked about the Black Confederate Body Servant as a Combatant During the Civil War. I was well received by the group and even had my picture in the *Winchester Evening Star*. My host was Rotarian Harry Lovett. I believe that I was the first person of color to ever speak to those wonderful club members.

The Soldiers' General, 1973

The Late Brigadier General Roscoe Cartwright

The Race Relations School was located briefly in Chiemse, Germany, a resort area that was used by United States Army Europe for the Welfare and Recreation facility for the military and their families. The school occupied a portion of the resort area. The facility was used during World War II as a rest facility for the SS officers. I occupied a large spacious office that was once used by a high ranking German officer. I had invited two generals of color to visit the school, and they gave a speech to the graduating class. Brigadier General George Shuffer represented the USAEUR's Office of the Assistant Chief of Staff of Personnel, and Brigadier General Roscoe Cartwright was the Comptroller of United States Army Europe at Heidelberg. Their presence attracted the attention of a news reporter from the nearby town of Bernau and his photographer photographed the two generals together. The caption of the picture read, "Zwei Farbige Generale", two colored generals.

I had an interesting chat with General Cartwright in my office, and it seems that at that first meeting he was to become my mentor and advisor. Several months later when I was visiting my family at Heidelberg, he invited me and my wife to his house for dinner. He had just been promoted to Brigadier General and he had been assigned a house orderly. While we were enjoying a delicious dinner, his orderly was showing the General, and his wife, and their guests how he would be serving a formal dinner at the house. We all enjoyed the rehearsal dinner. I called it a privilege and honor. General Cartwright appreciated my writings in 1973, and we even had discussed the possibilities some day of writing a book on the Black officer, his trials and tribulations in an integrated army. Unfortunately, the untimely demise of the General and Mrs. Cartwright in a fatal airplane crash made that book impossible.

General Cartwright was asked by the Stuttgart Chapter of The NAACP to be their keynote speaker at their Inaugural Banquet on February 11, 1973, in Stuttgart, Germany. At that time, General Cartwright was serving as Assistant Division Commander, 3rd Infantry Division, Germany. The General asked me to assist him in the writing of his address. I was invited to attend the banquet, a memory I will always cherish of my mentor whom I call "the soldier's general". He delivered an outstanding address and did not delete what I sometimes call my mentally militant writings. The General's boss, the Commanding General of the Seventh U.S. Corps was in the audience as well as with the, young women and men soldiers of all ranks and races, officers, civilians and the German guests. I had included in the speech some very direct race related paragraphs that I am recalling after 25 years. The General told the vast audience that "we must understand the early Black ideologies that were expressed by the Black leadership tripartite as we examined some of the divergent views of Booker T. Washington, Marcus Garvey and W.E.B. Dubois. Also we must remember that when the boats of immigrants of all colors arrived in America, that Blacks were housed in the third class section and even today we are still attempting to reach the first class berths. The remarks were similar to what I had written, but the General's style of delivery impressed the young soldiers most of whom had similar beliefs.

I tell many young Blacks today, that the military had a race problem in Germany in the 1970's. But to the best of my knowledge, you would not learn about it from any type of a "night line" program. Yet, the Frankfurt and Stuttgart, Germany, NAACP Chapter was a welcome presence. That was the way we were in Germany 1972-1975.

United States Army Europe - Race Relations School (USAUER)

In May 1972, I officially requested an assignment in the equal opportunity field, if necessary in the Washington, D.C. area. However, the Chief of the Equal Opportunity Division of the Department of the Army at that time, Colonel Harry W. Brooks Jr., later promoted to Major General, coordinated with U.S. Army Europe. ODCSPER, and I was accepted as Equal Opportunity Staff Officer in the Equal

ODCSPER, and I was accepted as Equal Opportunity Staff Officer in the Equal Opportunity Division. I was quite elated over being selected in May, 1972 for this challenge for several reasons. My past 17 years in the military at that time had glorious and inglorious experiences in the areas of human relations, race relations and equal opportunity. Unfortunately, I had experienced the acquaintances of senior officers, junior and senior NCO's and enlisted men who could not see and did not attempt to recognize the injustices and unequal opportunities that prevailed within the United States Army at all echelons. Therefore, I was quite indebted to Brigadier General Brooks, Major General Harold I. Hayward, Colonel Edward F. Krise, LTC Patrick Chisolm, LTC James Revels, LTC Don Phillips, Major Herman Fitzgerald, SSG Larry J. Hamilton and SP4 David Wright who received me in a most friendly and sincere manner and welcomed me as a part of a realistic team that was striving to correct the many race relations problems of the U.S. Army.

I received a most unusual but challenging task on 19 July, 1972, to establish the first USAREUR Race Relations School. At the time I never realized or could not predict that I would receive one of the most extensive exposures to divergent personalities and observe significant behavioral changes in the 426 students that completed the school during my tenure.

United States Army Europe Race Relations School (URRS)

The major purpose of the school was to train qualified military how to teach, and resolve racial ethnic problems by non-violent procedures and to increase the numbers of Race Relations Officers/Non Commissioned Officers (RRO/NCO's) in the USAREUR command. The mission was to conduct training for USAREUR military personnel to become instructors in race relations, develop doctrine and curricula in education for race relations, conduct research, perform evaluation of program effectiveness and disseminate race relation educational guidelines and materials for utilization throughout the USAREUR command.

The original organization of the school consisted of the chain of command: Major General Hayward, Deputy Chief of Staff, Personnel, his deputy, Brigadier General Shuffer; Colonel Krise, Chief, Equal Opportunity, and the Director, Major Greene. The instructional staff included: Behavioral Science instructors: Lt. Lentz, Capt Shaefer, SP-5 Petroff, Minority studies instructor, Lt. McCord, SSG Whitehead, SP-4 Gomez, Administrative staff, SP-5 Roach, PFC Bergan, PFC Leon-Guerrero and PFC Russell. The educational consultants were Dr. June Holmes and Mr. John Thornbons. The student selection criteria were: Grades E4 to E7, W1-4, and O1 to O5. Students had to volunteer for the program and have at least one year of service in USAEUR remaining after completion of school. They were required to possess an outstanding record and leadership attributes, and have demonstrated the ability to complete college level courses successfully. The student had to possess instructor potential and an awareness of current social issues and interest in the USAEUR Race Relations Program. The school's curriculum innovations were: maximize participation during lecture or seminar by use of specific training aide, use of film resources, emphasis on scholarship and two graded book reports and methods of teaching.

Students were required to complete a total of 120 hours of instruction. The minority studies curriculum included the subjects of African Heritage, Institution of Slavery, Abolitionist Movement, Pre-Civil War, Civil War and Reconstruction, Separate but Equal, New Militancy of the 20th Century and the Black Revolt (1954-1972). Mexican Americans Studies included, History and Culture of Mexican people, Contemporary Mexican American Situation, and Contemporary Mexican American Organizations. The Puerto Ricans Studies were history, people and society, and culture and life on the mainland. The Appalachian Studies were of the southern mountain folk culture. The American Indian Studies Were History and Cultural Overview and Contemporaries Situation. The Oriental American studies were Chinese Americans and Japanese Americans. We also included in the curriculum: History of the Black Soldier.

Some of the other subjects taught were Behavioral Science, Racial Problems of the Military in Germany, Educational Techniques, Practice Teaching, Role Playing Lesson Plan Development, Stereotypes, Group Discussion. White Contemporary Thought, Communication Skills, Instructional Aids, German Customs, and Book Report Preparation. The school prepared a list of reading material for our German guests, "Understanding America's Minorities, a recommended reading list. It was prepared in the German language.

When the Race Relations School opened in September 1972, at Oberammergau, Germany, the German news media was present in full force. But unfortunately, our honored guest speaker, Jesse Owens, 1936 Olympic star, became ill and had to cancel his appearance. He was in Germany for the 1972 Olympics and was also being honored by the German government. later, the German news media and television showed a great interest in the Army's Race Relations School on German soil.

We were fortunate to have some distinguished visitors who expressed their sincere appraisal and impressions of our school. The Honorable Roger T. Kelley, Assistant Secretary of Defense Manpower and Reserve Affairs sent me a personal letter, it was dated November 16, 1972. The letter read, "I want to thank you and your staff in a special way for the satisfaction of my recent visit to your Race Relations School. Your charter is a vital one and will shape the behavior and attitudes within the Army for generations to come. I am pleased that you have organized so well for the task and this is remarkable in the limited time you have had to do it. My regard to your program is such that I have recommended its scope expanded including some Navy as well as Army students." The Secretary's letter gave me and my staff more encouragement to accomplish our mission. We appreciated the fact that we had been observed and praised by the Pentagon in the guise of Secretary Kelley. We did receive some Navy personnel for our next class. We also had a visit from the Honorable Carl S. Wallace, Assistant Secretary of the Army for Manpower and Reserve Affairs. He was very impressed with the thoroughness of the briefing and tour of the school in September, 1973. There was a definitive effort to invite U.S. Army Europe Commanders and General Officers to be our guest speakers for our graduating ceremonies. Some of our distinguished keynote speakers were Brigadier General Gannon, Major General Cobb, Lieutenant General Arthur Gregg, Major General McLaughlin, Major General Frederic Davison, Brigadier General Shuffer, Brigadier General Cartwright, and Major General Haywood. On December 12, 1972, the Race Relations School was honored with the visit of Vice Admiral Gerald E. Miller, Commander of the Sixth U.S. Naval Fleet. He was given a briefing and a tour of the school. We also had lunch with him.

I often remarked in later years that my numerous interviews by German newspapers and television probably would never have happened in America. Some of the German newspapers that carried stories about the new school were the *Augsburger Zeitung, Stuttgarter Zeitung, Abend Zeitung, Munich, Augsburger Allegemein, TZ newspaper, Munich, Garmisch-Parten Kirchner, Tagblatt and the Speigel and Weltbild Magazine.* Some of the German television stations that interviewed me were Zweites Deutches Fernsehen, Bayern, (Second German Television), and WURR, a large broadcast corporation with some 17 million listeners with eight stations. (I was interviewed by a Frederick Quest).

As Director of the school, I was utilized by my headquarters as a guest speaker for Martin Luther King's Birthday, Black History Month, Race Relations Conferences, Black Expos and an English class at the University of Augsburg. The School's first location was Oberammergau, then Chiemse and Munich. Later the School was moved to Bremerhaven.

I would receive letters from German citizens who were curious and interested in learning about the Race Relations School and also sharing their comments. I received an interesting letter from a German lady who had observed a television interview which began with the title "Colored members of the Army are disadvantaged everywhere". I would use the following excerpts from her letter in classes sometime to show how she offered her personal observations and impressions of the American Black. "Prejudice -- from my childhood days (about 40 years ago), I remember that my grandmother was pointing to Black people and explaining, these were often only beggars who had painted their faces, and one has to look at the fingernails and inside of the hands in order to see if the person is a real Negro. Besides, the real Negroes get really mad when one looks at them so closely. And thus it was impressed upon me - and probably not only on me, - "don't look at a Negro, or he will become mad". She also said, "Based upon happenings in the First and Second World Wars, one still considers a colored man unpredictable when he drinks alcoholic beverages (exactly as one thinks about a Russian or Italian), and thus is afraid to let him enter a bar or to give him an apartment. Of course this is a one-sided fear because many white people and many Germans are worse with alcohol, but one knows how to handle them and from a colored man one does not know it, he is unknown to us. But the main reason is probably that one does not have any opportunity to get to know Negro or Chinese etc.. And now I can talk about the Gentleman who complains that he is being stared at in a gasthaus with his wife and child."

"This, certainly, is no staring in a bad, meaning. One just would like to see how people of other origins are eating, drinking, talking, and treating their family. One does not know it. I myself would, for instance, like to look really at a Negro's face, without having to fear that he will become irritated. These faces are so strange for us, no one has learned to read in them and so one can only judge as one hears It. It is beautiful to see a little Black baby, who is so different with his smile and big eyes. But also for this there is no opportunity".

The German lady wrote the letter 26 years ago. I wonder how do some new immigrants in America today perceive Blacks if they never had an opportunity to engage in a normal conversation with Blacks.

I received a letter from a gentleman in Lucerne, Switzerland, and he had read about the School from an article in the German magazine *Spiegel*. He said that he was studying the discrimination of workers of a foreign origin. There was a German who sent me a letter after reading an article in the *Weltbild* Magazine. He was interested in our race relations curriculum. He said that someone was presenting a sequence of classes on racism at a German trade school. He believed race relations should be addressed in German schools.

The various German newspapers would include some descriptions of the race relations program as they viewed it, just as the American public in recent years have coined or developed new terms related to race problems, such as "race card", and "politically correct". I developed a positive approach that I would use at the School and during media interviews. I was somewhat amazed when I saw my creative phrase in German newspapers as the byline for their articles on the Race Relation School. I used the saying "The color makes no difference", translated in German "Die Farbe ist egal".

TRAINING FOR A BETTER WORLD
THE COLOR MAKES NO DIFFERENCE

"School for Race Relations" of the U.S. Army.

Report by Uta Koning from TZ newspaper of Munich, 1972

"What America, home of Human Rights, Declarations of Independence and Pledges for Liberty and Freedom, has not been capable of overcoming for the last centuries, it is trying now to solve in a three-weeks-course: to reduce racial tensions between Blacks and Whites in American uniforms.

"How serious the ministry considers or how concerned it is about the race problems, also among the troops in European Garrisons, is now to be demonstrated to the citizens of the Federal Republic: For one week now, in the U.S. Barracks of Oberammergau, 32 soldiers, from private to major, Black and white people have been drilled up for a "better world", the first school for race relations in Europe". Major Greene is especially concerned with assisting in problems of every-day-life. He stated, "You see, we want to point out to the Black soldiers, German habits, too, so that no misunderstanding will arise." A Black man is to be convinced that not because of his color that he was not allowed to enter the nightclub, but because of his sloppy way of being dressed." "Here in the Federal Republic, colored people need not have any inferiority complexes, and this we want them to understand by making them familiar with the habits in our host-country", emphasizes Major Greene".

THE UNDERSTANDING OF PEOPLE AMONG NATIONS
"Abend Zeitung", Munchen, 14 September 1972

The color makes no difference!" This motto is displayed prominently at the desk of the U.S. Major R.E. Greene, located on the U.S. Base in O'gau. It demonstrates the spirit of a scholastic attempt, unique in Europe, which was initiated by the colored officer Greene this week in the Passion Play town.

Sponsor of the School is the U.S. Army. The School's goal: Elimination of racial discrimination within and outside the American (military) bases. The teaching program ranges from the history of American minority groups (Negroes, Indians., Puerto Ricans, Mexicans, Chinese) and the "Black Power" movement to the racial problems in the host nation. This last teaching point discusses towards favorable relations between colored U.S. soldiers on one side and German guest-house and hotel owners and landlords on the other. For many Americans no longer consider the FRG the "paradise with its "untroubled highlights" of German beer and "Frauleins". In the past years, members of the military (community) and their families more and more got the feeling that they are not wanted in many guest houses, bars, and by landlords. A commission of the civil rights movement NAACP which in the spring of 1971 conducted an information tour of the 300 U.S. military installations in the FRG, sized up their findings in this sentence: "Blacks and minorities find that the amount of discrimination, to which they are subjected to here, is often greater than in the U.S. nowadays." This German-American racial problem, which, in the opinion of MAJ Greene and his instructors mainly stems from misunderstandings, is to be resolved in this new School by providing information about German habits and the German mentality. Until now, the U.S. soldiers who come to the FRG, within NATO agreements, had been insufficiently prepared for the habits, and local customs and traditions of their host nation. Language difficulties contribute to further tensions.

Maj Greene: "If for example, a Bavarian guest house owner makes a colored soldier move from the "Stamtisch*" in his place to another table, it is not meant as racism. The same applies if a German girl refuses to dance with a Black GI because she is either tired or generally does not dance with soldiers. But this has to be first explained to the upset colored who feels degraded in this moment because of his color of skin. The lesson plan, which is presently still "in the mill", ranges from the Pueblo Revolt in 1680 to the student riots in Berkeley, from the "Uncle Tom" philosophy to the Eldridge-Cleaver ideology.

Even between White and Black, a subject which even today is still "tabu" in the U.S., are being brought up in O'gau. The 3-week course in the "mutual understanding" consists of 120 lecture hours which interested troops from Private to Major may volunteer to attend. The instructors, themselves members of various minority groups, were trained for their task in a similar school in Florida. Their students in Germany are to become "pioneers" for better relations between the races among the U.S. troops stationed in Europe.

*This is a table reserved for "regular customers" only.

Augsburger Allgemeine Newspaper
April 3, 1973

NEW TASK NOT ONLY FOR OFFICERS

INSTRUCTION COURSES FOR BLACKS AND WHITES

US Army opens School for Race Relations in Munich - denial to violence

"Munich - Not multiplications, but fellow-human questions will be taught in the "School for Race Relations" (URRS) which was opened in a ceremony on Monday in the theater on McGraw Kaserne in Munich. This organization was already established by the US Army in Oberammergau in September 1972, but has now obtained its new station in Perlacher Forst in Munich a place appropriate to the importance of their endeavors for a racial settlement. 169 students were already trained in courses in Oberammergau, who are presently working with the US Army in the Federal Republic of Germany as instructors for race relations.

What this is essentially all about was explained on Monday by Major Robert E. Greene, director of this school and colored himself, by example of a personal experience. When he went shopping last weekend in Munich and later on noticed that the sales clerk forgot to charge him for one item, he naturally went back and pointed this mistake out to her. Her reaction, according to Greene, was typical. Instead of being happy, the employee was speechless from astonishment. "Black and honest, that seemed to be too much for her", commented the US officer about this incident with a bitter smile.

Discrimination also in Europe

When the "School for Race Relations" opened on 11 September 1972 in Oberammergau, the American Army in the Federal Republic assumed the task of training qualified military personnel, who would be capable of detecting racial minority problems and who could solve them without violence. The number of officers and noncommissioned officers was also to be increased in order to improve and to loosen the tense relations between the races within the command of the European Theater. That racial discrimination does not only exist in the southern states of America, but also in Europe, was made clear by Major Greene by many examples. The exploration of the reasons for this deplorable state of affairs and the examination of the planned program is the task of the "Race Relations School" in Munich's McGraw Kaserne, where about 5000 American soldiers live with their families, among them many Blacks, in a ghetto which also the often mentioned German-American friendship could not tear down.

Psychology Classes

With the enrollment of Course 6 on Monday, the URRS hopes to have placed a new milestone in their endeavors for a genuine racial settlement. The newly founded School at the outskirts of Munich will attempt to reduce the tension between Blacks and Whites with conduct guidance, explanations of characteristics, for example in a German bar - and psychology classes. However, a one-sided willingness to get to know the problems and characteristics of the other person brings up the question whether in this case the host does not need thorough instructions as well. Major Robert E. Greene had enough material at a press conference on Monday to show how strong the misunderstanding between the races in the Federal Republic is, starting with literature and ending with the "charming" Negro group with sticking out tongues."

RACE RELATIONS DIALOGUE

When I conducted the 18 hour race relations seminars in the military Munich Community, Germany, in 1975, I asked the participants to write their honest comments about the seminars. Some of their remarks were:

"Discuss prejudices in all forms.

Have more people to participate.

Increase the seminar type.

This is my first exposure to any type of race seminar and I feel captivated by the whole concept.

I did not realize that there were so many different prejudices.

I believed that the minorities have as many opportunities in 1974 as the lower class white. If minorities want to succeed, we cannot be expected to take them by the hand and lead them to success, they must work for it like the rest of us whites.

Combine more discussion on the minority problems of Indians, Mexicans, Puerto Ricans, Japanese and Chinese.

Do not let the Blacks influence the audience.

Discuss the issues at home of busing, equal opportunity and education.

Less emphasis on Blacks.

Race relations education should not be forced upon the individual. I believe that all the US civilian citizens and foreigners of the European Exchange System should attend the seminars.

The freedom that was given to communicate with each other was good.

It is a pity that this seminar lasts only six hours and not three days.

Invite non Americans to the seminar.

Enjoyed the realistic examples we have today in America as a people.

I did not realize all my own prejudices

I feel the discussion opened the people's mind somewhat, but not enough to change them.

Yes, I found it very interesting to hear a Black discuss their problems. it gave me an insight I had not received in reading.

Most of the discussion had no meanings to me, because I came to most of the present conclusions several years ago.

TRUE STORIES OF SEGREGATION

I have learned some facts that will help me in understanding the struggles of minority groups.

Before the seminar, I had been aware of most but certainly not all of the aspects presented.

I do not know about different minorities because I have not been around them. I'd like to find out more. It makes people more interesting to associate with.

I do not think the oriental problem is so serious as the Black or Mexican.

The seminar starts you thinking about areas you would not normally think about.

The seminar was an awareness.

Although I was aware of multiracial problems, being a minority myself, I became more aware of the problems faced by other minorities.

I have been aware of many problems, I also found problems I was not aware of.

Definitely one tends to believe one is well informed. I was not as well informed as I had thought. Some of the plain facts were extremely illuminating.

Awareness can be like dawn and it comes gradually and has to be absorbed.

You need to taste other people's experience to have a total awareness.

I learned a lot from other people's experience and opinions that made me alert to what my fellow workers are concerned about.

One is aware but not to everything.

I feel the seminar should not be a requirement and every individual should be able to decide whether he wants to go or not.

I feel that continued efforts must be made to overcome the problems of prejudice.

My feelings are as before I have always been a defender of individual rights.

The seminar offered more than I expected.

I enjoyed the seminar and I was impressed.

I do not consider myself a prejudiced person. I accept people for what they are and not by color.

The course did not change or affect me much.

I feel that I have a broader perspective of racial prejudice in America.

I have always tried to be aware of race relations problems and this course helped to update me.

Prejudice originates from the most tangible asset an individuals' color. In order to become involved for harmony, I must judge by merits not color.

Most of us are learning the problems a little too late.

It is very important for every American citizen to go through this course. I am fully impressed.

I was against this seminar at first, but now I think it is very needed.

It was all very good, but I do not feel in the long run it will do much to accomplish change and improvement.

Most people do not understand racism and even after discussing it today, some people still do not understand some of the topics discussed.

Some people just cannot realize the problem even after you tell them in simple language. Very informative, however too much attention to the Black group and not enough to the yellow and red.

I feel people could unite if they would recognize each group, accept people for what they are and try not to change them.

The race problem should be called human relations because this is the most important aspect.

A greater awareness to the color problem is prejudice, but color is not a critical issue for me.

My feelings did not change other than I appreciate the efforts which are elevated to the important feature in our daily life.

The course was very interesting and probably helped people who are trying to discriminate even less but I doubt that it will influence those who have been discriminating all of their lives.

I am glad to have been a part of the seminar. it is a chance to think of things I do not always take time for.

The seminar was a better understanding of minorities and their problems.

I enjoyed having a group discussion with people of different nationalities. I feel that lack of communications between race is our major problem.

The seminar dealt too much on Black or colored related problems than other minorities.

There are race problems but they will not be completely solved for many years.

I feel more aware of the reality of the situations.

The lectures should not address itself to Blacks mainly.

No matter what color a person is or walk of life, they cannot improve or progress in society unless they apply themselves.

I would like to attend more discussion groups of this sort.

I am going to continue living and thinking of myself as human and putting no less of a class on others.

I am glad I attended this seminar.

I have a greater awareness of the problems of minorities, although I don't think people were open enough to express how they feel toward minorities.

I was glad to give my opinions and also glad that others were forced to come out and give theirs.

I received a broad aspect of majority feelings toward the minority problems.

There should be an option to attend the seminar.

The seminar reminded me that problems exist.

I am more willing to examine and question myself in an objective way about my true feelings about other people.

I feel anxious to learn and discuss more about the problem.

I would like to attend the seminar again.

I enjoyed the discussion and became interested and would like to learn more.

The seminar was definitely worthwhile, but only as a start, surely too short a period of time to do more than scratch the surface.

The seminar covered the basic race issue. I stated in an interview with Mr. Speck Reynolds of the Oklahoma City *Black Dispatch* newspaper in May 1974 my views of the value of race relations education program in the U.S. Army. I said, "Since I have seen Mexican Americans, Native Americans, Asians, Blacks and Whites' attitudes change after attending a race relations school, that it will also work if we could spread our race relations curriculum into the civilian community. One of the most important things race relations education attempts to do is to eradicate fears which many persons have against minorities". I also said that the military is able to relate more in race relations than the civilian community and that I saw a strong need for race relation courses in public and private schools. I went on to state that if the civilians could adopt some of the Army Race Relations concepts like we were doing in Europe, some of our race problems in America would be lessened.

THE MILITARY

Significant Gains Since Integration

The late Colonel John Cash's outstanding performances of Military duties reflect some of the significant gains that people of color have made in the United States Military services.

Cash was a native of Atlantic City, New Jersey and was a graduate of Rutgers University where he received degrees in history and the University of Wisconsin where he received a degree in Latin American Studies. During his active military service, he served as a Unit Commander in Vietnam and served as Defense Attache in El Salvador and Brazil.

Colonel Cash taught history at the U.S. Military Academy, West Point, New York and Morgan State University, Baltimore, Maryland. Cash wrote a book, *Seven Fire Fights in Vietnam* and contributed to the *Exclusion of Black Soldiers From the Medal of Honor in World War II* and *Black Soldier - White Army: The Twenty-Fourth Infantry Regiment in Korea.* Colonel John Cash was a soldier, scholar and a very personable individual who was admired by all. He was truly "A Black Defender of America".

CHAPTER 5

MEMORIES OF SEGREGATION

I personally asked some people to recall and tell me some of their experiences of living in a legal segregated environment prior to the 1960's. and I asked a young man to tell me his personal experiences of living in a predominantly white environment. These stories will portray some truths about the race relations dialogue, sincere Whites and Blacks, either sustaining polarization or trying to move toward a more integrated society in America.

"Ma'm You Are On the Wrong Side"

During World War II, the Black men from the south who were in the Navy, received their basic training at the Great Lakes Naval Training Station. The Black sailors were trained at Camp Robert Smalls. A mulatto southern lady had made plans to travel to New York to visit her husband when he completed "boot camp" at the training center. He would meet her in New York. She travelled to Rocky Mount, North Carolina, from Enfield, N.C. to catch her train. The train was scheduled to arrive in the station at 3:45 p.m. She went to the ticket counter and purchased her ticket. Then she went to the "colored" waiting room. Suddenly the colored porter appeared; He was working for the Atlantic Coast Line and his major duty was to assist the white people with their baggage. The porter came over to the mulatto lady and in a very soft voice said to her "Miss, I think you are on the wrong side". There was a wall that divided the white waiting room from the colored waiting room. The porter told the lady, "You know Miss, when that train comes in here they won't let no colored people on it; no Ma'm, only the white folks is going to get on that train. Now if you want to get on that train, you have to move over to the other side." The lady told the porter that she had lived in New Jersey and was now living in North Carolina. She also said that her husband was in the Navy, and she was going to meet him in New York, at eleven o'clock that night. The porter then said, well come with me. He picked up her bags and walked over to the ticket agent desk and said, "Bossman, this lady was on the wrong side of the waiting rooms and she is going up North". The agent gave the lady a quick glance and told the porter, very well you know what to do. He then opened the swinging doors and pushed the bags on the other side and the lady went on into the white waiting room. She thanked him and gave him fifty cents. He said, "No thank you Ma'm, go on to meet your sailor and enjoy yourself". She said two hours later the train arrived in the station and everyone got in line, first the white people in a long line. She said that she was at the end of the white line where seven colored were standing behind her. When the conductor got to her, he took her ticket and waved his hand for her to get on the train. The conductor said in a loud clear voice, "The rest of you people will have to wait for the next train", which was due to arrive at 2:45 a.m. in the morning. The other colored people had to return home or remain in the train station ten to twelve hours. The lady said that she felt very terrible about it; however she wanted to meet her husband on time. She got on the train and went on to New York. The lady told me that she met the same porter six years later and he remembered her. She also learned that he was married to her cousin.

"The Case of Two Photographs"

A Black serviceman in World War II asked his wife to send him a photograph of their four year old son and also one of her. She dressed her little boy in his "Sunday best" and went to a photo studio in Rocky Mount, North Carolina. She was not able to call and make an appointment because in those days, few people in the country had telephones. She lived with her parents who did not have a telephone; therefore, she was hoping that she would be able to get the pictures taken. She arrived at the studio and found that it had closed at 12 o'clock. She then went around the corner to a small studio that she believed was okay. She and her son walked into the studio and she rang a bell to announce their arrival A young white woman came out of a small dark room and said in a friendly voice, "Can I help you'? The lady said "Yes, would you be able to take a picture of me this afternoon, as I live 20 miles out of town, and I do not know when I could come back again". Of course, the white lady said, "Come right this way". At the same time the lady's little son stood up on "tip toe" and tried to look over the counter and the white lady spotted his little "curly hair". She stopped in her tracks according to the mulatto lady, and looked at him and then her. She then emphatically said, "Oh I am sorry we do not take colored people's pictures in here". The lady told me that of course she was very upset, but she told the white lady "Do your realize that my husband left his home and family to fight for this country and people like you? This true story was not completed in the 1940's. In 1997, this lady said that she was in the same studio (just a curious visit) and observed a large picture on the wall of a Black man she knew. She decided to relate the story and experience of 1940's to the person who asked to help her, who politely asked her to stay for a "sitting" after hearing the story; She declined.

"I Am Colored Also", 1940's

There were some Black Americans during segregation who demonstrated their problem in dealing with color obsession. A southern mulatto lady from North Carolina moved to Newark, New Jersey. One Sunday, she decided to visit a Black church in the town. She said that she was so ridiculed that she finally got up and left the church before the services were over and never returned to that church again.

TRUE STORIES OF SEGREGATION

"Catch The Next Train North"

A mulatto Black left North Carolina, and went North to live. In later years, he decided to visit his home town during the years of segregation. When he arrived on the morning train in Rocky Mount, North Carolina, he was met by his father. When his father saw him with his white wife, he told him to go over to the hotel that was near the station and to stay there until the next train going North would arrive. He and his wife could stay at the segregated hotel, because he could easily pass as white. However, his father knew that once he left Rocky Mount and went to his home town, 20 miles away, the white people who knew him would become enraged with his bringing a white wife home. His father literally said "Son, please catch that next train North".

A Soldier's True Stories

I interviewed First Sergeant Mark Matthews in 1994 and he related to me several interesting true stories relating to segregation and Black pride. With God's continual blessings, he was 104 years, on August 7, 1998, a real "Buffalo soldier".

A Black Jockey at Lexington

"When I was living in Lexington, Kentucky, I would go down to the race track. I loved horses. I could ride almost any horse. I was comfortable with them because I was raised up with them. The man in charge of the horses at the race track was Jack Terrell. He gave me a job where I would exercise the ponies and horses. Sometimes I would ride a single rooter. You see a single rooter is a horse that when it is running, he will watch each step as he moves. Now, a pacer will not do that. He is a gallop horse. I trained a pacer that was also fast. If you wanted to stop him, just talk to him. I could handle him so nice. The man in charge would always pat me on the shoulder and say I was riding very good with the horses. He would also take a strap and tie it around the horse and around my knees, because the horse could run so fast that I could have fallen if I did not have the straps tied around me. I would train and exercise the horses to be ready for the jockey. Yes, they had a few Black jockeys. There was one Black jockey that was so good, that some English people saw him perform and took him to England, and he never came back to the race track."

Today we read in the newspapers about the U.S. government considering the use of military troops at the Mexican borders to assist in the drug interdiction program and illegal bordering crosses. I wonder how many of the policemen and laypersons are aware of the Black presence on the borders 75 years ago.

"Service On The Border"

During segregation, Black troops were assigned to one geographical area of the Mexican border and Whites to another. First Sergeant Matthews relates his experience. "I left for New Mexico to serve on the border with the immigration officer at Naco, Arizona. Later, I would do patrol duty.

"Sometimes there would be little uprisings on the Nogales side in Mexico. There were two men trying to be mayor of the towns in Mexico. They had a gold mine at Cananea. The gold would be taken to Bisbee to be cooked and prepared for solid gold. This was around 1921. The two men, Escobel and Escapia, wanted to be mayor of the Sonora State. The Governor of Arizona wanted protection for residents in the area because there was fighting on the Mexican side. Fort Huachuca was 68 miles from Nogales. It was in 1919 when the Tenth Cavalry was involved the last time in those uprisings on the Mexican side. Governor Churchill of Arizona had received complaints from residents on the American side. They claimed that bullets were coming on their side from Mexico and going through their homes. They wanted protection. One night while we were in the theatre, an announcement was made. All men of the machine gun troop report at once to your orderly room. When we arrived at the orderly room, the first sergeant was standing there and had a pad in his hand. He said "Saddle up". We immediately obtained our rifles. We arrived at Nogales and made a show of force. Orders were issued to the Mexicans to move 5 miles back into Mexico."

"After World War 1, I was assigned to an immigration office along the border. For a long time all I had to do was to get up in the morning, eat my breakfast, shine my boots and then report to the immigration officer. I did duty with the immigration officer for a pretty good while. When a Mexican wanted to enter the United States, especially if he was running from some trouble he had in Mexico, all he had to do was show his passport. The passport had the necessary information, his picture and the right for him to enter and leave U.S. However, the immigration officer could not stop him. The military could stop him. In those days the immigration officer did not have that authority. As a military man on duty, I could stop the Mexicans and have them returned to Mexico. The white cavalry units were stationed in El Paso, Texas and were performing the same duties we were."

"Cemetery Segregated, But a Black Firing Squad Could Fire Volleys at White Funerals"

"On June 25, 1930, 1 received orders to report to Fort Myer, Virginia. When we arrived the all white Third U.S. Cavalry Regiment and a white artillery unit were stationed there. Within a week we were doing the same duties that the white cavalry unit were performing. We drilled on the large parade field at Fort Myer and used the riding hall. I had duty at Arlington National Cemetery at times. Many times, I would take enough ammunition to remain the entire day. The superintendent of the cemetery or my lieutenant would say; Here comes another one, referring to the funeral processions. We would then prepare to fire the rifle volleys at the appropriate time. The cemetery was segregated, but we were still detailed to fire the volley for all funeral procession, Black or white. The bugler and pall bearers were white. I could play the bugle. I was a bugler for seven years. I could play taps and all the calls."

"Black Performers Before The Royalty"

We performed for the late Emperor Haile Selassie of Ethiopia. We were scheduled to perform for him on another visit to the United States but he was ill. Therefore, we performed for his nephew Ras Desta, in the Fort Myer large Riding Hall. Our officers were sitting erect in the stands and other people were watching the Tenth Cavalry members perform, using their horses. We made a picture like model of a ship on water. The men using their horses had a man standing on each others shoulders forming a very high level. Ras Desta was very impressed, because later he left the stands and just looked, probably trying to understand how we were able to do the act. After we had dismounted, Ras Desta approached each man, asked their name and where they were from in the United States. There were three men from Howard University acting as translators for the Ras. However, Ras Desta could speak English very well and he then asked was anyone from Chicago, Illinois? Several men raised their hands. Ras Desta said very fine, because I went to school in Chicago. He also said that the performance was the best he had ever seen. The soldiers of the regiment were very proud to see and perform before an African royal family member. The next visitor we performed for was Queen Mary of England. We had to meet her at the Washington, D.C. Union Station and escort her to the White House. Later, we gave a performance for her at Fort Myer. The men would remark about her beauty. She was small at that time and a beautiful queen."

The U.S. military would demonstrate some aspects of integration when they deemed it was necessary or for other reasons. First Sergeant Matthews told me the following:

"Black and White Together"

"There were times we would be marching along with all white units. Sometimes we would be marching on maneuvers with the Seventh and Eighth Cavalry Regiments. They came from El Paso, Texas and we came from Kansas. Some days during a march, there would be a white platoon and Black platoon together. One time we marched from Fort Huachuca to El Paso, Texas, 279 miles, the white cavalry and Black cavalry together. If nobody looked at them, they were the same as one, so proud to be cavalrymen.

We marched in President Franklin D. Roosevelt's parade with whites in 1939, February 2. That was Roosevelt's Second Inaugural. When I went to Fort Leavenworth, Kansas and received my horse, I named it "Franklin D". He was a tall horse.

A Glass Of Water, Please

A Nigerian student who had a part-time job working in a nursing home was asked to take a glass of water to a very elderly white lady. When he brought the lady the water, she told him, "No, you cannot bring my water because your hands are very dirty". She was referring to his skin color. Later she decided to take the water. When her daughter heard about the incident, she told the Nigerian man that she was sorry about her mother's remarks. She also told him that if she was not married that she would be happy to date him. Just another true story about the segregation days.

Antone Bailey's True Story

"My name is Antone Bailey and I was born on October 15, 1917 in a small Black community, Meacham Park, near Kirkwood, Missouri, not far from St. Louis, Missouri. Recently, I went to a four o'clock Mass at my parish church. A Vietnamese seminary student related an interesting story about his family's fortunate immigration to the United States. He stated that his father had been a soldier in the army and when conditions worsened, his family decided to leave Saigon. They were able to crowd on a large barge which was sighted by an American ship. They were rescued and brought to America. While listening to the student, I realized that when his family was able to arrive int he U.S., they were given a place to live and did not have to worry about legal segregation because of skin color. Their ancestors were not in the American institution of slavery. During the Mass, I began to think about my family, especially my mother. I offered a special prayer for her as I realized the hardships she faced in her successful efforts to raise me and my sister, Juanita and brother Clifford. Therefore when my cousin Robert asked me to record a narrative of my memories of segregation I decided to discuss my memories of my mother and her ordeals, my childhood, World War II military service, and adult employment through the years.

My mother worked and ironed for white families. She would earn three dollars for the washing and two dollars for the ironing. She worked for many years for a family in Webster Groves, Mo. Unfortunately, my father was involved in a shooting and a person was shot and later died. My Dad had to spend some time in the State Prison in Jefferson City, Missouri. I visited him one time when I was very small. Since my mother was separated from my father, it was necessary for her to assume a very responsible role as the head of our household. We were living in a small house that was owned by a postman. He had told my mother that she would have to move out of the house. I can remember very clearly that for two weeks we had to live in a small building which was a simple chicken coup, that had been cleared out to make room for us. Mother was able to cash in on a small insurance policy and with 300 dollars was able to purchase a vacant lot on Saratoga street in Meacham Park. Ironically, she purchased the lot from the postman. I had an uncle whose mother-in-law had a garage that she built for her 1928 Chevrolet, but was not using the garage and sold it to my mother. The garage was moved to our lot and a relative, Henry Spears along with some other men, helped in securing the garage on the lot. They used lumber and railroad ties to build a firm foundation. It took them some two weeks to complete the task. I sincerely believe that my sister and I had a very loving and caring mother who did the best she could in those days of enforced segregation and economic and job deprivation for Black people.

I started school when I was six years old and my sister started when she was four years, because the teacher needed twelve children in order to conduct the class in our one room school. I graduated from the eight grade in 1929. I learned about the work ethic at a very young age. I would earn some change as a youngster by cutting wood, carrying out ashes and hauling coal for people. I also worked briefly for five dollars a week for some people in Webster Groves, Missouri. Sometimes I would ride the buses and street cars looking for work such as sweeping floors, collecting old rags to sell to the ragman, selling empty whiskey bottles (that you could sell for a few pennies) and when I was older I would wait tables. My Uncle Oliver had a little paper hanging business and I would assist him. He had a paste table, cutting board and ladders. We could hang paper for two rooms 8 x 12 in a day, and earn four dollars a room. During the winter months, I would wash automobiles in a service station for fifty cents a vehicle. I also had to wash very carefully the wheel spokes, under the fenders, hub caps, and the tires. I even worked on a trash truck as a young boy.

Now as a young man, I worked briefly for a white man who was a credit manager for the Goodyear Tire Company. I drove for him and did some household chores. When he moved to Kansas City, Missouri. I drove his 1932 Ford car along with him and his family who were traveling in another car. The weather was quite severe as we were riding on highway 50. We ran into a snow storm and with no defrosters on the cars, we could hardly see through the windshields. We obtained some candles and placed them on the dashboard in order to make a little opening through the windshield. We arrived in Kansas City, Missouri safe at 2:00 a.m. in the morning. My boss had moved into a house at 7111 Warnell Road in the Country Club area of the city. I stayed with the Kelley family for six months. One day Mr. Kelley left the house and to everyone's dismay, he never returned. Mrs. Kelley had no money to keep the house and also retain my services; so I was out of a job and a place to stay. I happened to go down to the colored section of Kansas City and was able to see my Cousin Moses Perkins. I was able to stay with him briefly. I got a job at the Paseo Cab Company washing cars and received ten cents each for fixing flat tires. When I received enough money for a bus ticket, cost three dollars, I returned to St. Louis, Missouri.

After returning to St. Louis, I met a wealthy white man, Dr. O'Malley and was hired to work for him as a chauffeur. Dr. O'Malley owned a large farm and the two major crops that were grown on the farm were tomatoes and string beans. He was originally from Rochester, New York, and had some property in Pomokey, Maryland where he had docked a thirty foot Richardson boat cruiser. He would visit Maryland during the summers and travel by boat to New York. One summer, I drove him and his family to Maryland. When he was trying to start the boat's engine along with some friends, I was standing near observing them. Suddenly, the doctor turned to me and said "Antone do you know anything about motors? I said, yes. I examined the Chrysler Marine engine. This was first time that I had worked on a Chrysler engine, but I knew some things about an engine, because as a youngster I would observed the mechanics working on cars. I removed the distributor cap, and noticed the presence of some moisture; there was water on the points and I wiped them thoroughly, blew into them and sand papered them. I also scraped the rotary. This took me some 35 minutes. I then told the men to turn on the key and immediately that boat engine started and they all thought that I was the best mechanic.

Dr. O'Malley's wife told her husband that I must go along with them to Rochester, New York because I knew how to start the boat's engine. So I did go along with them. They had their navigational maps and charts, and we observed water markers such as buoys and bell lights along the water routes. I would listen to the boat captain and I was able to learn about the compasses, degrees, latitude and longitude. We travelled from Pomokey, Maryland to Delaware on to New York. We passed through the Chesapeake to Delaware Canal Bay to Cape May on out into the Atlantic Ocean and after two weeks landed in Rochester, New York. As we travelled along the Hudson River, I could see Father Divine's mansion and President Franklin D. Roosevelt's Estate in Hyde Park. I also saw the Statue of Liberty as we proceeded toward Albany, New York. While working for the O'Malley family in the 1940's, I received a draft notice to report for Army service. I was able to obtain a brief deferment, but I was finally told to report to Jefferson Barracks, Missouri for induction. I was given a physical examination and some intelligence tests. I had a good IQ and passed the physical examination with my weight at that time being 129 pounds. The descriptions of segregation was evident when the colored soldiers reported to some old barracks and the Whites were housed in new barracks. Later, we were given orders to report to Scott Field Air Force Base, Illinois.

When I received my first weekend pass, I went home to Meacham Park, Missouri. I visited a girl friend of mine, and she suggested that we should go to church and get married before I return to camp. I agreed and we were married and spent several days together. I would go overseas and return back home and I never saw that young lady again. After returning to Scott Field, I received military orders to report to Camp Stewart, Georgia. I was assigned to an anti-aircraft unit in the segregated camp area of Camp Stewart for Negro soldiers. I went to a post school to receive training as an aircraft machine gunner. During my stay at Camp Stewart, a race riot occurred when some Black soldiers went to town.

The next orders that I would receive were to Fort Campbell, Kentucky. The Black troops were sent to the field for their training. We stayed out in the field for months. The soldiers were living like dogs all winter long. Sometimes a white General would visit us and have a marching band to accompany him when he would review the colored troops. I will always remember that band playing a song called "Big Fat Mother". The conditions in the field were causing some morale problems, because one day a soldier confronted a white colonel and began to beat him. After Easter, the officials decided to bring us out of those deplorable field conditions. Upon returning to the main post area, I was sent to a mechanic's school, where I was able to become proficient in tearing an engine down and rebuilding it again. Later my unit was shipped to Europe. We had to load our equipment and vehicles aboard the ship. All of the colored soldiers were assigned to a segregated area on the ship, of course below the main deck and other levels. We did have all white officers. I was only a private first class, but had been given the responsibility to be in charge of six men. There was one soldier who was quite upset because his mother had just died and he was not able to attend her funeral. He was trying to jump overboard and I was successful in talking him out of such a dreadful action.

We traveled across the Atlantic Ocean for 13 long days and nights. We were aboard a British ship with an all British crew. The ocean was quite rough. The soldiers were required to man their training post and had anti aircraft practice daily. Our ship landed in Liverpool, England and when we went across the gang plank, we boarded another ship and went to Glasgow, Scotland. There we boarded a train that took us to a camp area where we pitched our two man pup tents. There were guard towers surrounding the camp area. There was an officer who gave the troops a daily lecture on venereal diseases. While stationed in England, I was able to visit the cities of Liverpool, Manchester and Southhampton, England.

During a conversation with my Cousin Robert recently, he asked me had I heard about a statement that many Black soldiers had said over the years about English ladies asking Black soldiers "Do they have tails"? Well, I was able to verify that subject for him, because I was sitting in an English Tavern or bar when an English woman asked me "Do you really have a tail; the white GI Joe said you do, please let me see your tail". She had actually informed me where the story actually originated. Yes, it was a real example of transplanted white racism during segregation.

We landed at Omaha Beach when it was quiet. We did not have any food for several days. Some soldiers found some canned apples and after eating them, became ill. As we moved through France, I was almost killed in the town of Metz. One night while I was walking down a hill and a dirt mover bomb landed just ahead of me. Our captain was killed. While moving toward Germany our units were responsible to haul ammunition guns and gasoline for the white combat units. I was assigned to a Howitzer 105 outfit. The unit moved toward the battle of St. Lo and we had to wear the First Army patch. The Negro units experienced housing problems overseas, because we were placed anywhere in a village or a town. Sometimes we had to sleep outside, in our trucks and we were constantly in fear of the enemy and could hardly sleep with the continuous gun fire. One night we were able to stay in a house in a village. A soldier happened to look down in the basement in the morning and he immediately ran back up the steps. He had observed some German soldiers sleeping in the basement. We immediately left the house and found some open basement windows and dropped some grenades through the windows and that house and those German soldiers were in a burning inferno.

Our unit had to travel through the Black Forest, because we were in the Battle of the Bulge. We crossed the Mossele, Lohr and Rhine Rivers. At one time a bridge had to be built several times. It was an engineer pontoon bridge. The enemy had knocked it out for four days.

I remember one day when we came across an old root cellar, some 35-50 feet underground. There was a senior citizen about 90 years of age who was sitting in an old fashioned wheel chair. She was quite frightened and crying. There were also some German soldiers lying around who were seriously wounded and some were begging us to shoot them. The senior citizen and the soldiers were turned over to the appropriate authorities.

TRUE STORIES OF SEGREGATION

The news of an atomic bomb being dropped in Japan was an instant revocation of our orders to ship out to the Philippines. Everyone was jubilant because we got our new orders to return home at last. We boarded ship in Marseilles, France. The name of the ship was the Marine Robin, and for nine days on the ocean, it was like a bouncing rowboat. When the ship docked at the Boston, Massachusetts, Harbor, we could observe from our main deck, the roaring reception the white solders were given as they left their ships to be greeted by the white citizens. Later the Black soldiers were able to leave their ship, and we were sent to New York City and stayed a few days. Then I was given my orders to report to Jefferson Barracks, Missouri for my discharge from the U.S. Army. I was given 134 dollars muster out pay and 30 cents carfare. A friend from Kirkwood, Austin Massey came to the barracks to drive me home. I saw my mother and family. Then I had to attend several welcome parties with my friends. I stayed with my mother for a short while, she now had an additional room on our house. A week after being home, some friends gave me a hay ride party. We were on our way to a farm in Chesterfield, Missouri when suddenly a car leaving a tavern hit our truck, full of people, in the back. Unfortunately, those riding in the back were injured and one lady was killed. I was also hurt. I received a compound leg fracture, breaking two bones. Some 13 people had to be admitted to the hospital. I had to remain in the hospital for two weeks.

After my leg began to heal, I realized that I needed a job. I went to St. Louis, Missouri and was hired by a Mr. Leech, a white man who owned the Egyptian Ties and Timber Company. He made ties for the railroad. He also owned some oil wells in Shawnee, Illinois. We became very close friends, even though he was my boss. Mr. Leech owned some saw mills in Arcadia, Missouri and he would send me to Arcadia to check the saw mills and to take care of some minor business for him in the town. When I first visited the town, the white folks began to watch me and wonder who was the colored man with such responsibility to handle a white man's business. Later they changed their attitudes and probably satisfied their curosity when they learned that I really did work for Mr. Leech. During segregation, Whites would refer to you and call you, not necessarily in your presence but to their friends "Oh that colored boy is Mr. Leech's nigger". The citizens were very concerned when they first saw me because Mr. Leech had several cars and I was permitted to drive all of the cars at certain times. Therefore, I could visit Arcadia in Mr. Leech's 1942 Ford sedan, 1946 Mercury station wagon, 1936 Mercury sedan, 1941 Packard 2 door coupe or his 12 cylinder Lincoln cars. I was responsible for keeping all those cars in good maintenance.

I was talking to Mr. Leech one day about how I used to assist Dr. O'Malley on his boat trips to Rochester, New York. He then said that he had a boat docked in Illinois, a V-eight engine boat with a state room with a bar. Mr. Leech gave me an opportunity to pilot his boat on the Ohio River to Paducah, Kentucky. Sometimes I would cook for his guests at boat parties and even pick up some of his business partners at dock ports along the river. I was paid fifty dollars a week and I travelled all the time. This wealthy man who was from Evanston, Illinois, also owned a wild turkey and hog farm in the Ozarks. He would send me there to feed the hogs and also to slaughter some. He had a very beautiful large house there, but his wife did not want a colored man staying in their house; so Mr. Leech had me to build a small log cabin where I could stay over night. My Uncle Allen helped me to build the cabin, and also assisted me in butchering the hogs. All Mr. Leech wanted was the hams, sausage and lard from the hogs. Therefore, I was able to keep the rest of the meat. I would place it in brine and in a smoke house. Later, I would take some of it home to my friends and family in Kirkwood, Missouri.

During a visit to Paducah, Kentucky, I met a very nice young lady, and I knew that I wanted to marry her. Her name was Frances. When I returned home, I told Mr. Leech that I was going to get married. He gave me 100 dollars and permitted me to use his boat to go to Paducah, Kentucky, where we were married. After I ended my employment with Mr. Leech, my family was living in a one room apartment with a bathroom, two burner gas stove and ice box. Later, the manager of the building asked me to manage several of his buildings. He offered me free rent and 45 dollars every two weeks. I was also responsible for stoking the furnaces.

During segregation many Blacks would move from job to job to try to improve their living conditions and of course, earn more money. I was able to meet a man named Clifford Seigmaster who was a Benrus Watch Company salesman. He was responsible for sales in the areas of Missouri, Illinois, Arkansas, Kansas, Nebraska and Iowa. I was hired as his chauffuer and assistant. He paid me 55 dollars a week and also paid my room and meals when we travelled. He had a Cadillac car. Sometimes we would be on the road 3-4 days at a time. Then I would return home for a brief time. I was not able to stay in the white hotels where Mr. Seigmaster stayed. I had to stay at the colored YMCA's, small Black hotels and rooming houses. When the boss was selling the watches, I would help him to write the orders and also I would polish the watches at times. The practices of segregation were very evident when travelling in the Midwestern part of the country. We would stop to eat and use the restrooms, but I was not allowed to go into the restaurants. I would have to find a place in the back to urinate and sometimes the only water I was able to get was when we stopped at a gas station and I would drink from a water hose laying on the ground, because there were no separate water fountains to be found. On several occasions, Mr. Seigmaster would have to bring my sandwiches out to the car and it was necessary for us to park the car out of sight of the restaurant because the owners did not want colored people sitting in front of their businesses eating their food.

During segregation, some white people would have some strange race customs, because I recall when I worked in a white restaurant once and the owner would allow some of the Black employees to sit at his table with him while they were eating their meals. One day he told us while we were eating, not to eat too much and save some room for a delicious dessert. He then said that his "wife had baked a good old nigger and white folks cake". He was actually referring to what some white people called a marble cake. Those were the times when you wanted to say something, but in those days you had to sit and listen to those remarks if you wanted to continue to work in that place. Mr. Clifford Seigmaster had received a promotion in the Benrus Watch Company as a vice president, and was assigned to Long Island, New York. He asked me to go to New York with him. He offered me to bring my wife and family to live in his home where there was a residence for the chauffeur. Unfortunately, an incident occurred that would eventually end my employment with Mr. Seigmaster, and I would not be able to accept his offer.

I returned one day from our road trips and when I arrived home, my wife told me one evening that she was going out to play cards with her friends. She came into our apartment building at 3:00 a.m. in the morning. When I opened the door and saw her coming up the stair ways, she was continuing to the next stair level. I asked her where was she going? She then turned around and ran. Suddenly someone hit me over the head. Eventually my wife left. After that situation, I had several part-time jobs. Later, I was able to chauffeur for a white family in the 1950's. I would drive them at times to Miami Beach, Florida. They would give me a railroad ticket to return home.

We would stop in Atlanta, Georgia, overnight and I would have to find a room or Black hotel in the colored area of the city. As we were traveling through the deep South, I would have to buy a soda when I could not find a "colored" water fountain. Many times the white doorman at the hotel where I would leave the white family, would be cordial enough to direct me to the colored part of town where I could find a room for the night. Sometimes we would arrive in Miami Beach very late at night. The white family would slip me on the beach and let me stay with them until morning. After 9:00 p.m. no Black people were allowed in the Miami Beach resort areas. Early in the morning they would take me to the train station.

I remember an interesting conversation that occurred one time while I was waiting for a late train to arrive in Miami, Florida. A white lady asked the white conductor, "Why is the train late"? The conductor replied "Sometimes there is a breakdown or an automobile accident on the tracks". Just the day before yesterday, said the conductor", there was an accident where a nigger on a motorcycle was hit".

My sister was living in Minnesota and I decided to move there. I was able to obtain a job in a factory where I had to work in a basement area with little air present. I asked the boss to give me a job upstairs in the factory. I worked in an area where I had to pull auto parts aside and prepare them for another assembly line. I decided to find another job and I worked briefly at a country club cleaning golf shoes. I met a Dr. Porter who owned a veterinary clinic. He hired me, and his brother taught me how to trim ponies. I worked there for a brief time. I applied for a job at the Post Office and at first I was not accepted, because my grade on the examination was 90 and another person was hired. They later called me and said that there was an error because I was not given six points for my veterans preference and I actually had the highest score. I was given a job as a garage man. I would pick up trucks in need of repair, and later I was assigned as a mailhandler in the main building. I also worked as a truck driver, driving the 5 ton mail trucks. A neighbor of my sister assisted me in obtaining a job in the parts department of the Post Office garage as a parts clerk. I was able to retire from the Post Office in Minneapolis, Minnesota. In later years I moved to Denver, Colorado after living briefly in California.

Cousin Robert, I have given you some memories of my 81 years of life and many of them were lived in a period of United States history which was called separate but equal. Now you and the future readers might understand what I said about some honest and innocent foreigners coming to America in 1998 and not having to experience what my mother, relatives and millions of colored people had to face prior to the 1960's. Your Cousin Antone Bailey, Denver Colorado, June, 1998.

Memories of Segregation

A man of color who was visiting a rural public school in Burlington, Iowa, in 1966 encountered some racism from young students. While walking up the stairs with a white friend, he overheard the following:

"Who is that"? A young student replied, "That's the new Nigger Speech teacher". The teacher said that he ignored it realizing that there was little he could do or say, since they were students and he was an adult. He said that he simply ignored it as if he did not hear it. He was the first Black Speech Pathologist to work at that school. He also said that he learned years later that when one rural school found out that an African American was hired, they asked that he not be assigned to their district. This person of color stated that when he arrived in Burlington, he also had difficulty in obtaining an apartment. When he would appear at the rental offices, they would always tell him that even though he had called, all apartments had been rented. After several more similar responses, he believed that his color was the problem. Finally, he was able to find an apartment. These incidents did not occur in the deep South but in Burlington, Iowa in 1966.

CHAPTER 6

Memories of Integration

David's True Story

My name is David; my close friends call me Dave. I was asked to express some of my personal experiences and feelings about being raised in an integrated environment and my continual living among the white majority society. The way I perceive my living in an integrated community is that it is not that I chose to, but my parents did, because my late brother Rob and I had no choice in the way we grew up. We lived in Northern Virginia, Reston, in Fairfax County and also in a predominantly white military environment at times.

Young Blacks who grow up in a white community have to communicate with Whites, listen to their music and watch their kind of movies. Now the situation with my brother Rob was that he grew up around whites all his life, and in some ways he did not see himself as a Black man. Most of his friends were White; he loved their music and life styles. Sometimes, I become alienated but I am very conscious that I am a Black man and there are times I try to be more Black. I often ask what is the definition of being Black? Is it speaking Black, listening to Black music, responding to some whites pre conceived perceptions that I am not supposed to be educated, listening to Black music and being obsessed about sports? The reality is that one receive criticism from both sides. There are Blacks who will tell me, "You are not Black enough", and there are whites who will say to me "You are trying to act white". Recently, I went to a social event and a white friend introduced me to her date. The young man said "Oh, this is the Black fellow who talks like white people". The actual situation is that I try to be the best person that I can. What some people do not realize is that regardless of how Robert or I would speak, when we walk down the street and before we would say a word or anything, the significant fact is that we were Black.

I can remember when I was ten years old and lived in an upper class white neighborhood in Reston, Virginia. I had been playing with my white friend, Todd; and he was leaving to go home. I rode him on my bicycle up to the main roadway. As I was returning home, I made a wrong decision by riding out toward the moving traffic. A Volkswagen almost hit me. Just as I was moving out of the way toward a safe area, very nervous, excited, with my heart pounding and realizing that I narrowly escaped being seriously injured, a more traumatic incident occurred. The white man who was driving the Volkswagen car put his head out the window and screamed back toward me shouting "You dumb little nigger, you dumb little nigger". This was the first time in my life that anyone referred personally to me as a "nigger". I had a little understanding of the word but never the reality of it. But it left a lasting memory. I have always had a feeling about it after that situation. I do not see white children often finding themselves in that kind of situation. When I became a teenager and even now, I in no way can tolerate racism directed, not just to Blacks and Whites but also to Jews, Asians, Hispanics, and Native Americans also. My point is that when someone calls a person's child a "nigger" he could say to an eight year old child, your are a "kike, chink, or even dago" also. That is not right, because when I was ten years old and was called a "nigger" it did leave a tremendous residual emotional scar. Now suppose in later years, I have a son, little Robert; and he is seven years old, and some adult calls him a "nigger". Of course, I would be very angry. We should not call anyone a derogatory name and especially a little child. I do not believe in that. Ironically, I never told my story to my parents, only to my brother, Rob.

In later years, I experienced a situation in the 1980's that probably happens to some youngsters today. I had returned home one weekend to visit my brother, Rob, who was ill in a Northern Virginia hospital. As my friend Chris and I were leaving the parking lot in my car, we observed a Fairfax County police car several blocks away. Just as we were proceeding down the street, suddenly we were surrounded by 4-5 police cars. The officers who were all white had their hands firmly on their weapons. They told us to get out of the car, place our hands in front of us and to give them our driver's license or identification. Every time we would ask what this is all about? They would say "Shut up, and give us your identifications". While this was happening, there were some firemen across the street, standing in front of their fire station looking at us and there were people coming out of stores who were observing the situation. After the policemen had checked our identification, one of the officers said "They are not the Black males who just robbed the Seven-Eleven Store". Then they told us we may return to our car. I decided to approach one of the officers and I asked him, "Do we get an apology?" He replied, "Do you know how many policemen are killed each year?" I said, No, and that is not the question I asked you." I was able to obtain his badge number, but I did not pursue it further, I meant to obtain an apology. I later called my father and told him about the event. My Dad said "I was right in asking the officer for an apology because I was standing up for my rights". But another person that I told the story to said that I should never talk back to a police officer". I do realize that all police officers do not perform their duties as those officers did in the 1980's. We must realize that there are situations where everybody is an individual. They can be a doctor, teacher, store clerk and police. Sometimes they carry a baggage of racism with them.

When I was a student at Longwood College, Farmville, Virginia. I had a poster in my room with pictures of some 8-9 white ladies that I had previously dated and there was a caption on the poster that read "Gone with the Wind". One day my white roommate and six white dormitory friends were gathered in the room. One fellow was looking at the pictures and said, "David, is there any difference between being with a white woman and a Black woman? Now, I had previously dated some very beautiful and attractive Black ladies and I knew that the only difference was in the melanin of the skin. But to me, this question was totally absurd. Therefore, I answered by saying, that question is ridiculous."

Then the conversation changed to the subject of "White and Black dating". I asked my white friends two questions. The first question was "Would you let your sister date a Black man"? There was only one of the seven fellows who said yes to that question. Then I asked them "What if a Black man had a good job, was a respectable person in the community, neatly dressed and wanted to date your sister, and there also was a white man who dressed very shabbily, had tattoos, long hair, and had no job, which one would you select for your sister to date? All of their responses except one were that they would select the white man. One, my roommate, would have selected the Black man. The interesting thing is that none of those white youngsters was from the deep South but all were from Northern Virginia.

I was able to observe some interesting characteristics of the town's people. I noticed that the white people were very polite and would say good morning and how are you? They might not have you over to their house for dinner because they probably felt that as a Black person you were not up to their standards. There were some Blacks in the city who appeared to have a certain mentality in respect to the white race customs. But I would always carry myself in a self confident manner and not in a subservient way. I must say that the southern whites were at least honest by letting you know how they felt about race relations. I can respect that because that was better than stabbing a person in the back and then saying something that they do not mean. I knew in many instances that they were wrong, but they were being frank about it. That experience and a later experience when I was attending George Mason University revealed the fact that there is just as much racism in Northern Virginia as there was in Farmsville, Virginia. One day when I went into the male restroom at George Mason University, I happened to observe some racial graffiti on the toilet stall doors, not just one door, but almost 15 stall doors. Some of the writings were: "Niggers get off campus" . "Asian Chinks go home", "Niggers and Crackers keep on fighting because the Asians will rule the world one day" and " A good Nigger is a dead Nigger". I thought this was really something because Fairfax County, Virginia, is one of the richest counties in the state and possibly the country. The citizens are privileged people but some appear to be very angry. Many Americans believe racism is present only in certain places, but it is all around us and in places you would least expect.

I recall an incident when I was 16 years old and in high school. One day, I was driving my mother's car with my good friend Chris, and I decided to give two white classmates a ride. This was during the time when the citizens of Atlanta, Georgia, were confronted with the unfortunate horrible child murders. One of the white fellows in the car remarked about the Atlanta murders by saying, "It is too bad that they did not kill more of them". I believe that I made some comment. But it bothered me later because I did not tell them to get out of the car. After that incident, I would not let something like that get past me again, because while at Longwood College, I had a roommate who was going to put up a Confederate flag in the room. I told him that he was not going to put that flag up. He then said "Are you not like Dr. Martin Luther King Jr., a non violent man"? I said if you put that flag up, I might have to hit you because I believe in some peace and some violence sometimes; you know like Malcolm X said "By any means necessary". I guess we reached a mutual truce between a possible war among the North and the South. The flag never went up.

I once dated a white blond young lady from Canada. She is a graduate registered nurse. We had driven from Los Angeles to San Francisco, California, to visit my aunt and uncle. She was a little hesitant to visit my relatives, but she decided to visit them. My aunt is a retired senior counselor and vice principal of a middle school and my uncle is a retired Air Force officer and pilot. He also has retired from a very prestigious position with the San Francisco Bart Metro System. My friend enjoyed the visit, and as we were leaving the house, she said to me " You know your uncle spoke so well and he is very articulate". We must realize that people's perceptions are powerful measurements of what they think of people and there is also that element of stereotypes. With my uncle's outstanding accomplishments and achievements, it is obvious that he is an articulate person.

I realize that I am in this white environment almost every day of my life. Even if I had grown up in an all Black environment and lived in a Black neighborhood, I would still have to go into the white job community. That is how one has to adapt to the changing situations of life. But you cannot lose your perspective as to who you are; you must be proud of where you come from. Some people will say you must be proud that you are Black. Yes, you must be proud that you are Black; however, I do not think that being proud that you are Black means that you must wear a certain hairstyle, certain clothes and speak a certain way. I am proud of being Black and that means to me that I am proud of my family and they are Black. One should be proud of where he comes from and of his ancestors. The history that my father has taught me about my family makes me very proud to have relatives like the Hendersons, McAfees, Sanford's and the Greene's, all well-educated people.

I have been very fortunate to have met some of my late great uncles and aunts. I was raised by a strong and supportive family and I am very proud of my mother and father. I was taught to believe that I am just as good as anyone and possibly better. The color of my skin makes no difference to me, as my Dad says and also my God Father, Fritz Lang, who would say it in German "Die Farbe ist egal". I have stated some sincere memories of my living in an integrated society with some optimism for a true "One America" someday.

    The above narrative was provided to me by a young man of color who was born on August 23, 1967 in Frankfurt, Germany at the United States Army 97th General Hospital. He was delivered by a Turkish obstetrician, treated by a Yugoslavian pediatrician and cared for by a German nurse. His early education was in the U.S. Department of Defense Overseas Dependent School System. Later in his young life, he attended predominantly white schools in Reston and Herndon, Virginia. He has never attended an all Black school. The majority of his childhood life was spent in a white environment. His college experiences included white roommates and fraternity brothers. Recently, he was the best man for his college roommate at a very impressive wedding Mass at a Fairfax, Virginia, Catholic Church. He has traveled abroad on trips with his white friends. He also enjoys several trips a year at resorts with his friends. This young man continues to live comfortably in a white society because his self-concept, knowledge of who he is and an awareness of his strong family heritage of proud people of color will always sustain him in times when he might be one among many. I thank you again for sharing these personal memories for my book, my loving son, David Arthur Friedrich Greene.

PICTORIAL REVISIT

CHAPTER 7

A Pictorial Revisit

The pictures in this Chapter portray the genetic diversity and different amounts of melanin deposits of people of color prior to the 1960's. These pictures will not depict the current illustrations that advertisers, television commercials, magazines, and news media used in depicting people of color in a typical commonality stereotyped setting.

A picture is really worth a thousand words because these photographs will show that the African American, Black, Afro American, Negro and Colored persons do not all look alike. Many of these pictures will also depict that all Blacks do not dress alike, act alike and have the same physical features such as hair texture, eye color, nose shape, skin color and lip size.

This pictorial revisit will portray to some Blacks that many of us do look like many non Blacks, namely, Native Americans, Europeans, Hispanics, Asians and Jewish. However one must not forget regardless of how a Black might look, in America the beautiful, he is still a Black person.

This chapter contains pictures of the Black family in church, in education, in sports and in the community, Shades of color (genetic diversity), the U.S. Military, and the United States, Army Europe (USAEUR) Race Relations School (URRS) are all represented in photograph of peoples of color, living in the years of segregation and some during the beginning years of integration.

R.E.G.

SEGREGATED YEARS

Howard
University
1923 Law
School Class

Howard
University
Law School, 1917

**When College Football
was segregated
Howard University, 1918**

**New York Schools were integrated,
Not in Harlem, only the White
Teacher, 1940's**

TRUE STORIES OF SEGREGATION 347

SOUVENIR OF

SMALLS PARADISE ★ ★ ★

"The Talk of the Town"

★

135th Street and 7th Avenue
New York City

Home From World War II, 1940's

Segregated Military, World War II, 1940's

TRUE STORIES OF SEGREGATION

The Lynching Tree During Segregation

Segregated Public Facilities

TRUE STORIES OF SEGREGATION

"A Picture is worth a Thousands Words"
The Burning

**Segregated School Science Fair
St. Louis, Missouri, 1948**

TRUE STORIES OF SEGREGATION

**Segregated University Dormitory Room
Missouri, 1953**

Two Years After the 1954 School Decision, The English Bishop said: "You Remind Me of My Children In Africa".

**ROTC Cadet 1953
Segregated Unit, Lincoln University of Missouri**

STEREOTYPES

"CARRY ME BACK TO OLD VIRGINNY"

SONG

WORDS & MUSIC
BY
JAMES A. BLAND

WHALEY, ROYCE & CO., Limited
237 YONGE STREET   TORONTO, ONT.

Cover of an Original Sheet Music

Cover of Bert Williams' Original
Sheet Music, 1911

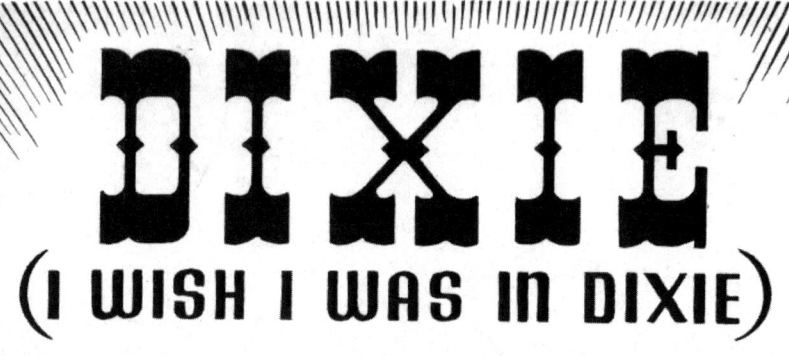

Cover of Original Sheet Music, 1936

TRUE STORIES OF SEGREGATION

Boy Eating Watermelon, 1930's

The TOM THUMB MINSTRELS

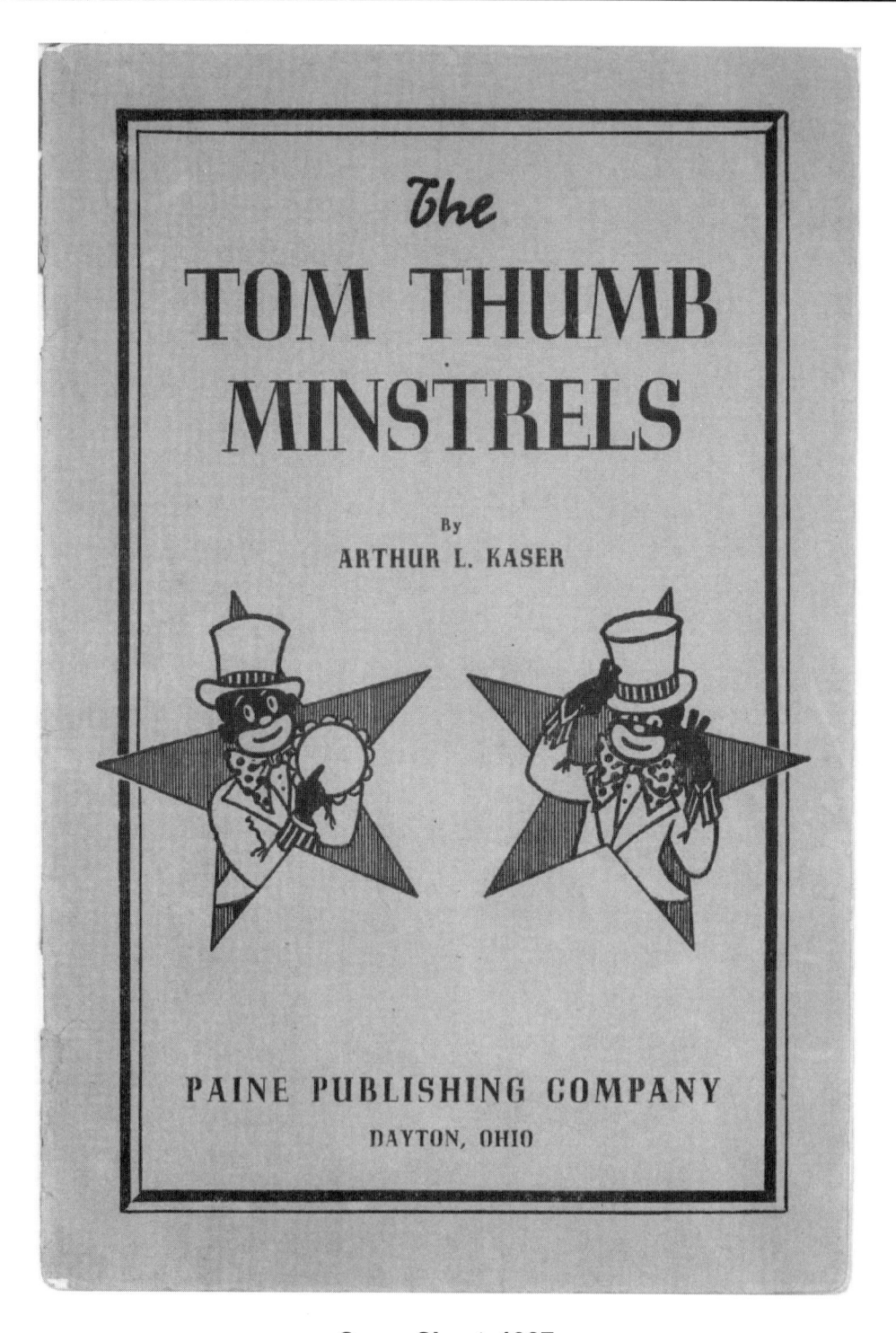

By
ARTHUR L. KASER

PAINE PUBLISHING COMPANY
DAYTON, OHIO

Cover Sheet, 1937

TRUE STORIES OF SEGREGATION

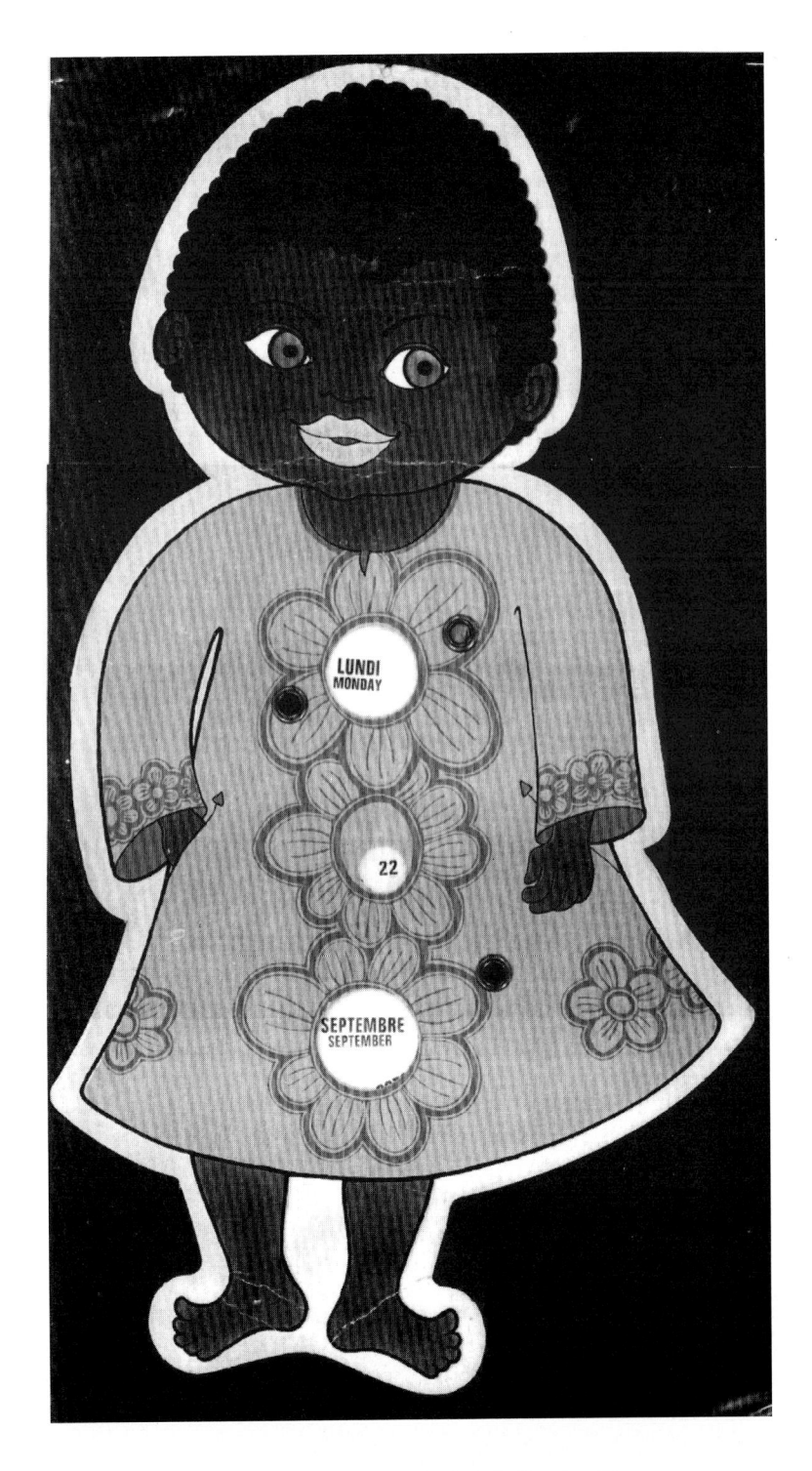

**French Calendar purchased, Paris, France
December, 1974**

THE BLACK EXPERIENCE

Nineteenth Street Baptist Church
Washington, DC, 1930
Church Missionary Society

Bessie Coleman
Pioneer Pilot, 1922

**Hampton Institute, Virginia
Class of 1916
(Note the Presence of Native Americans)**

TRUE STORIES OF SEGREGATION

**Judge William Hastie, Former Governor,
U.S. Virgin Islands, and Army Officer**

**Carver Community Center
Kansas City, Missouri
Board Members, Award Night 1950's**

Mary McLeod Bethune and Eleanor Roosevelt
1940's

**Lincoln University of Missouri
"Did Not Use Deliberate Speed in 1954"**

TRUE STORIES OF SEGREGATION

Twelfth Street Young Mens' Christian Association
Washington, DC, 1940's
Professional Community Members

374 TRUE STORIES OF SEGREGATION

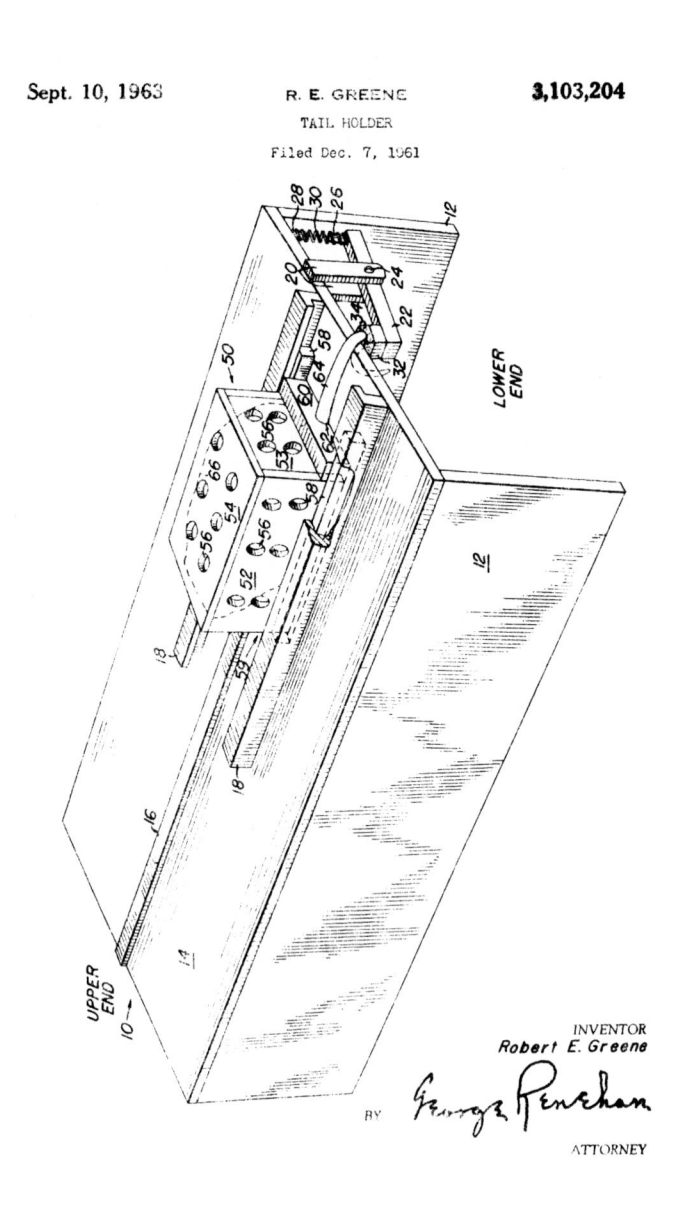

Sept. 10, 1963   R. E. GREENE   3,103,204
TAIL HOLDER
Filed Dec. 7, 1961

INVENTOR
Robert E. Greene

BY *George Renehan*
ATTORNEY

**R.E. Greene Small Animal Restrainer Invention
Patented September 10, 1963**

TRUE STORIES OF SEGREGATION 375

**George Washington Carver Community Center
Kansas City, Missouri, August, 1958
"Sightless Club"**

Daughters of the American Revolution (DAR)
Black Courage **Book Signing, 1985**

TRUE STORIES OF SEGREGATION

**DAR Book Signing
Present Were DAR President, Mrs. King
and U.S. Vice President Al Gore, 1985**

Director, National Selective Service, Gil Coronado
Presents an Award to Author.
At Left is Janice Wood Hunter

Black Defenders
Book Signing, 1974

Sister Beatrice Jeffries Assist
Haitian Woman in Florida

TRUE STORIES OF SEGREGATION

John H. Johnson, Johnson Publishing Company,
Doris Saunders, and Author

TRUE STORIES OF SEGREGATION

**Integrated Schools, U.S. Military
1974-1975**

TRUE STORIES OF SEGREGATION

**Integrated German School
Ruckingen, Germany, 1965**

TRUE STORIES OF SEGREGATION

"Two Brothers"
California
and
Paris France,
1974

Black Owned Business
St. Louis, Missouri, 1940's
Proprietors, Arthur A. Greene Sr. and Ruth N. Greene

FORD BROTHERS PHONOGRAPH CO.
100% NEGRO OWNED AND OPERATED)
"SERVICE WITH SATISFACTION"

CPL. ALFRED J. FORD

ELLIS V. FORD

LAFAYETTE FORD, JR.

JESSE DOWDY

ELLEN M. FORD

Black Owned Business
St. Louis, Missouri, 1950's

BLACK CULTURE

"THE FAMILY"

The Black Culture
The Early Black Family

TRUE STORIES OF SEGREGATION

**A Black Family During Segregation
1905 and 1930's**

Black Culture "The Family"
1930's and 1950's

TRUE STORIES OF SEGREGATION

**Black Culture
A Black Family, 1980's
The Anderson's**

Black Culture
Black Families, 1900's and 1970's

TRUE STORIES OF SEGREGATION

The Queen Family

The Wood Family

Black Culture - Black Families

Black Culture - Black Families
Greene, McAfee and Sanford

TRUE STORIES OF SEGREGATION

Black Culture
Sisters, 1920's

TRUE STORIES OF SEGREGATION

**Black Culture
The Greene's of Indiana**

Black Culture
The Conways, McCalla's, and Browns

TRUE STORIES OF SEGREGATION

**Black Culture
The Weddings**

**Black Culture
The Wills of North Carolina**

SPORTS - RECREATION

Sumner High School St. Louis, Missouri
Football Team, 1902 First Team

Sumner High School, St. Louis, Missouri
Football Team, 1905

Sumner High School's 1910 Team

Sumner High School's 1914 Team
One of the Greatest in Sumner History

We played Tennis in 1912-1913 at
Virginia Union University

M Street High School, Washington, DC
Girls Junior Team

Garrison Elementary School
Basketball Team, 1913, Washington, DC

Wissahickon School Club Basketball Team
Philadelphia, Pennsylvania, 1913

Livingstone College Football Team, 1912

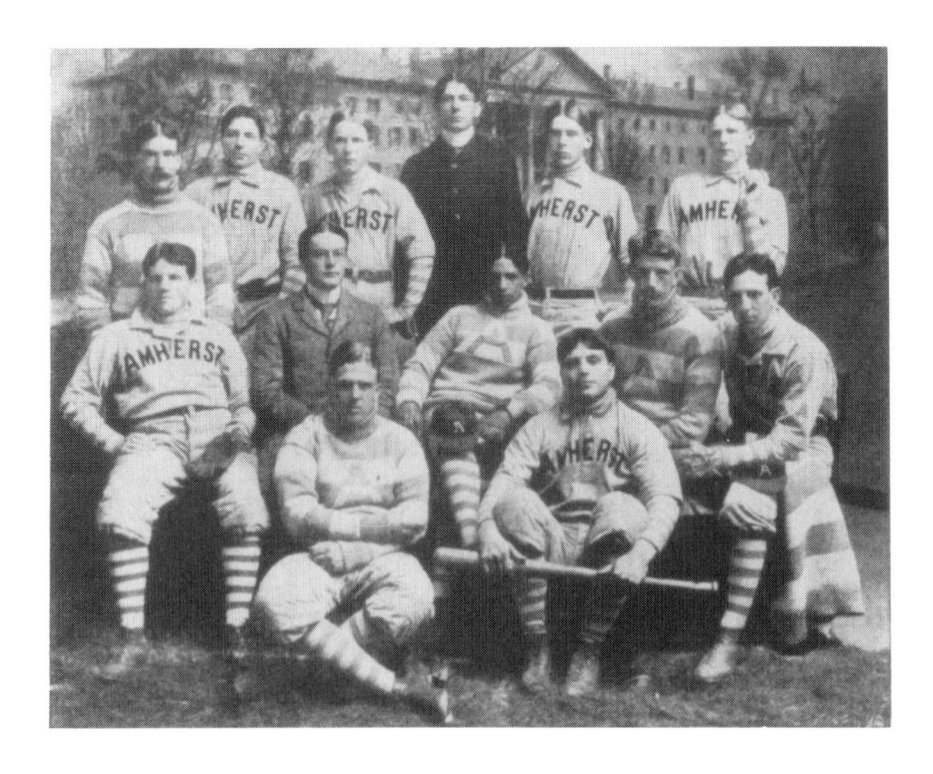

**Amherst College Baseball Team, 1898
included Man of Color, J. Francis Gregory**

M Street High School, Washington, DC
and Baltimore Colored High School
Basketball Teams, 1913

West Virginia Colored Institute
Third Girls Basketball Teams, 1912-1913

**West Virginia Colored Institute
Baseball Team, 1913**

Hilldale, Pennsylvania Baseball Club, 1913

**West Virginia Colored Institute
Basketball Team, 1913**

**Claver Catholic Club Basketball Team
Philadelphia, Pennsylvania**

**West Virginia Colored Institute
First Girls Basketball Team, 1912-1913**

**West Virginia Colored Institute
Second Girls Basketball Team, 1912-1913**

Hampton Institute Basketball Team, 1913
(Note: Two Native Americans)

Alpha Physical Culture Club Heavyweight
Basketball Team, New York Champions, 1912-1913

**Virginia Union University Baseball Team,
1913**

**Biddle University Baseball Team
Charlotte, North Carolina, 1913**

**Independent Pleasure Club
Basketball Team
East Orange, New Jersey, 1913**

**Tuskegee Institute, Alabama
Basketball Team, 1912-1913**

**Cardinal-Hiawatha Basketball Team
1913**

**Lincoln University Basketball Team
1912-1913**

TRUE STORIES OF SEGREGATION

**Commercial High School Track Team
Washington, DC, 1913**

**Jones School Basketball Team
1912**

Carver Center's Young Ladies Basketball Champs

**George Washington Carver Community Center
Kansas City, Missouri Adult Evening
Cooking Class, 1950's**

**The Eastern Board of Officials
1940's**

Carver Center Activities, 1950's

**Win or Lose, Donut Party
Carver Center, Kansas City, Missouri, 1950's**

TRUE STORIES OF SEGREGATION

Jesse Owens Berlin, 1936

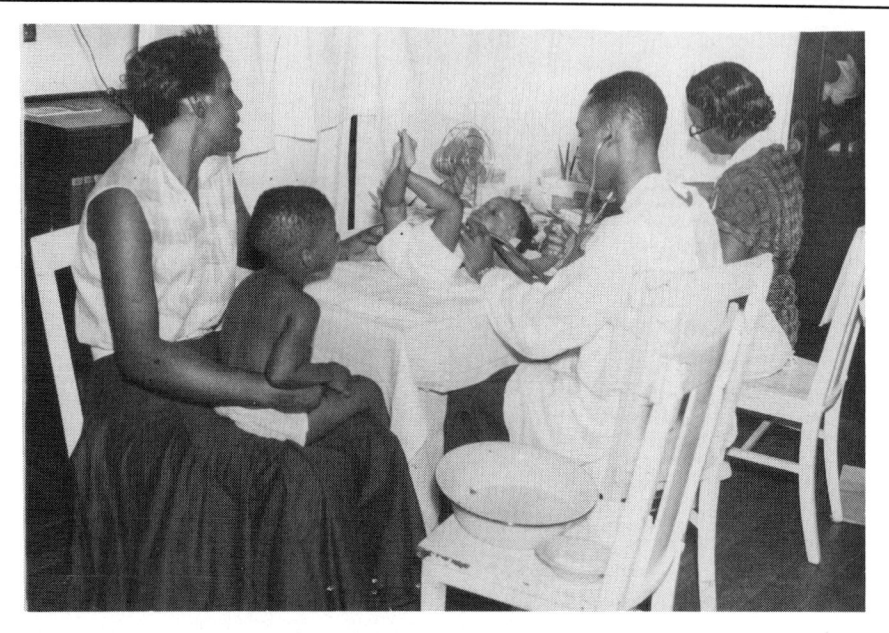

**Well Baby Clinic, Carver Center
Kansas City, Missouri, 1950's**

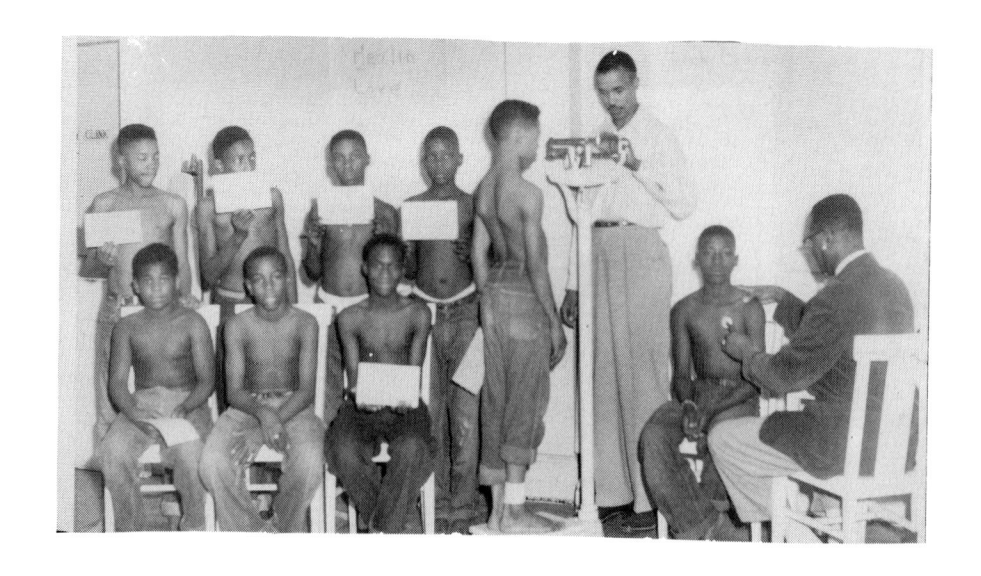

Physical Examination

TRUE STORIES OF SEGREGATION

Washington, DC's Segregated 12th Street YMCA, 1930's Volleyball, Y-Spikers

**Sports Integration, 1950's
Carver Center, Kansas City, Missouri**

Camp Fire Girls, 1954
Carver Center, Kansas City, Missouri

GENETIC DIVERSITY

Shades of Color

Annie Pryor Conway and daughters

**Genetic Diversity - Shades of Color
African, European, Jewish and Egyptian
The Conway Family**

Mary Conway Johnson
Father - English, Jew
Mother - Egyptian
Lived 100 years in America as a person of color

Genetic Diversity - Shades of Color
Harriet Proctor Smith
Mother of Thomas Sewell Inborden.
It has been inferred that he was
possibly the son of Robert E. Lee

**Shades of Color
Thomas Sewell Inborden Family**

TRUE STORIES OF SEGREGATION

Shades of Color - The Inbordens

Shades of Color
Murray Family, Washington, DC

Daniel Murray

Shades of Color - Oberlin, Ohio

TRUE STORIES OF SEGREGATION 431

**Wilson Bruce Evans, a Free Man of Color
And His Children, Oberlin, Ohio**

Shades of Color
Julia Evans Johnson and children

TRUE STORIES OF SEGREGATION

**Shades of Color
Julia E. Inborden Gordon and
Her mother, Sarah Jane Inborden**

Walter White

W. Hunton

Shades of Color

Shades of Color
Carmen Murray Bonde

**Shades of Color
Faculty, Brick School, North Carolina**

"I See the Colored Man Did Not Come"

Shades of Color
Oberlin College Students, 1880's

Shades of Color
Actor, Richard Harrison

TRUE STORIES OF SEGREGATION

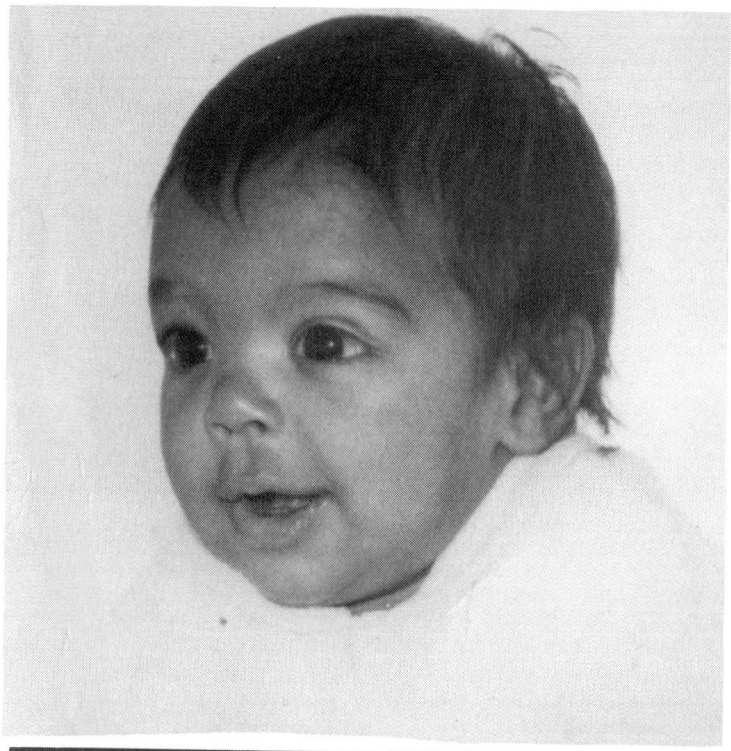

Zayne Grooms, Baby and Teenage pictures
Genetic Diversity, Shades of Color

Shades of Color

**Genetic Diversity
Father and Son**

TRUE STORIES OF SEGREGATION

441

**Genetic Diversity - Shades of Color
Jones - Boone Families of
North Carolina**

**Genetic Diversity - Shades of Color
Boone - Pittman Families
of North Carolina**

TRUE STORIES OF SEGREGATION

**Shades of Color
Brick School Students
North Carolina**

**Carey Pittman, Front Row,
Second right**

**Almyra Pittman Wills
Enfield, NC**

Genetic Diversity - Shades of Color

TRUE STORIES OF SEGREGATION 445

Shades of Color
Almyra Pittman Wills
1939   **1942**

TRUE STORIES OF SEGREGATION

**Shades of Color
Wills Family, Enfield, NC
1940's**

**Genetic Diversity
Spears of Alabama
African, Indian, European**

**Genetic Diversity-Shades of Color
Seminole Negro Indian Scout
Charles Daniels and Family**

Genetic Diversity - Shades of Color
Joseph Greene, Arthur A. Greene, Adam Greene
Evergreen, Alabama, 1920

Genetic Diversity - Shades of Color
Cecilia Spears Green
African, Indian and European

**Genetic Diversity - Shades of Color
The Green, Sisters
1930's**

**Genetic Diversity - Shades of Color
The Lum Family
African-Chinese and European**

TRUE STORIES OF SEGREGATION

**Genetic Diversity - Shades of Color
The Lum Family**

**Shades of Color
The Lums**

Brimming with Beauty

**Shades of Color
Howard University Ladies
1941**

**Genetic Diversity - Shades of Color
Wills and McAfee Families**

TRUE STORIES OF SEGREGATION   457

Genetic Diversity - Shades of Color

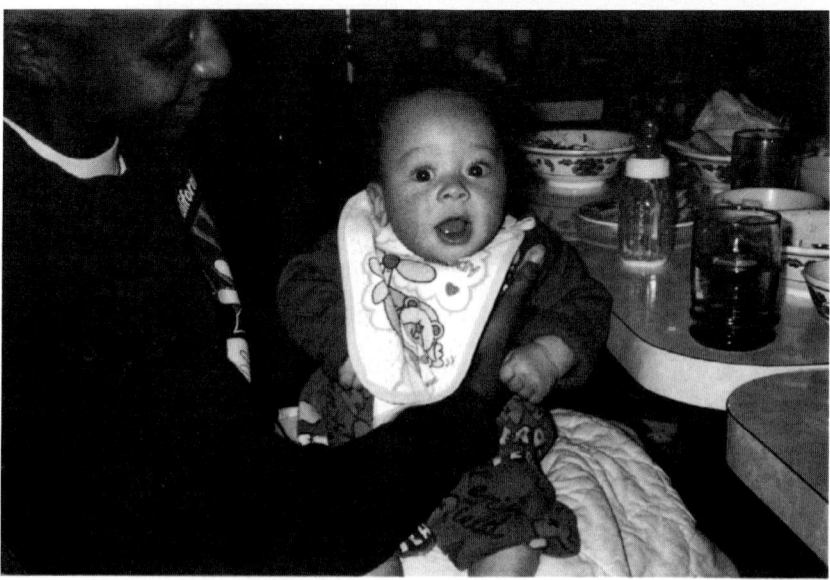

Genetic Diversity - Shades of Color

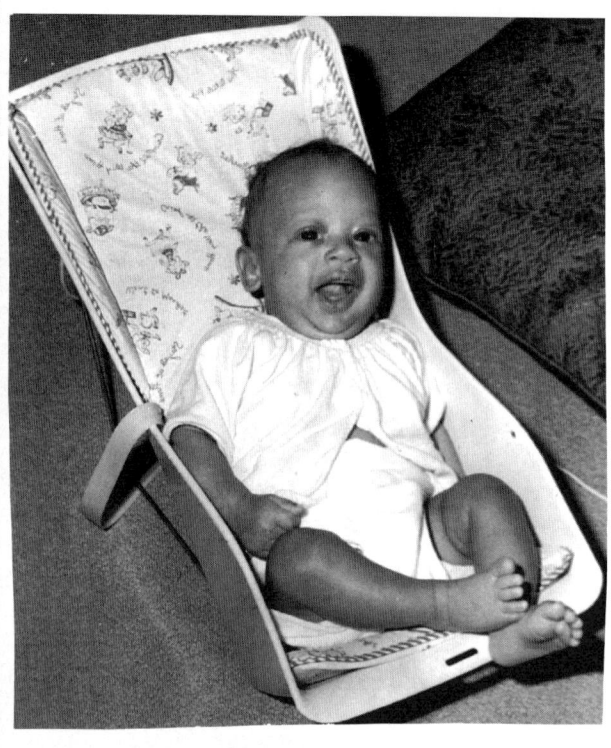

Genetic Diversity - Shades of Color

A Sorority, 1946

**A Sorority, 1970
Shades of Color**

TRUE STORIES OF SEGREGATION

Howard University Students, 1944

**Howard University Charter Day Committee, 1941
Shades of Color**

Genetic Diversity - Shades of Color

THE MILITARY

The Civil War Gunboat "Planter"
Charleston, South Carolina, 1862

**Tenth U.S. Cavalry Regiment
Polo Team, 1930's
The Segregated Years"**

**Hampton Institute, Virginia, 1900's
Student Cadets
(Native American Students were present)**

TRUE STORIES OF SEGREGATION

WINGS OVER JORDAN "OVERSEAS" CHOIR

World War II, They Entertained the Troops

184th Field Artillery Staff Officers

Great Lakes Negro Varsity, 1944
Back Row, R-L, Second Member, Larry Doby

TRUE STORIES OF SEGREGATION

**Chief Master Sergeant, Calvin McCoy
First Black Chief Master Sergeant of
U.S. Air Force**

**Admiral Samuel L. Gravely
First Black Admiral
U.S. Navy**

**Colonel Ruth Lucas, First Black Woman
In the U.S. Air Force. Promoted to Colonel
November 27, 1968
"They Paved The Way"**

TRUE STORIES OF SEGREGATION

Corporal Harold Johnson
U.S. Army, World War II

Technical Sergeant
Arthur Alonzo Greene, Jr.
U.S. Army, World War II

Heavy weight Champion (Sergeant) Joe Louis
with Mike Jacobs, presents his check of $89,000
to the World War II Effort to Admiral Andrews
"They Paved The Way"

TRUE STORIES OF SEGREGATION

**First Black Commander of the 3rd U.S. Infantry "Old Guard"
Fort Myer, Virginia**

"The Segregated Military"
Members, 372nd Infantry, Columbus, Ohio
leave for Fort Dix, New Jersey
March 16, 1941

TRUE STORIES OF SEGREGATION

**First Place Blood Award
Presentation
Fort McClellan, Alabama, 1965
"The Integrated Years"**

TRUE STORIES OF SEGREGATION

1st ENGINEER OFFICER BASIC CLASS
Fort Belvoir, Virginia
Ent 11 Jul 55 - Grad 14 Oct 55

1st Row	2nd Row	3rd Row	4th Row	5th Row	6th Row	7th Row	8th Row	9th Row	Row 10
Lt Arnette	Lt Walter	Lt Feldbruegge	Lt Ross	Lt Sokolich	Lt Ream	Lt Claxton	Lt LaBelle	Lt Woods	Capt Halliburton
Lt Stonehocker	Lt Carlson	Lt Arndt	Lt Strzeleck	Lt Allen	Lt Collins	Lt Ator	Lt Holland	Lt Minker	Lt McGhee
Lt McCray	Lt Bauer	Lt Carnahan	Lt Muncy	Lt Brunkow	Lt Smith D A	Lt Moses	Lt Clark	Lt DeGraw	Lt Carter
Lt Iwamoto	Lt Bailey	Lt Phelps	Lt Dillon	Lt Hickey	Lt Manson	Lt Corr	Lt Sorensen	Lt Day	
Lt Caputo	Lt Pouls	Lt Kautz	Lt Ferrini	Lt Gump	Lt White	Lt Prendergast	Lt Dzubak	Lt Harper	
Lt Mellegaard	Lt Williams	Lt Carson	Lt Horn	Lt Pigg	Lt Flynn	Lt York	Lt Rundle	Lt Saro	
Lt Rygh	Lt Blankinship	Lt Foster	Lt Hollis	Lt Walters	Lt Paxton	Lt Nutting	Lt Jones	Lt Perry	
Lt Lippman	Lt Falco	Lt Raymond	Lt Pierce	Lt Keating	Lt Colaianni	Lt Kaminski	Lt Jacobs	Lt Crull	
Lt Young	Lt Miles	Lt Wheeler	Lt Kellner	Lt Senft	Lt Greene	Lt Preisendorfer	Lt Colley	Lt Anderson	
Lt Ritchie	Lt Gavito	Lt Hamilton	Lt Valk	Lt Cochrane	Lt Wagoner	Lt Carpenter	Lt Fraher	Lt Borchers	
Lt Manson	Lt Bryant	Lt Wartur	Lt Palmer	Lt Nall	Lt Seldon	Lt Giambruno	Lt Haelig	Lt Pollock	
Lt Cruickshank	Lt Robbins	Lt Goodlett	Lt Casella	Lt Perkins	Lt Wood	Lt Smith H D	Lt Schwamm		

"The Early Days, an Integrated U.S. Military, 1955"

TRUE STORIES OF SEGREGATION

**Lieutenant General Arthur Gregg presents
the "Legion of Merit" to the Author,
Munich, Germany, 1975**

"An Integrated Military"
12th Chemical Maintenance Company
First Place Drill Team
Fort McClellan, Alabama, 1965

U.S. ARMY EUROPE

RACE RELATIONS SCHOOL

Germany, 1972

School Emblem

TRUE STORIES OF SEGREGATION

US-Soldaten auf der Schule Völkerverständigung

Donnerstag, 14. September 1972 Seite 3

"DIE FARBE IST EGAL": Dieser Botschaft will Major Robert E. Greene in seiner Schule zum Durchbruch verhelfen.

Fotos: Christine Strub

Vorurteile sollen abgebaut werden

Die Hautfarbe ist egal

Major Green plädiert im Rahmen der "Woche der Brüderlichkeit" für Verständnis

"Viele Deutsche wissen kaum etwas über den amerikanischen Neger, und einige Deutsche fürchten ihn sogar." Diese Feststellung traf der Direktor der Schule für Rassenbeziehungen der amerikanischen Streitkräfte in Europa, Major Robert E. Green aus München, bei seinem Vortrag im Rahmen der "Woche der Brüderlichkeit", zum Thema "Gedanken Deutscher über schwarze Soldaten" im oberen Rathausfletz. "Schaue keinen Neger an, sonst ist er verärgert", charakterisierte Major Green die Gedanken vieler Deutscher über die amerikanischen Neger. Der Hauptgrund für diese Angst liege jedoch daran, daß ihnen der Farbige fremd sei, weil sie keine Gelegenheit hätten, ihn kennzulernen.

Ferner hätten, so Green, die Deutschen viele amerikanische Vorurteile übernommen. Dennoch dürfe man es nicht als ein Vorurteil gegen die Farbigen verwenden, wenn man in Deutschland "Mohrenpuppen" oder "Negerpuppen" für Kinder kaufen könne, was heute in Amerika als Gegenstand des Anstoßes oder der Rassenbeleidigung betrachtet werde.

Major Green zählte dann einige Vorurteile der Deutschen gegenüber Farbigen auf: "Die Deutschen haben noch ihre Empfindungen aus den Tagen von Onkel Tom und der Sklavenperiode, einige haben einen angeborenen Rassenhaß, viele sind neugierig auf das "Schwarze" und wollen Neuland erforschen, andere glaubten ernsthaft, daß es in Deutschland keine Rassenvorurteile gegenüber Schwarzen gibt, Angst und mangelnde Kenntnis der amerikanischen Schwarzen erschweren das Rassenproblem."

Dennoch, so Green, versuchten viele Deutsche die Beziehungen zwischen den Rassen zu verbessern. Man müsse die individuellen Eigenarten der Schwarzen, wie farbenfrohe, spektakuläre Kleider und anderen Haarstil, akzeptieren, da sie damit ihre ursprünglichen Beziehungen zu Afrika zeigen wollten. In den letzten Jahren seien Fortschritte in der Integration der Schwarzen gemacht worden. Green: "Wir müssen aber auch sehen, daß die Abstempelung einiger Deutscher zu weißen Rassenfanatikern das Problem nicht lösen kann. Deutsche und Amerikaner aller Farben dürfen keine Mühe scheuen, um zu erkennen: Die Farbe ist egal."

it

DIE FARBIGEN KENNENLERNEN: Major Green plädierte für den Abbau der Vorurteile gegenüber schwarzen Amerikanern.

AZ-Bild: Studio Müller

**German Press Coverage of
the Race Relations School's opening, 1972**

Guest Speaker, Major General Frederic Davison

Guest Speaker, Major General Haywood
Graduation Exercises, Race Relations School

Race Relations School Slogan
1972
Painting by artist, Ruth Greene Richardson

Major General Hayward
Deputy Chief of Staff for Personnel
U.S. Army Europe, 1972
The Architect of the Race Relations School
Germany

TRUE STORIES OF SEGREGATION

**U.S. Army Europe Race Relations School
German Press Conference, Oberammergau, Germany, 1972**

**Race Relations School
Munich, Germany, 1973-1975**

TRUE STORIES OF SEGREGATION

Zum Arbeitsbeginn der Schule für rassische Beziehungen der US-Armee im Rasthaus Bernau waren auch die beiden farbigen Generäle Cartwright (links) und Shuffer (rechts) anwesend, die unser Bild im Fachgespräch mit Major Robert Greene, dem Leiter der Schule, zeigt.

Foto Berger

„Die Farbe ist egal"

**Guest Speakers, Race Relations School
Bernau, Chiemse, Germany, 1973
Brigadier Generals Cartwright and Shuffer**

BIBLIOGRAPHY

BIBLIOGRAPHY

PRIMARY SOURCES

Manuscript Collection

Thomas Sewell Inborden papers
Manuscript Division, Library of Congress, Washington, DC

- Newton D. Baker Papers
- W.H. Coston Collection
- Frederick Douglass Papers
- Christian Fleetwood Papers
- NAACP Collection
- Beverly Perea Papers
- John W. Pershing Papers
- Carter G. Woodson Papers

Moorland Spingarn Research Center, Howard University, Washington, DC

- Anna J. Cooper Papers
- Colonel Campbell C. Johnson Papers
- Mary Ann Shadd Papers
- Lucy Slowe Collection
- Mary Church Terrell Papers
- Mary O.H. Williams Papers

National Archives, Washington, D.C.

- Military Intelligence Division Papers (Colonel Charles Young), RG 165
- Military Pension Files, RG15 of the Adjutant General's Office
- Miscellaneous Navy Records, (Robert Smalls) RG 45
- Records of The Commission of Claims, Southern Claims Commission, 1871-1886

State Archives

Alabama State Archives and History, Montgomery, Alabama
Miscellaneous Manuscript Papers

Hall of Records, Maryland Archives, Annapolis, Maryland
Miscellaneous Manuscript Papers

Mississippi State Archives, Jackson, Mississippi
Miscellaneous Manuscript Papers

Ohio Historical Society
Paul Laurence Dunbar Papers
George Meyer Papers

South Carolina, Department of Archives and History,
    Columbia, South Carolina
Miscellaneous Manuscript Papers

Tennessee State Archives
Miscellaneous Manuscript Papers

Virginia State Archives, Richmond, Virginia
Miscellaneous Manuscript Papers

Newspapers

Afro American (Baltimore and Washington)
Arizona Informant (Phoenix)
Atlanta Journal and Constitution
Baltimore Sun
Black Chronicle (Oklahoma)
Boston Globe
Boston Guardian
Chicago Defender
Chicago Tribune
Cleveland Plain Dealer
Dallas Morning News
Detroit News

Enfield Progress
Hartford Courant
Helena Montana Newspaper
Houston Chronicle
Indianapolis Star
International Herald Tribune
Kansas City Call
Kansas City Star
Los Angeles Sun
Los Angeles Times
Miami Herald
New Orleans Times-Picayune
Newark Star Ledger
New and Observer (Raleigh, NC)
News Tribute (Oberlin, Ohio)
New York Age
New York Times
Norfolk Journal and Guide
Norfolk Virginia - Pilot
Orlando Sentinel
Pentagram News
Philadelphia Inquirer
Pittsburgh Courier
Pittsburgh Post-Gazette
Portland Oregonian
Prince George's Journal (Maryland)
Richmond Times Dispatch
Rocky Mount Telegram (North Carolina)
San Francisco Chronicle
St. Louis American
St. Louis Argus
St. Louis Post Dispatch
USA Today
Washington Post
Washington Times
Winston Salem Chronicle

Periodicals and Magazines

Journals

Army and Navy Journal
Cavalry Journal
Congressional Record
Journal of American Medical Association
Journal of the American Pharmaceutical Association
Journal of American History
National Medical Association
Negro History Bulletin
Negro History Journal
Utah Historical Quarterly

Magazines

Colored American
Cosmopolitan
Crisis
Ebony
Jet
Messenger
Opportunity
Southern Workman

Interviews

Allen, Harriet, conversations, 1988, 1989, 1991-2, Washington, DC
Miller, Inborden Dorothy, Conversations, 1976-1979 and 1992, Washington, DC

Personal Notes

Class lectures, unpublished and published manuscripts, and photographs from the Library of Robert Ewell Greene

Secondary Source

Books

Abingdom Press. *Songs of Zion*. Nashville, Tennessee: Abingdom Press, 1981

Bigglestone, William E. They *Stopped In Oberlin, Black Residents and Visitors of the Nineteenth Century*. Arizona: Innovation Group Inc., 1981.

Blackson, Augustus P. et. al. *Affray At Brownsville, Texas*, 1900.

Brandt, Nat. *The Town That Started The Civil War*, Syracuse: University Press, 1990.

Brawley, Benjamin. *A Short History of The American Negro*. New York: MacMillan Company, 1931.

Brown, Letitia. *The Negro in The District of Columbia*. New York: Oxford University Press, 1972.

Butcher, Margaret Just. *The Negro In American Culture*. New York: Alfred A. Knopf, 1956.

Davis, Arthur P. *Here and There with the Rattler*. Detroit: Harlo Press, 1929.

Cheek, William and Cheek, Annie Lee. *John Mercer Langston and the Fight for Black Freedom*, 1829-65. Chicago: University of Illinois Press, 1989.

Coston, Hilary W. *The Spanish American War Volunteers*, 1899.

Cox, Oliver C. *Caste, Color and Race*. New York: Modern Readers, 1970.

Cullen, Contee. *Color*. New York: Harpers and Brothers Publishers, 1925.

Dann, Martin E. *The Black Press, 1827-1890. The Quest For National Identity*. New York: G.P. Putnam and Sons, 1971.

Davis, Cyprian. *The History of Black Catholics in the United States*. New York: The Crossland Publishing Company, 1992.

Director of Selective Service. Selective Service In Wartime 2nd Report 1941-1952. Washington, DC: US Government Printing Office, 1945.

Director of Selective Service. Selective Service. *As the Tide of The War Turns, 3rd Report 1943-1944.* Washington, DC: US Government Printing Office, 1948.

Director of Selective Service. Selective Service and Victory, 4th Report 1943-1944. Washington DC: US Government Printing Office, 1948.

Dubois, W.E.B. *Black Folk, Then and Now: an Essay on the History and Sociology of the Negro Race.* New York: Henry Holt and Co., 1939.

Editors of Ebony. *The Ebony Handbook.* Chicago: Johnson Publishing Co., 1974.

Fleming G. James and Burckel Christian E. *Who's Who In Colored America.* New York: Christian E. Burckel and Associates, 1950.

Foley, Albert S. *Beloved Outeasts.* New York: Farrar, Straws, 1955.

Foy, Felician ed. 1992 *Catholic Almanac.* Huntington, Indiana: Our Sunday Visitor, Publishing Division, Inc., 1992.

Franklin, John H. and Isidore Starr eds. *The Negro In the 20th Century America.* New York: Vintage Books, Random House, 1967.

Franklin, John Hope ed. *Color and Race.* Boston: Beacon Press, 1969.

Franklin, John Hope. *From Slavery To Freedom, A History of Negro Americans.* New York: Alfred A. Knopf Inc., 1980.

Frazier, E. Franklin. *The Negro Family in the United States.* Chicago: University of Chicago Press, 1939.

Garland I., et. al. *The University of Life or Practical Self Educator.* Nashville, Tennessee: Southwestern Company, 1900.

Greene, Robert E. *Black Defenders of America, 1775-1973.* Chicago: Johnson Publishing Co., 1974.

Greene, Robert E. *They Rest Among The Known.* Washington, DC: Yancy Graphics, 1981.

Greene, Robert E. *Delta Memories A Historical Summary.* Washington, DC: Yancy Graphics, 1981.

Greene, Robert E. *Black Courage 1775-1783.* Washington, DC: National Society of the Daughters of the America Revolution, Washington, DC, 1984.

Greene, Robert E. *The Saga of Sydney A. Moore.* Washington, DC: R.E. Greene Publisher, 1985.

Greene, Robert E. *Colonel Charles Young, Soldier and Diplomat* Washington, DC: R.E. Greene Publishers, 1985.

Greene, Robert E. *Teach Me To Learn Biology, Simple To The Complex.* Washington, DC: R.E. Greene Publisher, 1987.

Greene, Robert E. *True Tales For Children, Young Adults and Adults.* Washington, DC: R.E. Greene Publisher, 1987.

Greene, Robert E. *Robert A. Thornton, Master Teacher, Scholar, Physicist and Humanist.* Fort Washington, Maryland: R.E. Greene Publisher, 1988.

Greene, Robert E. *Leary-Evans, Ohio's Free People of Color.* Washington, DC: Hickman Printing, Inc., 2nd edition, 1989.

Greene, Robert E. *The Conway, McAfee, People of Color.* Fort Washington, Maryland: R.E. Greene Publisher, 1989.

Greene, Robert E. *A Biographical Study of the 54th Massachusetts Regiment, Swamp Angels*: Fort Washington, Maryland: Bo/Mark/Greene Publishing Group, 1990.

Greene, Robert E. *Black Defenders of the Persian Gulf War, Desert Shield Desert Storm.* Fort Washington, Maryland: R.E. Greene Publishers, 1991.

Greene, Robert E. *They Did Not Tell Me True Facts About African Americans In the African and American Experiences.* Fort Washington, Maryland: R.E. Greene Publisher, 1992.

Greene, Robert E. *They Did Not Tell Me True Facts About African Americans In the African and American Experiences.* Fort Washington, Maryland: R.E. Greene Publisher, 1992.

Greene, Robert E. *A Pictorial Tribute To The Tuskegee Airmen of World War II.* Fort Washington, Maryland: R.E. Greene Publisher, 1992.

Greene, Robert E. *The Ebony Matriarch Mothers of Color Through The Years.* Fort Washington, Maryland: R.E. Greene Publishers, 1993.

Greene, Robert E. *The Way We Were True Stories of Yesteryears.* Fort Washington, Maryland: R.E. Greene Publishers, 1993.

Greene, Robert E. *Who Were The Real Buffalo Soldiers?* Fort Washington, Maryland: R.E. Greene Publisher, 1994.

Greene, Robert E. *Thomas Sewell Inborden, Early Educator of Color.* Fort Washington, Maryland: R.E. Greene Publisher, 1996.

Greene, Robert E. *Physicians and Surgeons of Color Real Image Models For Youth and Adults* Fort Washington, Maryland: R.E. Greene Publisher, 1996.

Greene, Robert E. *Black Presence In World History* Fort Washington, Maryland: R.E. Greene Publisher, 1997.

Gunnar, Mydral. *An American Dilemma, The Negro Problem and Modern Democracy* New York: Harper and Brothers, 1944.

Hare-Cuney, Maude. *Negro Musicians and Their Music.* Washington, D.C.: The Associated Publisher, Inc., 1936.

Harris, James I. (compiler) *Biographical Directory of the America Congress 1774-1949.* Washington, DC: United States Government Printing Office, 1950.

Henderson, Edwin B. *The Negro In Sports.* Washington, DC: The Associated Publisher, 1949.

Hickok, Charles Thomas. *The Negro In Ohio 1902-1970.* New York: AMS Press Inc., 1975.

Huggins, Nathan. *Harlem Renaissance.* New York: Oxford University Press, 1974.

Hutchinson, Louise Daniel. *Anna J. Cooper, A Voice From The South.* Washington: Smithsonian Institution Press, 1987.

Isaacs, Edith. *The Negro In the American Theatre.* New York: Theatre Arts, 1947.

Lamb, Daniel Smith. *Howard University Medical Department* Washington, DC: Beresford Printers, 1900.

Lawson, Jesse. *How To Solve The Race Problem.* Washington, DC: Beresford Printer, 1904.

Lee, Ulysses. *The Employment of Negro Troops.* Washington, DC: US Government, 1966.

Logan, Raymond. *Howard University, The First Hundred years 1867-1967.* New York: New York University Press, 1969.

Lum, Maria C. *A Gift From God: The Story of a Mongoloid Boy.* New York: Vantage Press, 1971.

Major, Gerri and Saunders, Doris. *Black Society.* Chicago, Illinois: Johnson Publishing Co., 1976.

McCorkle, Lucy Helena Howell. *The Anatomy of the Howell Family Descendants of Harry and Mary Howell 1808-1982.* Washington, DC: R.E. Greene Publisher, 1982.

Murray, Florence, ed. *The Negro Handbook, 1949.* New York: The Macmillian Co., 1949.

Murray, Paula, ed. *State Laws On Race and Color.* Cincinnati, Ohio: The Women's Division of Christian Service. Board of Missions and Church Extension, the Methodist Church, 1951.

Pipkin, J.J. *The Negro In Revelation in History and in Citizenship.* St. Louis, Missouri: A.D. Thompson Publishing Co., 1902.

Quillan, Frank U. *The Color Line In Ohio.* Anne Arbor, Michigan: George Wahr, 1913.

Richardson, Clement. *The National Encyclopedia of the Colored Race.* Montgomery, Alabama: National Publishing Co., 1919.

Rogers, Joel A. *Amazing Facts About The Negro.* New York: J.A. Rogers Publisher, 1934.

Stewart, Theophilus G. *The Colored Regulars in the United States Army. Philadelphia: AME Book Concern, 1904.*

Smith, Augustine H. *Lyric Religion, The Romance of Immortal Hymns.* New York: The Century Co., 1931.

U.S. Army Service Forces Manual. *Training Leadership and the Negro Soldier. Headquarters Army Service Forces.* Washington, DC: U.S. Government Printing Office, 1944.

Vroman, Mary Elizabeth. *Shaped To Its Purpose: Delta Sigma Theta. The First Fifty Years.* New York: Random House, 1965.

Watkins, Sylvester C. *Anthology of American Negro Literature.* New York: Random House, 1944.

Wesley, Charles H. *The Negro In Our History.* Washington, DC: The Associated Publishers Inc. 1966.

Wilkinson, Frederick (ed.) *Dictionary of Graduates Howard University 1870-1963.* Washington, DC: Howard University, 1963.

Woodson, Carter G. *The Negro In Our History.* Washington, DC: The Associated Publishers, Inc., 1931.

Work, John W. *American Negro Songs and Spirituals.* New York: Dover Publications Inc., 1940.

Work, Monroe Ed. *New Year Book: An Annual Encyclopedia of the Negro, 1937-1938.* Tuskegee, Alabama: Negro year Book Publishing Co., 1937.

Young, Charles. Little Handbook of French Creole As Spoken in Haiti, 1905.

INDEX

A

Abyssinian Baptist Church, 154
Acadians, 237
Adams Family, 281
Adams, Frank, 47, 166
Adams, John Quincy, 281
Adams, Louis, 65
Admission Black Physicians, 165-166
Affirmative Dialogue, 106-107, 108
African American's Obsession of Color, 271-273
Agricultural Adjustment Administration, 144
"Aint No Kin To Her", 256
Airport Homes Riot, 23
Alabama Legal Zoning Cases, 23
Alcorn, Senator, 140, 141
Alexandria, Virginia, 303
Alzheimer Disease, 266
"All God's Chillum Got Wings", 194
Allen, Grace, 170
Allen-Grove Rosenwald School, 296
Allen, Harriet, 2
Allen, Shep, 71
Allensworth, Allen, 33
Almost an Aggie Alumnus, 261
Alpha Xi Delta Sorority, 52
Amalgamation Georgia Style, 250
"Amazing Grace", 198
American Bar Association, 183, 184
American Correctional Association, 181
American Indian Citizens of California, 21
American Jewish Committee, 21
American Missionary Association, 49, 50, 54, 206, 213, 255, 269, 270
American Red Cross, 184, 185
American Tennis Association, 128
American Trapshooting Association, 130
American Veterans Committee, 21
Ames, Chester, 165
Ames, J.W., 165
Ames, Senator, 140, 141
Amos and Andy, 73, 74
Amsterdam, 74, 74
Anderson, Marian, 187, 190
Anderson, William, 30
Andrews, Attorney, 210-212
Andrews, John, 262
Anniston, Alabama, 98, 158
Antone Bailey's True Story, 326-334
Anthropological Investigation, Mulatto Type, 240-242
Arcadia, Missouri, 331
Archdiocese of Northern Virginia, 304
Are you going to examine me?, 163-164
Arizona, Naco, 324
Arlington County, Virginia, 304
Arlington County, Virginia Medical Society, 186
Arlington National Cemetery, 325
Arlington VA Public Schools, 41, 42
Armwood, George, 181
Arnell, Ellis, 177
Artis, Lucinda, 295
Arthur, John P., 307
Asian Perceptions, 81
Auburn, New York, 182
Augusta, Alexander, 109
Atlantic Coast Line Railroad, 321
Atlantic City, New Jersey, 320
Atlanta, Georgia, 333, 337
Atlanta University, 54

B

Babbitt, Dean, 274
Badger, Roderick, 171
Bailey, Antone, 4
Bailey, Clifford, 4, 326
Bailey, Frances, 332
Bailey, Juanita, 4, 326
Bailey, Sadie, 4
Bakke, Allen, 43
Bald Heads and Stocking Caps, 222
Ball, Pat, 129
Baltimore Orioles, 127
Baltimore Western High School, 214
Banks, Dennis, 65
Banks, Porter, 261
Banks, William, 261
Barker, Oner, 166
Barnes, William, 156-157
Bassett, Angela, 1
Battle, Cullen, 268
Battle, Mark, 268
Battle of the Bulge, 330
Battle of St. Louis, 330
Battlesboro, North Carolina, 293-295
Bauer, John, 290
Baumunk, John, 47
Bavaria, Germany, 265
Baylies, George Mrs., 188
Beach Segregation, 101
Beaches, 202
Beale, John C., Jr., 276
Beard, Dr., 213, 268
Beaufort County, South Carolina, 282
Becker, Noerg, 79
Beckett, W.H.J., 131-135
Becroft, Marie, 264
Becroft, William, 264
Beecham, Grandma, 204
Belasco Rialto Theatre, 187, 188
Bell, Pittman Ozette, 295
Belvedere, 24

Benjamin Franklin Hotel, 104
Benrus Watch Company, 332,333
Berea College, 54
Berea College v. Kentucky, 31
Bergan, P.F.C., 309
Bernadotte, Count Folks, 150
Bernau, Germany, 307
Berry, Leonidas, 165-166
Bethune, McCleod Mary, 208
Birmingham, Alabama, 266
Bisbee, 324
Bishopville, NC, 214
Black, Arnold, 280
Black and Korean Proverbs, 72
Blacks and Sports Obsession, 131-134
"Black Body Problem", 223, 224
Black Caucus, 190-247
Black, Charles, 280
Black Communication, 73
Black Confederate Combatant, 307
Black Culture, 206, 107
Black Culture and African Awareness, 218, 219
Black Culture-Genetic Diversity, 199-
Black Disenfranchisement, 148
Black Dispatch Newspaper, 320
Black Families, 275
Black Forest, 330
Black, George, 280
Black, Gordon, 280
Black Horace G., 280
Black Jockey at Lexington, 323
Black, Julia, 280
Black Ministers, 203
Black Pete, 74
Black Social Problems, 216-217
Black, Sidney, 280
Black Sports Officials, 130
Black, Stanley, 280
Black, William, 280
Black Women Athletes, 129

Blackstone Club, 183
Blaylock, Albert, 166-167
Blackwell's Island, NY, 181
Blockbusting Policy, 25
Blood Banks, 306
Blue-baby Syndrome, 167
B'nai B'rith, 21
Boaz, Sophia, 184
Bolding, 15
Boler, William, 1
Bolling Air Force Base, 297
Bolton, Francis, 189
Bomop, 15
Bond, Caroline, 240, 241, 242
Boone, Dolly, 294
Boon, Elizabeth, 295
Boon, Jesse, 295
Boone, Laura S., 295
Boone, Octavius, 295
Boone, Pittman, Viola, 295
Bonner, Lyncia, 122
Bowen, J.W.E., 54
Bragg, Thomas, 294
Brandeis, Louis, 267
Brandeis, Susan, 267
Brandeis University, 267
Brandywine Area, 238
Brazil, 320
Breast Feeding and the Brain, 168
Bremerhaven, Germany, 311
Brick School, NC, 175, 214, 268, 271
Broker's Agreement, 21
Bromley, Ernest, 65
Brooks, Harry W. Jr., 308-309
Brooks, Walter, 43
Brown, Anne, 195-196
Brown, Dorothy, 155-156
Brown, Fielding 289
Brown, Harry, 196
Brown, John, 290
Brownsville Community, 22
Bruce, B.K., 140, 141, 143, 213

Brucker, Wilbur, 137
Bruer, Alice, 247, 248
Boston, Massachusett, 331
Bullock, Benjamin, 215
Bullock, George, 215
Bullock, Joseph, 215
Bullock, Lula, 215
Bruce, William, 289
Bunche, Joan, 6
Bunche, Ralph, 127, 148, 149, 150, 151, 221, 250
Bureau of Pensions, 223
Burger, Chief Justice, 190
Burgoin, Mary O., 109
Burlington, Iowa, 334
Burr, Johnny, 6
Bush, President, 306
Busing, 35
Butler, William, 71
Burton, Harold, 64
Bryan, Albert V. Jr., 42
Bryan, Albert V. Sr., 42
Byone, Ida, 129

C

Cady, Secretary, 270
Calbert, Sadie, 33
Calbert, William, 33
California Bar Association, 183
Calhoun, John, 77
Callender, Maurice, 104
Callender, Stanton, 104
Cambridge University, 250
Camden, Alabama, 274
Camp Columbus, New Mexico, 299
Camp Funston, Kansas, 172
Camp Robert Smalls, 321
Camp Stewart, Georgia, 329
Campbell, Charles, 287
Camper, John, 166

Cananea, 324
Cantonese Chinese, 293
Cantor, Eddie, 72
Cape, Hatteras, 286
Cape May, New Jersey 282
Cape Verdians, 231, 236-237
Capitilization, Word Negro, 236
Carnegie Library, 42
Carroll, Charles, 264
Carroll, E. Mae, 165
Carroll, Joseph, 55, 56
Carrs Beach, 101
Carson, Mr. and Mrs., 15
Carter, Arthur, 276
Carter, Jimmy, 143
Cartwright, Mrs., 308
Cartwright, Roscoe, 307, 308
Carver, George Washington, 207
Cary, Lieutenant, 290
Casablanca, 301
Casablanca Conference, 300
Case, Clifford, 178
Case of Two Photographs, 322
Cash, John, 320
Caste System, 199
"Catch The Next Train North", 323
Catholic Immaculate Conception
  School, 293
Catholic Sisterhoods, 62
Caucasian Definition of an African
  American, 250-253
CCC, 67, 68, 69
Cemeteries, 108
Centenary United Methodist
  Church, 293
Chambers, H.H., 142
Chambers, Jordan, 10, 13
Chaney, 295
Chapel Hill, North Carolina, 211
Charles County, MD, 258
Charleston, South Carolina, 195, 196,
  283, 284, 286, 292, 293

Charlotte, NC, 215
Chase, Julia, 280
Chatham, Canada, 280
Chesapeake Bay, 286
Cherokee County, Georgia, 221
Chesterfield, Missouri, 331
Chestnut, W. Calvin, 103
Chicago Defender, 8
Chicken Bone Beach, 101
Chico, California, 117
Chiemse, Germany, 307
China, 292
Chinese, 293
Chinese Consulate, 293
Chinese Interpreter, 293
Chinese Laundry, 292
Ching, Lem Yu, 292
Chisolm, Patrick, 309
Chung, Lem Yu, 292, 293
Church, Robert, 94
Church Statistics, 55
Churchill, Governor, 324
Churchill, Winston, 301
CIAA, 130
Ciognani, Amleto, 52
Circle Theatre, 12
City Called Heaven, 196
Clark, Frances, 223
Clark, John, 222
Clark, Pittman Geraldine, 295
Clark University, 54
Clarke, David, 189
Class System, 199-201
Clay, Henry, 276
Clement, Rufus, 70
Cleveland, Grover, 142, 143
Cleveland, Ohio, 190, 194
Clifford, Colonel, 17
Clifford, Maurice, 166
Clifton, Sweet Water, 123
Clinton, William, 143
Club Membership, 21

TRUE STORIES OF SEGREGATION

Club Rivera, 10
Cobb, General, 311
Cobb, James, 24
Coates, Juliet, 42
Cobb, Montague, 94, 137-139
Cohen, Charles, 187
Cole, Nat King, 11
Colgate University, 154
Colonia Dublan, 299
Color Change, 263
Color Designation, 229-245
Color Me Black, 161, 162
Color Me White, 261
Color Obsession, 238-245
Color White-The Obsession of Color, 255-274
Colored Doctor, 162
Columbus, New Mexico, 300
Columbus, Ohio, 223
Comiskey, Charles, 127
Command and General Staff College, 305
Confronting the Smithsonian Institution, 245-249
Congress of Industrial Organizations, 21
Congress of Racial Equality, 65
Congressional Restaurant Segregation, 69, 70
Congressional Stereotypes, 77
Conkling, Roscoe, 140
Constitution Hall, 187, 190
Conway, Annie, 2, 3
Conway, Bessie, 3
Conway, Burnetta, 3
Conway, Daniel, 2
Conway, Esther, 3
Conway, Ewell, 3
Conway, Ewell Jr., 101
Conway, Jessie, 101
Conway, Maria, 3
Conway, Mercer, 3

Conway, Ruth, 3
Coolidge, President, 172
Cooper, Chauncey, 12
Cooper, Chuck, 123, 124
Cooper, Richard, 276
CORE, 65, 103
Cornish, Samuel, 54
Corps of Engineers, 120
Cosby, Bill, 98
Cotillion, 265
Court Martial, 285
Courtney School, 293
Covington, Harold, 69
Cowpers, William, 197
Cravath, President, 213
Creoles, 237
Crock, David, 277
Croom, A.S., 215
Cubana, 237
Culver, James, 102
Cummins, David, 153
Cumming v. Board of Education, 31
Curley, Mayor, 108
Curry, Nurse, 158
Cyprus, 151

D

Daddy Grace's Church, 203
Dalits, 230, 298
Danville, Illinois, 176
Daughters of the American Revolution, 187-193
David's True Story, 335-339
Davis, Benjamin Sr., 145
Davison, Frederic, 311
Dawson, Ms., 195
Dawson, William, 49
Decatur, Illinois, 256
Deckard, Julia, 92
DeFrantz, Robert, 70

de Gaule, General, 301
Delaney, Colonel, 281
Delaware Bay, 286
Delaware State College, 32
Delta Airlines, 305
Demarest, Granville, 223
Dendy, John, 128, 129
Dennis, Esther, 129
Denver, Colorado, 288, 289, 334
Derricotte, Juliette, 157
Deutscher Presserat, 107
Detroit, Michigan, 149, 188
Devores Neck, South Carolina, 288
Dialect and Slang, 201
Dickey, Bill, 127
Din, Seyed, 150
Diop, Cheikh, 248, 249
District Grocery Stores, 121
District of Columbia Public Schools Basic Track, 37
Distinguished War Correspondent, 300
Diversity of African Americans, 224-229
Dixon, Frank, 104
Dogan, Matthew, 42, 292
Dominickers, 237
Do Not Forget Payday, 258
Do Not See Your Color, 259
"Do Not Tell Them Your First Name", 217-218
Dorsey, George, Mr. and Mrs., 177
Douglas, Helen G., 178
Douglass, Frederick, 63, 175, 213, 168, 274
Douglass, Haley, 131
Douglass Hospital, 164
Dowell, Miss, 268
Downing, Ann, 276
Downing, James, 276
Downing, John, 276
Downs Syndrome, 168

Dozier, Benjamin, 293
Dozier, Charlotte, 293
Dozier, Julius, 293
Dozier, Martha S., 293
Dozier, Thomas, 293
Dravidians, 298
Dravidian Type, 241
Drew, Charles, 101
Drew Smith School, 303
Druid Hill park, 128
Dubissette, M.E., 175
Dubois, W.E.B., 30, 212, 243, 308
Dunbar, Alice, 208
Dunbar Hospital, 165
Dunbar, Paul L. Mrs., 208
Dunbarton Oaks Conference, 149
Duncan, Todd, 195
Dupont, Commodore, 284
Durant, Sadie, 27
Dyson, Geraldine, 301

E

Early Affirmative Action, 93
Early Black Organizations, 186-187
Early, Stephen, 144
Eaton, Dr., 6
Eckert, Frederick, 22
Edgecombe County, North Carolina, 293-295
Edmund, Senator, 141
Edwards, Charles, 177
Edwards, Pearl, 129
EEOC, 119
Egyptian Ties and Timber Company, 331
Eisenhower, President, 17, 118, 150, 195
Einstein, Albert, 215, 112, 163
Ellis, Georgia, 184
Ellis, Raymond, 56
El Paso, Texas, 324, 326

El Salvador, 320
Ely, Priscella, 287
Emergency Treatment, High Blood Pressure, 158-160
Emperior Haile Selassie, 325
Enfield, North Carolina, 175-321
Englehart, Otto, 47
English Tavern, 330
Escapia, 324
Escobel, 324
Escort Officer's Change In Orders, 305
Ethiopian-Italian, 220
Evans, Bertha, 3
Evans, James C., 17
Evans, Wilson, 48
Evans, Wilson B., 94, 268
Evansville Bar Association, 183
Evanti, Lillian, 194, 195
Executive Order 11063, 26

F

Faiks, Walter, 17
Fairfax County School System, 303
Fairfax County, Va., 303, 304, 336, 337
Falkner, Emeline, 292
Falkner Family, 291-292
Falkner, Fannie Forest, 292
Falkner, Frances, 292
Falkner, William C., 291, 292
Falls Church Proposed Ordinance, 24
Falls Church Virginia Segregated School, 43, 44
Fanon, Franz, 274
Farmer, Karen, 188
Farmers' Meeting, 208-209
Farmville, Virginia, 336
Farris, Freddie, 4
Farris, Leslie, 4
Farris, Sarah, 4
Farris, Walter, 4
Faulkner, William, 291-292
Fechner, R., 67
Federal Bar Association, 184
Felmet, Joseph, 65
FEPC, 117, 118
Ferguson, Adelaide, 286
Ferguson, John, 283, 286
Ferguson, Lena, 189, 191
Ferguson, William, 285
Fernwood Project Riot, 23
FHA, 25
Fields, Chris, 336, 337
Filipinos, 302
Fisher, Hebie, 281
Fisk Students, 48
Fisk University, 54
Fitzgerald, Herman, 309
Fitzpatrick, Sarah, 162
Flenning, Thomas, 117
Folly Island, 286
Foote, Reverend, 290
Forest, Nathan B., 292
Fort Belvoir, VA, 303, 304
Fort Campbell, Kentucky, 329
Fort Gordon, Georgia, 305
Fort Jackson, South Carolina, 305
Fort Leavenworth, Kansas, 305
Fort McClellan, Alabama, 306-307
Fort Myer, Virginia, 304-325
Fort Pierce, Florida, 111
Fort Riley, Kansas, 195
Fort Sumter, 284
Foster, J.G., 262
Foster, John, 287
Foster, Stephen, 34
Fox, Caroline, 281
Fox, Curtis, 281
Fox, Daisy, 269, 281
Fox, George, 281
Fox, Hebie, 281
Fox, Henry, 281

Fox, Leslie, 281
Fox, Lillie, 281
Fox, Roal, 281
Fox Theatre, 97, 98
Fox, Waynefield, 281
Fox, William, 97
Frankfurt, Germany, 339
Frankfurt, Ohio, 294
Frazier, E. Franklin, 242
Frederick Douglass High School, 196
Frederick Memorial Hospital, 158
Freedmen's Bureau, 286
Freedmen's Hospital, 5
Freeman, Field, 146
Freeman, Henry, 128
Freedman's Village, 109, 110
French Directive, 82
Frissell, H.B., 48
Fung, Lem Yu, 292

G

Gaines, Lloyd, 31
Gannon, General, 311
Gant, Anita, 129
Gantt, Geary, 177
Garfield Hospital, 5, 157
Garfield, James, 142
Garfield, President, 155
Garner, Dr., 271
Garrison, Lindley, 109
Gates, President, 213
Gathings, Roosevelt, 166
Garvey, Marcus, 308
General Council of Congregational Churches, 21
Genetic Marks, 240
Genetic Surprise, 270
George Mason University, 337
Georgetown Day School, 220
Georgia Tech., 126
Gershwin, George, 195-196

Gillen, A.G. Jr., 301
Gillespie, Dizzy, 11
Gillis, Homer, 104
Gladden, James, 156, 157
Gladstone, W.E., 130
Glasgow, Scotland, 329
"Glass of Water Please", 326
Glen Echo Park, 93, 94
Golfers, 128, 129
Gomez, SP-4, 309
Gong Lum v. Rice
Goodyear Tire Company, 327
Gordon, Bart, 192
Gore, Albert, 190
Gould, Joan, 42
Government Segregation, 116
Graduations of Color, 261
Granger, Lester, 302
Grant, U.S., 142
Grant, William, 191
Gray v. University of Tennessee, 32
Gregg, Arthur, 311
Gregory, Dick, 12
Greenbriar Area, 22
Green, P.H., 153
Greene, Adam, 3, 4
Greene, Adam R., 47
Greene, Arthur A. Sr., 1, 3, 6, 47, 48, 75, 131-134, 183
Greene, Cecelia, 3
Greene, Daisy, 4
Greene, Hazel, 204
Greene, John, 3
Greene, John A., 153
Greene, Joseph, 4, 47, 204
Greene, Katie, 4
Greene, Mae, 4
Greene, Nathaniel, 268
Greene, Phyllis, 3
Greene, Robert II, 335, 336
Greene, Robert M., 4
Greene, Rosie, 4

TRUE STORIES OF SEGREGATION

Greene, Sylvia, 3
Greene, Tyler, 3
Greene, Wilma, 3
Greenridge, Robert, 165
Greensboro, North Carolina, 261
Greenville, South Carolina, 283
Grimke, Francis, 213
Grisson, Joe, 96, 97
Grovey v. Townsend, 148
Guerrero, Leon, 309
Gum Springs, Virginia, 303

H

Hackett, Grace, 33
Hairston, Juanita, 102
Halifax Company 4-H Rural Life Center, 296
Halifax Company, NC, 294
Hall, Basil, 123, 124
Hall, Jacques, 245, 246, 247
Hallowell, R.P., 287
Hamilton, Larry Jr., 309
Hampton Institute, 54
Hampton Roads, 286
Hancock, Samuel, 285
Hand, Fred, 187
Handy, William C., 157
Hanley, Daniel Jr., 102
Harding, Warren, 181
Harlem, 297
Harris, Albert, 177
Harris, Benjamin, 292

Harris, Romona, 129
Harrisburg, Ohio, 287
Harrison, A.S., 51
Harrison, J., 177
Harrison, N.B., 290
Harrison, President, 142

Harry Lovett, 307
Hastie, William, 208
Hawkins Act, 20
Hawthorne School, 220
Hayes, George, 24
Hayes, Lula, 129
Hayes, Rutherford, 142
Haynes, O.B. Jr., 177
Hayward, Harold, 309
Healy, Alexander, 54
Healy, Eliza, 54
Healy, James, 54
Healy, Mary, 54
Healy, Patrick, 54
He Could Still Be a Colored Man, 268
He Made It Out of The Inner City, 296
Henderson, Elmer, 64
Henderson, Edwin, 24, 131, 132, 134, 270
Henderson, Elmer, 64
Hershey, General, 145
Heyward, Dubose, 195, 196
Hicks, Hollow, 24
Hill-Burton Act, 167
Hill, William, 9
Hines, J.H., 262
Hogansville, Georgia, 117
Holland, Bird, 289
Holland Family, 389-290
Holland, James, 289
Holland, Milton, 289,290
Holland, William, 289
Holmes, June, 309
Holmes, Talley, 128
Holmes, William, 283
Holocaust, 218
Hong, Lem Yu, 293
Hood, William, 188
Hoover, Edgar, 5
"Hope He Will Be Light", 265
Hord, Dr., 264
Hord, Samuel, 264

Horne, Lena, 195
Horne, Nina, 290
Horse Racing, 123
Houser, George, 65
Houston Riot, 1917, 299
Houston, Texas, 97, 299, 300
Howard Theatre, 10, 11
Howell, Arthur Jr., 156
Hudnall, Albert, 275, 276
Hudnall, Alexander, 275
Hudnall and Mann Families, 275
Hudnall, Ann, 276
Hudnall, Athelia, 275
Hudnall, Blucker, 278
Hudnall, Elizabeth, 275
Hudnall, Fanny, 277
Hudnall, Greenwood, 275
Hudnall, Harriet, 275
Hudnall, James, 275, 276, 277, 278
Hudnall, John, 275, 278
Hudnall, John W., 275
Hudnall, Joseph, 275
Hudnall, Molly, 275
Hudnall, Nancy, 275
Hudnall, Polly, 275
Hudnall, Richard, 276
Hudnall, Romulus, 278
Hudnall, Sarah, 275
Hudnall, Thomas, 275
Hudnall, Tucker, 278
Hudnall, William, 275, 276, 277, 278
Hudnall, William H., 275
Hughes, Alfreda, 292
Hughes, Bernice, 303
Hughes, Dogan Blanche, 292
Hughes, Faulkner, 292
Hughes, Langston, 269-270
Hughes, Miriam, 292
Hughes, Solomon, 129
Hughes, William A.C., Jr., 292
Hughes, William A.C., Sr., 292
Humphrey, Hubert, 123

Hunter, Janice, 42
Hurd, James, 20
Hurd, Joy, 102-103
Hurok, Sol, 187
Hutchinson, Judge, 47

J

Jack, Homer, 65
Jackson, Harry, 129
Jackson, S.I., 173
Jackson, Stonewall, 3097
Jackson, W.G., 209, 210
Jackson Whites, 237
Jacksonville, Florida, 157
Jacobs, Mike, 125
James, Lieutenant., 300
Japan, 330
Jaybird Association, 148
Jefferson Barracks, Missouri, 331
Jefferson City, Missouri, 305, 306, 327, 329
Jeffries, Everett, 4
Jennings, Peter, 190, 192, 193
Jernagin, W.H., 71
Jet Magazine, 191
Jewish Americans, 218
Jewish War Veterans, 21
Jim Crow Car, 218
Jim Crow Travel, 63
Johnson, Andrew, 65, 141
Johnson, Campbell, 145
Johnson, Gertrude, 129
Johnson, James W., 76
Johnson, John H., 221
Johnson, Lyndon, 221
Johnson, Mary, 2
Johnson, Max, 300
Johnson, Mordecai, 33, 70
Johnson, Octave, 291
Johnson, P.H., 69
Joliet, Illinois, 181

Jones, Colonel, 17
Jones, Dolly, 294
Jones, Elizabeth, 294
Jones, Esther, 294
Jones, George, 294
Jones, John, 294
Jones, John C., 177
Jones, John Q., 170
Jones, John W., 190
Jones, Laurence Jr., 170-171
Jones, Leroy, 152, 153
Jones, Lewis, 294
Jones, Lucy, 294
Jones, Lydia, 170
Jones, Matthew, 294, 295
Jones, Sally, 294
Jones, Shirley, 42
Jones, Sydney, 294
Jones, Turner, 170
Jones, Wallis, 152
Jones, William, 223, 295
Jordan, Alex, 104
Jordan, Michael, 127
Journalism, 118, 119
Journey of Reconciliation, 65
Juitt, James, 290
Juillard School of Music, 196
Jujitsu, 173
Junior American Citizens Clubs, 189

K

Kansas City Call, 296
Kansas City, Missouri 296, 297, 327-328
Kansas City, Missouri Airport, 305
Kansas City Star, 257-258
Kaufman, Rudolph, 4
Kelly, Mr., 328
Kelley, Mrs., 328
Kelley, Roger, 310, 311
Keokuk, 286

Kennedy, John, 143
Kenslow, Jim, 270
Ketchens, M.P., 262
Knights of Columbus, 62
Kiawh River, 286
King, Martin L. Jr., 23
King, Sarah, 189, 191, 192
Kirkwood, Missouri, 332
Koning, Uta, 313
Korea, 99, 259
Krise, Edward, 309
Ku Klux Klan, 194

L

Labor Unions, 118, 119, 120
Ladd, Mary, 30
Lafayette, Mississippi, 291
Lamar, Mr., 143
Lamar, Mr. and Mrs., 10
Lancaster District, South Carolina, 261
Lancaster, South Carolina, 110
Lang, Fritz, 338
Langston, John M., 287 289
Langston, John Mercer, Illinois, 7
Langston University, 31
Laurence, Paul, 102
Law, Charles, 102
Law Enforcement, 169-184
Lawless, Dr., 271
Leasehold System, 21
Lee, Asher, 280
Lee, Horace, 280
Lee, Robert E., 235-236, 279-280
Lee, Yee, 292
Leech, Mr., 331-221
Legal Injustice, 172-172
Legal Quotas, 302-303
Lehman, Herbert H., 305
Leiper, Henry, 270, 271
Len, Lem Yu, 293

Lentz, Lt., 309
Levitt, William, 24
Levittown, 24
Lewis, Judge, 42
Lewis, William 183, 184
Lexington, Kentucky, 323
Lie, Trygve, 150
Lloyd, Earl, 123
Lincoln University, 13, 187
Lippincott, LTC., 305
Lisner Auditorium, 98
Liuzzo, Viola, 175
Liverpool, England, 197, 329, 330
Lofton, Isaiah, 117
Lofton, Williston, 117
Logan, Myra, 155
Logan, Walter, 300
Lohr River, 330
Long Island, New York, 333
Longwood College, 336, 338
Louis, Joe, 10, 125
Louis, Julia, 280
Louisiana Cajuns, 237
Louisville, Kentucky, 299
Loving, Walter, 256
Lowell, Massachusetts, 213
Lower Class, 201, 208-209, 218
Luce, Clare, 189
Lucerne, Switzerland, 312
Lum, Benny, 293
Lum, Charles, 293
Lum, Charlie, 292, 293
Lum, Ernest, 293
Lum Family, 292-293
Lum, Louis, 293
Lum, Mamie, 292, 293
Lum, Maria, 293
Lynch, John, 140, 141, 142
Lynching, 176-181
Lynching Facts, 181
Lynn, Conrad, 65
Lyons, Georgia, 181

Mc

Macbeth, Hugh Sr., 183
McAfee, Michael, 2
McAfee, Michelle, 2
McAfee, Monica, 2
McAfee, Phyllis, 1
McAfee, Travis, 2
McAlester, Oklahoma, 182
McDonald, Colonel, 300
McCord, Lieutenant, 309
McDonald, John, 299-300
McGhee, Orsell, 20
McGraw, John, 127
McKee, Henry, 282
McKee, Mrs., 282
McKinley, President, 117
McKissick v. Carmichael, 32
McLaughlin, General, 311
McLaurin, G.W., 31, 32
McNutt, Paul, 70
McPhaer, John, 166
McWilliams, Pittman Selda, 295

M

Mackey, Thomas Jr., 28
Mackey, Thomas D., III, 28
Madden, Samuel St., 177
Malone, Crystal, 52
Malvin, Catherine, 278
Malvin, Dorsey, 278
Malvin, John, 278
Malvin, Laura, 278
Malvin, Roberta, 278
Malvin, Rosabel, 278
Malvin, Solomon, 278
Malvin, Sophia Mann, 278
Malvin, Zeph Turner, 278
"Man From Mars", 199
Manassa Regional High School, 303
Manchester, England, 330

Mann, Blucker, 277
Mann, Columbia, 278
Mann, Drayton, 276, 277
Mann, Edward, 276, 278
Mann, Eliza, 276, 277
Mann, Elizabeth, 277, 278, 279
Mann, Frances, 277
Mann, John, 276, 277
Mann, Julius, 277
Mann, Ludwell, 276, 277, 278
Mann, Mildred, 276, 277, 278
Mann, Polly, 264, 279
Mann, Richard, 278
Mann, Rush, 276
Mann, Sophia, 276, 278, 279
Mann, Susanna, 276
Mann, Thomas, 276, 277, 278
Mann, Tucker, 277
Mann, West, 277
Mann, Westwood, 276, 278
Mann, Wilfred, 276, 277
Mann, William, 277
Manning, South Carolina, 292
Marathons, 75
Marine Robin, 331
Marry and Get a Job, 263
Mary Washington Chapter, DAR, 189
Marsh, James, 286
Marshal, George, 107, 108
Marseilles, France, 330
Marsh, David, 286
Martha's Vineyeard, 7
Massey, Austin, 331
Matthews, mark, 324
Matthews, Samuel, 23
Mayo, Pearl, 4, 5
Maysville, South Carolina, 208
Meacham Park, MO, 326, 327, 329
Medicine - Hospitals, 154-168
Melungeons, 237
Membership Card Trick, 105
Memorial Hospital, Frederick,

Maryland, 158
Memories of Segregation, 321-334
Merchant, Claude, 104
Mercy Hospital, 165
Meredith, James, 36
Merryweather, Andrew, 102
Metcalfe, Ralph, 124
Metropolitan Insurance Company 21
Metz, France, 330
Miami Beach, Florida, 333
Michaels, David, 40
Middleburg College, 30
Middleburg, Virginia 269, 279, 281
Midland, Texas, 146
Miledge, Stanley, 22
Milgram, Morris, 26
Milholland, Jean, 212, 213
Milholland, John, 212
Military, 299-308
Military Affirmative Action, 1956, 305
Military Quotas, 301
Military Reserves Bill, 304
Miller, Dorothy, 229, 244, 269, 279, 280
Miller, Gerald, 311
Miller, Kenneth, 47
Millikin, 256
"Million Man March", 219
Minden, Louisiana, 177
Minnaepolis, Minnesota, 208, 334
Missionaries, 216
Mississippi, 296
Mistaken Identity, 262
Mitchell, Arthur, 66
Mitchell, Clarence, 304
Mitchell, Juanita, 166
Mob Action, Chicago, Illinois, 169
Mobile, Alabama, 291
Monde, Aristide, 291
Monde Family, 290
Monde, Joe, 290
Monde, Marsaline, 290

Monde, Octave, 290
Monumental Tennis Club, 128
Moore, Ben, 102
Moore, George, 290
Moore, Mae, 301
Moore, Peter L., 183, 290
Moors, 237
Mordecai, Mr., 287
More, John, 290
Morgan, Irene, 64, 65
Morgan State College, 292
Morocco, 300
Mormon Church, 3, 57
Morris Island, South Carolina, 222, 223
Morris, William, 183
Morrow, Dr., 49
Morse, Wayne, 178
Mortgage Device, 21
Mossele River, 330
Moton, R.R., 212, 271
Mount Vernon High School, 303
Murfreesboro, Tennessee, 190, 192, 193
Mullins, Clarence, 23
Murphy, Henry, 36
Murray, Donald, 31
Murray, John, 191
Music, 194-198
Mydral, Gunnar, 148, 251, 252
My Identity is Black, 256

N

Nabrit, James Jr., 6
Nabrit, James Sr., 5
"Name Game", 243
Narragansetts, 237
Nash County, NC, 293-295
Nash, Janet, 283
Nasser, President, 150

National Association of Colored Graduate Nurses, 184-185
National Association of Real Estate Boards, 21
National Association of Women Lawyers, 184
National Bar Association, 184
National Iron and Ship Builders, 286
National Lawyers, Guild, 21, 184
National Negro Business league, 184
National Recovery Administration, 144
National Symphony, 187
Neal, Claude, 180
Negro Domination, 141
Negro National Opera Company, 195
Nelson, Wallace, 65
Nettingham, Frank, 71
New Albany, Mississippi, 291
Newbold, Mr., 270
Newbold, North Carolina, 185
New Deal Era, 144, 145
New London Submarine Base, 126
New Orleans, Louisiana, 290
Newton, John, 196-198
New York Times, 191
Nice, Henry, 292
Nicklaus, Jack, 137
"Nigger and White Folks Cake", 333
Ninety Second Division, 172
Nixon v. Condon, 148
Nixon v. Herndon, 147-148
Nogales, 324
No Rights as a Citizen, 264
No Time For Darkness, 266
Norris, Elizabeth, 290
North Africa, 301
North Carolina, 296, 323
North Carolina A and T, 126
North Carolina Mutual Life Insurance Company, 171

North Carolina Negro Teachers Association, 185
North Carolina's Unequal Schools, 49
Northcross, David, 165
Northern Dining Policies, 95
Northern Virginia Community College, 36, 40
Northern Virginia Segregated Transportation, 63, 64
Northrop, Claudian, 290
Norway, 196
Not Completely Senile, 266
Not Even If Painted With Gold, 265
Nova Scotia, 283

O

Oberammergau, 310
Oberlin College, 269, 287
Oberlin, Ohio, 218
Oblate Catholic Sisters of Providence, 264
Ohio River, 331
Ohio State, 124
Oliver, Dr., 47
Omaha Beach, 330
O'Malley, Dr., 328, 331
Office of Management and Budget (OMB), 229, 230, 231
One Drop of Blood Theory, 240
One Sixteenth White, 265
Optimist Camp, 14
Organizations, 184-193
Our Lady of Mercy Catholic Church, 293
Owens, Jesse, 11-12, 124-126, 138-139, 310
Oxford, Mississippi, 291

P

Pacer, 323

Paducah, Kentucky, 331-332
Palisades Park, 103
Palmer, Edward, 4, 80
Parker, Harry, 69
Parker, Milford, 104
Parkin, Lieutenant, 15
Paris, Kentucky, 280
Paris Opera Company, 194
Paris, Virginia, 279
Parks and Playground Segregation, 96, 97
Parks, Rosa, 66
Passing As Whites, 269
Passing In the White Society Column, 257-258
Patterson, Frederick, 70, 188
Patton, George, 1, 80
Patton, Mrs., 79-80
Payne, Ethel, 118, 119
Peabody Conservatory, 196
Pearson v. Murray, 31
Pedro, Don, 277
Pemberton, General, 284, 285
Pennington, James W.C., 54
Pension Bureau, 262
Perea, Beverly, 108
Perea, Missouri, 108
Perkins, Francis, 67
Perkins, Helen, 3
Perkins, Henry, 3
Perkins, Jane, 3
Perkins, Moses, 3, 5, 328
Perkins, W.D., 177
Perry, Christine, 129
Perry, H.E., 177
Perry, J. Edward, 164
Pershing Expedition, 299
Person, James, 176
Pet boys, 277
Petroff, SP-5, 309
Philadelphia, Pennsylvania, 286
Philippines, 225, 330

Philippine Constabulary Band, 256
Phillips, Don, 309
Pickens, William, 45-46, 175, 207
Pierce, Chester, 126
Piney Woods Country Life School, 170
Pitcher, S.Z., 285
Pittman, Boone Almyra, 295
Pittman, Carey, 295, 296
Pittman, Carey Jr., 295
Pittman, Doris, 295
Pittman, Gerald, 295
Pittman, Olivia E., 295
Pittman, William J., 295
Pittman, Winton V., 295
Pitts, Helen, 213
Planter, 283-286
Planter Hotel, 282
Platonic Interracial Relationship, 256-257
Poindexter, Maria, 280
Polish, 260
Polite, Amanda, 290
Polite, John, 290
Politics, 140
Pollard, Judge, 42
Pomokey, Maryland 328
Ponder, Prince, 265
Poor, Tapscott Elizabeth, 291
Poor, Telam, 291
Population Biologists, 240
Porgy and Bess, 195, 196
Porter, Dr., 333
Porter, Lewis, 263
Post, Richard, 240
Povich, Shirley Sr., 127
Powell, Adam C. Jr., 28, 153-154, 165, 188, 302-304
Prettyman, Arthur, 301
Price, Leontyne, 196
Princess Anne Company, MD, 181
Prince William County, 303

Pritchard, Alabama, 173
Proctor, Hannah, 239
Proctor, Levi, 239
Proctor, Dr., 271
Pulaski, Tennessee, 174
Purvis, Charles, 155
PWA, 34

Q

Quest, Frederick, 311

R

Race and Intermarriage in Politics, 143
Race Relations Dialogue, 316-320
Race Relations School, 307
Radcliffe College, 240
Raleigh, North Carolina, 211, 293
Randle, Worth, 65
Randolph, A. Philip, 117
Randolph, J., 286
Rankin, E. Neremiah, 56
Ras Desta, 325
Ravenel, William, 286
Ray, Marcus H., 108, 236
Real Estate Law 1946, 20
Reck, James, 65
Reconstruction Finance Corporation, 211
Rector, Hannah, 239
Red Caps, 67
Religion, 202-206
Relyea, C.J., 285
Remember the Children, 259
Remington, Frederic, 75, 75
Reston, Virginia, 335
Restrictive Covenant, 20
Revels, James, 309
Reverse Discrimination, 53
Reynolds, Benjamin, 295

TRUE STORIES OF SEGREGATION

Reynolds, Jones Sarah, 294
Reynolds, Mary, 295
Reynolds, Sally, 295
Reynolds, Speck, 320
Reynolds, William, 295
Rhetta, B.M., 128
Rhine River, 330
Rhodes, Jerry, 12
Richardson, Ruth, 1
Richmond Company Public Schools Georgia, 305
Richmond, Virginia, 218, 288
Riddle, Gladys, 280
Riley, Margaret, 42
Ritter, Joseph, 52
River, Francis, 184
Roach, SP-5, 309
Robert, Henry Mrs., 187
Robeson, Paul, 194
Robinson, Hugh, 6
Robinson, James, 6
Robinson, Merton B., 131
Robinson, Remus, 165
Rochester, New York, 328
Rocky Mount, NC, 321, 322, 323
Rod and Gun Clubs, 130
Roger, Malcolm, Mr. and Mrs., 176-177
Rommey, Kenneth, 69
Roodenko, Igal, 65
Roosevelt, Eleanor, 117, 195
Roosevelt, Franklin D., 67, 117, 144, 300, 326
Rosenwald, Julius, 333, 296
Ross County, Ohio, 294
"Rowan Oaks", 291
Rowe, Absalom, 263
Rowe, Robert, 20
Roxabel, Ohio, 294
Rush, Dean, 221
Rush, Margaret, 222
Rush, Virginia, 221

Russell, PFC, 309
Rustin, Bayard, 65
Rutgers University, 320

S

"Salute To Ghana", 195
Sancho, Rupert, 35
Sanford, Comelia, 2
Sanford, Daisy, 2
Sanford, Jaymie, 2
Sanford, Johnson, 2
Sanford, Karla, 2
Sanford, Oscar, 281
Santa Fe Railroad, 14, 97
Saunders, Jordan W., 276
Saunders, Lillie, 278
Savage, Herbert
Savoy, A., 131
Sayers, Arthur, 166
Sayings Related To Color, 274-275
Schulman, S., 300
Scott, Emment, 70, 213
Scottfield Airforce Base, Illinois, 329
Scott, Hazel, 188
Sears Roebuck, 100
Seattle, Washington, 221
Segregated Hospitals Kansas City, Missouri, 164
Segregation In Northern School, 51, 52
Segregated Ordinances, 29
Segregated Prisons, 181-182
Segregated Stores, 95, 95
Segregated USO, 70
Segregation, Veteran Hospitals, 165
Segregation vs. Integration, 208
Seifer, Lynn, 56
Seigmaster, Clifford, 332, 333
Sensitive Surveillance, 161
Separate Employee Training, 51

Separate Lifestyles, 273-274
Separate Teaching Licenses, 44
"Service On The Border", 324
Shaefer, Captain, 309
Shanks, Ann, 288
Shanks, Fannie, 288
Shanks, George, 288
Shanks, Mary, 288
Shanks, Willis, 288
Shawnee, Illinois, 331
She Passed As White At Times, 269-270
Shell Gasoline Station, 98, 99
Shelley, J.D., 20
Shertor, Moshe, 150
Shippen, Cyrus, 128
Shippen, John, 128
Shirley "K" Resort, 101
Shuffer, George, 307, 309, 311
Simpson, O.J., 177
Singh-Sidat, Wilmer, 126
Single Rooter, 323
Sipuel, Ada, 31
Sixty-Fifth Infantry Battalion, 300
Slem, Lem Gong, 292
Sloan, Edward D. Jr., 283
Smalls, Robert, 283, 284, 285, 286
Smead, Edith, 280
Smith, Artenia, 221
Smith, Ashton, 279, 280
Smith, Cain, 263
Smith, Clarence, 221
Smith, Clifford, 172
Smith College Faculty, 208
Smith, Guy, 222
Smith, Harriet, 239
Smith, Judson, 288
Smith, Louisa, 290
Smith, Sarah, 2, 129
Smith v. Allwright, 148
Smith, William, 103
Smithey, Corporal, 236

Soldiers Descriptive Complexions, 254-255
Soldier's General, 307-308
Soldier's True Stories, 323-326
Some Look Like Blacks, 264
Sonora State, 324
South Carolina, 269
South Carolina National Guard, 283
Southhampton, England, 330
Southern Justice, 172
Southern Railroad, 64
South Pacific Islands, 232-236
Sparrows Beach, 101
Spaulding, C.C., 171
Spears, Allen, 3
Spears, Allena, 3
Spears, Alonzo Jr., 4
Spears, Alonzo Sr., 3, 4
Spears, Arthur, 3
Spears, Bertha, 3
Spears, Della, 4
Spears, Eugene, 3
Spears, Florence, 4
Spears, Frank, 4
Spears, Hannah, 3
Spears, Helen, 3, 4
Spears, Jane, 3
Spears, Josephine, 4
Spears, Manassa Jr., 3
Spears, Manassa Sr., 3
Spears, Mollie, 4
Spears, Oliver, 3
Spears, Robina, 4
Spears, Sadie, 3
Spears, Sandy, 4
Spears, Sarah, 3
Spears, Sophia, 3
Spears, Stella, 3
Spears, Uriah, 3
Spears, Viola, 3
Spears, Walter, 3,4
Speech Language Pathologist, 297

Speech Pathologist, 334
Spiegel Magazine, 312
Spinney, Al, 281
Sports Stereotypes, 137
Stainback, John, 242
Stanford University, 136
Stanley, Eugene, 65
Stanton, Secretary, 262
States' Rights, 172
Steiner, Professor, 239
Stevens, General, 284
Stevens, Rutherford, 166
Steward Branch, 302
Stewart, Ollie, 300-301
Stewart, Pauline, 20
Stills, Joseph, 287
Stokes, Louis, 190
Stone, River, 286
Straight University, 54
Stress, 145
Stubb, Frederick, 156
Stuttgart Chapter NAACP, 308
Stuttgarter Nachricthen, 105
Stuyvesant Town, 21
Subculture, 218
Sulper Lick Springs, Ohio, 294
Sumner, Charles, 43
Sumner High School, 7, 8
Supreme Court of North Carolina, 210
Surinam, 74
Swails, Stephen, 262
Sweatt, Herman, 32
Sweatt v. Painter, 32
Syracuse University, 126

T

Taft, President, 49
Taft, William, 246
Tageblat, Heidelberg, 105
Talladega College, 54
Talmadge, Julius Mrs., 188

Tapscott Family, 291
Tapscott, Elizabeth, 291
Tapscott, Mack, 291
Tapscott, Maggie, 291
Tapscott, Mary Francis, 291
Tapscott, Nancy, 291
Tapscott, Randolph, 291
Tapscott, Robert, 291
Tapscott, Telam, 291
Tapscott, Virginia, 291
Tapscott, William, 291
Tate, Etta, 129
Taussig, Helen, 167
Tavenner, Frank, 146
Taylor, Lottie, 65, 66
Taylor, Lucy, 149
Taylor, Ruth, 305
Terrell, Esther, 129
Terrell, Jack, 323
Terrell, Mary C., 94
Terry v. Adams, 148
Texas, 296
Texas A and M College, 261
Texas Primary Cases, 147-148
Texas State Legislature, 289
Thant, U, 151
They Never Knew She Was Black, 269
This is one Colored Passenger, 260
Thomas, Ada, 185
Thomas, Bernice, 173
Thomas, Judith, 42
Thomas, Secretary, 302
Thomas, Viven, 166-167
Thomasville, Georgia, 110
Thompson, Elizabeth, 276-277
Thornbons, John, 309
Thornell, Harold, 165
Thornton, Jessie Bullock, 215
Thornton, Robert, 215, 223, 263, 267
Thurmond, Strom, 306
Tibbs, Evans Lillian, 194-195

Tidewater Planters, 284
Tidrington, Ernest G., 183
Tokohama, 127
Tomasi, Andrew, 306
Tougaloo University, 54
Trams, 286
Travis, Connie, 280
Treasury Department, 286
Trigg, Joseph, 1
Triracial Groups, 237-238
Truman, Harry, 150, 189, 195
Tucker, Francis, 277
Tucker, Herbert L., 13
Tucker, William, 278
Tulane University, 137
Turks, 237
Turner, Alexander, 165
Turner, D.H., 274
Turner, Theodore, 23
Turner, Thomas, 54, 55
Tweed, A.R., 166
Twenty-Fourth Infantry Battalion, 299-300
Twilight, Alexander, 30
Twilight, Ichabod, 30
Twilight, Mary, 30

U

Uline Arena, 94, 95
Unfortunate Visit To The Dentist, 266
United Golf Association, 129
United Negro College Fund, 188
United States Disciplinary Barracks, 18
University of Arkansas, 32
University of Augsburg, 311
University of California, 126
University of Delaware, 32
University of Illinois, 12
University of Kentucky, 32
University of Maryland, 126
University of North Carolina, 32
University of Oklahoma, 31
University of Tennessee, 32
University of Texas, 32
University of Vermont, 52
University of Virginia, 126
University of West Virginia, 31
University of Wisconsin, 320
Unthank, Thomas C., 164
U Thant Secretary, 151
Untouchables, 230, 298
Upper and Middle Class Blacks, 201-203, 206-212, 217, 218
Upperville, VA, 269, 279, 281
Uricola, Raphael, 20
U.S. Army Europe Race Relations School, 308-312, 314-315
U.S. Army General Hospital, 339
U.S. Census, 229
USAREUR Housing Referral Srevice Report, 2, 8

V

Vardaman, James K., 77
Vashon High School, 7
Vietnamese Student, 326
Villa, Pancho 299
Virginia Academy of Science, 55
Virginia State Legislature, 270

W

Waggoner, Joe D. Jr., 302
Walker, Mel, 124
Walker, Obezine, 6
Wall, Albert, 287, 288
Wall, Barbara, 288
Wall, Benjamin, 287
Wall, Caroline, 287
Wall Family, 287, 289
Wall, George, 288

Wall, Horton, 288
Wall, Hugh, 288
Wall, John, 287, 288, 289
Wall, John W., Jr., 289
Wall, Mary, 288, 289
Wall, Napoleon, 287
Wall, O.S.B., 287
Wall, Rody, 287, 288
Wall, Sarah, 287, 288
Wall, Stephen, 287, 288
Wallace, Carl S., 311
Wardlow, James, 104
Warfield, W.A., 288
Warfield, William, 196
Warrenton, Virginia 275
Wartime Industries, 121
Washington and Jefferson College, 126
Washington and Lee College, 126
Washington, Benjamin, 131
Washington, Booker T., 175, 207, 212, 271, 308
Washington, Booker T. Mrs., 182
Washington, Porter, 129
Washington Technical High School, 7
Waterford, Pennsylvania, 188
Watermelon Story, 80
Watson, Samuel, 184
Watts, Julia, 280
Watts, Martha, 280
Weaver, Jennie, 188
Weaver, Robert, 144
Webster, Daniel, 277
Webster Groves, Missouri, 327
Wedlock, Lunabelle, 173
Wellington, Kansas, 97
Weltbild Magazine, 312
West, Charles, 126
West, Dorothy, 7
West Newton Academy, 283
Westside, Tennis Club, 149

West, William, 79, 80
Western Golf Association, 101
Wetmore, Ernest, 130
Wetmore, Kay, 130
What About the Mother and Children?, 84-88
What's In a Name?, 258
What is Your Race?, 270
"What Would Daddy Think", 222-223
Where is the Colored Man?, 255-256
White as Anyone, 263
White Gangs, 100, 101
White, James, 295
White or Mulatto, 262
White, Selah, 295
White Thought, 88-91
White, Walter, 178-180
White, Yvonne, 6
Whitehead, SSG, 309
Who Am I?, 260
Wilberforce University, 126
Wilder, James, 160, 161
Wiggins, Mary, 196
Wiley College, 42, 191
Wilkinson, Garnet C., 131, 134
Wilkinson, John, 128
Williams, Ben, 31
Williams, Franklin, 236
Williams, Georgia Ann, 290
Williams, James, 67
Williams, John, 104
Williams, Lum Ewella (Cookie), 293
Williams, Sidney, 301
Wills, Pittman Almyra, 295
Wilson, Buther, 183, 184
Wilson, Emma, 208
Wilson High School, 220
Wilson, Ivy, 129
Wilson, J. Franklin, 71
Wilson, Woodrow, 116
Winchester Evening Star, 307
Winchester Rotary Club, 307

Winchester, Virginia, 151, 307
Wing, Lem Yu, 292
Women and Race Adjustment, 182
Wood, James, 42
Wood, Marguerite, 42
Woodbury, Dr., 214
Woods, Frances, 223
Woods, Tiger, 128
Woodson, Carter G., 9
Worldwide Color Obsession, 271
Worthy, William, 65
Wright, David, 309
Wright, Jane, 156
Wright, Louis, 156
Wright, Nathan, 65
Wright, William, 128
Wyatt, Donald, 301
Wycoff, Frank, 138

Y

YMCA Ecumenical Spirit, 56
"You Are On the Wrong Side", 321-322
You Were Not My Kind, 259
Young, Charles, 111-116
Young, Nellie V., 279
Young, Coleman, 145-146
Younger, Charles, 136
Younger V. Judah, 136
Younger, Simpson, 136
Youth Track Meet, 126
Yugoslavian Lady, 271

Z

Zydeco, 237